D1029621

# THE BILL OF RIGHTS

MAGILL'S CHOICE

# THE BILL OF RIGHTS

## Volume 1

## The Bill of Rights
## The Amendments
## Issues

*edited by*
Thomas T. Lewis
*Mount Senario College*

SALEM PRESS, INC.
Pasadena, California     Hackensack, New Jersey

Essays in these volumes first appeared in *Encyclopedia of the U.S. Supreme Court* (2001), *Censorship* (1997), and *American Justice* (1996). Many essays have been updated, and new material has been added.

∞ The paper used in these volumes conforms to the American National Standard for Permanence of Paper for Printed Library Materials, Z39.48-1992 (R1997).

**Library of Congress Cataloging-in-Publication Data**
The Bill of Rights / edited by Thomas T. Lewis.
    p. cm. — (Magill's choice)
Includes bibliographical references and index.
    ISBN 1-58765-062-2 (set : alk. paper) — ISBN 1-58765-063-0 (v. 1 : alk. paper) — ISBN 1-58765-064-9 (v. 2 : alk. paper)
    1. United States. Constitution. 1st-10th Amendments 2. Civil rights—United States. I. Lewis, Thomas T. (Thomas Tandy) II. Series.
    KF4750 .B55 2002
    342.73'085–dc21
                                                              2002002007

# TABLE OF CONTENTS

**Appendices**

# PUBLISHER'S NOTE

This two-volume contribution to the Magill's Choice series of reference works is an encyclopedic guide to the first ten amendments to the U.S. Constitution—those amendments collectively known as the U.S. Bill of Rights because of the important rights and liberties they were framed to protect from government abuses. The set's purpose is to provide information that is comprehensive, accessible, accurate, and up to date. Articles in these volumes focus on the first ten amendments and have little to say about other parts of the Constitution; however, the Bill of Rights alone is such a large topic that it easily fills these two volumes.

For the convenience of the readers, essays are divided under four broad headings: Overviews, Amendments, Issues, and Court Cases. The first three sections fill volume 1. The fourteen essays in the first section survey the history and significance of the Bill of Rights within the broader contexts of the principles of constitutional law and U.S. legal history. Special attention is paid here to the subject of *incorporation*—the term applied to the process through which the U.S. Supreme Court has used the Fourteenth Amendment to extend most of the rights enumerated in the first ten amendments to the states. The Fourteenth Amendment is not, by definition, part of the Bill of Rights; however, it may be considered the key to the Bill. When the Founders adopted the first ten amendments to the Constitution in 1791, the amendments' protections were generally understood to apply only to the federal government. It would not be until many years after the Fourteenth Amendment was adopted in 1868 that the Supreme Court began incorporating into that amendment's due protection clause protections of the Bill of Rights, thereby holding the states to the same standards as the federal government.

The second section of essays contains individual articles on each of the first ten amendments, arranged in numerical order. The full text of each amendment can be found in the U.S. Constitution, which is reprinted as an appendix at the back of both volumes.

The eighty-one essays in the third section of the set address specific issues relating to the Bill of Rights. These articles cover subjects ranging from "Academic freedom" to "Zoning," with essays on subjects as broad as censorship, civil rights and liberties, due process, and freedom of religion, and as narrow as chilling effect, the right to counsel, and Miranda rights. Readers can find the subjects they seek under their alphabetically arranged titles or by consulting the comprehensive index in volume 2.

The fourth section of essays, which accounts for the bulk of volume 2, consists of 281 brief articles on the individual court cases through which the rights in the Bill of Rights have been defined and extended. It is through these cases that the Supreme Court has provided authoritative interpretations of the Bill of Rights, thereby establishing doctrines and principles of constitutional law. These articles cover Supreme Court decisions through June, 2001.

Essays in this set are written and formatted to be accessible to high school and college students and other nonspecialist readers. Each essay opens with labeled "Description" and "Significance" paragraphs that briefly explain the subject and summarize its significance in constitutional history. Essays in the Issues and Court Case sections contain additional top matter lines identifying the Bill of Rights amendments that are most relevant to the essays' subjects. Because of the close relationship between the Bill of Rights and the Fourteenth Amendment, many "Relevant Amendment" lines also cite that amendment.

As is the case with all Magill's Choice sets, the bulk of the material in *The Bill of Rights* is taken from earlier Salem Press publications. Most of the articles come from the recent *Encyclopedia of the U.S. Supreme Court* (2001), a recipient of the American Library Association Reference and Adult Services Division award for "Outstanding Reference Source for 2001." Most of the remaining articles come from *American Justice* (1996), and *Censorship* (1997)—both earlier winners of the same award. Additionally, the set's Editor, Thomas T. Lewis—who was coeditor of *Encyclopedia of the U.S. Supreme Court*—has written entirely new articles on such subjects as the Virginia Declaration of Rights, the English and the Indian bills of rights, inverse incorporation, blasphemy, and the so-called Nuremberg files. Professor Lewis has also updated and expanded many other articles from the earlier sets.

Four appendices from the *Encyclopedia of the U.S. Supreme Court* have been brought further up to date and adapted to be more pertinent to the Bill of Rights. These appendices include a glossary, a time line, an annotated bibliography, and a table summarizing the stances on the Bill of Rights taken by every justice who has sat on the Supreme Court. The appendix material also includes the complete texts of the Declaration of Independence and the U.S. Constitution and its amendments—all of which appear at the end of each volume. The final item in volume 2 is a comprehensive subject index.

The Editors of Salem Press wish to express their thanks to Professor Lewis for the enthusiasm and dedication that he brought to this project. We also wish to thank the many contributors who wrote the articles. Their names are signed to each article and are listed in the front of volume 1.

# CONTRIBUTOR LIST

Nobuko Adachi
*Illinois State University*

Charles F. Bahmueller
*Center for Civil Education*

Bernard W. Bell
*Rutgers Law School*

Steve D. Boilard
*Sacramento, California*

P. J. Brendese III
*State University of New York at Albany*

Beau Breslin
*Skidmore College*

Joseph V. Brogan
*La Salle University*

Michael H. Burchett
*Limestone College*

William H. Burnside
*John Brown University*

Beau David Case
*Ohio State University*

H. Lee Cheek, Jr.
*Brewton-Parker College*

Alisa White Coleman
*University of Texas at Arlington*

Rebecca Davis
*Georgia Southern University*

Steven J. Dunker
*Northeastern State University*

Philip A. Dynia
*Loyola University*

Jennifer Eastman
*Clark University*

Daryl R. Fair
*College of New Jersey*

John Fliter
*Kansas State University*

Michael J. Garcia
*Arapahoe Community College*

Evan Gerstmann
*Loyola Marymount University*

Richard A. Glenn
*Millersville University*

Robert Justin Goldstein
*Oakland University*

Diana R. Grant
*California State University at Stanislaus*

Steven P. Grossman
*University of Baltimore School of Law*

John Gruhl
*University of Nebraska at Lincoln*

Timothy L. Hall
*University of Mississippi*

Sarah E. Heath
*University of Cincinnati*

Eric Howard
*Los Angeles, California*

John C. Hughes
*Saint Michael's College*

Patricia Jackson
*Davenport College*

Robert Jacobs
*Central Washington University*

Dwight Jensen
*Marshall University*

Alan E. Johnson
*Brecksville, Ohio*

Gae R. Johnson
*Northern Arizona University*

Sugwon Kang
*Hartwick College*

Marshall R. King
*Maryville University at St. Louis*

Paul Lermack
*Bradley University*

Thomas T. Lewis
*Mt. Senario College*

Lester G. Lindley
*Nova Southeastern University*

Matthew Lindstrom
*Siena College*

James J. Lopach
*University of Montana*

William C. Lowe
*Mount St. Clare College*

William Shepard McAninch
*University of South Carolina School of Law*

Joseph M. McCarthy
*Suffolk University*

Priscilla H. Machado
*United States Naval Academy*

Patrick Malcolmson
*St. Thomas University*

Kurt X. Metzmeier
*University of Kentucky College of Law*

Wayne D. Moore
*Virginia Polytechnic Institute and State University*

Kenneth F. Mott
*Gettysburg College*

Bruce G. Peabody
*University of Texas at Austin*

John B. Peoples
*University of Tennessee at Chattanooga*

Stephen F. Rohde
*Los Angeles, California*

Paul F. Rothstein
*Georgetown University School of Law*

Christopher Shortell
*Los Angeles, California*

Christopher E. Smith
*Michigan State University*

Chuck Smith
*West Virginia State College*

G. Thomas Taylor
*University of Maine*

Susan L. Thomas
*Hollins University*

Dean Van Bibber
*Fairmont State College*

Donald V. Weatherman
*Lyon College*

Marcia J. Weiss
*Point Park College*

Richard L. Wilson
*University of Tennessee at Chattanooga*

# INTRODUCTION

Although Americans clearly cherish the many liberties and privileges enumerated in the first ten amendments to the U.S. Constitution, public opinion surveys have repeatedly shown that most citizens have only vague notions about the specific contents of the amendments collectively known as the Bill of Rights. Indeed, many confuse these amendments with other parts of the Constitution and with other documents, especially the Declaration of Independence. However, no political or legal field is more interesting or worthy of study than the Bill of Rights and the twenty-seven liberties and privileges they enumerate.

The provisions in the Bill of Rights, as interpreted, and re-interpreted, by the U.S. Supreme Court, frequently have significant consequences on the lives of real people. Examples of contemporary Bill of Rights issues include laws requiring students in public schools to take tests for illegal drug use, the application of capital punishment to minors and persons with mental disabilities, the right of women to obtain legal abortions, public funding of educational services in private sectarian schools, the prohibition of religious ceremonies in public school activities, and the right of individuals to engage in controversial forms of expressive behavior—such as exotic dancing and flag desecration. These are just a few of the fascinating topics discussed within these two volumes.

**Challenges to Liberties.** Throughout American history, international wars and fears of domestic violence have periodically surfaced and threatened to restrict the liberties guaranteed by the Bill of Rights. The dramatic terrorist attacks on Washington, D.C., and New York City on September 11, 2001, certainly had such an effect. Six weeks afterward, on October 25, the U.S. Congress enacted an omnibus law of some 342 pages called the USA Patriot Act. It was designed to expand the authority of law enforcement officials to monitor telephone conversations and Internet messages and to detain aliens on mere suspicion of terrorist activity. The American Civil Liberties Union and other libertarian groups alleged that the complex law undermined several constitutional guarantees, especially the Fourth Amendment's rules concerning probable cause and search warrants. Then, on November 13, President George W. Bush issued a military order that authorized military tribunals to try noncitizens accused of terrorism. The tribunals were to be allowed to conduct secret trials without juries, despite the Sixth Amendment, and to disregard many principles of due process that are normally considered Fifth Amendment rights. Critics of President Bush's order pointed to *Ex Parte Milligan* (1866), in which the Supreme Court rejected the use of military trials when the regular courts were in operation. Supporters of President Bush's order, on the other hand, looked to another case, *Ex Parte Quirin* (1942), in which the Court approved trying eight suspected German saboteurs in military tribunals. The legal disputes surrounding what in late 2001 was being called the new "war on terrorism" demonstrated once again that interpretations of the Bill of Rights can determine the freedom and future prospects of ordinary people.

**Other Rights.** These two volumes are devoted to the Bill of Rights and thus do not cover every right and liberty that Americans enjoy. The right to vote, for example, is not covered here, even though voting is considered a fundamental right of citizenship. Neither the original Constitution nor its first ten amendments addressed qualifications for the voting franchise, a matter that the Constitution left entirely up to the states. It is thus not the Bill of Rights, but the Fifteenth, Nineteenth, Twenty-fourth, and Twenty-sixth Amendments that authorize the federal courts to provide safeguards for the right to vote. Also, these two volumes do not include essays about the Thirteenth Amendment, which prohibits slavery, or about the various civil rights laws, which are designed to prohibit discrimination based on race, ethnicity, sex, and religion.

On the other hand, these volumes may at times appear to range beyond the twenty-seven specific rights and liberties enumerated in the Bill of Rights. The Fifth Amendment, for instance, has a clause requiring government to employ "due process of law" whenever depriving persons of their life, liberty, or property. The broad concept of due process is often related to other guaranteed rights in the Constitution, such as the writ of *habeas corpus*, and the concept also subsumes many common law principles, as well as substantive rights to life, liberty, and property. The requirement for proof beyond a reasonable doubt in criminal prosecutions is an example of a common law principle that is considered to be a part of due process. Much more controversial is the doctrine of substantive due process, which recognizes substantive rights to life, liberty, and property, and requires government to justify any deprivation of these rights with an appropriate rationale. The Supreme Court has expanded the concept of liberty, moreover, to include a generic "right of privacy," which refers to personal autonomy, family relationships, and a woman's right to terminate a pregnancy.

**The Ninth Amendment.** Because of the special characteristics of the Ninth and Tenth Amendments, many works about the Bill of Rights deal almost exclusively with the first eight Amendments. The Ninth Amendment, which suggests the existence of rights not enumerated in the Constitution, is especially enigmatic and open to numerous interpretations. Because of its vagueness, some lawyers have looked upon the amendment as a refuge for litigants without cogent legal arguments, so that the phrase "relying on the Ninth Amendment" is understood to be almost humorous. However, James Madison and the other framers of the Bill of Rights did choose to include the Ninth Amendment, and they must have assumed that it had some practical application. Some scholars have interpreted the amendment in light of the framers' commitment to the theory of natural rights, either based on a religious foundation or on an assumption of a shared human nature. Others have emphasized the provisions of the common law tradition, as in the establishment requirement that a criminal jury in a federal trial must be composed of twelve jurors. Still others have suggested that the amendment simply means that the absence of an enumerated right from the Constitution does not necessarily prove that such a right does not exist. In one significant Supreme Court case, *Griswold v. Connecticut* (1965), the Ninth Amendment's application was overlapping with the doctrine of substantive due process, and it is possible that this broad reading of the amendment may become more common in the twenty-first century.

**The Tenth Amendment.** Liberal critics of states' rights and federalism often prefer to ignore entirely the Tenth Amendment, which gives states authority over matters not delegated to the federal government in the Constitution. A common complaint is that the amendment has allowed the states to enact undemocratic laws and to oppress members of racial minorities, especially in the time of slavery and Jim Crow. Although there is abundant historical support for this point of view, it is also true that Madison and other framers looked to the Tenth Amendment as a means of preventing abuses by the federal government, and they assumed that the states were bastions of liberty. Historically, the Supreme Court has often considered the application of the Tenth Amendment in relationship to the original Constitution's commerce and elastic clauses—two clauses that have allowed for expansive interpretations of congressional power. Because of their relevance to the Tenth Amendment, these volumes include essays relating to these two clauses. In addition, the Fourteenth Amendment, which was ratified in 1868, has expanded federal powers and reduced the states' reserved powers within three broad areas: the privileges or immunities of citizens, the due process of law, and the equal protection of the laws.

**Incorporation.** During the twentieth century, most of the provisions of the Bill of Rights were "incorporated" or "absorbed" into the Fourteenth Amendment, thus making these provisions binding on the state governments. It seems quite clear that James Madison intended that the Bill of Rights would only apply to the federal government, because he expected that the amendments would be placed in Article I, section 9, which explicitly limited the powers of Congress. Madison also proposed am additional amendment that would have made four rights applicable to the states, and he assumed that this failed amendment should be placed in section 10, which lists prohibitions on the state governments. In view of this history, the Supreme Court, in *Barron v. Baltimore* (1833), recognized that the first nine amendments were not binding on the states. In formulating the Fourteenth Amendment, there is considerable evidence that its framers expected that its "privileges or immunities" clause would subsume at least a few (perhaps most) of the rights in the Bill of Rights. In the *Slaughterhouse Cases* (1873), however, the Supreme Court rejected such a construction of the privileges or immunities clause, and it was not until the 1920's that the Court seriously began to apply most of the Bill of Rights to the states by way of the Fourteenth Amendment's due process clause. This fascinating topic is covered in the overview essay on incorporation and a number of essays on individual Supreme Court cases in the second volume.

The most difficult choices about which materials to include in the guide relate to the Fourteenth Amendment's mandate that states must provide every person with the "equal protection of the laws." This equal protection clause, as its wording makes clear, was originally binding only on the state governments, not the national government. Racial segregation cases such as *Plessy v. Ferguson* (1896), were concerned with state statutes and did not have any real bearing on the federal government or the Bill of Rights. After World War II, however, the Supreme Court began interpreting the Fifth Amendment's due process clause to incorporate an equal protection requirement. Ironically, the Court cautiously endorsed this interpretation, often called "inverse incorporation," when approving of the discriminatory treatment directed at Japanese Americans during World War II, and it firmly established the doctrine in *Bolling v. Sharpe* (1954), the landmark case that held that Congress's own operation of segregated government schools in the national capital violated the Fifth Amendment. Since the *Bolling* ruling, many equal protection cases have directly applied to the Fifth Amendment, especially when the issues are gender discrimination and affirmative action. The various cases dealing with court-ordered busing, on the other hand, are not relevant to the Fifth Amendment, because none of them has ever dealt with federal policies.

**Controversies and Objectivity.** Throughout American history, applications of the Bill of Rights in particular circumstances have been extremely controversial. In addition to their practical consequences, the study of these applications are intellectually compelling. Few Americans can be detached or unemotional when considering matters such as freedom for unpopular religious practices (such as peyote smoking), restrictions on the public support of popular religious practices (such as Christmas Nativity scenes), rules for searches and seizures by the police, or reproductive liberty versus fetal rights. Such topics frequently produce angry exchanges and occasionally even lead to violent confrontations. Justice Hugo L. Black once stated that most Americans assume that the Constitution supports the particular views that they endorse and prohibits those ideas and practices they dislike. This common tendency, in fact, seems to be equally true of liberals, conservatives, and moderates. Recognizing the influences of unconscious bias, the authors of the articles in these volumes have tried to be as dispassionate and objective as humanly possible, and they have emphasized factual information and avoided expressions of personal opinions. To the extent that it is possible, moreover, they have made every effort to be fair to viewpoints with which they may disagree.

These volumes are not designed primarily for lawyers and scholars who possess a specialized knowledge in the field of constitutional law. Rather, they are intended for general readers and students attending high school or college. Thus, their writers have tried to use straightforward language and to define terms that are not part of the vocabulary of the person without advanced instruction. At the same time, the editors have not avoided difficult and challenging topics. While the writers and editors have tried to utilize an accessible style and a clarity of expression, they have not utilized misleading or overly simplistic analyses of complex legal issues.

It has been a true pleasure to work on this project and to select the essays for inclusion in the volumes. I wish to express appreciation to the many fine scholars who have written these essays. In addition, I wish to thank R. Kent Rasmussen and the other editors of Salem Press for developing the project, helping in the selection of essays, and doing much of the actual work.

*Thomas T. Lewis*
*Mount Senario College*

# THE BILL OF RIGHTS

# BILL OF RIGHTS

*Description:* The first ten amendments to the U.S. Constitution, guaranteeing individual rights, such as freedom of speech, freedom of the press, separation of church and state, the right to counsel, the right against self-incrimination, and due process.

*Significance:* The Bill of Rights has posed an endless series of challenges for the Supreme Court to interpret the scope of personal liberties and the limits of government power.

When the Constitutional Convention adjourned in September, 1787, and submitted its new Constitution to a curious public, three of the remaining delegates refused to sign the new charter. One, George Mason of Virginia, declared that he would "sooner chop off this right hand than put it to a constitution without a Bill of Rights." Fearing that Mason and other Antifederalists might scuttle the ratification of the new Constitution, James Madison promised his fellow Virginians that if they supported the new charter (and elected him to the First Congress), he would sponsor a Bill of Rights. Each side kept its end of the bargain.

In December, 1791, the Bill of Rights was ratified, launching more than two hundred years of Supreme Court decisions interpreting, defining, and refining the nature of the relationship between the government and its citizens.

The Constitution was essentially a plan of government, establishing the legislative, executive, and federal branches and delineating their powers and responsibilities. Although the Constitution purported to grant only limited powers to Congress to pass laws in specified areas, it also provided that Congress had the authority to "make all Laws which shall be necessary and proper for carrying into Execution the foregoing Powers, and all other Powers vested by this Constitution in the Government of the United States, or in any Department or Officer thereof." This elastic catch-all clause worried those who feared that the Constitution would install an all-powerful national government, free to dominate the people and the states. It was the Bill of Rights that gave these critics some measure of solace that the new federal government would not become the same tyrannical seat of power that they had so recently fought to escape.

From the outset, the Supreme Court played a special role in giving meaning to the Bill of Rights. In March of 1789, Thomas Jefferson wrote

*James Madison, the chief architect of the Bill of Rights.* (Library of Congress)

to Madison that "the Bill of Rights is necessary because of the legal check which it puts into the hands of the judiciary." Jefferson was referring to a "legal check" on unwarranted government interference with the rights of the citizens.

The Bill of Rights touches on every realm of human affairs. It has fallen to the Supreme Court to interpret its elusive and elastic language. In every generation, the Court has been called on to grapple with the challenge of applying its 413 words, written in the late eighteenth century, to circumstances unknown to the authors, arising in the nineteenth, twentieth, and twenty-first centuries. The Bill of Rights protects both substantive and procedural rights. In contrast to the Constitution itself, which says what the government *can* do, the Bill of Rights says what the governmen *cannot* do.

**First Amendment.** The most powerful articulation of individual rights against government intrusion is found in the First Amendment, which is considered by many to be the most important of all the Amendments. The opening words speak volumes about the purpose and intent of the Bill of Rights: "Congress shall make no law . . . " These five words set the tone for all that follows. However, the simplicity is deceiving and the Supreme Court has the responsibility of deciding which laws pass constitutional muster and which do not.

Specifically, under the First Amendment, Congress is prohibited from making laws "respecting an establishment of religion or prohibiting the free exercise thereof." In one phrase, the First Amendment simultaneously guarantees the right of individuals to follow the beliefs and practices of their chosen religious faiths, while at the same time, it prohibits the government from singling out any particular religious denomination as a state-sponsored church. The First Amendment built what Jefferson called a "wall of separation" between church and state.

The free exercise and establishment clauses generated great consternation for the Court on controversial issues. From prayer in school to religious symbols on public property, from religious invocations at high school graduations to vouchers using public funds to subsidize parochial schools, the Court struggled to ensure that government remains neutral, but not hostile, in matters of religion.

The First Amendment next prohibits Congress from "abridging the freedom of speech, or of the press, or the right of the people peaceably to assemble, and to petition the Government for a redress of grievances." No portion of the Bill of Rights has engaged the Court's attention with more intensity, drama, and public interest than its protection of freedom of expression and freedom of assembly. Volumes have been written about how and why the Court decided whether particular speech or gatherings are constitutionally protected.

No majority of Supreme Court justices ever treated the protections guaranteed by the First Amendment as absolute. Instead, the Court has recognized exceptions for obscenity, libel, criminal solicitation, perjury, false advertising, and fighting words. Within and beyond these categories, the Court has shifted, especially in times of war or during external threats, from the protection of wide-open, robust debate to the punishment of controversial ideas.

**Second Amendment.** The Second Amendment has been controversial; however, it has been addressed by the Court only on rare occasions. It is popularly known for guaranteeing "the right of the people to keep and bear arms." However, in its most significant pronouncement, the Court unanimously held that this right is qualified by the opening phrase which reads: "A well regulated Militia, being necessary to the security of a free State ... " In the light of that limitation, most recently the Court declined to hear an appeal from a lower court ruling upholding a municipal ban on hand guns.

**Third Amendment.** The Third Amendment, prohibiting the quartering of soldiers in private houses in times of peace without the consent of the owner, or in times of war, except as prescribed by law, while vitally important when it was written, is no longer the subject of serious Court review.

**Fourth Amendment.** The Fourth Amendment is a catalogue of important personal rights that the Court has sought to interpret by balancing the right of privacy against the legitimate needs of law enforcement. It begins by declaring that the "right of the people to be secure in their persons, houses, papers, and effects, against unreasonable searches and seizures, shall not be violated." The very presence of the undefined term "unreasonable" has required the Court to delve into every manner of search and seizure, developing specific rules that police must follow in order to avoid the exclusion of evidence at trial. The Court has repeatedly articulated that the consequence for an illegal search or seizure is suppression of the evidence, thereby creating an incentive for police to scrupulously follow constitutional requirements.

The Fourth Amendment also guarantees that "no Warrants shall issue, but upon probable cause." Here again the Court developed rules to determine whether probable cause exists. In essence, the Court uses a standard of reasonableness based on all of the facts and circumstances surrounding a challenged search or arrest. The Court places itself in the position of the reasonable police officer, relying on particularized suspicion and past experience, but rejecting mere hunches or guesswork.

**Fifth Amendment.** The Fifth Amendment also protects the rights of persons charged with crimes. It prohibits double jeopardy ("subject for the same offence to be twice put in jeopardy of life or limb"), self-incrimination (being "compelled in any criminal case to be a witness against himself"), denial of due process (being "deprived of life, liberty, or property, without due process of law"), and a taking without compensation (having "private property ... taken for public use without just compensation"). The Court takes these rights very seriously because they set critical boundaries on what government may do in prosecuting crime.

**Sixth Amendment.** The Sixth Amendment protects the rights of persons charged with criminal violations. Often mischaracterized as mere "technicalities" protecting the "guilty," Sixth Amendment rights were included in the Bill of Rights because the Founders had lived under a government that frequently arrested, jailed, convicted, and punished individuals without any semblance of fairness or justice.

Under the Sixth Amendment, the accused has a "right to a speedy and public trial." Both elements of this right are very important. The right to a trial is of little value if the accused is kept in jail for several months or years waiting to be tried. Generally speaking, unless the accused waives the time limit, he or she is entitled to go to trial within sixty days after arrest. Likewise, a "public" trial is vital to ensure that an overzealous prosecutor or corrupt judge does not trample on the rights of the accused. Exposing criminal trials to the bright light of public scrutiny allows the general public and the press to observe the proceedings and see for themselves whether the accused is getting a fair trial. The days of the notorious "Star Chamber," where Englishmen were tried in secret, are a thing of the past.

Anyone accused of a crime is also entitled to "an impartial jury" chosen from the geographical area where the crime was committed. The Sixth Amendment guarantees that no one may sit on a jury if he or she has a demonstrable bias or prejudice against the accused, either individually, or because of his or her gender, race, religion, ethnicity, or any other immutable characteristic. Generally, trial judges go to great lengths to question prospective jurors in order to ferret out those who cannot discharge their duties in an impartial manner.

Anyone accused of a crime has a right under the Sixth Amendment "to be informed of the nature and cause of the accusation." Obviously, in order to defend himself, the accused must know what he is being accused of so that he can establish an alibi or find witnesses who may assist in proving his innocence. Only by knowing the charges can the accused's attorney challenge the sufficiency of the indictment or the validity of the statute or regulation involved.

Closely allied to this right is the important right under the Sixth Amendment "to be confronted with the witnesses against him." An accused is entitled to know who will testify against him or her so that the accused and his or her lawyer can prepare adequate cross-examination. From experience, the Founders knew that it is more difficult to lie to another's face than to do so when the other person is not present.

Also, under the Sixth Amendment, an accused has the right "to have compulsory process for obtaining witnesses in his favor." In other words, the accused has the right to subpoena other persons and require them to come to court to testify and to bring papers and documents. Because the government already has this power, this right ensures a level playing field, where an accused can force reluctant witnesses to present evidence that may exonerate him or her or prove that a witness for the prosecution is lying. Without this right, an accused would be confined to presenting only testimony or documents from persons who voluntarily chose to take the time to come to court.

Finally, and perhaps most importantly, the Sixth Amendment guarantees the accused the right "to have Assistance of Counsel for his defense." No person should face a criminal trial without competent legal counsel at his or her side. Only attorneys trained in the rules of evidence and trial procedures can adequately navigate through the complexities of a criminal trial. Indeed, so vital is the right to legal counsel that the law requires the state to provide a lawyer free of charge for the most serious crimes where the accused cannot afford one.

It is worth noting, before leaving the Sixth Amendment, that it contains no reference to the fundamental principle—considered the very foundation of Anglo-Saxon law—that one is innocent until proven guilty. Indeed, the presumption of innocence appears nowhere in the Bill of Rights or the Constitution. Yet, this essential right has repeatedly been recognized by the courts and remains a vital guarantee of American justice.

**Seventh Amendment.** The Seventh Amendment provides that in civil cases in federal courts at common law, where the value in controversy exceeds twenty dollars, "the right of trial by jury shall be preserved." Essentially, any civil case that entitled a litigant to a jury in 1791 still entitles the litigant to a jury today. Numerous rules (too extensive to be discussed here) have been developed by the courts to determine which civil claims must be tried before a jury and which may not.

The Seventh Amendment also guarantees that once a fact has been decided by a jury, it may not be otherwise reexamined in any federal court, except as provided by common law. Here again, because juries were viewed by the Founders as a protection against injustice and tyranny, it was important to ensure that once a jury had decided the facts in a case, a judge could not overturn that finding, except in limited circumstances provided in the common law.

**Eighth Amendment.** Further protections for criminal defendants are found in the Eighth Amendment, beginning with the guarantee that "excessive bail shall not be required." Persons awaiting trial are entitled to be released from jail, provided they post reasonable bail, in cash or property, which will be returned as long as they appear in court where required. The prohibition against excessive bail ensures that an accused is not arbitrarily detained because a judge has set an unreasonably high bail.

Closely related is the Eighth Amendment's prohibition against "excessive fines." This provision ensures that once convicted, an individual will be fined in proportion to his or her crime or in keeping with guidelines for similar offenses under similar circumstances.

The most important provision of the Eighth Amendment states that "cruel and unusual punishment" shall not be inflicted. This prohibition limits the kinds of punishment that can be imposed on those convicted of crimes. It proscribes punishment grossly disproportionate to the severity of a crime, and it imposes substantive limits on what can be made criminal and punished as such. At its most basic level, the prohibition against cruel and unusual punishment was intended to eliminate torture and other barbaric methods of punishment, although as recently as 1963, twenty lashes as part of the sentence for robbery was found not to be in violation of the Eighth Amendment.

By far, the most serious—and controversial— application of the prohibition on cruel and unusual punishment came in 1972 when the Court used it to strike down the death penalty (which was then reinstated four years later). The Court found that to the extent the death penalty was administered in an arbitrary and capricious manner, amounting to little more than a lottery, it constituted cruel and unusual punishment in violation of the Eighth Amendment.

Generally, in determining whether a punishment is cruel and unusual, the courts consider a variety of factors, including the age of the defendant, the attitude of the defendant, the availability of less severe punishments, contemporary standards of decency, the frequency of imposition, the disparity in punishments for the same or lesser crimes, the proportionality to the offense, the inhuman shocking or barbarous nature of the punishment, and the totality of the circumstances.

**Ninth Amendment.** One of the least known but most important provisions of the Bill of Rights is the Ninth Amendment, which in simple but meaningful terms states that the "enumeration in the Constitution, of certain rights, shall not be construed to deny or disparage others retained by the people." In many ways, these twenty-one words speak volumes about the very nature of American constitutional democracy.

As set forth in the Declaration of Independence, people are born with certain inalienable rights. They are not granted their rights by a benevolent government; they are born with those rights and they establish governments in order to preserve and protect them. Thus, people speak of the Bill of Rights as "guaranteeing" constitutional rights, not "creating" them.

The Founders firmly believed in those principles. Indeed at first, the drafters of the Constitution did not include a Bill of Rights because they did not contemplate that the Constitution posed any threat to the inalienable rights of all citizens. However, as noted at the outset, many feared that a new and powerful national government would seize all the power it could, thereby jeopardizing personal rights and liberties.

However, when James Madison set about to draft the Bill of Rights during the First Congress in 1789, he faced a dilemma: How could he write a comprehensive list of *all* rights enjoyed by Americans without the risk of leaving some out? The solution was the Ninth Amendment. There, Madison, with utter simplicity, stated that the fact that "certain rights" were enumerated in the Constitution did not mean that "others retained by the people" were denied or disparaged. Consequently, any analysis of constitutional rights cannot stop by merely examining the specific rights; the "certain rights" spelled out in the first eight amendments. One must go further to determine whether there are "others retained by the people."

One of the most profound applications of the Ninth Amendment relates to the right of privacy. Few rights are more important to Americans than the right to be let alone, yet the right to privacy is nowhere mentioned in the Constitution or the Bill of Rights. To some extent, the entire Constitution and Bill of Rights express a right to privacy, that is, a set of limited and enumerated powers delegated to the government, with all other powers and rights held by the people. When the Supreme Court in the 1960's and 1970's began to address laws restricting contraception and abortion, it found that the right of privacy was rooted in several amendments, including the First, Fourth, Fifth, and Ninth, and what it called the "penumbras" emanating from all of the amendments.

Trivialized by certain judges and scholars as a mere "water blot" on the Constitution, the Ninth Amendment, on serious examination, may well reflect the true meaning of the Bill of Rights.

**Tenth Amendment.** Parallel to the Ninth Amendment, the Tenth Amendment rounds out the Bill of Rights. It provides that the "powers not delegated to the United States by the Constitution, nor prohibited by it to the States, are reserved to the States respectively, or to the people." Thus, as all *rights* not expressed in the Constitution are retained by the people, all *powers* not delegated to the federal government are reserved to the individual States or to the people. The Tenth Amendment reemphasizes the *limited* nature of the national government, underscoring the fact that the government possesses only the powers expressly delineated in the Constitution and no others.

The Tenth Amendment is rather obscure on the question of whether the reserved powers belong to the states or to the people. This was surely intentional. Having made his point that the national government was a creature of limited powers, Madison and his colleagues left it to others, including state legislatures, state courts, and the people themselves to sort out their respective relationships when it came to these reserved powers.

The Bill of Rights continues to serve the majestic purposes for which it was written more than two hundred years ago. Sometimes with intentional ambiguity, often with passionate eloquence and always with elusive simplicity, the Bill of Rights represents one of the most masterful declarations of individual rights and civil liberties in human history. Yet, as a charter written by people to last the test of time, the Bill of Rights demands continuous study and interpretation to meet the challenges of the next century.

**Further Reading**

Don Nardo's *The Bill of Rights* (San Diego, Calif.: Greenhaven Press, 1998) provides an overview of the original debate over the need for a bill of rights and explores some of the later debates about rights. Books that examine the origins of the Bill of Rights include Akhil Reed Amar's *The Bill of Rights: Creation and Reconstruction* (New Haven, Conn.: Yale University Press, 1998), Leonard Levy's *Origins of the Bill of Rights* (New Haven, Conn.: Yale University Press, 1999), and *The Essential Bill of Rights: Original Arguments and Fundamental Documents* (Lanham, Md.: University Press of America, 1998), edited by Gordon Lloyd and Margie Lloyd. Works that examine the legacy of the Bill of Rights include Ellen Alderman and Caroline Kennedy's *In Our Defense: The Bill of Rights in Action* (New York: Bard, 1998), *The Bill of Rights, the Courts and the Law: The Landmark Cases that Have Shaped American Society* (3d ed., Charlottesville, Va.: Virginia Foundation for the Humanities and Public Policy, 1999) by Lynda Butler et al., and Nat Hentoff's *Living the Bill of Rights: How to Be an Authentic American* (New York: HarperCollins, 1998). *1791-1991: The Bill of Rights and Beyond* by the Commission on the Bicentennial of the United States Constitution, edited by Herbert M. Atherton et al. (Washington, D.C.: Commission on the Bicentennial of the U.S. Constitution, 1990) provides an interesting look back at the Bill of Rights.

*Stephen F. Rohde*

# CASE LAW

*Description:* The entire body of reported cases forming all or part of the law in a particular jurisdiction.

*Significance:* Case law is a defining characteristic of common law legal systems, which use cases to declare rules and principles of law

The common law, as developed in England and transplanted to colonial America, was unwritten and based on custom. It had no authoritative statement in a code or statute such as may be found in civil law systems. Legal rules and principles were "found" or "declared" by judges as they decided cases. A judicial decision can be viewed in two parts: first, the decision on who won and the relief granted, and second, the reasoned explanation of the judge in reaching the decision. It is the reasoned explanation which gives rise to a case law system, even if the reasons must be skillfully extracted or inferred from the written decision.

Cases, including their explanations, are used to decide future cases. If the facts of a future case are similar to the facts of an old case, the rule or principle of the old case will be used to decide the new case. The old case is called a precedent, and the general procedure whereby courts use old cases to decide new ones is called *stare decisis*. Over time *stare decisis* causes a refinement of old rules and principles, adapting them to changes in law and society. In addition, judges will change an old rule or principle if they believe it is wrong, outdated, or otherwise unacceptable. For example, the law of products liability changed in the early twentieth century as judges rejected established legal rules which did not allow consumers to recover damages when injured by defective products except under the most extreme circumstances. Today, the common-law rules allow recovery in most circumstances.

Case law is also used to interpret positive law, such as constitutions, statutes, and administrative regulations. This is particularly true if the language of the positive law is open-ended, vague, ambiguous, susceptible to different interpretations, or simply ill-defined. A court which applies the positive law in a particular case will announce a decision accompanied by a reasoned explanation. This explanation will be read by lawyers to discover a legal rule or principle, which will then be applied to future cases arising under the same or a similar positive law. For example, cases arising under the free speech clause of the First Amendment to the United

States Constitution have created a rich case law defining the boundaries of protected speech. The Constitution does not define what is meant by freedom of speech, so it is up to the courts to give meaning to this concept as they decide individual cases.

# COMMON LAW

*Description:* Law generated from court cases and judicial decisions.

*Significance:* The U.S. Supreme Court is a common-law court in that it generally follows earlier decisions made by judges.

Common law, or judge-made law, is generated from a succession of judicial decisions or precedents. In common-law systems, courts are bound by the rule called *stare decisis,* or "let the precedent stand." In the United States, common law is distinguished from equity law, which is based on reasoning about what is fair or equitable. It also differs from law based on statutes enacted by legislatures.

Common-law systems are contrasted with civil-law systems found on the continent of Europe and elsewhere, which are based on legal codes. Some of these systems are based on the *Code civil* ("civil law") drafted in Napoleonic France, derived partially from Roman law. By contrast, the common-law system was developed in England and brought to the American colonies. By 1776 the colonial courts used common law as a matter of course. After the American Revolution, decisions made in U.S. courts added to the body of common law.

The Supreme Court is a common-law court. Its decisions are the basis of constitutional law and it generally adheres, except when changing cir-

*The Supreme Court Building, Washington, D.C.* (Library of Congress)

cumstances warrant creation of new rules, to *stare decisis.* When government under the Constitution began in 1789, questions arose as to whether federal courts had jurisdiction over common law cases. The question also arose as to whether federal cases would themselves become a kind of common law in civil or criminal cases. The Court's decisions regarding these questions had far-reaching consequences.

In *United States v. Hudson and Goodwin* (1812), the Court ruled that no federal court could exercise common-law jurisdiction in criminal cases. It therefore denied the existence of a federal common law of crimes. Whether a federal common law of civil cases exists, however, was another matter. In 1842 in *Swift v. Tyson,* the Court ruled that there is federal common law in commercial cases. This ruling prevailed for nearly a century; then the Court, departing from *stare decisis,* reversed itself, ruling in *Erie Railroad Co. v. Tompkins* (1938) that one of its own decisions—*Swift*—was unconstitutional. Speaking for the majority, Justice Louis D. Brandeis wrote: "There is no federal common law." Nevertheless, this ruling did not completely eliminate the idea of federal common law, though today it is limited to specialized subjects.

The common-law process of following precedent in making decisions has allowed the federal judiciary to assume the position it holds in the U.S. constitutional plan. When Chief Justice John Marshall rendered the key decision in *Marbury v. Madison* (1803) that established the federal courts' power to declare laws void, he was following the common law obligation to apply all relevant law. Because of the force of precedent in common law procedure, the Court's action in *Marbury* has reverberated through two centuries of legal tradition, helping to shape the theory and practice of U.S. government.

**Further Reading**
Farnsworth, E. Allan. *An Introduction to the Legal System of the United States.* 3d ed. Dobbs Ferry, N.Y.: Oceana Publications, 1996.
Friedman, Lawrence M. *A History of American Law.* 2d ed. New York: Simon & Schuster, 1985.
Plucknett, Theodore F. T. *A Concise History of the Common Law.* 5th ed. London: Butterworth, 1956.

*Charles F. Bahmueller*

# CONSTITUTIONAL INTERPRETATION

*Description:* Process by which general principles of a constitution are applied by officials to individual laws or actions.

*Significance:* The Supreme Court has traditionally had the last word on constitutional interpretation, which can change the powers of government and alter the degree of protection that individuals have from government action. In turn, the permissible scope of interpretation has been determined by what the Court did as it decided cases through its existence.

Chief Justice John Marshall noted, in *Marbury v. Madison* (1803), that the U.S. Constitution requires extensive interpretation. Although it was written and put into effect in the eighteenth century, its creators expected it to last for a long time and assumed that the three branches of the federal government it established would do different things at different times. Although the Constitution purports to control government action, the limits it creates are phrased in broad, general terms and are often vague. Therefore, questions about what each branch is constitutionally allowed to do and the rights of individuals are constantly recurring.

**The Need for Finality.** Of necessity, all three branches of the federal government, as well as state governments, must sometimes interpret the Constitution. A tacit part of the creation of any law is the assertion that the legislature has the power to pass it. Before the Civil War (1861-1865), when government exercised only traditional and well-explored functions, these interpretations were rarely controversial. After the war, however, because of national expansion and the Industrial Revolution, governments began to legislate in new areas, to impose new taxes, and in general to be more energetic. These new actions often raised questions over whether legislatures or the president had the constitutional power to make them. In the twentieth century, large businesses, political pressure groups, and litigious cranks often have incentives (and money) to file lawsuits to challenge interpretations with which they disagree.

If there is a question over what the Constitution means and it is properly raised in a federal lawsuit, usually the Supreme Court's interpretation prevails. As part of its power, the Court can declare that an action of another branch of government violates some limit on the power of that branch and is therefore void, or unconstitutional. This power of judicial review is the most important of the Court's powers. The Court thus serves as the "umpire" of the political game, telling the various elected "players"—Congress, the president, and the states—what they can and cannot do. Through the late 1990's, the Court declared more than two hundred acts of Congress unconstitutional and invalidated a much larger number of state laws. It is also the guarantor of individual rights, determining how much protection Americans enjoy from government action.

The Constitution does not explicitly grant the Court this interpretive finality, and it is by no means clear why the Court should have it. Marshall himself argued that if interpretation is needed, courts are best suited to the task because they have extensive experience interpreting written documents and because they are sworn to give the Constitution priority over ordinary legislation. Scholars have argued that because federal judges have lifetime appointments and are insulated from political pressure, they can interpret the Constitution relatively free of ambition and political bias. Further, because judges are trained in the law, they are more likely to base their interpretations on legal or moral principles than Congress or the president (who are more likely to be swayed by transitory political concerns). Finally, because courts are weaker than Congress or the president, they pose less danger of becoming tyrannical. If nothing else, a final arbiter is needed in a government with a separation of powers, and public opinion seems comfortable with the Court serving as that arbiter.

**Judicial Restraint.** However, the actions of elected presidents and legislators—who presumably try to do what the public wants in order to be re-elected—can be set aside by the undemocratic decisions of nonelected judges. For this reason, most Court justices believe that they must restrain themselves to avoid coming into conflict with the elected branches too often. Justice Felix Frankfurter argued for this philosophy of judicial self restraint in numerous texts between 1939 and 1962. He pointed out that courts have no financial or military power and depend on broad support from the public to persuade the other branches to enforce court decisions. If they set aside the democratic decisions of legislatures or presidents too often, this public support will evaporate. Moreover, judges typically have less education in the details of policy and taxation than legislators do.

Justices who follow the philosophy of restraint try to avoid or at least delay interpreting the Constitution. They raise procedural obstacles to prevent lawsuits from being brought or decide cases on nonconstitutional grounds. If interpretation cannot be avoided, they try to make their interpretations as narrow and case-bound as possible. Above all, they presume that the actions of other branches are valid and do not declare them unconstitutional unless absolutely necessary.

**Judicial Activism.** Justices who follow the philosophy of judicial activism have strong political preferences and believe that they should use constitutional interpretation to write these preferences into law, even if the elected branches disagree. Consequently, they are much more willing to invalidate actions of the other branches.

Activists who supported the economic ideology of laissez-faire controlled the Court between 1895 and 1936. Because they believed that business should be allowed to operate as free of government regulation as possible, they interpreted the commerce clause and other parts of the Constitution very narrowly. They struck down many laws designed to protect worker health and safety or to otherwise limit how businesses were allowed to operate. By 1936, neither the states nor the federal government had much economic regulatory power left; consequently, neither was able to deal with the Great Depression. Public opinion turned against the Court, and the activist position was discredited. Judicial restraint justices, who became a majority after 1936, overturned many of the activist economic rulings, leaving it to legislatures to determine how extensively they could regulate the economy.

After 1936, most justices have been suspicious of activism. However, that stance enjoyed a resurgence between 1954 and 1969, when activist justices struck down state laws mandating racially segregated public schools and created new court procedures designed to protect the constitutional rights of people accused of crimes. Professor John Hart Ely argued that although elected branches usually can be trusted to operate constitutionally when they deal with economic issues, they can sometimes be perverted by improper election procedures or other structural flaws. If legislatures are malapportioned or voting registration procedures are corrupted so that some people cannot register to vote, the public may not be able to make its wishes known at elections. Majority rule and democracy will not occur. Ely argued that judicial activism is needed to correct these structural flaws when legislatures are unable or unwilling to do so.

Following *Baker v. Carr* (1962), the Court ordered legislative reapportionment in many states to ensure that each person's vote counted equally in choosing legislators.

Some justices take compromise positions between activism and restraint. Justice Harlan Fiske Stone argued that courts can defer to legislatures when economics is involved but need to be especially vigilant when legislatures act to limit freedom of speech, press, or religion because these rights are fragile and easily lost. The Court must, in his words, give these political rights a preferred position. In the 1970's the Court used Stone's view as the basis for the strict scrutiny principle: Unlike economic legislation, laws that limit basic rights or that operate to harm politically weak minorities are presumed to be invalid unless they are indispensable to achieving some extremely important government goal. Through the 1990's, the Court continued to construe legislative power very narrowly in such cases.

**Interpretivism.** The dispute between judicial activists and restraintists is largely a dispute about when, or how often, the Court should interpret the Constitution. Justices are also divided over how the job should be done. Supreme Court justices have always assumed that they should function as a court of law, by applying principles of interpretation to individual cases in an objective and disinterested way and by treating like cases alike.

However, the Constitution does not contain principles for its own interpretation. These have to be discovered elsewhere, and justices and scholars disagree over the method. Interpretivists, sometimes called originalists, believe that the Constitution should be interpreted as intended by the people who framed and ratified the Constitution—the Founders. Interpretivists typically believe that there are eternal political principles, such as the belief that power corrupts, which must be controlled if government is to operate fairly. The wise Framers knew these principles, embodied them in the Constitution, and expected these principles to control all constitutional interpretation. Thus, interpretivists claim that they are following the path marked out by the Framers.

In addition, as Justice Clarence Thomas and many others argued, the legitimacy of the Constitution depends on its having been accepted by the people in the ratification procedure in 1789. In that "constitution-making moment," a contract was created between the rulers and the ruled. The Constitution, which is the written part of that contract, secured the consent of the governed for the limited government it set up. However, the people accepted the Constitution as the Framers expected it to be interpreted. The interpretations of the Framers. the unwritten part of the agreement, are thus equally binding. If the Court interprets the Constitution in some other way, governments may come to exercise more powers than the people granted.

When controversies arise about what the Constitution means, interpretivists try to determine what its Framers intended. Most try to learn about the values of the Founders by studying their records and papers. Others seek principles in the records of American and British common-law courts because courts discuss and apply the political values of their times. Still others study traditions and customs. For example, the practice of beginning each session of Congress with a prayer, which has existed since the first Congress wrote the First Amendment in 1790, has been cited as proof that the Framers did not intend that amendment to forbid all ceremonial prayer in government proceedings. Finally, others, called textualists, try to discover principles embedded in the language of the Constitution by studying how its words and phrases were used in the eighteenth century.

Sometimes the interpretive intent of the Framers can easily be discovered. For example, it is clear that the Framers did not intend the prohibition on cruel and unusual punishments to forbid the death penalty as such because they continued to use it. However, many parts of the Constitution remain stubbornly unclear. Sometimes the intent of the Framers cannot be discovered, and sometimes, they disagreed with one another. In more troubling cases, some values of the Founders, including their toleration of slavery, have become outdated or offensive. Professor Ronald Dworkin, for example, has observed that although the Founders overwhelmingly accepted racially segregated schools and many other governmental inequities, any constitutional interpretation that permitted these inequities to exist today would be overwhelmingly rejected by most Americans.

**Noninterpretivism.** For these reasons, noninterpretivists argue that the intent of the Founders should be given little weight in contemporary constitutional interpretation. Most noninterpretivists either deny that there are political principles of eternal validity or else believe that the few such principles that do exist are of such generality that they offer little guidance to dealing with concrete problems. As Chief Justice Earl Warren observed, the rule to "treat people equally except in exceptional cases" does not help a justice trying to decide whether segregated schools should constitute such an exception.

Nor, as Justice William J. Brennan, Jr., has noted, does the Constitution depend for its binding effect on the consent of people in 1789. Instead, he argues, the people must constantly accept the Constitution as it exists today. They do so tacitly, by obeying its requirements. They will continue to do so as long as the Constitution meets their expectations about what it should be like. If there is any conflict between what the law says the Constitution is and what the people want it to be at any moment, then the job of the Court is to sit as a "permanent constitutional convention" and, by interpretation, to revise the Constitution to fit the public expectations.

This is what the Court did in *Brown v. Board of Education* (1954), when it struck down the segregated schools that had long been legally accepted. Significantly, in *Brown*, the Court ignored the history urged on it by interpretivists, saying only that it could not "turn back the clock" to the Civil War or the colonial period. Instead, Chief Justice Warren emphasized sociology, stressing the importance of contemporary education to the ability of individuals to achieve their goals and function as citizens.

As compared with interpretivists, noninterpretivists assume that change is more rapid and cuts deeper into political values and beliefs. Though they insist that the values of contemporary citizens should be given priority, they offer little guidance on how to discover these values. Nor do they explain how to tell the difference between basic principles and values, which should govern views on many political issues over time, and short-term political principles specific to an issue. Finally, noninterpretivists do not explain the source of the power they claim to continually revise the Constitution. Though that document contains procedures for formal amendment, it nowhere gives the Court the right to serve as a "permanent amending convention."

**Other Views.** In an influential 1959 article, Professor Herbert Wechsler argued that any constitutional interpretation, to be fair, must be made on the basis of a neutral principle, a rule capable of being applied uniformly to all similar cases without creating an advantage for any particular political force. Neutral principles may be those of the Founders or may be discovered later. His examples are derived from moral principles and relate to controversies of the period: A state cannot escape limits on public action by transferring some government function (such as holding primary elections) to private control, and racial segregation (a denial of equality per se) may constitute a denial of freedom of association. Presumably, the neutrality of such principles can be tested by philosophers who study critical cases.

Neutrality has long been an important consideration in constitutional law. Therefore, the holding that the First Amendment guarantees the right to hold peaceable public parades cannot be considered fair unless it is applied impartially to Republicans and Democrats and civil rights activists and members of the Ku Klux Klan. Professor Wechsler suggests that interpretive principles can be similarly neutral and should not be used by the Court unless they are.

The neutral principles approach seems intuitively fair. In legal proceedings, neutrality seems achievable. Thus, courts insist that laws be knowable in advance, for example, and that lawyers for both sides in a lawsuit have adequate time to prepare their cases. However, it may not be possible to find nontrivial principles that are truly neutral. Wechsler suggests that equality may be such a principle, but others have disagreed.

Most of the individual rights guaranteed by the Constitution are not meant to be absolute. The public is protected, for example, against only "unreasonable" searches and seizures; the privilege of *habeas corpus* must not be suspended "unless the public safety requires." However, some parts of the Constitution are phrased to suggest that they allow no exceptions. For these, absolutists argue that the Constitution should always be interpreted to forbid government action. For example, absolutists interpret the First Amendment statement that Congress shall make no law abridging freedom of speech as meaning that Congress cannot regulate sedition, the utterance of threats, or the publishing of obscene literature.

Absolutists make it unnecessary to draw precise legal lines between things that may be vague and subjective. If they prevailed, it would be unnecessary, for example, for justices to distinguish between obscene material, which legislatures could ban, and nonobscene pornography, which is protected under the First Amendment. However, this would require the acceptance of extremes of behavior offensive to both Founders and contemporary Americans. In practice, absolutists tend to allow exceptions by casuistry. Uttering a threat, for example, is said to be a form of action, not speech. The publication of obscene material is seen as an incitement of violence against women, rather than as freedom of the press.

Finally, in cases in which rights conflict, the Court has created legal rules, or doctrines, for handling the conflict. Sometimes rights are placed in a hierarchy. Those rights of criminally accused persons that are necessary for courts to hold fair criminal trials, for example, have been preferred to individual rights to speak or publish. The latter, in turn, have been preferred to the rights of political leaders and bureaucrats to act with "administrative efficiency."

In other cases, rights have been balanced against one another. In *United States v. Nixon* (1974), for example, in which the president unsuccessfully sought to keep secret audiotapes that had been requested by former aides who needed them to defend themselves against criminal charges, the Court balanced the need of the president to keep information confidential against the constitutional rights of the defendants in a criminal court.

**Further Reading**

Lee Epstein and Jack Knight have described how the Court goes about its work in *The Choices Justices Make* (Washington, D.C.: Congressional Quarterly, 1998). The most comprehensive presentation of the various approaches to interpretation is Craig Ducat, *Modes of Constitutional Interpretation* (St. Paul, Minn.: West Publishing, 1978). Activism and restraint are examined in *Supreme Court Activism and Restraint* (Lexington, Mass.: Lexington Books, 1982), edited by Stephen C. Halpern and Charles M. Lamb, and Christopher Wolfe's *Judicial Activism: Bulwark of Liberty or Precarious Security?* (rev. ed., Lanham, Md.: Rowman & Littlefield, 1997). Leif Carter has written an accessible introduction to the problem of original intent, *Contemporary Constitutional Lawmaking* (New York: Pergamon, 1986). Judge Robert H. Bork argues for one form of interpretivism in *The Tempting of America* (New York: Simon & Schuster, 1990), and scholar Michael Perry examines noninterpretivism in *The Constitution, the Courts, and Human Rights* (New Haven, Conn.: Yale University Press, 1982) and interpretivism in *The Constitution in the Courts: Law or Politics?* (New York: Oxford University Press, 1994). Herbert Wechsler's views are best described in his own article, "Toward Neutral Principles of Constitutional Law," *Harvard Law Review* 73 (1959). Mark Tushnet demonstrates the difficulty of applying such an approach in practice in "Following the Rules Laid Down: A Critique of Interpretivism and Neutral Principles," *Harvard Law Review* 96 (1983): 781. Finally, the Court's traditional control of interpretation has not gone unchallenged. Tushnet takes a critical perspective in *Taking the Constitution Away from the Courts* (Princeton, N.J.: Princeton University Press, 1999).

*Paul Lermack*

# CONSTITUTIONAL LAW

*Description:* Dynamic body of law that defines and limits the powers of government and sets out its organizational structure.

*Significance:* As the fundamental law contained in the U.S. Constitution and in Supreme Court decisions interpreting that document, constitutional law blends legal decisions with elements of politics and political theory, history, economics, public policy, philosophy, and ethics.

A resilient document, the U.S. Constitution has endured with only twenty-seven amendments since its formulation in 1787. Its sweeping language and generalities allow change and interpretation in the face of altered circumstances, from the changing human condition to the changing composition of the Supreme Court. The Constitution contains few rules and is not self-explanatory. That lack of specificity was intentional.

The Constitution's original Framers outlined their general intent to create the fundamentals of a national government, prescribing how it should operate and limiting its scope of power. The ongoing interpretative process engaged in by the Court allows the provisions of the Constitution to change and adapt over time. The Court refers to the original Constitution because, by doing so, it can bring resolution of the new and often divisive issues of each generation. The genius of constitutionalism, therefore, lies in the opportunities provided in the document for change and continuity, the method of judicial interpretation, and the overall skill and sensitivity of the justices. The fact that the justices are lifetime appointees frees them from concerns about approval by political leaders and voters and permits concentration on the issues.

**Constitutional Decision Making.** Virtually all cases going before the Court involve seeking review of a decision by a federal court of appeals or a state supreme court. As the final authority on federal matters and questions dealing with the Constitution and treaties, the Court exercises appellate jurisdiction (appeals) and functions as a trial court (original jurisdiction) only in certain limited situations involving ambassadors or where a state is a party. Most of the cases reach the Court for review by means of a writ of certiorari, or through the exercise of the Court's discretion. This means that the Court has almost complete control of its docket. Of the 7,000 petitions for review annually, only 2 percent are granted. The

Court issues an average of 110 opinions per year, permitting a selected group of policy issues to be addressed.

The Court is shrouded in secrecy, assuming some of the awe and mystery of the document it interprets. Some have criticized the Court for remaining in an "ivory tower" far removed from "we the people" set out in the preamble to the Constitution. Decisions to grant or deny review are made in secret conferences attended only by the nine justices with no support staff. A traditional unwritten rule specifies that a case is accepted for review if four justices feel that it merits the Court's attention (rule of four) and that it would serve the interests of justice. The Court does not have to explain its refusal.

When the Court decides to hear a case, the clerk schedules oral argument during which the justices may interrupt and ask questions of the attorneys to clarify, debate, or explain the written briefs. Cases are discussed in secret conferences following oral argument. It takes a majority vote to decide a case.

Following the conference and ensuing discussion, an opinion or reasoned argument explaining the legal issues in the case and the precedents on which the opinion is based must be drafted. The manner in which a majority opinion is written can have a great impact on Americans. That impact depends in part on who writes the opinion and how it is written, and also on the extent of support or dissent by the remaining justices. A 5-4 plurality opinion does not demonstrate the firm conviction of the Court that is present in a unanimous or 8-1 decision.

Any justice can write a

*E. Robert Seaver, clerk of the Supreme Court in 1970. (Library of Congress)*

separate opinion. If justices agree with the majority's decision but disagree with its reasoning, they may write a concurring opinion. If they disagree with both the result and reasoning contained in the majority opinion, they may write a dissenting opinion or simply go on the record as dissenting without an opinion. More than one justice can join in a concurring or dissenting opinion.

Decision making or opinion writing is a painstaking and laborious process. The time involved varies from one justice to another depending on the complexity of the issues in the case. The actual reporting of decisions has changed from the days in which members of the Court read long opinions aloud, sometimes taking days to do so. When Charles Evans Hughes became chief justice in 1930, he encouraged the delivery of summaries of opinions. That practice has continued, and the justice writing the majority opinion delivers the summary. Dissenting justices deliver their own opinions. Computerization and Lexis and Westlaw legal databases have made newly decided opinions accessible to all within hours of their release.

**The Highest Court.** Decisions of the Court are final because there is no higher court to which to appeal. Its interpretation of statutes can be reversed only by congressional legislation, and its constitutional rulings overturned only by constitutional amendment. Absent these remedies, all courts are obliged to follow the Supreme Court in matters of federal law. In its decisions, the Court attempts to adhere to precedent, or *stare decisis*, and in that capacity serves as final authority in constitutional matters, thereby providing a uniform interpretation of the law, historical continuity, stability, and predictability. Just as the Court sets its own agenda and controls what it hears, accepting or rejecting cases according to individual and collective goals such as avoiding troublesome issues, resolving legal conflicts, and establishing policies favored by the justices, Court decisions are group products shaped by the law, the Court and the country's environment, and the personal value systems of and interactions among the justices.

The power to define the Constitution makes the Court unique among government institutions. Through the exercise of its constitutional role together with the rule of law, the Court has wielded far-reaching power. The proper functioning of federalism and the scope of the rights of the individual depend on the actions of the Court, whose words mark the boundaries of the branches and departments of government.

The justices function as "nine little law firms," autonomous but working as a collegial body to decide a case. In important cases, the opinions issued by the Court are often negotiated among the members, the result of a cooperative collaboration in which the end product is the joint work of all rather than the product of the named author alone.

**Self-Imposed Limitations.** The Court imposes certain limitations or barriers before accepting a case for review. It poses certain threshold questions to deal with tactical issues that must be resolved before the Court reaches the substance of the controversy. Referred to as "judicial restraint," if these elements are not overcome, the Court will not exercise jurisdiction over a case. Article III, section 2, of the Constitution requires that there exist an ongoing "case or controversy" at all stages of the proceedings, including appeal. As interpreted by the Court, these words limit the power of federal courts to resolving disputes between adversaries whose rights are truly in collision. Often called "justiciability," the requirement provides concreteness when a question is precisely framed. The case, therefore, must present a live dispute.

Precluded are advisory opinions, or giving advice on abstract or hypothetical situations, as the Court ruled in *Muskrat v. United States* (1911), and moot cases, or those that have already been resolved, settled, or feigned, or those in which circumstances or time have removed the dispute or conflict because there is nothing for a court to decide, as it ruled in *DeFunis v. Odegaard* (1974). Several narrow exceptions to the mootness rule exist where conduct is of short duration but capable of repetition such as election disputes or abortion cases such as *Roe v. Wade* and its companion case *Doe v. Bolton* (1973). In *Baker v. Carr* (1962), the Court determined that political questions or those matters more properly applicable to another branch of government will not be accepted, nor will friendly or collusive suits and test cases. Standing to sue requires that the litigants have a personal stake in the outcome of the case, having suffered an actual injury, in order to assure concrete adverseness. Ripeness requires the issues in the case to be clearly delineated and sharply outlined, not premature, in flux, or abstract. Moreover, the Court will not engage in speculation, contingencies, or predictions or issue extrajudicial advice.

**Judicial Review.** Courts participate in the development of constitutional law through judicial review. In the landmark case *Marbury v. Madison*

(1803), considered to be the point at which constitutional law begins, the Court held that Article III empowers courts to review government actions and invalidate those found to be repugnant to the Constitution by declaring them unconstitutional. The supremacy clause of Article IV states that no provision of state law and no legislative enactment may conflict with the national Constitution, which is the supreme law of the land.

The Framers of the Constitution decentralized control through federalism, considered one of the most important contributions to government. Federalism is a dual system in which powers are divided between national and state authorities.

**Bill of Rights.** Protecting the fundamental rights of individuals was considered of the utmost importance. The Framers believed that explicit enumeration of those rights would make the rights more secure. In order to achieve ratification of the main body of the Constitution, therefore, in 1791 the Framers appended to it a Bill of Rights, consisting of the first ten amendments of the present document. While the body of the main Constitution concerns government, the Bill of Rights represents the popular perception of constitutional guarantees.

Basic to American identity is the First Amendment and its central guarantees of freedom of speech, press, religion, assembly, and right to petition for redress of grievances. Despite language to the contrary, the rights contained in the Bill of Rights are not absolute. In the speech area, for example, certain categories of expression can be regulated; others are not protected at all. "Pure" speech that creates no danger to the public is protected. However, if speech advocates an imminent lawless action that presents a "clear and present danger," the speech loses its protection, as the Court ruled in *Schenck v. United States* (1919). In *Texas v. Johnson* (1989), the Court found that symbolic speech or use of actions as a substitute for words is generally protected, such as flag burning as a controversial but valid expression of political views. Obscenity or pornography, defamatory communications (libel and slander), and "fighting words" that provoke an immediate breach of the peace do not receive First Amendment protection.

Some rights that Americans consider basic to their fundamental freedoms are not mentioned specifically in the Constitution. Among these are the right of personal privacy, which protects the individual from state interference. The Court has struggled with the constitutional foundation of the right, suggesting various sources: the due process guarantee of the

Fourteenth Amendment and the penumbras or emanations from the interests protected by the First, Third, Fourth, Fifth, and Ninth Amendments (*Griswold v. Connecticut,* 1965).

**Further Reading**

Two well-written works containing detailed treatment with case references and quotations are Joan Biskupic and Elder Witt's *The Supreme Court and the Powers of the American Government* (Washington, D.C.: Congressional Quarterly, 1997) and *The Supreme Court at Work* (2d ed., Washington, D.C.: Congressional Quarterly, 1997), with biographical sketches of the justices and illustrations. Lawrence Baum's *The Supreme Court* (5th ed., Washington, D.C.: Congressional Quarterly, 1995) examines the role of the Court, the justices, the decision-making process, factors that influence the Court, activism in policy making, and the Court's significance. Organized by case themes, *Decision: How the Supreme Court Decides Cases* (New York: Oxford University Press, 1996) by Bernard Schwartz offers a behind-the-scenes look at how the Court decides cases. Archibald Cox's *The Court and the Constitution* (Boston: Houghton Mifflin, 1987) is a readable yet scholarly account of how the Court shaped constitutional law. Peter G. Renstrom's *Constitutional Law and Young Adults* (Santa Barbara, Calif.: ABC-CLIO, 1992) is a guide to the Constitution, the court system, and key provisions of the Bill of Rights and Fourteenth Amendment with case references. It is comprehensive in scope and comprehensible to the general reader. David P. Currie's *The Constitution of the United States: A Primer for the People* (Chicago: University of Chicago Press, 1988) contains an overview of the document and the major concepts contained in it in language intended for the general reader.

*Marcia J. Weiss*

# CONSTITUTION, U.S.

*Description:* The fundamental document establishing the national government of the United States of America. (*The full text of the Constitution appears in this volume beginning on page 379.*)

*Significance:* This document describes the nature and limits of political power within the national government; it also describes how the different branches of government will be structured

The Constitution of the United States is an extraordinary document, both theoretically and historically. Knowing how this document was developed is important to understanding both its purpose and its success.

**Development.** The Constitution of the United States was not the first— and some would argue that it is not the most important—of the founding American documents. The Constitution was developed eleven years after the approval of the Declaration of Independence. After declaring and then winning independence from Great Britain, the new nation spent a number of years governed by the Articles of Confederation. The Articles created a loose federation of states which eventually proved too weak to serve the needs of the young nation. In 1787 delegates from twelve of the states (all but Rhode Island) met to discuss ways of revising the Articles of Confederation to create a more adequate government. The Constitutional Convention of 1787 quickly decided that the basic premise behind the Articles of Confederation rendered them inadequate for governing the nation. The Convention began discussing a far more centralized form of government than was possible under the Articles of Confederation. James Madison and Edmund Randolph, two Virginia delegates who had anticipated this possibility, arrived at the Convention with the rough outlines of a totally new form of government. After considerable debate and numerous compromises, the Convention approved the Constitution of the United States and sent it to the states for their ratification. After further debate and much political maneuvering, the Constitution was eventually ratified by all thirteen states.

**Basic Principles of the Constitution.** One of the most unique aspects of the Constitution was that it was (and is) firmly based on a clear set of theoretical principles. To describe the Constitution as a document of the En-

E, the People of the United States, in order to form a more perfect Union, eſtabliſh Juſtice, inſure domeſtic Tranquility, provide for the common Defence, promote the General Welfare, and ſecure the Bleſſings of Liberty to Ourſelves and our Poſterity, do ordain and eſtabliſh this Conſtitution for the United States of America.

A R T I C L E  I.

Sect. 1. ALL legiſlative powers herein granted ſhall be veſted in a Congreſs of the United States, which ſhall conſiſt of a Senate and Houſe of Repreſentatives.

Sect. 2. The Houſe of Repreſentatives ſhall be compoſed of members choſen every ſecond year by the people of the ſeveral ſtates, and the electors in each ſtate ſhall have the qualifications requiſite for electors of the moſt numerous branch of the ſtate legiſlature.

No perſon ſhall be a repreſentative who ſhall not have attained to the age of twenty-five years, and been ſeven years a citizen of the United States, and who ſhall not, when elected, be an inhabitant of that ſtate in which he ſhall be choſen.

Repreſentatives and direct taxes ſhall be apportioned among the ſeveral ſtates which may be included within this Union, according to their reſpective numbers, which ſhall be determined by adding to the whole number of free perſons, including thoſe bound to ſervice for a term of years, and excluding Indians not taxed, three-fifths of all other perſons. The actual enumeration ſhall be made within three years after the firſt meeting of the Congreſs of the United States, and within every ſubſequent term of ten years, in ſuch manner as they ſhall by law direct. The number of repreſentatives ſhall not exceed one for every thirty thouſand, but each ſtate ſhall have at leaſt one repreſentative; and until ſuch enumeration ſhall be made, the ſtate of New-Hampſhire ſhall be entitled to chuſe three, Maſſachuſetts eight, Rhode-Iſland and Providence Plantations one, Connecticut five, New-York ſix, New-Jerſey four, Pennſylvania eight, Delaware one, Maryland ſix, Virginia ten, North-Carolina five, South-Carolina five, and Georgia three.

When vacancies happen in the repreſentation from any ſtate, the Executive authority thereof ſhall iſſue writs of election to fill ſuch vacancies.

The Houſe of Repreſentatives ſhall chuſe their Speaker and other officers; and ſhall have the ſole power of impeachment.

Sect. 3. The Senate of the United States ſhall be compoſed of two ſenators from each ſtate, choſen by the legiſlature thereof, for ſix years; and each ſenator ſhall have one vote.

Immediately after they ſhall be aſſembled in conſequence of the firſt election, they ſhall be divided as equally as may be into three claſſes. The ſeats of the ſenators of the firſt claſs ſhall be vacated at the expiration of the ſecond year, of the ſecond claſs at the expiration of the fourth year, and of the third claſs at the expiration of the ſixth year; ſo that one-third may be choſen every ſecond year; and if vacancies happen by reſignation, or otherwiſe, during the receſs of the Legiſlature of any ſtate, the Executive thereof may make temporary appointments until the next meeting of the Legiſlature, which ſhall then fill ſuch vacancies.

No perſon ſhall be a ſenator who ſhall not have attained to the age of thirty years, and been nine years a citizen of the United States, and who ſhall not, when elected, be an inhabitant of that ſtate for which he ſhall be choſen.

The Vice-Preſident of the United States ſhall be Preſident of the ſenate, but ſhall have no vote, unleſs they be equally divided.

The Senate ſhall chuſe their other officers, and alſo a Preſident pro tempore, in the abſence of the Vice-Preſident; or when he ſhall exerciſe the office of Preſident of the United States.

The Senate ſhall have the ſole power to try all impeachments. When ſitting for that purpoſe, they ſhall be on oath or affirmation. When the Preſident of the United States is tried, the Chief Juſtice ſhall preſide: And no perſon ſhall be convicted without the concurrence of two-thirds of the members preſent.

Judgment in caſes of impeachment ſhall not extend further than to removal from office, and diſqualification to hold and enjoy any office of honor, truſt or profit under the United States; but the party convicted ſhall nevertheleſs be liable and ſubject to indictment, trial, judgment and puniſhment, according to law.

Sect. 4. The times, places and manner of holding elections for ſenators and repreſentatives, ſhall be preſcribed in each ſtate by the legiſlature thereof; but the Congreſs may at any time by law make or alter ſuch regulations, except as to the places of chuſing Senators.

The Congreſs ſhall aſſemble at leaſt once in every year, and ſuch meeting ſhall be on the firſt Monday in December, unleſs they ſhall by law appoint a different day.

Sect. 5. Each houſe ſhall be the judge of the elections, returns and qualifications of its own members, and a majority of each ſhall conſtitute a quorum to do buſineſs; but a ſmaller number may adjourn from day to day, and may be authoriſed to compel the attendance of abſent members, in ſuch manner, and under ſuch penalties as each houſe may provide.

Each houſe may determine the rules of its proceedings, puniſh its members for diſorderly behaviour, and, with the concurrence of two-thirds, expel a member.

Each houſe ſhall keep a journal of its proceedings, and from time to time publiſh the ſame, excepting ſuch parts as may in their judgment require ſecrecy; and the yeas and nays of the members of either houſe on any queſtion ſhall, at the deſire of one-fifth of thoſe preſent, be entered on the journal.

Neither houſe, during the ſeſſion of Congreſs, ſhall, without the conſent of the other, adjourn for more than three days, nor to any other place than that in which the two houſes ſhall be ſitting.

Sect. 6. The ſenators and repreſentatives ſhall receive a compenſation for their ſervices, to be aſcertained by law, and paid out of the treaſury of the United States. They ſhall in all caſes, except treaſon, felony and breach of the peace, be privileged from arreſt during their attendance at the ſeſſion of their reſpective houſes, and in going to and returning from the ſame; and for any ſpeech or debate in either houſe, they ſhall not be queſtioned in any other place.

No ſenator or repreſentative ſhall, during the time for which he was elected, be appointed to any civil office under the authority of the United States, which ſhall have been created, or the emoluments whereof ſhall have been encreaſed during ſuch time; and no perſon holding any office under the United States, ſhall be a member of either houſe during his continuance in office.

Sect. 7. All bills for raiſing revenue ſhall originate in the houſe of repreſentatives; but the ſenate may propoſe or concur with amendments as on other bills.

Every bill which ſhall have paſſed the houſe of repreſentatives and the ſenate, ſhall, before it become a law, be preſented to the preſident of the United States; if he approve he ſhall ſign it, but if not he ſhall return it, with his objections to that houſe in which it ſhall have originated, who ſhall enter the objections at large on their journal, and proceed to reconſider it. If after ſuch reconſideration two-thirds of that houſe ſhall agree to paſs the bill, it ſhall be ſent, together with the objections, to the other houſe, by which it ſhall likewiſe be reconſidered, and if approved by two-thirds of that houſe, it ſhall become a law. But in all ſuch caſes the votes of both houſes ſhall

A portion of the U.S. Constitution printed in the Pennsylvania Packet two days after the document was sent to the states for ratification. (Library of Congress)

lightenment—an eighteenth century movement in European thought that celebrated the capacity of reason to solve human problems—would be to tell the truth but not necessarily the whole truth. Alexander Hamilton, a delegate to the Constitutional Convention from New York, claimed that the U.S. Constitution reflected what he described as a "new science of politics." According to Hamilton, this new science was based on principles either unknown to or not fully understood by previous generations. It is generally acknowledged that the most fundamental principles of the Constitution are separation of powers, federalism, and republicanism.

Each of these principles is critical to a clear understanding of the American system of government, but each was developed because of the commitment of the Framers of the Constitution to a prior principle—the principle of limited governmental power. A government founded on the principle of limited powers must develop safeguards to ensure that the people who wield the powers of government do not go beyond the limits. Within the American constitutional system this is accomplished by the three principles cited above.

**Separation of Powers.** Separation of powers was a political principle advocated by English philosopher John Locke and French philosopher Baron de Montesquieu. The Constitution of the United States was the first national political document to apply this concept of government. Distinct governmental powers had long been recognized, but the Constitution of the United States was the first to place these powers in separate branches of government. The first three articles of the Constitution describe the location and authority of the legislative, executive, and judicial powers of government.

Article I, section 1 of the Constitution begins by stating: "All legislative Powers herein granted shall be vested in a Congress of the United States, which shall consist of a Senate and House of Representatives." In addition to establishing the location of the legislative powers, this statement declares that those powers will be shared by two separate legislative chambers. Bicameralism (the term used to describe a two-chambered legislature) permits the two legislative chambers to provide internal checks on each other.

The notes taken at the Constitutional Convention reveal that disagreements over how the representatives to Congress would be apportioned and selected were the most difficult for the delegates to settle. At one point, delegates threatened to withdraw from the convention over this issue. The solution to this dispute produced one legislative chamber that represents states equally (the Senate) and another that represents states according to their population (the House of Representatives).

The Senate consists of two senators from each state in the Union. Senators are elected for six-year terms; the long term was intended to give them relative freedom from the passing whims of the electorate. One of the rationales for such long terms was that the Senate would be freer to speak to the long-term needs of the nation. The Constitution requires staggered terms for the senators so that a third of the Senate seats are up for election every two years. This requirement provides a degree of stability and continuity in the national government.

In contrast, the members of the House of Representatives hold two-year terms. These shorter terms keep House members in much closer contact with the American voters. By requiring that House members seek reelection every two years, the Constitution provides the voting public with regular access to national lawmakers.

Legislators who desire new laws or want to alter old ones must be able to persuade a majority of the lawmakers in both legislative chambers of Congress. By design, this process was not intended to be quick or easy. The legislature was meant to be a deliberative group that carefully examines all proposed laws. In a bicameral legislature, proposals that might be rushed through one chamber may be examined carefully in the second chamber. The Framers of the Constitution believed that it was more important that laws be carefully and thoughtfully examined than that they be approved quickly.

Article II, section 1 of the Constitution places the executive powers of the United States government in the hands of "a President." The Constitutional Convention had considerable difficulties developing the executive branch of government. In part, this was attributable to their basic suspicion of executive power. They also realized, however, that one of the greatest shortcomings of the Articles of Confederation was the absence of a clearly defined executive branch. The first question was whether the executive authority should be placed in a single executive or multiple executives. The second question, and one of the last to be settled at the Convention, concerned the method for selecting the executive.

After much debate, the Convention settled on a single executive. In the words of Alexander Hamilton, only a single executive would provide the "unity and dispatch" modern governments required. This sentiment prevailed, and the Convention then had to determine how "the President of the United States" would be selected. The electoral college was the method upon which they eventually settled. This system utilizes the states as electoral units and follows the representative principle devised for Congress to distribute the votes among the states.

The president's basic responsibilities are to see that national laws are faithfully executed, to serve as the commander in chief of the national armed forces, to appoint the executive officers of the different federal agencies, and to recommend judges to serve on the Supreme Court and the lesser courts established by Congress. In addition to these responsibilities, the president has a limited veto over the acts of Congress.

Article III of the Constitution describes the judicial branch of government. More specifically, it establishes the Supreme Court and any additional courts Congress may establish. One of the more unusual aspects of the Constitution is its establishment of an independent judiciary. Judges receive lifelong appointments, so they are as free from political influences as is humanly possible. The only qualification to this independence is that Congress has the power to impeach and remove judges if they behave in a manner that would warrant such removal. In this respect, judges are subjected to the same kind of scrutiny as are members of the executive branch of government.

One aspect of the separation of powers that is often given particular consideration is the concept of checks and balances. The Constitution provides that each of the three branches of government has certain "checks" on its power that are under the control of another branch. Congress, for example, controls the budget of the president and the judiciary. The president, on the other hand, can veto acts of Congress (Congress, in turn, can override a veto with a two-thirds vote in both houses). The president also appoints justices to the Supreme Court (with congressional approval). Finally, the Supreme Court can rule that the laws of Congress or the actions of the president are unconstitutional.

**Federalism.** This aspect of the Constitution is one of the more ingenious creations to grow out of the Constitutional Convention. Historically, national governments had been either unitary governments or confederal governments. Unitary governments place all power in the hands of a centralized authority. The British government is an example of such a system. In a confederal system, the ultimate power is decentralized among member states. Some responsibility may be given over to a centralized authority, but the real power remains with the decentralized units of government. This was the case under the Articles of Confederation. The federal system established by the Constitution was unique in that it created a governmental system in which the real powers of the political system were truly divided between the centralized and decentralized units of government.

The distribution of powers between the states and the national government has created considerable political tensions during the course of American history. It is important to realize that these tensions were largely intended by the Framers. Federalism, like the separation of powers, was built into the constitutional system as a check on governmental powers. Article VI establishes the Constitution, acts of Congress, and treaties as the "supreme Law of the Land," but the Tenth Amendment to the Constitution declares the limits of that supremacy: The states and the people possess all powers not delegated to the United States by the Constitution.

*John Jay, one of the authors of the* Federalist *papers, later became the first chief justice of the United States.* (Collection of the Supreme Court of the United States)

**Republicanism.** Article IV of the Constitution guarantees that every state in the union will have a republican form of government. The Federalist Papers, a collection of essays written by Alexander Hamilton, James Madison, and John Jay in 1787 and 1788, explain why a republican system of government was considered preferable to a democratic system. The tenth essay of this collection provides a detailed comparison of these two popular systems of government. The first advantage of republicanism is that governmental authority is delegated to a small group of citizens. The second is that republican governments can cover a much larger geographical area than a direct democracy can.

When a smaller group has the responsibility of representing a larger group, each of the representatives must speak for a variety of interests. By learning the interests and needs of a diverse number of groups, representatives approach governmental decision making with a broader perspective than they would if they were simply advocating their own interests and needs. Public opinion is thereby filtered through a select group of representatives who must keep the many needs of their district in mind.

The advantage of a large geographical area is that it produces a great diversity of interests. This diversity decreases the likelihood that a single interest will constitute a majority on any given issue. For example, while chicken processors may hold a majority interest in Arkansas or oil producers may be a major political force in Texas, neither of these groups can dominate a large geographical area such as the entire United States. Together, these factors increase the likelihood that governmental decisions will serve the general interests of the nation instead of one or a few dominant groups.

The existence of these basic principles within the Constitution creates a significant barrier to government guided by passion as opposed to government guided by reason. The many checks within the system provide numerous obstacles to laws that are not in the interest of a fairly wide and diverse group of citizens. The system also places a substantial burden of proof on those who want to change existing laws or develop new laws. The cumbersome nature of the political process exposes any legislative initiative to a series of examinations before a number of different bodies.

**Amendments.** The Constitution has been a remarkably stable political document. The method described in Article V for amending the Constitution has not been utilized very often. By 1995 there were only twenty-seven amendments to the Constitution. The first ten amendments, known as the Bill of Rights, were passed within three years of the Constitution's ratification.

Three amendments (thirteen through fifteen) were passed at the end of the Civil War to make the institution of slavery unconstitutional and to extend certain citizenship rights to African Americans liberated by the Civil War. One of these, the Fourteenth Amendment, through its requirements of "due process" and "equal protection of the laws," has been instrumental in expanding basic civil rights to a number of other groups as well. The Seventeenth Amendment instituted the direct election of senators, the Twenty-second Amendment limited presidents to two terms, and the Twenty-fifth Amendment provided for the transfer of power in cases of presidential disability. A number of amendments (fifteen, nineteen, twenty-three, twenty-four, and twenty-six) have expanded the electorate.

One of the reasons often cited for the Constitution not having gathered more amendments through the years is the role the federal courts have played in determining questions of constitutionality. This process, known as judicial review, has permitted the courts to clarify and fine tune aspects of the Constitution. At times the courts have been accused of taking undue advantage of this authority. President Woodrow Wilson, for example, once referred to the Supreme Court as an ongoing constitutional convention.

The Constitution has proved to be one of the most durable political documents of all time. One of the key reasons for this durability is the document's brevity. The Framers had a sense of what a constitution needed to specify and what it did not. Leaving many details unsettled, the Framers recognized that statutory laws, administrative law, and precedents could handle the more specific and transient details of government.

**Further Reading**

The most important work describing the Constitution is the collection of essays written by Alexander Hamilton, James Madison, and John Jay, *The Federalist Papers*. The Clinton Rossiter edition (New York: New American Library, 1961) is probably the most readily available. One of the most thorough volumes is edited by the late Allan Bloom, *Confronting the Constitution* (Washington, D.C.: AEI Press, 1990). A clearly written and thoughtful examination of some of the theoretical aspects of the Constitution can be found in Harvey C. Mansfield's *America's Constitutional Soul* (Baltimore:

Johns Hopkins University Press, 1991). The most readable constitutional history available is probably Alfred H. Kelly, Winfred A. Harbison, and Herman Belz's *The American Constitution: Its Origin and Development* (6th ed. New York: W. W. Norton, 1983). For a well-reasoned and well-written intellectual history, see Forrest McDonald's *Novus Ordo Seclorum: The Intellectual Origins of the Constitution* (Lawrence: University Press of Kansas, 1979).

*Donald V. Weatherman*

# DECLARATION OF INDEPENDENCE

*Description:* The document in which a group of colonial American leaders declared themselves independent of Great Britain and King George III (*The full text of the Declaration of Independence appears in this volume beginning on page 375.*)

*Significance:* The Declaration of Independence was the legal basis for the formation of the United States; it has significantly influenced American political thought, as well as that of other emerging nations, through the years

When in the Course of human events, it becomes necessary for one people to dissolve the political bands which have connected them with another, and to assume among the powers of the earth, the separate and equal station to which the Laws of nature and of Nature's God entitle them, a decent respect to the opinions of mankind requires that they should declare the causes which impel them to the separation.

So begins one of the most famous documents in political history. The American Declaration of Independence has had broad and sweeping historical effects. Believing in self-government, the signers of the declaration also believed they were providing the legal basis for organizing a new government—provided that the new republic, with the help of its allies, could win control of the field in battle. The endeavor marked the origins of what eventually became the most powerful nation in the world. In the twentieth century the United States had great significance in world history, and the origins of that historical effect can be traced back to Philadelphia, Pennsylvania, and July 4, 1776.

**The Declaration and the Revolution.** Many nations have found in the Declaration of Independence inspiration and ideological support for their own revolutions. Some of the wording and many of the ideas have found their way into later, more modern declarations of independence in various parts of the world. The American Revolution was not really a revolution in the modern sense of the word, but was a separatist war seeking independence rather than seeking to overthrow an existing government. In that sense the war could more accurately be called the American war for independence from Great Britain.

*Currier and Ives print of the signing of the Declaration of Independence on July 4, 1776.*
(Library of Congress)

The colonists claimed they were fighting a defensive war for the preservation of English liberties in the American colonies. There was indeed a continuity with the past, and many of the prewar political leaders in America continued as leaders in the new republic, but major changes also took place, including the writing of the Constitution of the United States in 1787. English customs, traditions, and the continuity of the English common law in the United States helped to preserve stability and minimize the upheaval of such momentous change. In several states the colonial charters were kept largely intact, changing only terms to meet the new political realities.

The Declaration of Independence was not entered into lightly, as the preamble and first paragraph explicitly state: "Prudence, indeed, will dictate that Governments long established should not be changed for light and transient causes." The Americans, though, were convinced that there was a design on the part of King George III of Great Britain to "reduce" the American colonies to rule under "absolute Despotism." For that reason they decided to declare independence and risk their lives, fortunes, and "sacred Honor" in the pursuit of freedom and independence. They stood on principle and they stood together, for as Benjamin Franklin so aptly put it, "We must all hang together or surely we will all hang separately." Obviously the British did not consider the Declaration of Independence to be a legal document. The risks were great and so was the courage of the patriots. In the end the British had no choice but reluctantly to acknowledge American Independence as declared.

The Americans declared that they were fighting for certain things besides independence. Thomas Jefferson, the author of the Declaration of Independence, penned the views of the assembled Continental Congress. His famous words expressed their views on the purpose for, and basis of, government:

> We hold these truths to be self-evident, that all men are created equal, that they are endowed by their Creator with certain unalienable Rights, that among these are Life, Liberty, and the pursuit of Happiness. That to secure these rights, Governments are instituted among Men, deriving their just powers from the consent of the governed; That whenever any Form of Government becomes destructive of these ends it is the Right of the People to alter or to abolish it, and to institute new Government, laying its foundation on such principles and organizing its powers in such form, as to them shall seem most likely to effect their Safety and Happiness.

**"Unalienable Rights."** All Americans (indeed all people, according to the implication of these words) have "certain unalienable Rights." Where did those rights come from? Certainly not from the state—or else the state could change and take them away, and they would not be "unalienable." They came from "their Creator," from "the Laws of nature and of Nature's God." The Declaration of Independence then acknowledges a higher law, or natural law, to which government and human laws must conform. Jefferson was a leader of the American Enlightenment and so used "natural law" terminology. Many of the other leaders were orthodox Christians and so used biblical terminology. John Dickinson, a leader of the Stamp Act Congress, for example, wrote that "Our liberties do not come from charters; for these are only the declaration of preexisting rights. They do not depend on parchments or seals; but come from the King of Kings and Lord of all the earth." Enlightenment or traditional Christian, both groups agreed that Americans are born with certain God-given rights, including life and liberty.

The concept of inalienable rights for the individual presupposes limitations on the power of the state, and that idea is the basic assumption involved in writing a constitution. During the American Revolution the main constitutional authority in the United States rested in the thirteen state constitutions. The Continental Congress acted as the extralegal representative assembly that attempted to hold the states together and to conduct the war and diplomatic relations. It was not until 1781 that the first "constitution" of the United States was adopted, the Articles of Confederation. Both the Continental Congress and the Confederation Congress lacked sufficient authority to act as a central government, however, and in due time the United States Constitution was written, adopted, and put into effect in 1789.

Thomas Jefferson did not claim originality in writing the Declaration. "All American whigs [Patriots]," he wrote, "thought alike on these subjects." He wrote the declaration "to place before mankind the common sense of the subject, in terms so plain and firm as to command their assent, and to justify ourselves in the independent stand we are compelled to take. . . . It was intended to be an expression of the American mind, and to give to that expression the proper tone and spirit called for by the occasion. All its authority rests then on the harmonizing sentiments of the day, whether expressed in conversation, in letters, printed essays, or in the elementary books of public right, as Aristotle, Cicero, Locke, etc."

The Declaration of Independence is not a constitution. It was partially designed to attract international support to the American cause. Yet if its basic presuppositions are correct and "the people" have a right to change their form of government, then the declaration is extremely important as a representative expression of the collective will of the people.

*Thomas Jefferson, principal author of the Declaration of Independence.* (White House Historical Society)

**Further Reading**

A good starting point for further reading on the Declaration of Independence is a collection of essays on the subject (and related matters), Earl Latham's *The Declaration of Independence and the Constitution* (3d ed. Lexington, Mass.: D.C. Heath, 1976). The ideas leading to the signing of the Declaration of Independence are brilliantly discussed in Bernard Bailyn's *The Ideological Origins of the American Revolution* (Cambridge, Mass.: Belknap Press of Harvard University Press, 1967), and in Gordon S. Wood's *The Creation of the American Republic, 1776-1787* (Chapel Hill: University of North Carolina Press, 1969). Dumas Malone's *The Story of the Declaration of Independence* (New York: Oxford University Press, 1975) is a pictorial book prepared for the bicentennial of the signing of the Declaration of Independence and is useful not only for the story but also for its sketches of the lives of the signers of the declaration. Those are given in more detail in C. Edward Quinn's *The Signers of the Declaration of Independence* (2d ed. The Bronx, N.Y.: The Bronx County Historical Society, 1988). Carl L. Becker's classic account, *The Declaration of Independence: A Study in the History of Political Ideas* (New York: Vintage Books, 1922, reprint 1960), is still useful. Russell Kirk has a chapter on the ideas implied in the Declaration of Independence in his *The Roots of American Order* (3d ed. Washington, D.C.: Regnery Gateway, 1991). Many biographies of Thomas Jefferson are available, including Merrill D. Peterson, *The Jefferson Image in the American Mind* (New York: Oxford University Press, 1960).

*William H. Burnside*

# ENGLISH BILL OF RIGHTS

*Description:* Adopted in 1689, the bill was one of the great charters of English liberties that limited the power of the monarch, repudiated the notion that kings rule by divine right, protected the prerogatives of Parliament, and recognized a significant number of individual rights.

*Significance:* An important component of England's unwritten constitution, the English Bill of Rights included six rights later enumerated in the U.S. Bill of Rights, and it accustomed American colonists to the notion of a constitution that explicitly limits governmental powers and protects fundamental rights and liberties.

The English Bill of Rights was a product of the Glorious Revolution of 1688, which resulted primarily from the stubborn attempts of England's King James II to restore Roman Catholicism as the dominant religion and to limit the powers of Parliament. Refusing to enforce the Act of Uniformity, he appointed Catholics to important positions in the government and army. Judge Jeffreys's infamous Bloody Assizes, in which some two hundred supporters of the Monmouth Rebellion were executed, convinced many people that James was a tyrant determined to emulate the absolutist model of France's Louis XIV.

Three developments of 1688 ignited the rebellion. First, James issued a new royal proclamation of religious toleration, suspending parliamentary statutes, and ordered the clergy to read it in the churches. Second, when seven bishops petitioned for permission to refuse the order, they were arrested and tried for seditious libel. Third, during the trial, James's Catholic wife gave birth to a son, meaning that his Protestant daughter, Mary, would no longer be heir to his throne. In response, seven prominent leaders of Parliament invited Mary and her Dutch husband, William of Orange, to restore Protestantism and the constitutional position of Parliament. When William invaded England with fourteen thousand troops, popular support for his cause soon became overwhelming. In desperation, James fled to France, where he lived the rest of his life. Parliament, its powers restored, declared the throne vacant and invited William and Mary to serve as constitutional co-monarchs.

Anglo-American colonists enthusiastically celebrated the change in England's government. James's consolidation of the northern colonies under a single royal colony had been highly disliked. On April 18, 1689, the people of Massachusetts arrested their governor, Sir Edmund Andros, and sent him back to England in chains. The leading Congregational minister, Cotton Mather, drafted a manifesto justifying the action. In New York City, Jacob Leisler led a revolt in the name of the new monarchs, while John Coode staged a popular uprising in Maryland.

William and Mary were crowned king and queen of England in Westminster Abby on April 11, 1689. They were required to swear that they would obey all laws of Parliament. A proposed Bill of Rights was read during their coronation ceremony. Parliament formally enacted the bill after the coronation, and the king and queen endorsed it on December 16, 1689.

Provisions in the English Bill of Rights can be grouped into three broad categories. First, several items related to the doctrine of parliamentary supremacy, including frequent sessions of Parliament, freedom of speech for its members, repudiation of the royal prerogative to suspend legislation, and the necessity of Parliament's consent for levying taxes and for the keeping of a standing army. Second, the document established rules for succession and restricted the crown to Protestants. Third, it asserted a number of individual liberties and procedural safeguards against arbitrary government, including the right of petition, the right of Protestants to "have arms for their defense," the importance of "duly impaneled" juries, and the repudiation of "cruel and unusual punishments" and "excessive bail,"

A century later, the English Bill of Rights served as a major source for the first eight amendments to the U.S. Constitution. In fact, the 1689 document contained provisions similar to six clauses in those amendments: the document's condemnation of cruel punishments and excessive bails closely resembles the Eighth Amendment; its recognition of the limited right to keep arms is similar to the Second Amendment; its right of petition is almost identical to this guarantee in the First Amendment; its condemnation of peacetime "quartering soldiers contrary to law" is also found in the Third Amendment; and its endorsement of jury trials is reaffirmed in the Sixth and Seventh Amendments, although the latter contain greater specificity about procedures. In contrast to the more absolutist language in the American amendments, the English document usually employed the terms "ought to be" or "ought not to be."

More important than its specific wording, the English Bill of Rights provided Americans of the revolutionary generation with the idea that a well-designed constitution should include a listing of the basic privileges and immunities of citizenship. Without the English model, it is entirely possible that the U.S. Constitution would not include the first ten amendments.

*Thomas T. Lewis*

# FEDERALISM

*Description:* Political union and the resulting constitutional structures that configure relationships among the states and institutions of national governance.

*Significance:* Problems of federalism involve questions of constitutional structure. The Supreme Court has expressed its position on relationships among institutions of national and state governance and enforced federal constitutional limitations against the states.

Even before the U.S. Constitution went into effect, there were serious debates about what type of political system it would create—and what type of union had already been formed. Part of the problem was multiple and shifting word usages. Those advocating the Constitution's ratification identified themselves as Federalists, described the new structures as partly federal, and claimed those structures were necessary to preserve the federal union. At the same time, members of the founding generation identified federalism with a confederation of sovereign states, as distinct from a consolidated or national government. Relying on these distinctions, James Madison in *The Federalist* (1788), No. 39, argued that the proposed Constitution was neither purely federal nor entirely national but instead included features of each.

Federalism in the American context has since become identified with this hybrid political system—especially the Constitution's configuration of national and state governing powers. Unlike the Articles of Confederation, the Constitution establishes a centralized government, which has institutions that directly represent the people and are capable, in turn, of acting directly on them. As a result of the Constitution's delegation of limited powers to these institutions, however, the states continue to hold independent governing powers. The states also play other important roles within the constitutional order, through, among other mechanisms, their equal representation in the Senate and their participation in constitutional amendment.

Not surprisingly, controversies involving problems of federalism survived the Constitution's ratification. Some such controversies—but certainly not all those of constitutional significance—have arisen in the context of litigation. Accordingly, the Supreme Court played an important role in the development of American federalism on several fronts. In the process, the Court articulated a range of competing conceptions of the constitutional design.

**Questions of Federal Jurisdiction.** One set of issues centered on problems of jurisdiction and matters of interpretive or decisional authority. Article III of the U.S. Constitution defines the jurisdiction of federal courts as including cases or controversies "between Citizens of a State and Citizens of another State." In *Chisholm v. Georgia* (1793), the Court held that this provision authorized federal courts to decide a suit against Georgia brought by two citizens of South Carolina. Two years later, Congress and the states overturned this holding by passing the Eleventh Amendment, which restricts federal courts from hearing suits against states brought by citizens of other states or by citizens of foreign nations. In subsequent decisions, the Court held that this amendment also bars suits against a state by its own citizens without its consent. However, the significance of these exceptions has been diluted by the Fourteenth Amendment, along with distinctions between the states and state officials. As explained below, a fertile area of constitutional litigation involves federal courts' enforcing the U.S. Constitution and federal laws against the states and state actors.

Article III delegates to federal courts the authority to decide some cases based on the identity of the litigants, as with lawsuits between citizens of different states. Federal courts also have authority to decide controversies based on the subject matter, including cases "arising under th[e] Constitution, the Laws of the United States, and Treaties." Especially during the republic's first century, substantial conflict surrounded the Court's assertions of appellate power to review decisions by state courts in cases raising such "federal questions." Most prominently, in *Martin v. Hunter's Lessee* (1816), a civil case, and *Cohens v. Virginia* (1821), a criminal case, the justices insisted that they had final authority to review decisions by state courts. In both contexts, state courts denied that the Supreme Court had authority to review or reverse their decisions.

Challenges of federal authority by state judges, legislatures, and others continued through the antebellum period and into the twentieth century. The Court responded to one such challenge in *Ableman v. Booth* (1859), in the context of efforts by the Wisconsin supreme court to authorize the release of prisoners from a local jail based on the state judges' position that the federal Fugitive Slave Act of 1850 was unconstitutional. In response, Chief Justice Roger Brooke Taney unflinchingly reasserted the Supreme Court's interpretive supremacy. He claimed that "no power is more clearly conferred by the Constitution and laws of the United States, than the power of this court to decide, ultimately and finally, all cases arising under such Constitution and laws." (Ironically, however, the Court's position on the constitutional status of slavery was soon overruled by the Civil War and Reconstruction amendments.)

Almost one hundred years later, Chief Justice Earl Warren echoed Taney's position on the preeminence of the Court's interpretive powers in *Cooper v. Aaron* (1958). In that case, the justices sought to overcome resistance to their previous ruling in *Brown v. Board of Education* (1954). Collapsing the constitutional text into its interpretation by the justices, Warren proclaimed that "the interpretation of the Fourteenth Amendment by this Court in the Brown Case is the supreme law of the land, and Article 6 of the Constitution makes it of binding effect on the States."

**Early Views of Federal-State Relations.** Woven through these cases raising questions of jurisdictional and decisional authority were controversies over the scope of Congress's powers (or federal powers more generally) and their relationships to state powers, along with efforts to enforce other limitations on the states. Among other things, the Supreme Court justices took positions on the constitutional status of slavery, the scope of the Constitution's delegation of commercial powers and their negative implications, implied powers, and taxing and spending powers. The Tenth Amendment was at the center of these debates because it both presupposes that federal powers are intrinsically limited and refers to reserved powers of "the states" and "the people." The Fourteenth Amendment was also centrally relevant, as it was the vehicle for the Court's applying much of the Bill of Rights to the states, along with additional guarantees of due process and equal protection.

During the republic's early years, the federal government's role was relatively limited compared to that of the states. Nevertheless, in cases such as *McCulloch v. Maryland* (1819) and *Gibbons v. Ogden* (1824), Chief Justice John Marshall offered a vigorous conception of federal powers and emphasized the supremacy of delegated over reserved powers. He presumed that federal powers were intrinsically limited and thus were consistent with the states' continuing to have substantial regulatory autonomy. However, he did not regard state powers as affirmative limitations on congressional powers or as capable of interfering with their exercise. Therefore, he claimed that state powers must give way to legitimate assertions of federal power.

Taney, Marshall's successor, developed the idea of state police powers and placed greater emphasis on the limited scope of federal powers. Beneath the surface if not always transparently, there was recurring concern during Taney's tenure with problems of slavery. In some contexts, he and his colleagues treated federal and state powers as potentially overlapping, as with powers of commercial regulation in general. At the same time, the justices treated some federal and state governing powers as mutually exclusive and reciprocally limiting. Taney relied on a version of the latter approach, characteristically dual federalist, in *Scott v. Sandford* (1857). Among other things, he argued that limitations on Congress's powers relating to slavery corresponded to—and protected—powers reserved exclusively to the states.

The predominant view during the antebellum period, as articulated by Chief Justice Marshall in *Barron v. Baltimore* (1833), was that federal judges lacked authority to enforce the Bill of Rights against the states. Other parts of the constitutional text, such as Article I, section 10, imposed limitations directly on the states. The Court interpreted some constitutional delegations of power to Congress as preempting state regulations within certain "spheres." However, the Court, along with Congress, allowed large measures of state autonomy. Accordingly, dual federalism largely prevailed in both theory and practice.

**Constitutional Transformations.** The Civil War and Reconstruction substantially altered these relationships between institutions of federal and state governance, along with their respective relationships to the people at large. During the war itself, governing power became increasingly centralized, supporting further consolidations of national power after the war. These tendencies were exacerbated, moreover, by problems of reconstruction. The Thirteenth, Fourteenth, and Fifteenth Amendments altered representational structures, imposed additional limitations on the states, and otherwise sought to reduce state autonomy and enhance national powers.

During these transformative periods, the Court's role was mixed. In *Ex parte Merryman* (1861), the Taney Court denied that President Abraham Lincoln had authority to suspend the writ of *habeas corpus.* However, the president refused to comply with this decision, and in the *Prize Cases* (1863), a majority of the justices upheld Lincoln's blockade of Southern ports. After the war, in *Ex parte Milligan* (1866), the Court reasserted itself, with Salmon P. Chase as chief justice, by invalidating the military trial of a civilian when civil courts were open. In *Mississippi v. Johnson* (1867),

*Georgia v. Stanton* (1868), *Ex parte McCardle* (1869), and *Texas v. White* (1869), however, the justices refrained in various contexts from taking a position on the validity of military reconstruction. In the last of these cases, Chase supported the cause of the Union by proclaiming that "the Constitution in all its provisions looks to an indestructible Union com-

*The post-Civil War Reconstruction years were a time of both political and legal upheaval in the United States.* (Library of Congress)

posed of indestructible states." Thus, he denied that states could legitimately secede from the Union, claimed that the war had altered relationships between the rebellious states and the Union, and affirmed congressional power to restore republican governments in the South.

The judges initially interpreted the Thirteenth, Fourteenth, and Fifteenth Amendments as supporting Congress's power to secure civil rights from abridgement by the states or individuals. However, soon the justices joined a broader retreat from Reconstruction, as signaled by the opinions in *Slaughterhouse Cases* (1873) and *Civil Rights Cases* (1883). Justices Samuel F. Miller and Joseph P. Bradley wrote the respective majority opinions. In the former case, the Court upheld a monopoly on the slaughtering of meat in New Orleans; in the latter, it invalidated the Civil Rights Act of 1875. From opposite directions, these two decisions perpetuated models of dual federalism.

**Dual Federalism.** In *Slaughterhouse Cases*, Miller claimed that the "one pervading purpose" of the Thirteenth, Fourteenth, and Fifteenth Amendments was "the freedom of the slave race, the security and firm establishment of that freedom, and the protection of the newly-made freeman and citizen." Though he suggested that other races might benefit from their guarantees, Miller denied that these amendments "radically changed the whole theory of the relations of the State and Federal governments to each other and of both these governments to the people." More specifically, he denied that the privileges or immunities clause of the Fourteenth Amendment "was intended to bring within the power of Congress the entire domain of civil rights heretofore belonging exclusively to the States." Nor did that clause "constitute this court a perpetual censor upon all legislation of the States, on the civil rights of their own citizens." He staked out corresponding positions on the Thirteenth Amendment and the Fourteenth Amendment's due process and equal protection clauses.

In *Civil Rights Cases*, Bradley likewise argued that the Fourteenth Amendment did not "invest Congress with power to legislate upon subjects which are within the domain of State legislation." In his view, the amendment provided remedies for abridgements of rights by states, not individuals. Relying on the Tenth Amendment, a majority of the justices claimed that the law regulating individual actions exceeded Congress's delegated powers.

Although the Court would subsequently adhere to aspects of the majority opinions in these two cases, many of the dissenters' arguments

would eventually prevail in
one form or another. The
dissents of Justices Stephen J.
Field and Bradley in *Slaughterhouse* anticipated judicial
enforcement of commercial
rights as limitations on the
states in reliance on the due
process clause of the Fourteenth Amendment. Federal
judges went even further by
relying on that clause as the
primary vehicle for enforcing much of the Bill of Rights
against the states, making
prescient Justice Noah H.
Swayne's characterization of
the amendment as "a new
Magna Charta." Justice John
Marshall Harlan's dissent in
the *Civil Rights Cases* likewise

*Justice Noah H. Swayne called the Fourteenth
Amendment a "new Magna Charta."* (Collection
of the Supreme Court of the United States)

anticipated national regulation of individual actions. Relying on the
Fourteenth Amendment and Article I's delegation of commercial powers, Congress in the twentieth century asserted—and the justices upheld—sweeping national civil rights legislation, economic regulations,
and other expansions of national power.

In the meantime, the Court enlisted the Fourteenth Amendment,
along with the Fifth and Tenth, to promote economic laissez-faire.
*Lochner v. New York* (1905) and *Hammer v. Dagenhart* (1918) epitomize the
restrictive decisions of this era. Both dealt with matters of federalism: the
first through the justices' invalidation of a state law in reliance on the U.S.
Constitution; the second because the majority relied on dual federalist
premises to strike down an act of Congress. In *Lochner*, the Court held
that a state maximum-hour workday law for bakers deprived them of liberty without due process of law in violation of the Fourteenth Amendment's due process clause; and in *Hammer*, they argued that a federal law
regulating child labor exceeded Congress's powers, conflicted with the
Fifth Amendment, and encroached on powers reserved exclusively to the
states. The combined result of such decisions was to treat a wide range of

commercial transactions (but not all) as beyond the legitimate reach of governmental restriction, federal or state.

**The Modern Era.** Controversy over this issue erupted during the New Deal. In response to intense pressure from President Franklin D. Roosevelt, Congress, state legislatures, and various constituencies, the Court shifted its posture in the late 1930's and early 1940's. *West Coast Hotel Co. v. Parrish* (1937) and *United States v. Darby Lumber Co.* (1941) both signaled and epitomized this change, often described as "revolutionary." In *West Coast*, the Court employed deferential reasoning to uphold a state minimum-wage, maximum-hour law, and in *Darby*, it affirmed Congress's powers to regulate terms of employment. In the process, the Court rejected dual federalist premises: Instead of presuming that federal and state powers were mutually exclusive and reciprocally limiting, they treated such powers as substantially overlapping, in many ways complementary, but with federal powers supreme.

The Court did not, however, entirely withdraw from enforcing constitutional limitations on the states. On the contrary, *United States v. Carolene Products Co.* (1938) suggested that the Court would continue to enforce enumerated rights, seek to guard political processes, and ensure fidelity to requirements of equal protection. Such efforts and their extensions gained momentum through the Civil Rights and women's movements and social change more generally, culminating in Warren and post-Warren Court precedents such as *Brown v. Board of Education* (1954), *Mapp v. Ohio* (1961), *Miranda v. Arizona* (1966), *Griswold v. Connecticut* (1965), and *Roe v. Wade* (1973).

Chief Justice Earl Warren's successors, Warren E. Burger and William H. Rehnquist, led modest retreats from these overall trends toward the Court's upholding greater concentrations of central governing power along with increased supervision of state actions. For example, in *National League of Cities v. Usery* (1976), the Court invalidated provisions in the Fair Labor Standards Act (1938) as they applied to the states. However, a majority of the justices overruled this decision nine years later in *Garcia v. San Antonio Metropolitan Transit Authority* (1985). Once again invoking principles of federalism, the Court in *United States v. Lopez* (1995) invalidated a federal law limiting possession of guns near schools. For the first time since 1937, a majority of the justices held that Congress had exceeded its commercial powers. Then in *Seminole Tribe v. Florida* (1996) and *Printz v. United States* (1997), respectively, the justices revitalized the

Eleventh Amendment and held that Congress could not command state and local officials to enforce a federal law. These cases, along with others involving issues of affirmative action, term limitations, criminal processes, and other matters, have been at the center of ongoing debates involving matters of federalism in the United States.

Cases from the founding period exemplify ways that constitutionalism in the United States rests on a premise that the states and the people may act through representational structures in some capacities while acting independently of them in others. Principles of federalism are at the heart of these interactions, forming and being reformed by ongoing commitment to constitutional governance. Rather than being settled by more than two hundred years of practice, these principles have remained radically contestable.

**Further Reading**

Charles Warren's "Legislative and Judicial Attacks on the Supreme Court of the United States: A History of the Twenty-fifth Section of the Judiciary Act," *American Law Review* 47 (1913-1914):1-34, 161-189, reviews the history of jurisdictional problems confronted by the Court. Edward S. Corwin's "The Passing of Dual Federalism," *Virginia Law Review* 36 (1950): 1-23 contains a concise account of the Court's shifting approach to federalism during the New Deal, and the special 1985 issue of the *Georgia Law Review* titled "Federalism: Allocating Responsibility Between the Federal and State Courts" explores subsequent constitutional developments. Federalism is placed in its historical and theoretical context in *A Nation of States: Essays on the American Federal System* (Chicago: Rand McNally, 1963), edited by Robert A. Goldwin; Raoul Berger's *Federalism: The Founders' Design* (Norman: University of Oklahoma Press, 1987); and *How Federal Is the Constitution?* (Washington, D.C.: American Enterprise Institute for Public Policy Research, 1987), edited by Robert A. Goldwin and William A. Schambra. Similar treatments of federalism can be found in Wayne D. Moore's *Constitutional Rights and Powers of the People* (Princeton, N.J.: Princeton University Press, 1996) and Daniel J. Elazar's *Covenant and Constitutionalism: The Great Frontier and the Matrix of Federal Democracy* (New Brunswick, N.J.: Transaction, 1998). For a progressive approach to federalism, see the essays in "Constructing a New Federalism: Jurisdictional Competence and Competition," Symposium Issue, *Yale Law and Policy Review/Yale Journal on Regulation* (1996).

*Wayne D. Moore*

# FUNDAMENTAL RIGHTS

*Description:* The idea that a select number of constitutional rights are so essential to American traditions of liberty and justice that they deserve special recognition and protection.

*Significance:* The Supreme Court utilized the doctrine of fundamental rights as a basis for deciding which provisions of the Bill of Rights should be binding on the states through incorporation of the Fourteenth Amendment. After the 1950's, moreover, the Court began applying "strict scrutiny" standards when examining governmental restrictions on those rights deemed to be fundamental.

James Madison, when making his proposal for a bill of rights in 1789, did not declare that all of his suggested amendments were of equal significance. Indeed, he wrote of his special concern for his rejected proposal that would have prohibited the states from violating "the equal rights of conscience, nor the freedom of speech, or of the press, or the trial by jury

*At the beginning of the American Revolution, Patrick Henry delivered a speech before the Virginia Assembly containing the famous phrase, "Give me liberty, or give me death!" As an expression of one of the most fundamental rights, that line became a war cry of the Revolution.* (Library of Congress)

in criminal cases." He clearly considered these particular rights to be more basic than some of the other provisions, such as those enumerated in the Third and Seventh Amendments.

The term "fundamental rights" entered American jurisprudence in Justice Bushrod Washington's circuit court opinion, *Corfield v. Coryell* (1823), which focused on Article IV's entitlement of "privileges and immunities of Citizens in the several states." Washington, who was influenced by the natural law tradition, wrote that this entitlement included a few rights which were "in their very nature, fundamental; which belong of right, to the citizens of all free governments." While he wrote that it was impossible to list all fundamental rights, he gave a few examples, such as the rights to own property and to travel through the states.

John Bingham and the other framers of the Fourteenth Amendment often quoted *Corfield* when discussing the "privileges or immunities" clause (commonly known as the "P or I clause") which they inserted into the new amendment. Although it is doubtful that most framers expected the privileges or immunities clause to make each and every provision in the Bill of Rights binding on the states, many of them suggested that it would prohibit the states from violating the more fundamental of these rights, such as the First Amendment's guarantee of free speech. The Supreme Court, however, gave an unusually restrictive interpretation to the clause in the *Slaughterhouse Cases* (1873), an interpretation that has never been directly overturned.

During the years from 1897 to 1937, the majority of the justices held that the freedom to enter into contracts was one of the fundamental rights guaranteed by the Fifth and Fourteenth Amendments. They based this right on a substantive interpretation of the due process clause, as in *Adkins v. Children's* Hospital (1923), which overturned a federal minimum wage requirement as an unconstitutional infringement on a protected liberty. Beginning in 1937, however, a majority of the justices accepted that government might restrict the freedom of contract in order to promote reasonable public interests. At the same time, the liberal members of the Court became increasingly concerned for the civil liberties enumerated in the first eight amendments.

For a number of years, the judges had been arguing about which, if any, of these rights should be incorporated into the Fourteenth Amendment, thus making them applicable to the states. In the seminal case, *Palko v. Connecticut* (1937), Justice Benjamin Cardozo argued for the incorporation of those rights that were "fundamental," either because they were "of the very essence of a scheme of ordered liberty," or because they were "principles of justice so rooted in the traditions and conscience of our people as to be ranked fundamental." In later years, the majority of the justices endorsed some variation of Cardozo's approach to incorporation.

A related question was whether the Court should apply the same standards of scrutiny when considering fundamental rights that they applied when considering less essential rights. In the famous "footnote four" of *United States v. Carolene Products, Co.* (1938), Justice Harlan Stone suggested that it might be appropriate to utilize a heightened level of scrutiny when examining three kinds of policies: (1) those appearing to contradict an explicit constitutional prohibition; (2) those appearing to interfere with political processes, such as a limitation on the right to vote; and (3) those that discriminate against members of racial or religious minorities. Years later, the footnote's advocacy of a double standard would provide ammunition for proponents of liberal judicial activism.

During World War II, beginning with *Murdock v. Pennsylvania* (1943), the Court's majority accepted the doctrine of "preferred freedoms," extending special judicial protections for the freedoms of the First Amendment. Similarly, in *Korematsu v. United States* (1944), the majority opinion declared that public policies discriminating on the basis of race were "immediately suspect," therefore requiring "the most rigid scrutiny."

Building on these precedents, the Warren Court established the use of the "strict scrutiny" standard during the 1950's and 1960's, whenever examining public policies with suspect classifications of persons, or public policies restricting fundamental rights. When dealing with the second category, the justices first asked whether the policy could be justified by a compelling public interest, and then they demanded the government to show that it could not achieve its purpose with a policy that was less restrictive of the fundamental right.

A good example of the Warren Court's approach to protecting fundamental rights was *Sherbert v. Verner* (1963), which overturned a state unemployment compensation law that only indirectly placed a burden on a religious practice. In *Griswold v. Connecticut* (1965), moreover, the Court declared that the right of privacy was a fundamental right, even though the term was not in the Constitution. The Court also held that the right of interstate movement was fundamental in *Shapiro v. Thompson* (1969). These activist decisions prepared the way for the monumental case, *Roe v. Wade* (1973), in which the justices expanded the right of privacy to include a woman's fundamental right to terminate an unwanted pregnancy.

After William Rehnquist became chief justice in 1986, the Court's conservative majority overturned several precedents concerning fundamental rights and strict scrutiny. In *Planned Parenthood v. Casey* (1992), for example, the Court endorsed a more permissive "undue burden" standard for evaluating restrictions on the abortion rights of women. In *Employment Division v. Smith* (1990), likewise, the majority of the justices announced that they would no longer use the standard of strict scrutiny when examining legislation of general applicability that placed an incidental burden on religion practices. When evaluating racial preferences in affirmative action programs, however, the Rehnquist Court applied the demanding standard of strict scrutiny.

*Thomas T. Lewis*

# INCORPORATION DOCTRINE

*Description:* Process by which the Supreme Court has gradually nationalized the Bill of Rights, requiring state governments to extend to residents much the same rights as the federal government must.

*Significance:* The Court held that some of the rights protected by the first eight amendments to the Constitution are also safeguarded by the due process clause of the Fourteenth Amendment.

In *Barron v. Baltimore* (1833), the Supreme Court ruled that rights enumerated in the Bill of Rights restrained the actions of the United States government, not the actions of the state governments. Specifically, the Court held that the eminent domain clause of the Fifth Amendment did not apply to a dispute over whether the city of Baltimore had taken Barron's property for public use without just compensation.

After the passage of the Fourteenth Amendment in 1868, lawyers began to seek ways to use its provisions to undermine *Barron*. The two provisions that lent themselves to this effort were the privileges and immunities clause and the due process clause. These two clauses appear next to one another in the amendment: "No State shall make or enforce any law which shall abridge the privileges or immunities of citizens of the United States; nor shall any State deprive any person of life, liberty or property, without due process of law."

In the *Slaughterhouse Cases* (1873), the attorney for the petitioners argued that engaging in a lawful and useful occupation was a privilege or immunity of U.S. citizenship and an aspect of liberty or property that could not be taken away without due process of law. At issue was an act of the Louisiana legislature creating a corporation and bestowing on that corporation a monopoly over the New Orleans slaughterhouse industry. Butchers disadvantaged by the law asked the courts to declare it unconstitutional. Failing to get a favorable result in the state courts, they appealed to the U.S. Supreme Court.

Justice Samuel F. Miller wrote an opinion that differentiated between privileges or immunities of U.S. citizenship and privileges or immunities of state citizenship. Only the former were protected by the Fourteenth Amendment, and engaging in a lawful and useful occupation was not among them; it was an aspect of state, not national, citizenship. In a similar vein, Justice Miller argued that due process protected persons against

*Justice Samuel F.
Miller, who served
on the Court from
1862 to 1890, held
a narrow view of
the Fourteenth
Amendment's
relevance to the
Bill of Rights.*
(Collection of the
Supreme Court of
the United States)

takings of life, liberty, or property by improper procedures but did not place limitations on the substance of laws themselves.

**The Due Process Clause.** The Court continued its narrow interpretation of the privileges or immunities clause in subsequent cases, but its view of the due process clause gradually changed. In *Hurtado v. California* (1884), the Court rejected the contention that the Fifth Amendment right to indictment by a grand jury in serious criminal cases was part of Fourteenth Amendment due process. However, in *Chicago, Burlington, and Quincy Railroad Co. v. Chicago* (1897), the Court held that the Fifth Amendment right to just compensation when private property is taken for public use is part of the Fourteenth Amendment protection against property being taken without due process. The Court continued to view criminal procedure rights as less important in *Maxwell v. Dow* (1900) and *Twining v. New Jersey* (1908). In *Maxwell*, the Court found trial by jury not to be incorporated into Fourteenth Amendment due process, and in *Twining*, the justices reached a similar conclusion with respect to the immunity against compulsory self-incrimination. In the latter case, the Court did recognize that it was possible that some of the rights safeguarded by the first eight amendments might be part of the concept of due process and therefore be protected against state action.

**Additional Incorporations.** It was some time after *Twining*, however, before the Court identified additional provisions of the first eight amendments to be incorporated into Fourteenth Amendment due process. In *Gitlow v. New York* (1925), the Court stated that it assumed that freedom of speech and of the press were among the liberties protected by the Fourteenth Amendment's due process clause, but nevertheless upheld Benjamin Gitlow's conviction for violating the New York law prohibiting language that advocated overthrow of the government by unlawful means. The Court subsequently held unconstitutional a conviction under a similar law in *Fiske v. Kansas* (1927) and overturned a state restriction on the press in *Near v. Minnesota* (1931), thereby confirming what it had assumed in *Gitlow*.

In 1932 the Court appeared to incorporate the right to counsel when it decided *Powell v. Alabama*, but it later ruled in *Betts v. Brady* (1942) that the *Powell* decision was limited to capital offenses. In a case reminiscent of *Gitlow*, the Court said in *Hamilton v. Board of Regents of the University of California* (1934) that freedom of religion was part of the concept of due process, but that a religious pacifist was not entitled to an exemption from the military training required by the university. The Court did clearly hold in *DeJonge v. Oregon* (1937) that the right to assemble peacefully was implicit in due process. This right barred the state of Oregon from convicting Dirk DeJonge for attending a peaceful meeting sponsored by the Communist Party.

A few months after the *DeJonge* decision, the Court attempted to provide a rationale for its incorporation decisions. The case was *Palko v. Connecticut* (1937). Frank Palko had been retried and convicted of first-degree murder after his conviction for second-degree murder had been overturned by the state supreme court. Prosecutors argued, and the state high court agreed, that the trial court judge had erred in excluding Palko's confession to robbery and murder in the first trial. Palko's attorney argued that the two trials constituted double jeopardy in violation of the Fifth Amendment, as incorporated by the due process clause of the Fourteenth. Justice Benjamin N. Cardozo wrote for the Court that only those rights "implicit in the concept of ordered liberty" were part of the notion of due process. These rights were so important "that neither liberty nor justice would exist if they were sacrificed." Justice Cardozo did not find the sort of double jeopardy involved in the *Palko* case inconsistent with the nation's fundamental principles of justice, and double jeopardy was, accordingly, not incorporated.

After *Palko*, the Court once again incorporated rights at a deliberate pace. It absorbed freedom to petition for redress of grievances in *Hague v. Congress of Industrial Organizations* (1939). *Cantwell v. Connecticut* (1940) confirmed the *Hamilton* statement that freedom of religion had been incorporated. The Court assumed that establishment of religion and the prohibition of cruel and unusual punishment were incorporated in 1947, although neither case, *Everson v. Board of Education of Ewing Township* and *Louisiana ex rel. Francis v. Resweber* respectively, resulted in state action being overturned. The Court confirmed its assumptions in these two cases in *Illinois ex rel. McCollum v. Board of Education* (1948), which struck down a religious education program conducted on school property as a violation of the establishment clause, and *Robinson v. California* (1962), which found a law that made being a drug addict a status crime, to be cruel and unusual punishment. In 1948 the Court incorporated the right to a public trial in the case of *In re Oliver* and the requirement of due notice of the charges against a criminal defendant in *Cole v. Arkansas*.

**An Alternative View.** In *Adamson v. California* (1947), the Court again confronted the matter of a rationale for its incorporation doctrine. In this case, the Court once again held that the immunity against self-incrimination was not a part of due process of law. In a lengthy dissent, Justice Hugo L. Black argued that the framers of the Fourteenth Amendment had intended to incorporate all of the provisions of the first eight amendments into the Fourteenth. The Court rejected his views by a 5-4 vote. Justices Frank Murphy and Wiley B. Rutledge, Jr., agreed with Black, but contended that the Court should not restrict the meaning of due process to the rights contained in the first eight amendments. Black, a textualist, wanted to limit the meaning of due process in this way. Justice William O. Douglas agreed with Black in *Adamson*, but in later cases adopted the Murphy-Rutledge position.

Two years later, in *Wolf v. Colorado* (1949), Justice Felix Frankfurter put forward an alternative view of what incorporation meant. At issue was the Fourth Amendment concept of unreasonable search and seizure. Frankfurter conceded that this right was part of due process but argued that only the essential core of the right—not the specific meanings of that right worked out by the federal courts for use in cases involving the U.S. government—restrained state action. Therefore the exclusionary rule, which meant that federal judges could not admit criminal evidence seized in violation of the Fourth Amendment, did not apply to the states. Instead, the courts would have to determine on a case-by-case basis whether states had violated the essential core meaning of the Fourth Amendment. Justice Black referred to this doctrine as applying a "watered down version" of the Bill of Rights to the states. The Frankfurter position dominated the Court in the 1950's, especially in criminal procedure matters such as search and seizure cases. Use of the case-by-case approach was brought to an end by *Mapp v. Ohio* (1961), in which the Court held that states were obliged to follow the exclusionary rule.

After the *Mapp* decision, the Court incorporated an additional seven rights in seventeen years. The Court first acted on the right to counsel in felony cases in *Gideon v. Wainwright* (1963) and expanded this right to include misdemeanors where a jail term was possible in *Argersinger v. Hamlin* (1972). Next it incorporated the immunity against self-incrimination in *Malloy v. Hogan* (1964) and the right to confront and cross-examine adverse witnesses in *Pointer v. Texas* (1965). The Court incorporated the right to a speedy trial in *Klopfer v. North Carolina* (1967) along with the right to compulsory process to obtain witnesses in *Washington v. Texas* (1968). It followed with the right to a jury trial in *Duncan v. Louisiana* (1968) and completed its incorporation jurisprudence with double jeopardy in *Benton v. Maryland* (1969). Only the Second Amendment right to keep and bear arms, the Third Amendment right against quartering soldiers, the Fifth Amendment right of grand jury indictment, the Seventh Amendment right to a jury trial in civil cases, and the Eighth Amendment protection against excessive bail and fines remain beyond the scope of due process.

The selective incorporation doctrine of *Palko* remains the majority view. However, Frankfurter's case-by-case approach continues to enjoy considerable support. Justice John Marshall Harlan II, Chief Justice Warren Burger, and Justice Lewis F. Powell, Jr., supported the doctrine when they were on the Court. Chief Justice William H. Rehnquist succeeded them as the strongest proponent of the case-by-case approach on the Court, and the doctrine seems to enjoy some favor among several other Court members as well. Justice Black's total incorporation approach and the total incorporation-plus doctrine of Murphy and Rutledge have had little support since such justices as Douglas and Arthur J. Goldberg left the Court.

**Further Reading**
An excellent basic source on incorporation doctrine is *Freedom and the Court: Civil Rights and Liberties in the United States* by Henry J. Abraham and Barbara A. Perry (7th ed., New York: Oxford University Press, 1998). Horace Flack made a case for total incorporation of the first eight amendments in *The Adoption of the Fourteenth Amendment* (Baltimore, Md.: Johns Hopkins University Press, 1908), as did Michael Curtis in *No State Shall Abridge: The Fourteenth Amendment and the Bill of Rights* (Durham, N.C.: Duke University Press, 1986). Two scholars who agree in part with the total incorporation doctrine but reject some of the historical generalizations made by Justice Black and Professor Flack are Jacobus ten Broek, *The Antislavery Origins of the Fourteenth Amendment* (Berkeley: University of California Press, 1951) and J. B. James, *The Framing of the Fourteenth Amendment* (Urbana: University of Illinois Press, 1956).

Raoul Berger's *Government by Judiciary: The Transformation of the Fourteenth Amendment* (Cambridge, Mass.: Harvard University Press, 1977) forcefully rejects the total incorporation doctrine. Raold Y. Mykkeltvedt discusses the Frankfurter case-by-case approach in *Nationalization of the Bill of Rights: Fourteenth Amendment Due Process and the Procedural Rights* (Port Washington, N.Y.: National University Publications, 1983). In *The Supreme Court and the Second Bill of Rights* (Madison: University of Wisconsin Press, 1981), Richard C. Cortner tells the story of the cases in which the Court incorporated various rights into the Fourteenth Amendment.

*Daryl R. Fair*

# INVERSE INCORPORATION

*Description:* The Supreme Court gradually came to the conclusion that the equal protection requirement of the Fourteenth Amendment is binding on the federal government through the due process clause of the Fifth Amendment.

*Significance:* Since the landmark case of *Bolling v. Sharpe* (1954), the Supreme Court has examined equal-protection claims against the federal government with the same standards of scrutiny that it uses when examining similar claims against the states.

In contrast to the Declaration of Independence of 1776, neither the original Constitution nor the Bill of Rights explicitly mentioned an inherent right to equality. The wording of the Fifth Amendment, however, implied a degree of legal equality: "no person" was to be deprived of "life, liberty, or property, without due process of law," nor was any person to be denied the privileges against self-incrimination or double jeopardy. The words "person" and "persons" apparently denoted human beings, and both words were used to refer to slaves in Articles I and IV of the Constitution. The same year that Congress approved the Bill of Rights, it expressed an egalitarian spirit in the Judiciary Act of 1789, requiring judges "solemnly [to] swear or affirm [to] administer law without respect to persons, and do equal right to the poor and to the rich."

Nevertheless, many federal laws mandated racial discrimination. The Naturalization Act of 1790, for instance, restricted naturalized citizenship to "any alien being a free white person." Despite the due process clause, the Fugitive Slave law of 1850 did not allow alleged fugitives in northern states to testify in trials or hearings that determined their freedom or enslavement, and the law was found to be constitutional in *Ableman v. Booth* (1859). In the *Dred Scott* ruling (1857), moreover, the Court asserted that persons of African ancestry possessed "no rights which the white man was bound to respect."

The Fourteenth Amendment, which was ratified after the Civil War, prohibited the states from denying any person the "equal protection of the laws." This important clause was not applicable to the federal government, apparently because the framers of the amendment were focusing on racial discrimination in the southern states. When debating the amendment, nevertheless, its framers often made moral allusions to the

Declaration of Independence and expressed a belief that all governments were obligated to respect a natural right to equality. But for about a hundred years, the Supreme Court interpreted the equal protection clause so narrowly that the question of a possible federal application seemed of little consequence.

*Gibson v. Mississippi* (1896) was probably the first case in which a Supreme Court justice unequivocally declared that the Fifth Amendment's due process clause prohibited the federal government from practicing racial discrimination. Justice John Marshall Harlan, a former slave owner, explained that the clause protected the life, liberty, and property of "all persons within the jurisdiction of the United States." Likewise, Justice Harlan Fiske Stone's "footnote four" in *Carolene Products v. United States* (1938) did not make any distinction between the federal and state governments when suggesting that the Court should use heightened scrutiny in the evaluation of legislation that discriminated against "discrete and insular minorities."

During World War II, the Court had to decide whether discriminatory policies toward persons of Japanese ancestry violated constitutional rights. Approving a curfew in *Hirabayashi v. United States* (1943), Chief Justice Stone wrote for the Court that racial distinctions were "by their very nature odious to a free people whose institutions are founded upon the doctrine of equality," and he also observed that precedents based on the equal protection clause would be "controlling" except for the dangers of espionage and sabotage. Although a 6-3 majority of the Court upheld the displacement program in *Korematsu v. United States* (1944), all the justices implicitly agreed that principles of due process prohibited the federal government from depriving persons of liberty simply because of their race or ethnicity. Justice Hugo Black's majority opinion asserted that "all legal restrictions which curtail the civil rights of a single racial group are immediately suspect," demanding "the most rigid scrutiny."

One member of the Court, Justice Frank Murphy wrote a dissent which articulated the concept of inverse incorporation: "Being an obvious racial discrimination, the [displacement] order deprives all those within its scope of the equal protection of the laws as guaranteed by the Fifth Amendment."

A decade later, in *Brown v. Board of Education* (1954), the Court ruled that segregated schools in the southern states were incompatible with the equal protection clause of the Fourteenth Amendment. In a companion case, *Bolling v. Sharpe,* the justices ruled that segregated schools operated by the federal government in the nation's capital were also unconstitutional. Unable to base the *Bolling* decision directly on the Fourteenth Amendment, they relied instead on a substantive due process interpretation of the Fifth Amendment. As historical precedents, Chief Justice Earl Warren referred to the earlier *dicta* (or statements) of justices Harlan, Stone, Black, and Murphy. In his argument, Warren utilized a broad definition of liberty, which was said to include "the full range of conduct which the individual is free to enjoy." Finding evidence that the policy of racial segregation denied African American children of basic life opportunities, he logically concluded that the policy constituted "an arbitrary deprivation of their liberty in violation of the due process clause."

Since the *Bolling* landmark, the Court has not recognized any distinctions between federal and state cases insofar as they relate to the standards of scrutiny for evaluating equal protection claims. In *Rostker v. Goldberg* (1981), for instance, the Court evaluated a gender classification of the federal government with an approach called "intermediate scrutiny," the same approach used in considering gender classifications by the state governments. Moreover, in *Adarand Constructors v. Peña* (1995), the Court utilized the strictest level of judicial scrutiny in striking down a racial preference mandated by the federal government, just as it had earlier done in a case involving a racial preference by a city government.

Federal cases dealing with equal protection under the Fifth Amendment have been relatively rare, compared to state cases relating to alleged violations under the Fourteenth Amendment.

*Thomas T. Lewis*

# STATE CONSTITUTIONS

*Description:* Supreme statements of state law, these documents outline fundamental political processes, set out the relationships between various governing institutions, and define a set of state-specific rights protected from government incursion.

*Significance:* For more than a century after ratification of the U.S. Constitution, state constitutions served as the primary source of protection from state power, a role that was temporarily eclipsed and then given new life when the Supreme Court pruned back some federally protected liberties during the 1970's, 1980's, and 1990's.

While the Supreme Court and the U.S. Constitution are sometimes thought of as the exclusive guarantors of legal rights, for many years, state constitutions provided citizens with their basic protections. Indeed, many of the rights secured by early state constitutions were ultimately included in the Bill of Rights, thus ensuring they could not be violated by the federal government.

Beginning in the twentieth century, however, the individual liberties in the Bill of Rights began to be applied by the Court to the states through the due process clause of the Fourteenth Amendment. By the late 1960's most of the rights protected in the federal Constitution were protected from encroachment by state government as well. As a consequence of this expanded reach of federal rights, the importance of state constitutional rights receded.

During the tenure of Chief Justices Warren E. Burger and William H. Rehnquist, the Court cut back on some of the liberties it had previously embraced, and citizens, politicians, and interest groups increasingly turned back to state constitutions for protection. State courts recognized a growing body of rights, including many that went beyond guarantees provided by the federal courts, giving rise to what some have called a new judicial federalism.

The Supreme Court monitors the judicial decisions of state courts, including decisions based on interpretations of state constitutions, through the independent and adequate state grounds doctrine. Under the doctrine, the Court refuses to examine a case decided by a state court if that case does not raise questions about federal law and as long as the state ruling is genuinely independent of federal law. In *Michigan v. Long* (1983), the Court elaborated on the doctrine and gave itself greater discretion in deciding when it could examine state court decisions.

Although this doctrine ultimately allowed for more intrusion by the federal courts into the judicial affairs of the states, it also affirmed the independent authority of the state court system and authorized the states to uphold greater protections in their constitutions than those in the Constitution. Although the Constitution and the Supreme Court establish a mandatory minimum for protected rights, state constitutions can be interpreted to secure additional rights.

**Protected Rights.** Generally speaking, state constitutions contain both rights similar to those found in the U.S. Constitution and rights that are unique to the state. Although state judges frequently use federal doctrine to apply state constitutional rights resembling those in the U.S. Constitution, they have also interpreted these rights more independently. Indeed, in a number of areas including free speech, equal protection, and criminal rights, state courts have offered protections that exceed those found at the federal level.

State constitutions also delineate rights that are distinct from those found in the U.S. Constitution. State constitutions have provided for special rights associated with education, welfare, health care, the environment, and collective bargaining, among others. In addition, a number of state constitutions include explicit privacy amendments, a right delineated by the Supreme Court but not explicitly mentioned in the U.S. Constitution. State court interpretations of these provisions have sometimes found them to guarantee greater protections than the federal right to privacy.

Although state judges are powerfully influenced by the jurisprudence of the Supreme Court, the unique nature of many state constitutional provisions and the unwillingness of the Court to provide rulings on numerous constitutional issues means that state constitutions demand specialized, state-based interpretation. In the absence of relevant guidance from federal judges, state courts have sometimes turned to cases and doctrine provided by judges in other states. This horizontal federalism is most often practiced between states with similar constitutions.

A number of scholars remain skeptical about the merits of the new judicial federalism, suggesting that state constitutions are often unwieldy and antiquated documents, more closely resembling ordinary legislation than fundamental charters of government. State constitutions, these critics maintain, are poor substitutes for the centralized, unified, and enduring system of law provided by the Supreme Court and U.S. Constitution.

Those applauding the reemergence of state constitutions as important sources of rights have argued that these documents have creatively and effectively bolstered liberties that have been undermined and ignored by the Court. In addition, state constitutions allow for greater popular expression, particularly since they are substantially easier to alter than the U.S. Constitution.

Whatever their merits and shortcomings, state constitutions continue to affect how state government is organized and conducted. This fact, combined with their historic and continuing contribution to protecting rights, especially those neglected by the federal courts, places state constitutions at the very core of the U.S. political system.

**Further Reading**

Brennan, William J. "The Bill of Rights and the States: The Revival of State Constitutions as Guardians of Individual Rights." *New York University Law Review* 61 (October, 1986): 535-553.

Friesen, Jennifer. *State Constitutional Law.* Charlottesville, Va.: Michie, 1996.

Tarr, G. Alan. *Understanding State Constitutions.* Princeton, N.J.: Princeton University Press, 1998.

Tarr, G. Alan, and Mary Cornelia Porter. "State Constitutionalism and State Constitutional Law." *Publius, Journal of Federalism* 17, no. 1 (Winter, 1987).

*Bruce G. Peabody*

# VIRGINIA DECLARATION OF RIGHTS

*Description:* The sixteen sections of the Virginia Declaration of Rights, adopted by the state of Virginia's constitutional convention in June, 1776, asserted the doctrine of inherent rights and enumerated a large number of specific rights and liberties that governments should respect.

*Significance:* The document profoundly influenced the content of the U.S. Bill of Rights, as well as the Declaration of Independence, the French Declaration of the Rights of Man, and various other bills of rights of other state constitutions.

On May 15, 1776, The Virginia Convention unanimously endorsed independence from Great Britain and authorized a committee to prepare a plan of government and a Declaration of Rights. George Mason, a wealthy landowner and a self-taught lawyer, was the principal author of both the resulting state constitution and its accompanying declaration, although his friend, Thomas Ludwell Lee, also played an important part in drafting the document. After making a number of rhetorical changes, the convention unanimously adopted the declaration on June 12, 1776.

Section 1 of the declaration asserted that "all men are born free and independent and have certain inherent rights," including "the enjoyment of life and liberty, with the means of acquiring and possessing property." It then acknowledged that governmental power "derived from the people," that the three branches of government should be separate, that elections of representatives "ought to be free," and that elective representatives should have the exclusive power of making or suspending laws.

At least seventeen items in the Virginia Declaration closely resembled provisions that James Madison would later include in the U.S. Bill of Rights. Section 8 specified "that no man be deprived of his liberty except by the law of the land," which was similar to the due process clause of the Fifth Amendment. In addition, Section 8 recognized a privilege against self-incrimination and other rights of criminal defendants that were found in the Fifth and Sixth Amendment. Section 11 proclaimed that the practice of trial by jury "is preferable to any other and ought to be held sacred." The prohibitions of "cruel and unusual punishments," "excessive bail," and "excessive fines" in Section 9 were identical to those of the amendment. Section 10 made requirements for search warrants that resemble the Fourth Amendment. Section 12 recognized the freedom of the press as "one of the great bulwarks of liberty." Section 13 proclaimed that people should be "trained in arms" in order to have a "well-regulated militia" and avoid the evils of standing armies. Finally, Section 16 acknowledged that "all men are equally entitled to the free exercise of religion, according to the dictates of conscience," a freedom which was expressed more concisely in the First Amendment.

The Virginia Declaration of Rights differed from the U.S. Bill of Rights in a number of particulars, especially its explicit recognition of inherent equality (despite the practice of slavery), its usage of the word "ought," and its references to the positive duties of citizenship.

In 1787, the man most responsible for Virginia's Declaration, George Mason, became one of the most vociferous critics of the new U.S. Constitution because of its lack of a bill of rights.

*Thomas T. Lewis*

# THE AMENDMENTS

# FIRST AMENDMENT

*Description:* Amendment guaranteeing freedom of speech, freedom of the press, religious liberty, separation of church and state, and the rights peaceably to assemble and to petition the government for redress of grievances. (*The full text of the First Amendment appears in this volume on page 391.*)

*Significance:* The wellspring of individual rights protected by the U.S. Constitution, the First Amendment presented the Supreme Court with endless challenges to decide the limits of governmental power and the scope of personal liberties.

Although the First Amendment, together with the other nine amendments known as the Bill of Rights, became part of the U.S. Constitution on December 15, 1791, the Supreme Court took little note of it until the beginning of the twentieth century. This was not for lack of federal laws impinging on free speech, from the Sedition Act of 1798 and the Comstock Act of 1873 to the Alien Immigration Act of 1930 and a wide variety of postal regulations. However, the Court never found that any of these laws violated the First Amendment. Indeed, in 1907 the Court upheld the conviction of an editor for contempt, rejecting a defense based on the First Amendment on the grounds that it only prohibited prior restraint.

It was inevitable that the Court and the First Amendment would travel together through U.S. constitutional law, frequently crossing paths, sometimes diverging, often forced by circumstances to retrace the same ground. Each clause of the First Amendment invites, indeed demands, judicial interpretation.

**Freedom of Speech.** Beginning at the end of World War I, the Court tackled the task of devising a series of tests to determine whether particular speech was constitutionally protected. The Court could not merely cite the general language of the First Amendment; it had to apply those opaque terms to the real world of real cases.

The first test was articulated by Justice Oliver Wendell Holmes in 1919 in a series of cases challenging the convictions of antiwar activists under the Espionage Act of 1917. The clear and present danger test looked at whether the speech posed a real and immediate risk of a substantive evil that Congress had a right to prevent. Holmes captured the test in a powerful, albeit often misquoted, metaphor that persists to this day: "The most stringent protection of free speech would not protect a man in falsely shouting fire in a theatre and causing a panic."

Later in 1919, Holmes and his ally, Justice Louis D. Brandeis, dissented in *Abrams v. United States*, arguing for greater constitutional protection for controversial or even subversive speech. The majority of the Court continued to use the clear and present danger test to uphold the punishment of such speech.

Six years later, the majority of the Court tightened the noose on free speech by focusing on whether the expression had a bad tendency. Over bitter dissent from Holmes and Brandeis, the Court upheld a conviction under the New York State Criminal Anarchy Act, stating that a "single revolutionary spark may kindle a fire," and therefore the state may "suppress the threatened danger in its incipiency."

In 1951 the Court used a slightly reformulated test to uphold the convictions of eleven members of the Communist Party under the Smith Act (1940). Chief Justice Fred M. Vinson, writing for the Court, asked "whether the gravity of the 'evil' discounted by its improbability" would justify government limits on speech.

In 1964 Justice William J. Brennan, Jr., introduced a test that was far more protective of free speech. In the landmark case of *New York Times Co. v. Sullivan*, the Court held that false criticism of public officials was constitutionally protected unless it was made with knowledge that it was false or in reckless disregard of the truth. Instead of tilting the constitutional balance in favor of the government, the *Sullivan* test gave the advantage to the speaker.

The Holmes-Brandeis view in favor of more robust protection for free speech was finally vindicated in 1967 in *Brandenburg v. Ohio*, in which the Court declared that mere advocacy of the use of force or violation of the law could no longer be punished unless "such advocacy is directed to inciting or producing imminent lawless action and is likely to produce such action."

**The Religion Clauses.** As in the field of free speech, the perplexing issues surrounding freedom of religion have required the Court to fashion several constitutional tests to ensure the free exercise of religion, without establishing a state-sponsored religion. As the twentieth century ushered in an era of secularization, the dominance of religion in public life began to be seen as inconsistent with the First Amendment's promise of neutrality

# FIRST AMENDMENT CONTROVERSIES

| Issue | Reasons to Limit | Reasons Not to Limit |
|---|---|---|
| Does the First Amendment protect the right of members of the Native American Church to smoke peyote as part of their religious rituals? | Peyote is a controlled substance. To permit its use might endanger the lives of the user and others. | The free exercise of religion by the Native American Church requires the use of peyote. Freedom of religion should not be infringed. |
| Does the First Amendment protect the right of art galleries to display publicly artworks that may be considered obscene or offensive? | The First Amendment does not protect pornography or obscenity. If a work is considered offensive by people in the community, it should not be displayed. | Freedom of speech and freedom of the press imply free expression. Art is in the eye of the beholder. |
| Does the First Amendment protect those who burn the American flag in violation of state laws? | The flag is the country's most important symbol. State governments ought to be allowed to protect it. | Burning the flag is as legitimate an act of protest as speaking out against a government policy. Preventing flag-burning would be banning a form of political expression. |
| Should schools and public libraries ban books that contain racially offensive terms? | Use of some racial terms is offensive and may lower the self-esteem of minority students. | Censorship restricts the flow of ideas. Students would be prevented from reading literature that was written in a time when such terms were considered more acceptable. |
| Should the press be allowed to print any government documents? | The press's freedom should be restricted to ensure national security. | Government decisions should be exposed to the will of the people. |
| Should newspapers and the media be allowed access to participants in a trial before a verdict has been delivered? | Unlimited discussion of trial-related matters in a public forum may infringe upon Fifth Amendment rights to due process. | Matters of public concern should be open for discussion. |

when it came to religious faith. Religion was seen as a part of the private sphere of life, leaving the public sphere, including most visibly public schools, free of religious symbols, let alone indoctrination.

In several decisions spanning more than twenty years, from *Everson v. Board of Education of Ewing Township* in 1947 to *Lemon v. Kurtzman* in 1971, the Court developed the test that any governmental action touching on religion would survive invalidation under the establishment clause only if it had a secular purpose that neither endorsed nor disapproved of religion, had an effect that neither advanced nor inhibited religion, and avoided creating a relationship between religion and government that entangled either in the internal affairs of the other. The *Lemon* test has been criticized by all ends of the political and constitutional spectrum, but it has provided lower courts and legislators with some level of guidance in dealing with such thorny issues as prayer in schools and financial aid to religious institutions.

Meanwhile, the Court had to interpret the free exercise clause of the First Amendment in numerous cases in which believers claimed a right to ignore laws that required them to perform an act that violated their religious beliefs or that prohibited them from performing an act that was required by their religious beliefs.

Beginning in 1879 in *Reynolds v. United States* and for almost a hundred years, the Court dealt with most free exercise cases by upholding laws that punished *actions* but struck down laws that punished *beliefs*. However, the easy dichotomy began to break down when, in *Sherbert v. Verner* (1963), the Court ordered a state to pay unemployment benefits to a Seventh-day Adventist even though she would not make herself available for work on Saturday (her Sabbath). In 1972, in *Wisconsin v. Yoder*, the Court held that the Amish were not required to send their children to public school past the eighth grade in violation of their religious beliefs.

By the 1980's, the pendulum had begun to swing against religious liberty as the Court issued a succession of decisions ruling against a Native American who sought to prevent the government from assigning his daughter a social security number, an Orthodox Jew who sought to wear a yarmulke in violation of Air Force uniform regulations, a Native American tribe that sought to prevent construction of a federal highway that would interfere with their worshiping, and two Native Americans who sought unemployment compensation after they were fired from their jobs for smoking peyote as part of tribal religious rituals.

The Court has found the religion clauses of the First Amendment fraught with interpretative dangers. Inevitably, the Court is criticized either for going too far in promoting religion or for exhibiting hostility toward religion. That alone may be evidence that the Court is doing its job as conceived by the Founders.

**The Right Peaceably to Assemble.** Although freedom of speech and freedom to worship protect highly personal rights, the First Amendment's guarantee of the right "of the people peaceably to assemble," protects the right of association. These are the rights of the people as a community to join together to achieve certain political, social, economic, artistic, educational, or other goals.

For the Court, interpreting the right to assemble has been even more difficult than construing other aspects of the First Amendment, because by its very nature, assembly involves both speech *and* conduct. At first blush, the First Amendment has nothing to do with conduct. However, when the Court is confronted with cases involving public demonstrations, protests, parades, and picketing, it is apparent that these activities are intended to send a message—and communicating messages is clearly protected by the First Amendment.

However, blocking traffic, littering the streets, or physically obstructing others from going about their business is not protected by the First Amendment. Consequently, when it comes to freedom of assembly, the Court has used a balancing test, seeking first to determine whether the law regulating assembly is in fact a ruse to suppress a particular viewpoint, and if not, whether the law serves a compelling state interest unrelated to the suppression of free speech.

For example, in 1940 in *Thornhill v. Alabama*, the Court struck down a state law that prohibited all picketing. Although the First Amendment does not afford an absolute right to picket, the Court overturned the statute because instead of regulating specific aspects of labor demonstrations, it prohibited "every practicable method whereby the facts of a labor dispute may be publicized."

Closely aligned with freedom of assembly is freedom of association or the right of the people to form and join organizations in order to educate themselves and influence public policy on important issues of the day. Even during the hysteria of the Cold War in the 1950's, the Court held in *Yates v. United States* (1957) that when membership in the Communist Party involved nothing more than the advocacy or teaching of the abstract doctrine of the forcible overthrow of the government (as contrasted with the advocacy or teaching of direct action to achieve that end) convictions under the Smith were unconstitutional.

In 1958, in *National Association for the Advancement of Colored People v. Alabama*, the Court found that the forced disclosure of an organization's membership list violated the members' rights to pursue their lawful interests and to freely associate with like-minded persons. Although freedom of association is not expressly set forth anywhere in the Constitution, the Court nevertheless found freedom of association to be an integral part of the First Amendment.

**The Right to Petition the Government.** The least controversial (and least litigated) right in the First Amendment is the right "to petition the government for redress of grievances." Aside from a doomed attempt in 1836 by the House of Representatives to impose a gag rule against the receipt of petitions from abolitionists who opposed slavery, Congress has not had the temerity to even attempt to restrict this quintessential right to write to your Congressperson, thereby sparing the Court the task of striking down such legislation.

**Further Reading**

Steven H. Shiffrin and Jesse H. Choper's *The First Amendment: Cases, Comments, Questions* (St. Paul, Minn.: West Publishing, 1996) provides a basic introduction to the First Amendment. *The First Amendment: The Legacy of George Mason* (London: Associated University Presses, 1985), edited by T. Daniel Shumate, focuses on the origin and meaning of the amendment. Louis E. Ingelhart's *Press and Speech Freedoms in the World, from Antiquity Until 1998: A Chronology* (Westport, Conn.: Greenwood Press, 1998) covers the concept of freedom of speech and press from ancient times until the modern period, and Margaret A. Blanchard's *Revolutionary Sparks: Freedom of Expression in Modern America* (New York: Oxford University Press, 1992) covers the concept from the beginning to the end of the twentieth century. The First Amendment and the freedoms of association and assembly are examined in *Freedom of Association* (Princeton, N.J.: Princeton University Press, 1998), edited by Amy Gutmann, and Paul L. Murphy's *Rights of Assembly, Petition, Arms, and Just Compensation* (New York: Garland, 1990). The First Amendment and religion are examined in *Toward Benevolent Neutrality: Church, State, and the Supreme Court*, edited by Ronald B. Flowers and Robert T. Miller (Waco, Tex.: Baylor University Press, 1998), *The Believer and the Powers That Are: Cases, History, and Other Data*

*Bearing on the Relation of Religion and Government,* by John Thomas Noonan, Jr. (New York: Macmillan, 1987), and *Religious Liberty in the Supreme Court: The Cases That Define the Debate over Church and State,* edited by Terry Eastland (Grand Rapids, Mich.: Wm. B. Eerdmans, 1995).

*Stephen F. Rohde*

# SECOND AMENDMENT

*Description:* Amendment that provided the right of people to keep and bear arms. (*The full text of the Second Amendment appears in this volume on page 391.*)

*Significance:* The Supreme Court's rare decisions on the Second Amendment have typically been narrowly drawn, leaving the broad issues of gun control and the intent of the Second Amendment unresolved.

The Second Amendment to the U.S. Constitution states: "A well regulated militia being necessary to the security of a free state, the right of the people to keep and bear arms shall not be infringed." In comparison to other controversial constitutional guarantees, such as freedom of speech, the Supreme Court has had little to say about the Second Amendment. The Court has generally upheld criminal laws regarding firearms, but it has done so without attempting to establish a guiding interpretation of the amendment. Although the Court overturned two federal gun laws in two decisions during the 1990's, it did not rule on the laws as they pertained to the Second Amendment. Rather, in keeping with the Court's states' rights conservatism under Chief Justice William H. Rehnquist, the Court ruled on the laws as they pertained to the limits of the federal government's power to impose its laws on state and local authorities.

In *Printz v. United States* (1997), Jay Printz, the sheriff of Ravalli County, Montana, challenged a federal law that required him to perform background checks on people in his jurisdiction who sought to buy guns. The Court accepted his argument that the federal government may not compel the states to implement federal regulations, overturning the portion of the federal act that required local law enforcement agencies to conduct background checks. Before that, *United States v. Lopez* (1995) reached the Court after a student, Alfonso Lopez, was charged with violating the Gun-Free School Zones Act of 1990 when he carried a concealed handgun into a high school. The Court upheld an appellate ruling that the federal act exceeded the authority of Congress to legislate under the interstate commerce clause. To allow the act to stand, the Court wrote, would "require this Court to pile inference upon inference in a manner that would bid fair to convert congressional commerce clause authority to a general police power of the sort held only by the States." *Printz* and *Lopez* did not address the Second Amendment or rule on how it is to be interpreted. Nor is the controversy settled by a review of Court decisions touching on the Second Amendment.

**Early Decisions.** In *United States v. Cruikshank* (1876), William Cruikshank, a member of the Ku Klux Klan, was tried in federal court for violating the federal civil rights laws protecting the African American victims of a murderous riot he led. The trial court found Cruikshank guilty of conspiring to deprive African Americans of their right to bear arms. The Supreme Court, however, ruled in favor of Cruikshank, arguing that the Second Amendment applied only to Congress and that people must look to local governments for protection against violations of their rights. The *Cruikshank* decision, like the *Slaughterhouse Cases* (1873), interpreted against use of the Fourteenth Amendment as a means to enforce the Bill of Rights at the state and local level. This interpretation of the Fourteenth Amendment, however, has since been abandoned in other decisions not relating to the Second Amendment.

The next major Second Amendment case was *Presser v. Illinois* (1886). Herman Presser led an armed group called the Lehr und Wehr Verein (Educational and Protective Association) on a march through the streets of Chicago. Presser argued that the Illinois law under which he was convicted was superseded by various provisions of federal law, including the Second Amendment. The Court upheld his conviction, arguing that to accept Presser's interpretations would amount to denying the rights of states to disperse mobs.

**Indications of Ambivalence.** The Court in *United States v. Miller* (1939) upheld the federal regulation against a shotgun's having a barrel less than eighteen inches long on the basis that the Court had no indication that such a weapon "was . . . ordinary military equipment or . . . could contribute to the common defense." It may be argued, therefore, that *Miller* indirectly defends the principle that a firearm that has some reasonable relationship to the efficiency of a well-regulated militia is protected by the Constitution. However, challenges to laws limiting civilian possession of machine guns and assault rifles, which are military weapons, have not met with success. A similar ambivalence can be inferred in *Cases v. United States* (1943), in which a lower court noted, "apparently . . . under the Second Amendment, the federal government can limit the keeping and bearing of arms by a single individual as well as by a group . . . but it cannot prohibit the possession or use of any weapon which has any reasonable relationship to the preservation or efficiency of a well-regulated militia." The Court made this observation, however, when declining to review a challenge to a provision of the Federal Firearms Act.

In *Quilici v. Village of Morton Grove* (1983), a circuit court refused to review a Second Amendment case and let stand a decision upholding an ordinance in Morton Grove, Illinois, banning possession of handguns. This decision has been cited to bolster the argument that the individual ownership of firearms is not a constitutional right, but the fact that the Court has done nothing to change the existing laws that allow individual possession of firearms undermines such an argument.

### Further Reading

Bijlefeld, Marjolijn, ed. *The Gun Control Debate: A Documentary History.* Westport, Conn.: Greenwood Press, 1997.

Cottrol, Robert J., ed. *Gun Control and the Constitution: Sources and Explorations on the Second Amendment.* New York: Garland, 1993.

Halbrook, Stephen P. *That Every Man Be Armed: The Evolution of a Constitutional Right.* Albuquerque: University of New Mexico Press, 1984.

Henigan, Dennis A. *Guns and the Constitution: The Myth of Second Amendment Protection for Firearms in America.* Northampton, Mass.: Aletheia Press, 1996.

Malcolm, Joyce Lee. *To Keep and Bear Arms: The Evolution of an Anglo-American Right.* Cambridge, Mass.: Harvard University Press, 1996.

*Eric Howard*

# THIRD AMENDMENT

*Description:* Amendment that denies quarter in private homes to soldiers during times of peace. (*The full text of the Third Amendment appears in this volume on page 391.*)

*Significance:* Contemporary use of the amendment by the Supreme Court has been simply as a reference exemplifying constitutional protections of property-based privacy rights against certain governmental intrusions.

The last time the Third Amendment had serious literal application was during the Civil War (1861-1865), when property owners were made to house, feed, and generally support both Union and Confederate soldiers. Today, such literal application is rare. However, in *Engblom v. Carey* (1982), a federal appellate court held that striking corrections officers had a lawful interest in their living quarters, located at the prison and provided in the course of their employment, which entitled them to a legitimate expectation of privacy protected by the Third Amendment.

For development of privacy rights, the Supreme Court usually relied on provisions of other amendments such as the Fourth Amendment protection against unreasonable search and seizure and used the Third Amendment simply as a nominal reference to general constitutional protections. For example, in a footnote to *Katz v. United States* (1967), a landmark decision regarding Fourth Amendment privacy rights, Justice Potter Stewart merely listed the Third Amendment in his enumeration of constitutional protections.

This contemporary reliance is typified by *State v. Coburn* (1974), in which the Montana supreme court cited the First, Third, Fourth, and Fifth Amendments as the "umbrella of constitutional protections" afforded individual privacy.

*Michael J. Garcia*

# FOURTH AMENDMENT

*Description:* Amendment that protects people against unreasonable searches and seizures. (*The full text of the Fourth Amendment appears in this volume on page 391.*)

*Significance:* In the early 1900's the Supreme Court began expanding the applications of the Fourth Amendment, balancing the rights of the accused against the safety of other people.

The framers of the Bill of Rights were concerned with the old English practice of issuing general warrants and writs of assistance. These two legal tools authorized searches with few stipulations on searching agents, allowing searches day or night on bare suspicion. Authorized by the monarch, they were valid for the duration of his or her lifetime. They were not required to name a specific person or place but could be stated in more general terms. No oath before a magistrate was necessary to secure a warrant, and probable cause was not required. Everything was left to the discretion of the holder of the warrant. The result was harassment. The colonists were victims of these general warrants and writs of assistance and purposely set out to outlaw them.

James Madison revised his initial draft of the Fourth Amendment, changing the word "secured" to "secure" and adding the clause "against unreasonable searches and seizures." Although Madison's goal was to eliminate general warrants and writs of assistance, scholars believe these alterations made the meaning of the amendment ambiguous. The Fourth Amendment outlaws only unreasonable searches and seizures, logically allowing those deemed reasonable. The framers envisioned that searches conducted with a warrant, which required specifics such as who is to be searched, what is to be seized, and when, were constitutionally permissible. The warrant clause stipulated what was expected of police when conducting searches. However, left unanswered were the questions of whether there are times when it is reasonable to search without a warrant, what constitutes probable cause, and whether the amendment restricts only police or other governmental agents with searching authority.

The Court in *Wolf v. Colorado* (1949) made clear that search warrants had to be supported by probable cause and issued by a neutral and impartial magistrate. However, often searches are conducted without a search warrant.

**Exceptions to the Warrant Requirement.** The Court created a number of exceptions to the search warrant requirement. Using the reasonableness clause of the amendment rather than the warrant provision, the Court rejected the idea of a bright-line rule in favor of a more fact-bound, case-by-case approach. The police do not need a warrant for searches incident to arrest; stop and frisk situations; when illegal or stolen items are in plain view during a legal search; administrative, consensual, and border searches; and searches involving exigent circumstances such as automobile searches.

When an individual is arrested on probable cause, a police officer is permitted to conduct a warrantless search of the person. This exception to the warrant requirement, search incident to arrest, rests on the understanding that the arresting officer must have the power to disarm the accused and preserve any evidence. Protecting the officer's safety and retaining probative evidence is reasonable. The officer may search not only the person but the areas of immediate control. In *Chimel v. California* (1969), the Court reasoned that the scope of a search incident to arrest included wherever the arrestee might reach to grab a weapon or piece of evidence.

If in the course of a valid search, an officer comes on stolen or illegal items in plain view, they may be seized and used as evidence. This inadvertent windfall is permissible and reasonable under the Fourth Amendment as long as the officer happens on the evidence in the course of conducting a legal search. Related is the plain feel exception. In *Minnesota v. Dickerson* (1993), the Court held that if an officer feels what seems to be contraband or evidence of a crime when patting down the outside of a suspect's clothing, the items can be seized.

In *Terry v. Ohio* (1968), the Court allowed for searches on the street that did not meet the standard of probable cause. In this case, it upheld the brief detention of a suspect for weapons on the grounds of reasonable suspicion rather than probable cause. Only a limited frisk was permitted with the lowered standard of cause. If the pat-down yielded a basis for an arrest, however, a full search incident to arrest could follow.

The Court has applied the Fourth Amendment to the increasing problems arising in a mobile society. Planes, buses, trains, and boats all raise exigency concerns because of the highly mobile nature of the place to be searched and the futility of the police in executing search warrants on moving objects. The most common exigent circumstance is created by the automobile. As early as 1925 in *Carroll v. United States*, the Court made clear that the automobile would not be afforded the same level of privacy rights protection as an individual's home or person. Stopping an automobile and searching it on the street without a warrant was reasonable. However, the particulars of the car have generated a volume of litigation aimed at answering questions such as whether the police can lawfully open the glove box, the trunk, or containers in the automobile or search the driver, passengers, and their personal items. Given the lower expectation of privacy in automobiles, the Court in *Michigan Department of State Police v. Sitz* (1990) allowed roadblocks to briefly stop all drivers to catch those driving under the influence of drugs and alcohol.

Employees of other governmental agencies, such as housing, fire, health, welfare, and safety inspectors, also have searching capabilities. These agents have a lesser standard than probable cause and often invoke an element of surprise, such as unannounced inspections of restaurants. Related to these types of searches are those to ensure safety in the workplace or school by drug-testing employees and students. In *National Treasury Employees Union v. Von Raab* (1989), the Court upheld suspicionless mandatory urinalysis testing for promotion on the grounds of safety (the employees would have access to firearms and secure information). By 1995 in *Vernonia School District v. Acton*, the Court upheld the right to drug-test all student athletes without requiring suspicion of individuals.

The courts have long recognized that individuals and items entering the United States may be searched at the international border without warrant or probable cause. The Court has placed some limits on these searches, such as the level of intrusion. Strip searches, for example, must be justified by real suspicion. In an attempt to stop the influx of illegal drugs, law enforcement developed the drug courier profile, a composite of variables that indicates the likelihood an individual is trafficking drugs. In *United States v. Sokolow* (1989), the Court upheld the use of the profile as a basis for detaining and searching individuals both at the border and within the continental United States.

In *Schneckloth v. Bustamonte* (1973), the Court acknowledged the use of consent searches, noting that individuals may waive their Fourth Amendment rights and allow a search without a warrant or probable cause. The key to the validity of such searches is that they must be voluntary; an individual must knowingly and freely consent to be searched. The waiver must be uncoerced, given without trickery or fear or promise of reward. Consent can be withdrawn at any time, and a refusal to give consent cannot then be used to establish probable cause.

The Fourth Amendment also applies to wiretapping and other forms of police surveillance. The Court in *Katz v. United States* (1967) reasoned that a person's expectation of privacy includes the seizure of intangible items such as words.

**Exclusionary Rule.** The Fourth Amendment describes the right to be secure against unreasonable searches and seizures without mentioning a remedy. The common-law remedy for search and seizure violations was a suit of trespass. This was used until *Weeks v. United States* (1914) when the Court adopted the exclusionary rule, which excludes illegally seized evidence from trials. The twofold purpose of the rule is to preserve the integrity of the judiciary and deter police misconduct. *Weeks* mandated the application of the exclusionary rule to searching agents of the federal government. In 1949 in *Wolf v. Colorado,* the Court incorporated the Fourth Amendment, thereby requiring states not to abridge the search and seizure rights of their citizens, yet allowing them to choose the remedy. This choice was eliminated in *Mapp v. Ohio* (1961) when the Court incorporated the remedy of exclusion from trials for all Fourth Amendment violations, by either state or federal officials.

*Mapp*'s scope was limited by the Court. In *Linkletter v. Walker* (1965), the Court refused to apply the exclusionary rule retroactively. The exclusion remedy was limited in scope so that it did not include grand jury proceedings in *United States v. Calandra* (1974). The Court ruled in *United States v. Havens* (1980) that illegally seized evidence could be used to impeach the credibility of the defendant at trial and in *Nix v. Williams* (1984) that it could also be admitted into evidence if the police would have inevitably discovered the evidence by lawful means. In 1984 in *United States v. Leon* and *Massachusetts v. Sheppard,* the Court allowed the use of illegally obtained evidence if the police error was made in objective good faith. The Court was unwilling to exclude reliable probative evidence when the error made by the police was unintentional and made in the course of attempting to follow the law.

**Further Reading**

One of the better historical treatments of the Fourth Amendment is Nelson B. Lasson's *The History and Development of the Fourth Amendment to the United States Constitution* (Baltimore, Md.: Johns Hopkins University Press, 1937). Several classic and often cited works about the Fourth Amendment are Jacob W. Landynski's *Search and Seizure and the Supreme Court*

(Baltimore, Md.: Johns Hopkins University Press, 1966), Wayne LaFave's *Search and Seizure: A Treatise on the Fourth Amendment* (Mineola, N.Y.: Foundation Press, 1978), Erwin N. Griswold's *Search and Seizure: A Dilemma of the Supreme Court* (Lincoln: University of Nebraska Press, 1975), and Telford Taylor's *Two Studies in Constitutional Interpretation* (Columbus: Ohio State University Press, 1969). A general treatment of Fourth Amendment rights can be found in David M. O'Brien's *Constitutional Law and Politics: Civil Rights and Liberties*. 3d ed. 2 vols. New York: W. W. Norton, 1997. Some law review articles debating the policy implications of the Fourth Amendment and its remedy are Anthony Amsterdam's "The Supreme Court and the Rights of Suspects in Criminal Cases," *New York University Law Review* 45 (1970): 785, Yale Kamisar's "Is the Exclusionary Rule an 'Illogical' or 'Unnatural' Interpretation of the Fourth Amendment?" *Judicature* 62 (1978): 67, and Malcolm Wiley's "Constitutional Alternatives to the Exclusionary Rule," *South Texas Law Journal* 23 (1982): 531. Warren E. Burger expressed his views on the Fourth Amendment in "Who Will Watch the Watchman?" *American University Law Review* 14 (1964): 1.

*Priscilla H. Machado*

# FIFTH AMENDMENT

*Description:* Amendment that provides a right to avoid self-incrimination, a right to a grand jury indictment in capital or infamous crime cases, a right to be free from double jeopardy, and a right to just compensation for property taken by the government. (*The full text of the Fifth Amendment appears in this volume beginning on page 391.*)

*Significance:* The Supreme Court has used the Fifth Amendment to protect citizens against government coercion.

The Fifth Amendment includes more than just a right against self-incrimination, yet it is virtually synonymous with the right against self-incrimination. This right reflected the framers' judgment that in a society based on respect for the individual, the government shouldered the entire burden of proving guilt and the accused need make no unwilling contribution to his or her conviction.

The Fifth Amendment is restricted on its face to "criminal cases." However, the Supreme Court ruled that the Fifth Amendment applies to criminal and civil cases and extends to nonjudicial proceedings, such as legislative investigations and administrative hearings. The protection of the clause extends only to people, not organizations such as corporations or unions, and is applicable to witnesses as well as to the accused.

The self-incrimination clause is violated if evidence compelled by the government incriminates the person who provides it. Given these standards, self-incrimination violations occur most commonly during police interrogations and government hearings. Although the purpose of the clause is to eliminate the inherently coercive and inquisitional atmosphere of the interrogation room, a person may voluntarily answer any incriminating question or confess to any crime, subject to the requirements for waiver of constitutional rights, even if his or her statements are intended as exculpatory but lend themselves to prosecutorial use as incriminatory.

**A Definition.** The Court first addressed the meaning of the self-incrimination clause in *Twining v. New Jersey* (1908). The question was whether the right against self-incrimination was "a fundamental principle of liberty and justice which inheres in the very idea of free government" and therefore should be included within the concept of due process of law safeguarded from state abridgment. The Court decided against the right. It reaffirmed this position in *Palko v. Connecticut* (1937), in which the Court held that the right against compulsory self-incrimination was not a fundamental right; it might be lost, and justice might still be done if the accused "were subject to a duty to respond to orderly inquiry."

The Court abandoned this position in its 1966 decision in *Miranda v. Arizona*, a tour de force on self-incrimination. The opinion announced a cluster of constitutional rights for defendants held in police custody and cut off from the outside world. The atmosphere and environment of incommunicado interrogation was held to be inherently intimidating and hostile to the privilege against self-incrimination. To prevent compulsion by law enforcement officials, before interrogation, people in custody must be clearly informed that they have the right to remain silent and anything they say may be used in court against them and that they have the rights to consult an attorney, to have a lawyer present during interrogation, and to have a lawyer appointed if they are indigent.

When Chief Justice Warren E. Burger replaced Chief Justice Earl Warren in 1964 and Justice Harry A. Blackmun replaced Justice Abe Fortas in 1970, they joined Justices Byron R. White, John Marshall Harlan II, and Potter Stewart in support of a narrow application of *Miranda*. These five justices constituted the majority in *Harris v. New York* (1971), indicating the beginning of a contracting trend for *Miranda*. Chief Justice Burger held that the prosecution is not precluded from the use of statements that admittedly do not meet the *Miranda* test as an impeachment tool in attacking the credibility of an accused's trial testimony.

The erosion of *Miranda* continued in several rulings in the 1970's. In *Michigan v. Tucker* (1974), the Court held that failure to inform a suspect of his or her right to appointed counsel before interrogation was only a harmless error in the total circumstances of the case. Then one year later in *Oregon v. Haas* (1975), the Court reaffirmed *Harris* and allowed the use of a suspect's statements for impeachment purposes though they had been made before arrival of counsel that he had requested before making any statements. And the next year in *Michigan v. Mosley* (1976), the Court did not construe *Miranda* as invoking a "proscription of indefinite duration on any further questionings . . . on any subject." This ruling approved an interrogation process in which a suspect had initially used the shield of Miranda rights to remain silent but several hours later in a different room was administered the Miranda rights again and proceeded to respond to questions about a different crime.

By the mid-1980's it was clear that the Court under Chief Justice William H. Rehnquist would continue to construe *Miranda* very narrowly. In *New York v. Quarles* (1984), for example, the Court held that when a danger to public safety exists, police may ask questions to remove that danger before reading Miranda warnings. Answers given to the police may be used as evidence. In *Illinois v. Perkins* (1990), the Court ruled that Miranda warnings are not required when a suspect is unaware he or she is speaking to the police and gives a voluntary statement. The case concerned a jailed defendant who implicated himself in a murder when talking to an undercover agent placed in his cell. Justice Anthony M. Kennedy wrote in the opinion, "*Miranda* forbids coercion, not mere strategic deception." Finally, in *Arizona v. Fulminante* (1991), the Court admitted that the defendant's confession was coerced by the threat of physical attack. However, the Court held that if such testimony is erroneously admitted as evidence, a conviction need not be overturned if sufficient independent evidence supporting a guilty verdict is also introduced.

At the turn of the century, the Court's decision to maintain the precedent with continued narrow application of *Miranda* appeared well entrenched. The majority of the justices appeared to be comfortable with that approach, and changes appeared unlikely.

**Double Jeopardy Clause.** Also under the Fifth Amendment, a person shall not be subject "for the same offense to be twice put in jeopardy of life or limb." The underlying premise of the double jeopardy clause is to prohibit the government from making repeated attempts to convict an individual. Acquittal acts as an absolute bar on a second trial. The meaning of acquittal, however, often divides the Court.

The Court ruled that there is no double jeopardy in trying someone twice for the same offense if the jury is unable to reach a verdict—in *United States v. Ball* (1896), the jury is discharged—in *Logan v. United States* (1892), or an appeals court returns the case to the trial court because of defects in the original indictment—in *Thompson v. United States* (1894). The Court also unanimously ruled in three cases—*Jerome v. United States* (1943), *Herbert v. Louisiana* (1926), and *United States v. Lanza* (1922)—that a person may be prosecuted for the same act under federal law and state law. The theory is that the person is being prosecuted for two distinct offenses rather than the same offense.

The double jeopardy clause also prohibits prosecutors from trying defendants a second time for the express purpose of obtaining a more severe sentence. However, in 1969 the Court decided that there is no constitutional bar to imposing a more severe sentence on reconviction (after the first conviction is thrown out), provided the sentencing judge is not motivated by vindictiveness. In *North Carolina v. Pearce; Chaffin v. Stynchcombe* (1973), it ruled that the guarantee against double jeopardy requires that punishment already exacted must be fully credited to the new sentence.

The double jeopardy clause also bars multiple punishments for the same offense. In *United States v. Ursery* (1996) and *Kansas v. Hendricks* (1997), the Court narrowly construed this right. The latter case involved a challenge to a statute that permitted the state to keep certain sexual offenders in custody in a mental institution after they had served their full sentence. The Court ruled that the civil confinement was not a second criminal punishment but a separate civil procedure, thus not a violation of the double jeopardy clause.

**Right to a Grand Jury.** The Fifth Amendment also provides that "no person shall be held for a capital, or otherwise infamous crime, unless on a presentment or indictment of a grand jury, except in cases arising in the land or naval forces, or in the militia, when in actual service in time of war or public danger." The grand jury procedure is one of the few provisions in the Bill of Rights that has not been incorporated into the due process clause of the Fourteenth Amendment and applied to the states. Instead the Court ruled that states may prosecute on a district attorney's "information," which consists of a prosecutor's accusation under oath in *Hurtado v. California* (1884) and *Lem Wood v. Oregon* (1913). The Court held in *Costello v. United States* (1956) that, unlike in a regular trial, grand juries may decide that "hearsay" evidence is sufficient grounds to indict. In 1992 the Court issued an opinion in *United States v. Williams* (1992) indicating that an otherwise valid indictment may not be dismissed on the ground that the government failed to disclose to the grand jury "substantial exculpatory evidence" in its possession. In 1974 the Court decided in *United States v. Calandra* that witnesses before a grand jury may invoke the Fifth Amendment privilege against self-incrimination. This privilege is overridden if the government grants immunity to the witness. Witnesses who then refuse to answer questions may be jailed for contempt of court. Witnesses may not refuse to answer because questions are based on illegally obtained evidence.

**The Takings Clause.** Finally, the Fifth Amendment provides that private property shall not "be taken for public use, without just compensation." This is referred to as the takings clause, or the just compensation clause. The Court incorporated the takings clause under the due process clause of the Fourteenth Amendment in *Chicago, Burlington, and Quincy Railroad Co. v. Chicago* (1897); therefore, states are also forbidden from taking private property for public use without just compensation. Not every deprivation of property requires compensation, however. For example, the Court held in *United States v. Caltex* (1952) that under conditions of war, private property may be demolished to prevent use by the enemy without compensation to the owner. When compensation is to be paid, a plethora of 5-4 decisions by the Court—including *United States v. Fuller* (1973) and *Almota Farmers Elevator and Wholesale Co. v. United States* (1973)—demonstrate fundamental disagreements among the justices about the proper method of calculating what is "just."

Court decisions in the early and mid-1990's underscore the complexity and reach of the takings clause. Several cases broadened the powers of the states, and others expanded property rights. In *Yee v. Escondido* (1992), a unanimous Court held that a rent-control ordinance did not amount to a physical taking of the property of owners of a mobile home park. A more significant ruling, *Lucas v. South Carolina Coastal Council* (1992), narrowed the rights of states to rely on regulatory takings that completely deprive individuals of the economic use of their property. To be exempt from compensating a property owner, a state must claim more than a general public interest or an interest in preventing serious public harm.

The Court broadened property rights by holding that land use requirements may be "takings." The decision in *Dolan v. City of Tigard* (1994) dealt with the practice of local governments giving property owners a permit for building a development only on the condition that they donate parts of their land for parks, bike paths, and other public purposes. These conditions are valid only if the local government makes "some sort of individualized determination that the required dedication is related both in nature and extent to the impact of the proposed development." This 5-4 decision underscores the Court's inability to reach agreement on constitutional principles under the Fifth Amendment.

## Further Reading

Two general works on the Fifth Amendment are Harvey Fireside's *The Fifth Amendment: The Right to Remain Silent* (Springfield, N.J.: Enslow,

1998) and Burnham Holmes's *The Fifth Amendment* (Englewood Cliffs, N. J.: Silver Burdett Press, 1991). David Bodenhamer's *Fair Trial: Rights of the Accused in American History* (New York: Oxford University Press, 1992) presents a useful account of double jeopardy and self-incrimination rights. Also recommended is Anthony Lewis's *Gideon's Trumpet* (New York: Vintage, 1964). A well-written and thorough account of the takings clause is found in Richard Epstein's *Takings: Private Property and the Power of Eminent Domain* (Cambridge, Mass.: Harvard University Press, 1985). A more scholarly account is James Ely's *The Guardian of Every Other Right: A Constitutional History of Property Rights* (New York: Oxford University Press, 1992).

*Susan L. Thomas*

# SIXTH AMENDMENT

*Description:* Amendment that specifies the trial rights possessed by criminal defendants. (*The full text of the Sixth Amendment appears in this volume on page 392.*)

*Significance:* Beginning in the 1960's, the Supreme Court actively interpreted and defined the provisions of the Sixth Amendment to ensure that criminal defendants receive their protected entitlements in both federal and state courts.

The Sixth Amendment, added to the U.S. Constitution in 1791, specifies the rights of defendants in the trial stage of the criminal law process, including the rights to a speedy and public trial, an impartial jury in the locale where the alleged crime was committed, information about the nature of charges being prosecuted, an opportunity to confront accusers and adverse witnesses, a compulsory process for obtaining favorable witnesses, and the assistance of counsel.

For most of U.S. history, the Sixth Amendment and other provisions of the Bill of Rights protected individuals against actions by the federal government only. However, during the twentieth century, the Supreme Court ruled that many provisions of the Bill of Rights, including the Sixth Amendment, also applied to state and local governments. Therefore, defendants in all criminal prosecutions came to benefit from the protections afforded by the Sixth Amendment.

**Right to Counsel.** Before the twentieth century, the right to counsel provided by the Sixth Amendment simply meant that the government could not prevent a criminal defendant from hiring an attorney when the defendant could afford to do so. Defendants who lacked the necessary funds were required to defend themselves in court without professional assistance.

The Court first expanded the right to counsel in *Powell v. Alabama* (1932). *Powell,* also known as the Scottsboro case, involved several African American defendants who were accused of raping two white women. The young men were convicted and sentenced to death in a quick trial without being represented by any attorneys. The case was heard at a time when African Americans were subjected to significant racial discrimination in the legal system, especially in southern states. There were troubling questions about the defendants' guilt, particularly after one of the alleged victims later admitted that she lied about what happened. Given the circumstances, the Court found the legal proceedings to be fundamentally unfair and declared that defendants facing the death penalty were entitled to representation by attorneys.

The Court expanded the right to counsel in *Johnson v. Zerbst* (1938) by declaring that all defendants facing serious charges in federal court are entitled to be provided with an attorney when they are too poor to afford to hire their own. The Court expanded this rule to cover all state and local courts in *Gideon v. Wainwright* (1963), a well-known case initiated by an uneducated prisoner who sent the Court a handwritten petition complaining about a judge denying his request for an attorney. In *Douglas v. California* (1963), the Court declared that the government must supply attorneys for poor defendants for their first appeal after a criminal conviction. Subsequently, the Court ruled in *Argersinger v. Hamlin* (1972) that regardless of the seriousness of the charges, criminal defendants are entitled to be represented by an attorney if they face the possibility of serving time in jail. Because people who possess the necessary funds are expected to hire their own attorneys, the Court's Sixth Amendment decisions primarily protected poor defendants who would not receive professional representation if it were not provided by the government. Although the Court expanded opportunities for poor defendants to receive representation during criminal trials, the right to counsel does not apply to civil trials or to cases pursued by prisoners after they have presented their first postconviction appeal.

**Trial by Jury.** The Court did not interpret the Sixth Amendment to apply the right to trial by jury to all serious cases in both state and federal courts until 1968. In *Duncan v. Louisiana* (1968), the Court overturned the conviction of an African American defendant whose request for a jury trial had been denied when he was convicted and sentenced to sixty days in jail for allegedly slapping a white man on the arm. After the conviction was overturned, the federal courts prevented Louisiana from prosecuting the man again because he and his attorney had been subjected to discrimination and harassment by local law enforcement officials during the course of his arrest and trial.

The right to trial by jury does not, however, apply to all criminal cases. In *Lewis v. United States* (1996), the Court ruled that the Sixth Amendment right to a jury trial does not apply to defendants facing petty offense charges with six months or less of imprisonment as the possible punishment for each charge. Therefore, defendants may be denied the opportunity for a jury trial if they face multiple petty offenses that, upon conviction, could produce cumulative sentences in excess of six months through separate sentences for each charge. Such defendants are entitled to a trial, but the trial will be before a judge rather than a jury.

In its early decisions, the Court expected that juries would be made up of twelve members who reach unanimous verdicts. However, the Court's interpretation of the Sixth Amendment changed during the 1970's. In *Williams v. Florida* (1970), the Court determined that juries could have as few as six members in criminal cases. In *Apodaca v. Oregon* (1972), the Court declared that states could permit defendants to be convicted of crimes by less than unanimous jury verdicts. It ruled that Oregon could convict defendants with 10-2 jury votes and Louisiana with 9-3 votes. The right to trial by jury is not implemented in identical fashion in all courts throughout the country.

**Other Trial Rights.** The Sixth Amendment's right to a speedy trial prevents the government from holding criminal charges over a defendant's head indefinitely without ever pursuing prosecution. People are entitled to have charges against them resolved in a timely manner. Because the Sixth Amendment provides no guidance on how long the government may take in pursuing prosecution, the Court had to establish guidelines through its Sixth Amendment rulings. The Court clarified the right to a speedy trial in *Barker v. Wingo* (1972), in which a defendant was forced to wait for more than five years for a trial after he was charged with murder. The delay occurred because the prosecution sought to convict a codefendant first but the codefendant's appeals led to orders for new trials. Therefore, it took several trials to obtain an error-free conviction of the codefendant. When the Court examined the claim that a five-year delay constituted a violation of the Sixth Amendment right to a speedy trial, the Court refused to set a firm time limit for speedy trials. Instead, the Court said the individual circumstances of each case must be examined. The Court ruled that judges must determine whether the right to a speedy trial was violated by considering four aspects of the delay: its length, the reason for it, whether the defendant complained about the delay, and whether it harmed the defendant's case, such as through the death or disappearance of a key witness. In this case, the Court found that because the defendant never complained about the delay and his case was not disadvantaged by the delay, the five-year wait for a trial did not violate the defendant's rights despite the fact that the prosecution caused the lengthy delay. Although the Court clarified the factors to be considered in evaluating a speedy trial claim, the exact nature of the right was not clearly defined.

The defendant's right to confront adverse witnesses is intended to prevent the government from holding trials without the defendant's knowledge or declaring the defendant guilty without permitting the defendant to challenge the prosecution's evidence. The adversary system underlying the U.S. criminal law process presumes that the best way to reveal the truth at a trial is to permit both sides to present their evidence and arguments to the judge and jury during the same proceeding.

The Court struggled with its attempts to provide a clear definition of the extent of the confrontation right. For example, in *Coy v. Iowa* (1988), the justices were deeply divided when they decided that it was not permissible for the state to place a screen in the courtroom to prevent a defendant from having eye contact with child victims who were presenting testimony about an alleged sexual assault. A few years later in *Maryland v. Craig* (1990), a narrow majority of justices approved the use of closed-circuit television to permit child victims to present testimony from a different room in the courthouse than the courtroom in which the trial was taking place. Thus the defendant could see the witnesses on television, but the children would not risk being traumatized by coming face to face with the person accused of committing crimes against them. The significant disagreements among the justices about the right to confrontation indicate that the Court may need to clarify the circumstances in which it is permissible to use devices to separate defendants from direct contact with witnesses testifying against them. Traditionally, defendants and witnesses were expected to be face to face in the same courtroom, but growing sensitivity to the psychological trauma experienced by crime victims who must testify in court has led to experiments with screens, closed-circuit television, and other techniques that collide with traditional conceptions of the right to confrontation.

Other Sixth Amendment issues to come before the Court include whether excessive pretrial publicity prevents the selection of an unbiased jury and in what circumstances judicial proceedings can be closed to the public. When addressing these issues, Court justices tend to focus on their assessment of factors and circumstances that may interfere with a criminal defendant's opportunity to receive a fair trial.

**Further Reading**

The development of trial rights is presented in Francis Heller's *The Sixth Amendment to the Constitution of the United States* (New York: Greenwood Press, 1951). Many landmark Sixth Amendment cases are presented in case studies examining the people and social contexts surrounding them. Of particular note are Anthony Lewis's *Gideon's Trumpet* (New York: Random House, 1964) concerning *Gideon v. Wainwright* and James Goodman's *Stories of Scottsboro* (New York: Random House, 1994) concerning *Powell v. Alabama*. Alfredo Garcia's *The Sixth Amendment in Modern American Jurisprudence* (New York: Greenwood Press, 1992) presents a discussion of the modern Court's decisions affecting the Sixth Amendment. A detailed presentation of the fine points of law concerning trial rights is available in Charles Whitebread and Christopher Slobogin's *Criminal Procedure* (3d ed., Mineola, N.Y.: Foundation Press, 1993). For an examination of the Court's decision making after the 1950's and the viewpoints of individual justices concerning the Sixth Amendment, see Thomas R. Hensley, Christopher E. Smith, and Joyce A. Baugh's *The Changing Supreme Court: Constitutional Rights and Liberties* (St. Paul, Minn.: West Publishing, 1997). A liberal critique of the Rehnquist Court's decisions affecting the criminal law process is presented in John Decker's *Revolution to the Right* (New York: Garland, 1992), which argues that the Supreme Court has diminished the protections of the Sixth Amendment and other rights with respect to criminal defendants.

*Christopher E. Smith*

# SEVENTH AMENDMENT

*Description:* Amendment that guaranteed the right to a jury trial in civil common law cases at the federal level. (*The full text of the Seventh Amendment appears in this volume on page 392.*)

*Significance:* The Supreme Court has interpreted this amendment to allow civil juries of six rather than twelve people but has not applied it to civil trials in state courts.

The Seventh Amendment was ratified in 1791. It guaranteed the right to trial by jury in federal civil cases. The amendment was designed to preserve the common law distinction between issues of law and issues of fact. In *Baltimore and Carolina Line v. Redman* (1935), the Court held that the judge should remain the trier of law, deciding unresolved issues of law, and the jury should remain the trier of fact, resolving issues of fact under appropriate instructions by the court.

The amendment's guarantee applies to all courts under the authority of the United States, including territories and the District of Columbia. Generally, the amendment does not apply to state courts, except when the state court is enforcing a federally created right. When a federal court is enforcing a state-created right, it may follow its own rules based on the interests of the federal court system.

In *Colgrove v. Battin* (1973), the Court held that a federal district court's authorization of civil juries composed of six persons instead of the traditional twelve was permissible under the Seventh Amendment.

*Patricia Jackson*

# EIGHTH AMENDMENT

*Description:* Amendment that forbids requiring excessive bail, imposing excessive fines, and inflicting cruel and unusual punishments. (*The full text of the Eighth Amendment appears in this volume on page 392.*)

*Significance:* The three clauses of the Eighth Amendment are the only provisions in the Constitution that place substantive limits on the severity of punishments in criminal cases. The Supreme Court's role has been to interpret these clauses.

The Eighth Amendment is derived almost verbatim from the English Bill of Rights (1689). Adopted in 1791 as part of the U.S. Bill of Rights, the amendment was intended to prohibit the abuse of federal government power, but the precise meaning of the amendment is unclear and requires interpretation by the Supreme Court.

The first two clauses of the Eighth Amendment (prohibiting excessive bail and fines) have not been applied to the states. Although the Court has never established an absolute right to bail, it has reviewed whether bail has been set higher than necessary to ensure that a defendant appears for trial.

The Court has taken a flexible interpretation of the cruel and unusual punishment clause, stating in *Trop v. Dulles* (1958) that punishments should be evaluated in light of the "evolving standards of decency" of a maturing society. The clause was formally applied to the states in *Robinson v. California* (1962). Barbaric punishments are prohibited, but the Court has refused to hold that the death penalty itself is cruel and unusual punishment. Punishments disproportionate to the crime, the treatment of prisoners, and conditions of confinement, may also violate the Eighth Amendment.

*John Fliter*

# NINTH AMENDMENT

*Description:* Amendment to the U.S. Constitution stating that the enumeration of certain rights in that document does not mean other, unenumerated rights should be denied. (*The full text of the Ninth Amendment appears in this volume on page 392.*)

*Significance:* Relying on the Ninth Amendment, the Supreme Court did not confine itself to rights directly stated in the Constitution but also enforced unenumerated rights, including the right of privacy.

The Ninth Amendment is among the most enigmatic parts of the Bill of Rights. At one level, the thrust of the amendment is relatively clear. The Bill of Rights and other parts of the constitutional text do not contain an exhaustive listing of the people's rights. However, the questions of what other rights the Constitution protects and from whom, as well as who may enforce such rights and how they relate to delegated and reserved governmental powers, raise complex interpretive problems.

**Historical Origins and Early Invocations.** Federalist James Madison apparently drafted the amendment to address concerns that adding a bill of rights to the constitutional text might imply that the people held only the rights listed in that document. Claims that the people held other rights were often linked to a premise that the Constitution delegated limited powers to the federal government. Accordingly, the Ninth Amendment was viewed as a companion to the Tenth Amendment, which reserved for the states or the people all powers "not delegated to the United States by the Constitution, nor prohibited by it to the States."

Even before the Bill of Rights was ratified by three-fourths of the states, Madison relied on the terms of these two amendments to support arguments that Congress had no authority to establish a national bank. In debates within the House of Representatives on February 2, 1791, Madison claimed the Ninth Amendment "guard[ed] against a latitude of interpretation" and the Tenth Amendment "exclude[ed] every source of power not within the Constitution itself."

The Supreme Court's decision in *McCulloch v. Maryland* (1819) had implications for interpreting the Ninth and Tenth Amendments. In arguing that Congress had authority to establish a national bank, Chief Justice John Marshall rejected a narrow rule of construction for interpreting the

Constitution's delegations of power. He argued instead that the Constitution gave Congress "vast powers," on whose execution "the happiness and prosperity of the nation so vitally depends."

Variations of this reasoning would eventually support expansive conceptions of federal power and correspondingly narrow conceptions of residuals—including reserved powers and retained rights. In *Fletcher v. Peck* (1810), however, Chief Justice Marshall suggested that judges might enforce unenumerated rights as limits on the states. In subsequent cases, the justices linked the idea of unenumerated rights to principles of limited federal power.

**The Ninth Amendment and Slavery.** In *Scott v. Sandford* (1857), Chief Justice Roger Brooke Taney argued in his majority opinion that the Missouri Compromise Act of 1850 was invalid because it exceeded constitutional delegations, encroached on reserved powers, and abridged retained rights. Referring to rights of slave ownership, Taney wrote, "The powers over person and property of which we speak are not only not granted to Congress, but are in express terms denied, and they are forbidden to exercise them." More specifically, he argued that Congress "has no power over the person or property of a citizen but what the citizens of the United States have granted."

Reinforcing Taney's arguments, Justice John A. Campbell quoted statements made by the authors of the Constitution intended to assure Antifederalists that the federal government would be limited to certain enumerated powers. Despite these assurances, the Constitution's critics demanded an "explicit declaration" that the federal government would not assume powers not specifically delegated to it. As a result, Campbell said, the Ninth and Tenth Amendments were "designed to include the reserved rights of the States, and the people . . . and to bind the authorities, State and Federal . . . to their recognition and observance." Claiming faithfulness to these interpretive premises, Campbell denied that Congress had power to prohibit slavery in the territories.

The Civil War Amendments (especially the Thirteenth and Fourteenth) overturned the central holdings of *Scott* and formalized the results of the Civil War by invalidating slavery and making all native-born people, including African Americans, citizens. However, these changes, along with others, did not end controversy over the scope of delegated powers or their relationship to reserved and retained prerogatives. Accordingly, the justices continued to deal with the problems of constitutional construction that were at the heart of the Ninth Amendment.

**Twentieth Century Precedents.** These problems came to a head again during the New Deal era. The mid-1930's inaugurated an increasingly deferential approach to assertions of national power and had corresponding implications for interpreting limitations on those powers. In this context, the Ninth Amendment made its first substantial appearance in a majority opinion for the Court.

In *Ashwander v. Tennessee Valley Authority* (1936), the justices upheld the operation of the Wilson Dam by the Tennessee Valley Authority, an agency of the U.S. government. Among other things, the plaintiffs argued that the sale of electric energy generated by the dam exceeded constitutional delegations of power and abridged rights protected by the Ninth Amendment. Chief Justice Charles Evans Hughes, writing the majority opinion, dismissed both arguments. Referring to the Ninth Amendment, he claimed that "the maintenance of rights retained by the people does not withdraw the rights which are expressly granted to the Federal Government. The question is as to the scope of the grant and whether there are inherent limitations which render invalid the disposition of property with which we are now concerned."

In this passage, Chief Justice Hughes relied on normative premises similar to those implicit in debates by the creators of the Constitution on matters of structure. Follow-ing Madison's example, the chief justice treated dele-gated powers and retained rights as mutually exclusive and reciprocally limiting pre-rogatives. However, Hughes suggested that a finding of delegated power precluded opposing claims of retained rights. He characterized the latter, like reserved powers, as residuals beyond the legit-imate reach of federal dele-gations.

Eleven years later, Justice Stanley F. Reed commented further on the Ninth Amend-ment in his opinion for the

*Justice Stanley F. Reed.* (Library of Congress)

majority in *United Public Workers v. Mitchell* (1947). In that case, the justices upheld a section of the Hatch Act (1939) that prohibited employees of the federal government from active participation in political campaigns. Reed accepted the employees' stance that "the nature of political rights reserved to the people by the Ninth and Tenth Amendments are involved. The rights claimed as inviolate may be stated as the right of a citizen to act as a party official or worker to further his own political views." The justice claimed, however, that "these fundamental human rights are not absolutes" and thus were subject to reasonable governmental restriction.

By this time, the Court had already enforced many of the guarantees of the Bill of Rights against the states through the Fourteenth Amendment's due process clause. In such cases, the Court repeatedly treated popular rights as "trumps" capable of preempting otherwise legitimate assertions of governmental power. The Court had also repeatedly interpreted enumerated rights as similar limitations on federal powers. In *Mitchell,* however, Justice Reed did not explore the possibility of judges' enforcing unenumerated rights as such limitations. Absent such a reconceptualization, the Ninth Amendment—along with the Tenth—would have diminished practical significance. Claims of unenumerated rights would be preempted by increasingly expansive conceptions of delegated powers.

**The Right of Privacy.** In the 1960's, the Court first relied on the Ninth Amendment to enforce unenumerated rights as limits on state powers. The Court made this move in the landmark case of *Griswold v. Connecticut* (1965). The majority opinion, written by Justice William O. Douglas, invoked the Ninth along with the First, Third, Fourth, Fifth, and Fourteenth Amendments, to support the Court's invalidation of a state law prohibiting the use of contraceptives by married couples. According to Douglas, the state law abridged a right of privacy that was "older than the Bill of Rights." He presumed that the government's purpose was valid but suggested that the means chosen "swe[pt] unnecessarily broadly and thereby invade[d] the area of protected freedoms."

Justice Arthur J. Goldberg in his concurrence offered his view of the Ninth Amendment's relevance in this context. In the most extensive explicit analysis of the Ninth Amendment in a Court opinion to date, Goldberg reviewed commentary on the amendment by Madison and Joseph Story, along with judicial precedents enforcing fundamental liberties in addition to enumerated rights. His central claim was that the Ninth Amendment supported interpreting the Fourteenth Amendment as embracing unenumerated along with enumerated liberties.

Justice Hugo L. Black in his dissent criticized both the majority opinion and Justice Goldberg's concurrence. He denied that the Constitution protected a right of privacy and claimed that relying on the Ninth Amendment to enforce such a right against the states turned somersaults with history. He stated that the Ninth Amendment was added to constitutional text "to assure the people that the Constitution in all its provisions was intended to limit the Federal Government to the powers granted expressly or by necessary implication."

In *Roe v. Wade* (1973), the Court extended its holding in *Griswold*. Justice Harry A. Blackmun, in the majority opinion, wrote, "The right of privacy, whether it be founded in the Fourteenth Amendment's concept of personal liberty and restrictions upon state action, as we feel it is, or, as the District Court determined, in the Ninth Amendment's reservation of rights to the people, is broad enough to encompass a woman's decision whether or not to terminate her pregnancy." Blackmun hesitated to rely squarely on the Ninth Amendment to strike down the challenged state law. Following Douglas and Goldberg's opinions in *Griswold*, however, he suggested connections between the Ninth and Fourteenth Amendments.

**A Saving Clause.** In *Richmond Newspapers v. Virginia* (1980), Chief Justice Warren E. Burger announced the Court's ruling that the First and Fourteenth Amendments guaranteed a right of the public and press to attend criminal trials. Burger relied on the Ninth Amendment to rebut arguments that such a right was not protected simply because it was nowhere spelled out in the Constitution. In his view, the Ninth Amendment was significant as a saving clause designed to allay fears that the explicit listing of certain guarantees could be interpreted as excluding others. The amendment prevented people from claiming that "the affirmation of particular rights implies a negation of those not expressly defined." Burger pointed out, moreover, that the Court repeatedly enforced fundamental rights going beyond those explicitly defined in the Constitution, including the rights of association, of privacy, to be presumed innocent, to travel freely, and to be judged by a standard of proof beyond a reasonable doubt in criminal trial.

It is impossible to ascertain with confidence the extent to which justices have relied on the Ninth Amendment as an interpretive guide but not cited it in their opinions. However, Chief Justice Burger's opinion in *Richmond Newspapers* is a reminder that justices have not confined themselves to protecting enumerated rights. They have also protected unenumerated rights and taken positions on what rights the people hold in connection with interpreting the character and scope of federal and state governmental powers.

**Further Reading**
The most comprehensive collection of materials on the Ninth Amendment is *The Rights Retained by the People: The History and Meaning of the Ninth Amendment* (2 vols., Fairfax, Va.: George Mason University Press, 1989-1993), edited by Randy E. Barnett. These two volumes include documentary sources, selections from books, reprints of law review articles, and a bibliography of writings on the amendment through 1992. Much of volume 2 reprints essays from a symposium on the amendment that were originally published in volume 64 of the *Chicago-Kent Law Review* (1988). Later works analyzing the Ninth Amendment include Calvin R. Massey's *Silent Rights: The Ninth Amendment and the Constitution's Unenumerated Rights* (Philadelphia: Temple University Press, 1995) and Wayne D. Moore's *Constitutional Rights and Powers of the People* (Princeton, N.J.: Princeton University Press, 1996). The latter explores premises of popular sovereignty and conceptions of constitutional structure, including how they inform interpretation of the Ninth Amendment.

*Wayne D. Moore*

# TENTH AMENDMENT

*Description:* Amendment that reserves for the states those powers not delegated to the federal government by the Constitution. (*The full text of the Tenth Amendment appears in this volume on page 392.*)
*Significance:* The Supreme Court's decisions involving the Tenth Amendment were not always consistent. At times the amendment was criticized as redundant and at others reaffirmed as a valuable part of the Constitution.

The Tenth Amendment protects the reserved powers of the state, those not delegated to the federal government by the U.S. Constitution. The First Congress received numerous requests to include a means of protecting the reserved powers of the states. These concerns arose in many quarters during the Constitutional Convention of 1787 and ratification process, especially among the Antifederalists, who feared that an overbearing national government would assume the authority of the states. Article II of the Articles of Confederation had contained explicit provisions for protecting states, initiating a system whereby "each state retains its sovereignty." Various early state constitutions included provisions outlining the primacy of states in the confederal arrangement.

**Federalists and Antifederalists.** The most popular form of amendment requested during the state ratification conventions and proposed to the First Congress concerned a reserved powers clause. The defenders of the Constitution argued that such a provision was unnecessary. James Madison suggested in No. 39 of *The Federalist* (1788) that each state was "a sovereign body," bound only by its voluntary act of ratification. Other Federalists at the Virginia ratifying convention, including James Wilson, Alexander Hamilton, and John Marshall, held that such a provision was already present in the Constitution and that the new government would have only the powers delegated to it.

Opposition to and suspicion of the proposed Constitution on the grounds that it would infringe on the privileged status of the states was widespread. The defenders of state authority viewed the states as the repository of reserved power, and many believed that states were invested with an equal capacity to judge infractions against the federal government. In the Virginia ratifying convention, George Nicholas and

*James Wilson was among the delegates at Virginia's ratifying convention who argued that the Tenth Amendment was unnecessary because its provisions were already inherent in the Constitution.* (Library of Congress)

Edmund Randolph, members of the committee reporting the instrument of ratification, noted that the Constitution would have only the powers "expressly" delegated to it. If Federalists disagreed with the stress on state authority, they generally viewed a reserved power clause as innocuous, and Madison included such a provision among the amendments he introduced in 1789.

In the First Congress, Elbridge Gerry, a Founder and Antifederalist elected to the House of Representatives, introduced a proposal reminiscent of the Articles of Confederation, leaving to the states all powers "not expressly delegated" to the federal government. Gerry's proposal was defeated, in part because of concerns about the similarity between the language of his amendment and that of the articles.

Others who took a states' rights or strict constructionist view of the Constitution, including Thomas Jefferson, persisted in defending state power. Before ratification of the Tenth Amendment, Jefferson advised President George Washington that incorporating a national bank was unconstitutional, basing his opinion on the amendment. Jefferson would later compose the Kentucky Resolutions, which defended the states as the sovereign building blocks of the American nation and noted that the states retained a means of protection when threatened. To describe the process of state action, Jefferson supplied a new term, nullification, to note the immediacy and severity of the "remedy" necessary to prohibit the federal government from absorbing state authority.

Defenders of the federal government, sometimes described as nationalists or loose constructionists, argued that Congress must assume more power if the needs of the country were to be met. Most prominent among the advocates of increased federal authority was Hamilton. For Hamilton, the Tenth Amendment was unnecessary as the political order already protected states. The Constitution, according to the nationalists, already contained provisions for the exercise of federal power, including the necessary and proper clause and supremacy clause.

**The Court and the Amendment.** The Supreme Court addressed the controversy in *McCulloch v. Maryland* (1819). The Court upheld the constitutionality of a national bank, even though such an institution was not specified in the Constitution. In dismissing a strict delineation of state and federal authority, the Court, under the leadership of Marshall, extended the powers of Congress at the expense of the states. However, the Marshall Court also affirmed the notion that police powers belonged exclusively to the states. Under Chief Justice Roger Brooke Taney, the Court assumed more of a strict constructionist posture.

With the Civil War and Reconstruction, the authority and influence of the federal government were greatly increased. The role of the Tenth Amendment was essentially disregarded as federal troops occupied southern states and Congress provided governance. The authority of the states continued to suffer, resulting in part from a series of Court decisions in the twentieth century. In *Champion v. Ames* (1903), the Court affirmed a congressional act that prohibited the sale of lottery tickets across state lines as an effort to limit gambling. Before *Champion*, decisions regarding gambling were made by the states. The decisions of the Court were not consistent, and it soon adopted a view of the relationship between states and the federal government that allowed each to be authoritative in its own sphere, exempting "state instrumentalities" from federal taxation. In *Hammer v. Dagenhart* (1918), the Court ruled in favor of state power in terms of commerce. The Tenth Amendment would, however, suffer its most severe criticism in *United States v. Darby Lumber Co.* (1941).

In this decision, Chief Justice Harlan Fiske Stone discredited the amendment as "redundant" and a "constitutional tranquilizer and empty declaration."

Although Stone dismissed the amendment, continued authentication of its importance can be seen in *Fry v. United States* (1975), in which the Court affirmed that the amendment "expressly declares the constitutional policy that Congress may not exercise power in a fashion that impairs the States' integrity or their ability to function effectively in a federal system." In *Printz v. United States* (1997), the Court again forcefully affirmed the amendment, noting that the amendment made express the residual state sovereignty that was implicit in the Constitution's conferring of specific governmental powers to Congress.

## Further Reading

Berger, Raoul. *Federalism: The Founders' Design.* Norman: University of Oklahoma Press, 1987.

Berns, Walter. "The Constitution as Bill of Rights." In *How Does the Constitution Secure Rights?*, edited by Robert A. Goldwin and William Schambra. Washington, D.C.: American Enterprise Institute, 1985.

_____. "The Meaning of the Tenth Amendment." In *A Nation of States*, edited by Robert A. Goldwin. Chicago: Rand McNally, 1963

Calhoun, John C. "A Discourse on the Constitution and Government of the United States." In *Union and Liberty: The Political Philosophy of John C. Calhoun*, edited by Ross M. Lence. Indianapolis, Ind.: Liberty Fund, 1992.

Hickok, Eugene W., Jr. "The Original Understanding of the Tenth Amendment." In *The Bill of Rights*, edited by Hickok. Charlottesville: University of Virginia Press, 1991.

Kaminski, John P., et al., eds. *The Documentary History of the Ratification of the Constitution, Volumes VIII-X: Ratification of the Constitution by the States, Virginia.* Madison: State Historical Society of Wisconsin, 1993.

Lofgren, Charles A. "The Origins of the Tenth Amendment, History, Sovereignty, and the Problems of Constitutional Intention." *Constitutional Government in America*, edited by Ronald K. L. Collins. Durham, N.C.: Carolina Academic Press, 1980.

Story, Joseph. *Commentaries on the Constitution of the United States.* Vol. 2. Boston: C. C. Little and J. Brown, 1833.

*H. Lee Cheek, Jr.*

# THE ISSUES

# ACADEMIC FREEDOM

*Description:* Ability freely to exchange ideas and concepts in an academic setting.

*Relevant amendment:* First

*Significance:* The Supreme Court has never granted academic freedom full constitutional status. It has ruled both for and against the protection of academic freedom on the basis of the First and Fourteenth Amendments.

In many rulings, the Supreme Court recognized that citizens possess constitutional rights of free speech and due process. However, when these citizens were faculty members at academic institutions, the Court also obligated them to respect their responsibilities to their students, their academic community, and society in general. In early cases such as *Gitlow v. New York* and *Whitney v. California* (1928), the Court struggled with the standard for judging constitutionality of state laws or actions that were being challenged as violations of the free speech clause of the First Amendment. The Court upheld convictions for subversive advocacy in both *Gitlow* and *Whitney* and ruled that the defendants' First Amendment rights had not been violated. The dissent issued in *Gitlow* by Justice Oliver Wendell Holmes joined by Justice Louis D. Brandeis became the test by which the Court determined what speech was allowable. The justices stressed that speech should be protected unless it creates a clear and present danger. In *Stromberg v. California* (1931), Stromberg's lawyers used the clear and present danger test in their arguments before the Court, which overturned Stromberg's conviction by a state court on a charge of displaying a red (communist) flag at a youth camp.

Two Supreme Court decisions in 1952 focused on the First Amendment rights of teachers. Both cases, *Adler v. Board of Education* and *Wieman v. Epdegraff*, involved teachers being discharged because of membership in subversive organizations. In *Adler*, the Court upheld New York's Feinberg Law, which banned teachers who belonged to subversive organizations from public schools. Justice Sherman Minton reasoned that because teachers shape the attitudes of young minds toward the society in which they live, the state has a vital concern in protecting schools from subversive organizations. In the dissent, Justices William O. Douglas and Hugo L. Black wrote of their concern for censorship and threat to First

Amendment rights. This concern for constitutional freedoms would be echoed by Justice William J. Brennan, Jr., in *Keyishian v. Board of Regents* (1967). In *Wieman v. Epdegraff*, the Court overruled an Oklahoma statute that disqualified people from teaching or other public employment solely on the basis of membership in a subversive organization and not whether they had knowledge of its purposes and activities. The Oklahoma statute was ruled unconstitutional under the due process clause. Justice Felix Frankfurter endorsed the issue of academic freedom for teachers at all levels.

**The Warren Court.** As chief justice, Earl Warren led the Court in landmark decisions guaranteeing First Amendment protections. In *Shelton v. Tucker* (1960), the Court declared unconstitutional a New York statute that required teachers to disclose all organizational affiliations. In *Keyishian v. Board of Regents*, it struck down sections of the Feinberg Law that had been upheld in *Adler* and established broad First Amendment protections for academic freedom for college faculty. In the majority opinion, Justice Brennan stressed the importance of academic freedom for all people, not just for teachers.

The Court's ruling in *Epperson v. Arkansas* (1968) extended academic freedom to precollegiate levels as it negated an Arkansas law prohibiting the teaching of evolution. The Court ruled on the basis of the First Amendment prohibition against religious establishment and therefore did not set a precedent for free speech rights for elementary and secondary schools. Free speech protection would not be extended to the precollegiate level until *Tinker v. Des Moines Independent Community School District* (1969).

**Burger-Rehnquist Eras.** Justices appointed by Presidents Richard M. Nixon and Ronald Reagan (Warren E. Burger, William H. Rehnquist, Lewis F. Powell, Jr., and Sandra Day O'Connor) formed the core of a new majority on the Burger and Rehnquist Courts. Under these chief justices, the Court would issue opinions contradicting rulings that had previously limited the authority of school-governing officials. In *Ambach v. Norwick* (1979), two teachers from Scotland and Finland challenged the New York statute that denied certification to foreign nationals who were not in the process of attaining U.S. citizenship. In writing the majority opinion, Justice Powell stressed the role of the school as an agency for socialization and the importance of the influence of the teacher in this process. The

## ATTEMPTS TO BAN BOOKS
## FROM U.S. SCHOOLS IN 1993-1994

The 1993-1994 school year saw a record number of efforts to ban books from U.S. schools. This map summarizes the number of such attempts in each state.

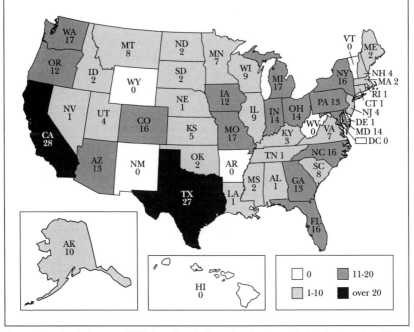

*Source: Parenting* (February, 1995), based on information from People for the American Way.

teachers argued on the grounds of academic freedom, but the Court ruled on the basis of an equal protection case under the Fourteenth Amendment rather than a free speech case under the First Amendment. The *Ambach* case, which describes the political socialization of schools, was cited by both sides in *Island Trees School District v. Pico* (1982). Justices Brennan and Harry A. Blackmun asserted in the majority opinion that judicial review of book removals from libraries is warranted in order to prevent First Amendment violations. In their dissent, Justices Burger, Powell, and Rehnquist argued that it is not unconstitutional for school officials to remove from the library books that contain expressions of values that are not shared by the community.

*Hazelwood School District v. Kuhlmeier* (1988) was a milestone in supporting the authority of school officials. The case involved a Missouri high school principal who removed articles from a school newspaper. The Court ruled that the newspaper was part of the school curriculum and was rightfully under the control of the school. The Court did not view the principal's action as a First Amendment violation.

*University of Pennsylvania v. Equal Employment Opportunity Commission* (1990) placed a different twist on the typical academic freedom argument. The University of Pennsylvania denied tenure to an associate professor who then filed a charge with the Equal Employment Opportunity Commission alleging discrimination in violation of Title VII of the Civil Rights Act of 1964. When a subpoena was issued requesting tenure-review files of the professor and of five other male faculty members, the university filed suit. The university argued that the files would jeopardize a common-law privilege against disclosure of confidential peer review materials and would violate the faculty members' First Amendment rights, including academic freedom. The Court rejected this position and ruled that a university does not enjoy a special privilege regarding peer review files.

**Further Reading**

Menard, Louis. *The Future of Academic Freedom.* Chicago: University of Chicago Press, 1996.

Poch, Robert. *Academic Freedom in American Higher Education: Rights, Responsibilities, and Limitations.* Washington, D.C.: George Washington University Press, 1993.

Whitson, James Anthony. *Constitution and Curriculum.* London: The Falmer Press, 1991.

*Gae R. Johnson*

# ASSEMBLY AND ASSOCIATION, FREEDOM OF

*Description:* The right of the people to gather peaceably and to associate with anyone they choose.

*Relevant amendment:* First

*Significance:* The Supreme Court has generally upheld the freedom of assembly and association, although it has upheld time, place, and manner restrictions on demonstrations, picketing, and similar gatherings.

The First Amendment to the Constitution prohibits Congress from making any law that limits "the right of the people peaceably to assemble," but the Constitution does not mention freedom of association. Freedom of association has been inferred, however, from freedom of assembly, and the guarantees of the Bill of Rights, of which the First Amendment is part, have been inferred to apply to the states. Therefore, subject to the interpretation of the Supreme Court, all laws, whether state or federal, that unduly restrict freedom of assembly and association are unconstitutional.

The only explicit restriction on these freedoms is the word "peaceably"; mobs and other groups intent on violence or destruction of property lie outside constitutional protection, as do picketers who physically

*Demonstrators attempting to exercise their right to assemble in front of the Capitol Building in Washington, D.C.* (Library of Congress)

oppose those who wish to cross picket lines. The freedoms also impinge on trespassing laws that protect the rights of private owners of property, resulting in issues of legal interpretation. Additionally, the Court has upheld laws requiring the licensing of parades and other large assemblies that, although taking place in public areas, may disrupt traffic or otherwise place an undue burden on local authorities. The Court has made further distinctions between public and private places. Quasi-public or quasi-private places, such as college campuses and privately owned areas open to the general public, have been defined regarding the limitations of the right of assembly. How such limitations are to be interpreted and applied have been and continue to be the subject of litigation that is often controversial.

**Interpretations.** The general standard that the Court applies to the question of the right of assembly is the same that it applies to speech: time, place, and manner. For example, the noisy demonstration that is legal in a park outside a public library may be considered illegal if it takes place inside the library. As the Court stated in *United States Postal Service v. Greenburgh Civic Associations* (1981): "The First Amendment does not guarantee access to property simply because it is owned or controlled by the government." This statement should be compared, however, with one from *Hague v. Congress of Industrial Organizations* (1939), that whether streets or parks are publicly or privately owned, "they have immemorially been held in trust for the use of the public for purposes of assembly and discussing public questions." The conflict between these two statements is to be resolved by examination of the intent that the government has in limiting the assembly in question. In *Perry Education Association v. Perry Local Educators' Association* (1983), the Court stated that the government may "reserve a forum for its intended purposes as long as the regulation is reasonable and not an effort to suppress expression merely because public officials oppose the speaker's view." *Perry* concerned a dispute between two teachers' unions. Under the employment contract, Perry Educational Association (PEA) had access to the interschool mail system and teacher mail boxes. The bargaining agreement also provided that access rights to the mail facilities were not available to any rival union. A rival union, Perry Local Educators' Association filed suit, contending that PEA's preferential access to the internal mail system violated the First Amendment. The Supreme Court ruled that the PEA's contract provision did not violate the First Amendment.

Freedom of association—in particular, political association, including membership in communist organizations—has been examined in similar ways. In such cases as *Yates v. United States* (1957), the Court explicitly rejected the idea that membership in a group indicates guilt by association. Communist groups are not the only ones whose memberships were subject to government scrutiny. In *National Association for the Advancement of Colored People v. Alabama* (1958), for example, the National Association for the Advancement of Colored People was able to enforce its right to free and private association, in particular to keep its membership rolls out of the hands of Alabama officials. Such protection, however, does not extend to groups that a government can demonstrate are engaged in illegal activities. The Court has upheld the careful application of federal antigang laws that make it a crime to belong to a group engaged in criminal enterprise.

Private organizations that discriminate according to sex, race, or other criteria have defended themselves on First Amendment grounds, with varying degrees of success. In general, the Court has placed greater emphasis on laws against discrimination than on the right to association, especially regarding large associations that have few restrictions on membership. In *Roberts v. United States Jaycees* (1984), the Court reasoned that the Jaycees lacked the distinctive characteristics, such as small size, identifiable purpose, selectivity in membership, and perhaps seclusion from the public eye that might afford constitutional protection to the organization's exclusion of women. In *Rotary International v. Rotary Club of Duarte* (1987), the Court upheld a California law that prevented Rotary International from excluding women from membership, and in *New York State Club Association v. City of New York* (1988), the Court upheld a New York City law prohibiting discrimination based on race, creed, sex, and other categories in places "of public accommodation, resort, or amusement." The court held that the law applied to clubs of more than 400 members providing regular meal service and supported by nonmembers for trade or business purposes.

A landmark case touching on freedom of association is *Griswold v. Connecticut* (1965). Griswold gave medical advice to married people regarding birth control and was convicted of breaking a Connecticut law prohibiting the use of birth control and the giving of medical advice about birth control. The Supreme Court declared the Connecticut law an unconstitutional violation of the right of privacy. The Constitution makes no mention of such a right, but in *Griswold* the Court reasoned that such a right flowed from the right to association. Put broadly, the government did not have the authority to tell people what they could talk about with whom. Thus the "right to be left alone is the beginning of all freedoms" could be inferred to freedom of association.

Abortion clinic protests, specifically the tactics employed by those opposed to abortion to prevent entrance to clinics, have generated various cases touching on freedom of assembly. In *Bray v. Alexandria Clinic* (1993), for example, the Court held that picketers in front of an abortion clinic did not violate the rights of those accessing the clinic to equal protection of the law because the picketers' methods did not rise to the level of "hinderance" considered illegal. On the other hand, the convictions of abortion clinic protesters who are too aggressive in their methods, particularly those that rise to physical confrontation, have been upheld in various courts.

**Further Reading**

Abernathy, M. Glenn. *The Right of Assembly and Association.* Columbia: University of South Carolina Press, 1981.

Gutmann, Amy, ed. *Freedom of Association.* Princeton, N.J.: Princeton University Press, 1998.

Murphy, Paul L. *Rights of Assembly, Petition, Arms, and Just Compensation.* New York: Garland, 1990.

Shiffrin, Steven H., and Jesse H. Choper. *The First Amendment: Cases, Comments, Questions.* St. Paul, Minn.: West Publishing, 1996.

*Eric Howard*

# AUTOMOBILE SEARCHES

*Description:* The inspection by police and other government agents of the interiors of motor vehicles to look for evidence of unlawful activity.

*Relevant amendment:* Fourth

*Significance:* Starting with its 1925 ruling, the Supreme Court made it progressively easier for police and other government agencies to engage lawfully in searches of motor vehicles by interpreting the search and seizure requirements of the Fourth Amendment in a manner that clearly distinguishes the search of a vehicle from that of a residence or a container.

The framers of the Fourth Amendment were concerned about protecting people from unlawful government searches and seizures of their "houses" and "effects" when they drafted the amendment in the late eighteenth century. When the automobile became prominent in U.S. society more than a century later, the Supreme Court had to decide how the words and principles of the Fourth Amendment should be applied to searches of cars and other motor vehicles.

Beginning with its decision in *Carroll v. United States* (1925), the Court has consistently held that where there is probable cause that an automobile contains evidence of a crime, the police may search that vehicle without a search warrant. Unlike houses, automobiles are mobile and therefore the police may not have time to obtain a warrant before the vehicle and any evidence contained within it disappear, the Court reasoned. As the Court applied the warrant requirement of the Fourth Amendment differently to automobiles than to houses, inevitably the question arose as to whether the search of a motorhome would be treated as that of a house or an automobile. In *California v. Carney* (1985), the Court held that in most cases, the potential mobility of a motorhome obviates the need for the police to obtain a search warrant.

Searches of effects, such as containers, generally are subject to the same warrant requirement that applies to house searches. The Court was thus confronted with the question of whether to require the police to obtain a warrant before searching a container located in an automobile. In a series of cases culminating in *California v. Acevedo* (1991), the Court held that when the police have probable cause that a container in an automobile contains criminal evidence or that the evidence is located somewhere in the automobile and can fit into the container, they may search the container without obtaining a warrant.

The Court has also authorized police searches of automobiles in situations in which there was no probable cause that there was criminal evidence within the automobile. After lawfully arresting the occupant of a vehicle, the police may search the passenger area of that vehicle, including the glove compartment or items within the passenger area. According to the Court's decision in *New York v. Belton*, (1981), such a search is permissible to prevent the arrested person from grabbing a weapon or disposing of evidence. Additionally, when police properly impound a vehicle, they are allowed to search all parts of the vehicle in order to inventory its contents, as the Court held in *South Dakota v. Opperman* (1976). In *United States v. Di Re* (1999), the Court held that officers who stopped a driver for a traffic violation and saw evidence of drugs were allowed to search everything in the automobile and the private effects of a passenger.

**Further Reading**

Quick, Bruce D. *Law of Arrest, Search, and Seizure: An Examination of the Fourth, Fifth, and Sixth Amendments to the United States Constitution*. Rev. ed. Bismarck, N.Dak.: Attorney General's Office, Criminal Justice Training and Statistics Division, 1987.

Regini, Lisa A. "The Motor Vehicle Exception: When and Where to Search." *FBI Law Enforcement Bulletin* 68, no. 7 (July, 1999): 26-32.

Savage, David G. "Privacy Rights Pulled Over: Cops Get More Power to Search Personal Effects in Vehicles." *American Bar Association Journal* 85 (June, 1999): 42-44.

*Steven P. Grossman*

# BAD TENDENCY TEST

*Description:* A test first applied by the Supreme Court in 1919 according to which speech that had a "tendency" to incite unlawful acts was not constitutionally protected.

*Relevant amendment:* First

*Significance:* Throughout much of the twentieth century, the Court used the bad tendency test broadly to restrict speech critical of the U.S. government or its policies.

Although usually associated with *Debs v. United States* (1919), the bad tendency test actually has its genesis in *Schenck v. United States* (1919). In that case, the Supreme Court decided that Charles Schenck, a leader of the Socialist party, was guilty of a conspiracy to violate the 1917 Espionage Act by distributing flyers denouncing the draft. As part of the opinion in *Schenck,* Justice Oliver Wendell Holmes made it clear that not all speech can or should be protected by invoking the now-famous example of a person yelling "fire" in a crowded theater. Drawing the line between protected and unprotected speech, however, has proven difficult. In *Schenck,* the Court established the following test for determining whether speech should be protected:

The question in every case is whether the words used are used in such circumstances and are of such a nature as to create a clear and present danger that they will bring about substantive evils that Congress has a right to prevent.

As applied, this test was far less protective of free speech than the term "clear and present danger" might suggest. No showing of present danger was required in *Schenck* or subsequent cases. The Court held that if the "tendency and intent" of the speech was to encourage illegal action, then the speech was not protected by the First Amendment. Furthermore, the Court was often willing to *assume* a bad tendency and intent if the speech was critical of the government or its policies. The bad tendency test was notoriously applied just weeks after *Schenck* in *Debs v. United States*, when the perennial presidential candidate Eugene Debs was convicted of conspiracy for telling a crowd that he was sympathetic toward those who were trying to obstruct the draft. He was sentenced to ten years in prison for the crime.

Almost immediately, the test came under fire, with Justice Holmes dissenting against the test's application in *Abrams v. United States* (1919). His was a lone voice, however, and the bad tendency test continued to be applied. For example, in *Gitlow v. New York* (1925), *Whitney v. California* (1927), and *Dennis v. United States* (1951), members of either the Socialist or Communist Parties were convicted of breaking the law because they were found to have advocated illegal action by distributing flyers or assembling in groups.

Although the Court employed various First Amendment tests after *Debs*, it did not begin to seriously move away from the substance of the bad tendency test until *Yates v. United States* in 1957. In *Yates*, the Court reversed

*Socialist Party leader Eugene Debs.*
(Library of Congress)

the conspiracy convictions of fourteen "second-string" Communist Party officials, drawing a line between advocacy of an abstract principle and advocacy of action. Even so, it was not until 1969, in *Brandenburg v. Ohio*, that the Court finally abandoned the bad tendency test completely and developed the modern, highly protective standard for freedom of speech.

**Further Reading**

Chafee, Zechariah, Jr. *Free Speech in the United States.* Cambridge, Mass.: Harvard University Press, 1941.

Downs, Donald. *Nazis in Skokie.* Notre Dame, Ind.: University of Notre Dame Press, 1985.

Greenawalt, Kent. *Speech, Crime and the Uses of Language.* New York: Oxford University Press, 1989.

*Evan Gerstmann and Christopher Shortell*


# BAIL

*Description:* Money posted by persons accused of crimes as security for their appearance at trial. The U.S. Constitution offers guarantees against excessive bail, which were interpreted and generally upheld by the Supreme Court.

*Relevant amendment:* Eighth

*Significance:* Because of the inherent unfairness of subjecting an unconvicted person to a long, indefinite period of imprisonment, the Court has attempted to ensure that the accused is not unreasonably detained. Denial of bail or excessive bail is also thought to be an unreasonable impediment to the accused person's right to prepare a defense.

The use of bail has been a part of the Anglo-American criminal justice system since the English Bill of Rights of 1689 gave protections against excessive bail. The Founders of the American republic counted the right to a just bail among the essential liberties. The Eighth Amendment to the U.S. Constitution guarantees that "excessive bail shall not be required." A stronger expression of the contemporary feeling about bail is found in the Northwest Ordinance of 1787, which declared that "all persons shall be bailable, unless for capital offenses, where the proof shall be evident, or the presumption great."

In 1895 the Supreme Court first affirmed the importance of a right to reasonable bail in *Hudson v. Parker*. Writing for the majority, Justice Horace Gray noted that a key principle of the U.S. justice system was "the theory that a person accused of a crime shall not, until he has been finally adjudged guilty . . . be absolutely compelled to undergo imprisonment or punishment." However, an earlier decision, *McKane v. Durston* (1894), limited the scope of this decision by ruling that the Eighth Amendment's bail provision did not apply to state courts.

*In a key 1895 Supreme Court decision, Justice Horace Gray affirmed the principle of bail in the U.S. justice system.* (Library of Congress)

The Court in *Stack v. Boyle* (1951), a case involving twelve Communist Party leaders accused of conspiracy, was concerned that excessive bail hampered the accused's right to a vigorous defense. The Court held that "the traditional right to freedom before conviction permits the unhampered preparation of a defense. Unless the right to bail is preserved, the presumption of innocence, secured after centuries of struggle, would lose its meaning." The Court determined that the purpose of bail is to "serve . . . as assurance of the presence of an accused. Bail set at a figure higher than an amount reasonably calculated to fulfill this purpose is excessive under the Eight Amendment." However, the next year, in *Carlson v. Landon* (1952), the Court in a 5-4 vote found that not all detentions were subject to bail, and Congress had the power to define cases in which bail was not allowed. The *Carlson* case was a civil case involving the detention of aliens before a deportation hearing.

**Preventive Detention.** Traditionally, the sole justification for jailing an accused but otherwise presumed innocent person before trial was to assure that the individual did not flee. It was generally not believed to be proper to deprive people of their liberty on the grounds that they may commit future crimes when they have not been convicted of a crime. The constitutional protection of the rights of the accused person clashed in the late twentieth century, with the desire by federal authorities to "preventively detain" persons accused of federal crimes to prevent them from engaging in criminal activities. One concern is the fear that members of criminal organizations freed on bail might harass and intimidate witnesses, thereby corrupting the judicial process.

The rise of international terrorism and drug trafficking led Congress to pass the Bail Reform Act of 1984, which allows a federal judge to consider preventive detention of a person accused of a federal crime if he or she finds that "no conditions or combination of conditions will reasonably assure the appearance of the [defendant] as required and the safety of any person before trial." The act allows a federal prosecutor to ask a judge to hold a defendant without bail indefinitely if the prosecutor can make a showing that the person poses a threat to others.

**The Act Examined.** The constitutionality of the Bail Reform Act was determined by the Court in *United States v. Salerno* (1987). *Salerno* involved two defendants indicted for racketeering and denied bail under the provisions of the act. One of the accused was alleged by prosecutors to be the "boss" of the Genovese crime family and the other a high-ranked "captain." The crimes included several counts of extortion and conspiracy to murder. The Court examined whether the bail reforms violated the defendant's constitutional right to be free from excessive bail, but it rejected the claim that *Stack* applied to the case. Limiting the scope of *Stack*, the Court found that the right to bail had never been considered absolute and that persons accused of capital crimes and at risk of flight had long been subject to bail restrictions and upheld the act. The Court noted that although "in our society liberty is the norm, and detention prior to trial or without trial is the carefully limited exception," the Bail Reform Act fell "within that carefully limited exception." The Count determined that the "numerous procedural safeguards" adequately protected against abuse of the act.

**Further Reading**
Duker, William F. "The Right to Bail: A Historical Inquiry." *Albany Law Review* 42 (1977): 33-120.
Goldkamp, John S. "Danger and Detention: A Second Generation of Bail Reform." *Journal of Criminal Law and Criminology* 76 (Spring, 1985): 1-74.
Metzmeier, Kurt X. "Preventive Detention: A Comparison of Bail Refusal Practices in the United States, England, Canada, and Other Common Law Nations." *Pace International Law Review* 7 (Spring, 1996): 399-438.
*Kurt X. Metzmeier*

# BIRTH CONTROL, RIGHT TO

*Description:* The right to use a method or object that aids in regulating or
preventing the birth of children
*Relevant amendments:* Fifth, Ninth, Fourteenth
*Significance:* Based on definitions of individual liberties and the right to
privacy, the American justice system has been involved in changing
notions of the permissibility of individual citizens' use of birth control

Throughout American history, midwives and health professionals have
always recorded ways in which couples could restrict or prevent pregnan-
cies. In the nineteenth century, however, increasingly stringent moral
standards and emphasis on women's domesticity led reformers to identify the prevention of pregnancy as a moral evil. Such moral views were
made a legal formality in 1873, when Anthony Comstock pressed for legislation that made illegal the possession, sale, or gift of any obscene materials or articles for the prevention of conception (Comstock Act). Comstock was made an assistant postal inspector, which gave him expanded
power to investigate and prosecute the dissemination of literature dealing with planned parenthood through the mail. In the 1870's and 1880's,
several states passed similar laws, making the use of contraceptives and
the spread of information about pregnancy prevention punishable under obscenity statutes.

**The Birth Control Movement.** Some reformers, however, viewed this legislation as damaging to the development of American families. Pointing
to large immigrant families and to mothers who were always in ill health,
they suggested that the spread of information about contraception would
help to prevent unchecked growth of American cities. One reformer in
particular, Margaret Sanger, was joined by Protestants, social reformers,
Malthusian scholars, and others who believed that American cities suffered from unchecked population growth. Sanger chose to confront the
Comstock Act. She founded planned parenthood clinics, and she repro-
duced contraception information to send to women by mail.

Although doctors could prescribe contraceptives for health reasons (to
prevent the spread of disease, broadly defined), Sanger and several other
reformers, including her sister, were arrested and jailed under the terms
of the Comstock Act. In spite of numerous penalties and court appear-

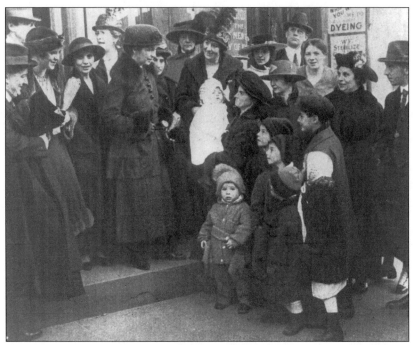

*Margaret Sanger (on step, facing baby) outside a Brooklyn courtroom during one of the many "birth control trials" to which she was subjected.* (Library of Congress)

ances, Sanger continually agitated for changes in the laws to permit the use of contraception by married couples. Eventually, activists in the state of Connecticut made a direct challenge to the legal validity of such statutes.

In 1935, the Birth Control League of Connecticut began to operate clinics for married women who could not afford doctors. Because this action violated Connecticut's obscenity statutes, the directors of the clinic were arrested and found guilty, and the clinics were closed. In the 1960's, however, Estelle Griswold, executive director of the Planned Parenthood League of Connecticut, opened another Planned Parenthood center for married women in the state. In *Griswold v. Connecticut* (1965), what was at issue were fundamental principles of individual freedoms and rights to privacy within the home. Griswold and her coworker both maintained that they had the right to practice their occupations and that the state's effort to limit their right to property was arbitrary. Even more important, attorneys maintained that obscenity statutes such as those in Connecticut were a violation of due process, since they unfairly invaded the privacy of the home and the private decisions of couples regarding their sexual practices and family planning. The Supreme Court, in a 7-2 ruling, agreed that laws passed under the terms of the Comstock Act were unfair invasions of privacy.

**Privacy and Birth Control After *Griswold*.** *Griswold v. Connecticut* was one of several decisions that have dealt with the question of rights to privacy. In *Mapp v. Ohio* (1961; the right to privacy within one's home), *Bowers v. Hardwick* (1986; permissibility of consensual sodomy), and *Roe v. Wade* (1973; the right of a woman to obtain an abortion), courts have had to address the extent to which the American judicial system protects individual liberties and citizens' rights to privacy.

After the *Griswold* case, contraception became widely available to individuals, through both private purchases and public programs. Later, the spread of venereal diseases and acquired immune deficiency syndrome (AIDS) added to public acceptance of the use of contraceptives. Nevertheless, public funding for the dissemination of information about contraception and of condoms and other preventive devices came under increasing criticism. Some groups have organized protests against the use of public monies for private relations. In particular, Roman Catholics and religious fundamentalists protest the spread of information and contraceptives on moral and religious grounds. Some cities have engaged in debates regarding whether the desire to protect public health outweighs the need to respect the religious and moral convictions of those opposed to the use of condoms and of family planning in general.

**Further Reading**

A good survey of the birth control movement which places birth control activism in historical perspective is Linda Gordon's *Woman's Body, Woman's Right: A Social History of Birth Control in America* (New York: Penguin Books, 1977). On Margaret Sanger, see Margaret Sanger, *My Fight for Birth Control* (New York: Maxwell Reprint, 1969); Vivian L. Werner, *Margaret Sanger: Woman Rebel* (New York: Hawthorn Books, 1970); Gloria Moore and Ronald Moore, *Margaret Sanger and the Birth Control Movement: A Bibliography, 1911-1984* (Metuchen, N.J.: Scarecrow Press, 1986); and David M. Kennedy, *Birth Control in America: The Career of Margaret Sanger* (New Haven, Conn.: Yale University Press, 1970).

*Sarah E. Heath*

# BLASPHEMY

*Description:* Contemptuous or irreverent expressions about God or matters held sacred in the dominant religion.

*Relevant amendment:* First

*Significance:* During the first half of the nineteenth century, state prosecutions of blasphemy occurred even when state bills of rights guaranteed freedom of speech and religion. Such prosecutions gradually ended because of the growth of secular and libertarian ideas. Under the Massachusetts blasphemy statute of 1782, "denying God" or "reproaching Jesus Christ or the Holy Ghost" were criminal acts. The state prosecuted and convicted a significant number of persons under the statute for about fifty years. In 1838, Abner Kneeland was sentenced to six months in the Suffolk County jail for his strong assertions of religious skepticism. Both the law and Kneeland's conviction were upheld by the state's supreme court.

In New York, blasphemy was occasionally prosecuted as a crime at common law. The crime was defined as "maliciously reviling God or religion." In 1811, a defendant was fined five hundred dollars and imprisoned for three months for "wickedly, maliciously, and blasphemously" saying in the presence of "good and Christian people" that "Jesus Christ was a bastard and his mother must be a whore." When upholding the conviction in *People v. Ruggles* (1811). The state's Chief Judge James Kent wrote that such language was "a gross violation of decency and good order." Allowing blasphemy to go unpunished, he asserted, would do great harm to the "tender morals of the young," eventually producing a culture in which oaths on the Bible would not be trustworthy.

The U.S. Supreme Court never had an occasion to review a prosecution for blasphemy because the First Amendment was not made applicable to the states until about a century after such prosecutions ended. In one related case, *Burstyn v. Wilson* (1952), the Court overturned a New York law that had authorized the censorship of "sacrilegious" movies.

*Thomas T. Lewis*

# CAPITAL PUNISHMENT

*Description:* The killing of a convict by the state for purposes of punishment or to reduce future crime.

*Relevant amendment:* Eighth

*Significance:* The death penalty, although infrequently applied, has symbolic importance and has sharply polarized public opinion. The Supreme Court entered this fray only briefly, first to restrict executions, then to permit capital punishment, increasingly free of federal court supervision.

During the colonial period and the founding of the United States, the execution of convicts was not only routine but also a public spectacle. The hangman's noose, a humane alternative to beheading, was employed with a liberality that would disturb modern sensibility. In eighteenth century England, for example, it is estimated that approximately 240 crimes were punishable by death, with the sentence commonly carried out in the town squares. In contrast to millennia of practice, the nineteenth and twentieth centuries have seen a gradual civilization of punishment. Incarceration replaced execution for most crimes. Hangings were removed from public view and placed instead behind prison walls. The abolition of physical torture as a legitimate part of punishment followed, eventually culminating in efforts to also circumscribe the infliction of psychological pain. Thus, the noose was replaced by electrocution, followed by the gas chamber, and later by lethal injection, all in a search of a humane method of depriving the convict of life, as the ultimate punishment. In the eyes of many ethicists, legal scholars, and moral leaders, the fulfillment of this historical trend would be the abolition of capital punishment altogether. In the United States, one of the last democratic nations retaining the death penalty, this debate has often acquired a constitutional dimension.

**The Death Penalty and the Constitution.** It is clear from the text of the Constitution that the Framers envisioned executions as a part of their legal regime. The Fifth Amendment provides that "no person shall be held to answer for a capital or otherwise infamous crime" absent an indictment by a grand jury. It further provides that no person shall "be subject for the same offense to be twice put in jeopardy of life and limb" nor be "deprived of life, liberty, or property without due process of law." The Fourteenth Amendment, adopted after the Civil War, similarly commands that no state shall deny any person "life, liberty, or property, without due process of law." Proponents of a contractual constitution, interpreted according to the historical intent of its Framers, are on apparently solid ground when they contend that the Constitution, in principle, sanctions capital punishment.

Opponents of the death penalty point to the same pair of due process clauses, promises of legal fairness, to condemn the application of the death penalty as arbitrary, capricious, even, in the words of Justice Potter Stewart, "freakishly imposed." They also point to the Fourteenth Amendment's requirement that states accord all persons the "equal protection of the laws" and raise questions concerning possible racial bias in the meting out of death sentences. Finally, and most tellingly, the Eighth Amendment's proscription of "cruel and unusual punishments" might provide a flat ban on capital punishment. The latter seems to have been adopted to end corporal punishments or the infliction of torture. However, in *Weems v. United States* (1910), the Supreme Court held that a constitutional principle "to be vital must be capable of wider application than the mischief which gave it birth." Abolitionists contend that these clauses create evolutionary constitutional rules, progressively driven by contemporary moral theory, that now proscribe the death penalty, regardless of accepted practice at the time of their adoption.

Judicial appeals to contemporary morality are always risky, especially regarding an emotionally contentious subject such as capital punishment. However, it is difficult to reconcile the death penalty, as practiced in the United States, with any of the common theoretical justifications for punishment. The death penalty is obviously not intended to accomplish the rehabilitation of the offender. There is little evidence in support of any general deterrence produced by the death penalty beyond that already achieved by incarceration and considerable evidence against the claim. Incapacitation of dangerous or repeat offenders can also be accomplished by means short of execution. Retribution, the theory that crime is a moral offense that must be redressed by the infliction of proportional pain to expiate the original offense, might justify capital punishment for heinous crimes, especially first-degree murder. The biblical injunction of "an eye for an eye and a tooth for a tooth" is a concise summary of retributive punishment. The problem is that retribution, if consistently followed, is a nondiscretionary punishment—a sentence proportional to the crime *must* be carried out, with no room for mercy or selection. Proponents of capital punishment who appeal to retribution would have to countenance the execution of all defendants convicted of crimes for which capital punishment is authorized. The result would be a rate of executions unprecedented in U.S. history. Public opinion overwhelmingly supports capital punishment. However, polls and jury behavior also show that Americans want the death sentence to be employed sparingly.

The modern Court's initial foray into death penalty law was not encouraging to abolitionists. In *Louisiana ex rel. Francis v. Resweber* (1947), the Court rejected the contention that a second attempt at executing a prisoner, the electric chair having malfunctioned the first time, was either double jeopardy or cruel and unusual punishment. Despite the Court's permissive attitude, the number of executions in the United States was already in decline. National statistics on executions date only from 1930, with 1935 the largest single year, with 199 executions. By the 1960's this number had declined to a trickle. Since the early 1980's, however, the number of annual executions in the United States has again been rising, especially in southern states. Sixty-eight executions were carried out in 1998.

**The Death Penalty Moratorium.** Encouraged by the Court's activism in civil rights and defendants' rights cases, death penalty opponents in the 1960's began a campaign to enlist the Court in the cause of abolition. The Legal Defense Fund (LDF) of the National Association for the Advancement of Colored People, later joined by the American Civil Liberties Union, orchestrated a threefold attack on capital punishment. First, the routine exclusion of "scrupled" jurors, those opposed to the death penalty on principle, was said to result in nonrepresentative juries skewed toward conviction and execution. Second, the determination of guilt and passing of sentence in a single trial procedure put defendants in an untenable position of having to offer evidence in mitigation of a crime they also contended they did not commit. Finally, the nearly complete discretion accorded juries in deciding when to impose death (the only sentencing question juries are called on to decide) resulted in an unpredictable, arbitrary, and discriminatory application of the death penalty.

In *Witherspoon v. Illinois* (1968), the Court banned the blanket exclusion of all scrupled jurors merely by virtue of their voicing objections to capital punishment. The state could still exclude those who would automatically or invariably vote against a death sentence, but not those expressing only "general objections" to capital punishment. The practical result of *Witherspoon* was to require commutation or resentencing of nearly all death sentences for prisoners then on death row. Until further litigation sorted out all potential *Witherspoon* claims, a de facto moratorium on capital punishment had been achieved. From 1967 until 1977, no executions were carried out in the United States.

Further LDF challenges to capital punishment were in the works. In *Furman v. Georgia* (1972), a fragmented Court adopted the third LDF critique of the death penalty as then practiced in all the states authorizing capital punishment, that unguided jury discretion produced arbitrary results. Only Justices William J. Brennan, Jr., and Thurgood Marshall held capital punishment to be cruel and unusual punishment per se in contravention of the Eighth Amendment. Dissenters William H. Rehnquist, Warren E. Burger, Lewis F. Powell, Jr., and Harry A. Blackmun found no constitutional prohibition to unbridled jury discretion to mete out death and would have deferred on the issue to state legislative politics (although the latter eloquently expressed personal misgivings concerning capital punishment). This left Justices William O. Douglas, Potter Stewart, and Byron R. White to cast limited but decisive votes against Georgia's capital punishment statute. Douglas expressed concerns that the death penalty was applied disproportionately to poor and socially disadvantaged defendants, in effect reading into the Eighth Amendment an equality requirement.

Stewart held that the rare imposition of death made capital punishment cruel and unusual in the minority of cases in which it was imposed. White agreed, arguing that its infrequency deprived the death penalty of any deterrent effect or ability to meet the test of retribution. For the first time, the Court had struck down a death sentence as cruel and unusual punishment. However, the long-term impact of *Furman* depended on the continued support of either Justice White or Justice Stewart, both centrists whose opposition to capital punishment seemed weak.

Public reception of *Furman* was immediate and hostile. Within a few years, thirty-five states had reenacted death penalty statutes purporting to meet the Court's objections. Three possibilities seemed available in the wake of *Furman*. States could enact mandatory death penalty statutes, imposing death in all cases where the death penalty was available, without discretion. This seemed to meet the objections of the Douglas, Stewart, and White bloc but would also have resulted in a large number of executions. A second option was to forgo death as a punishment altogether, but this seemed politically unlikely given the climate of public opinion. The third option was to enact guided discretion statutes, supplying juries with a host of aggravating and mitigating circumstances that would be considered in a separate sentencing phase of the trial, following a previous determination of guilt. This procedure met the LDF's second challenge to capital punishment, that the combined procedures for determining guilt and sentence imposed untenable choices on the defense. It also seemed to meet the issue of jury discretion head on, with neither the unpopular abolition of capital punishment nor the increased volume of executions that might follow adoption of mandatory capital punishment laws.

These laws came under the Court's scrutiny in *Gregg v. Georgia* (1976). Actually a compendium of five cases testing mandatory death penalty statutes in North Carolina and Louisiana and guided discretion statutes in Georgia, Texas, and Florida, *Gregg* also resulted in a badly fragmented Court. Justices Brennan and Marshall continued their per se opposition to the death penalty. Chief Justice Burger, along with Rehnquist, Blackmun, and White, voted to uphold all five death penalty regimes. As with *Furman*, the Court's decision rested on the centrists, now Justices Stewart, Powell, and John Paul Stevens. They approved of Georgia's death penalty regime, requiring a bifurcated procedure that separated the determination of guilt from the passing of sentence. In addition, before death could be imposed, a jury had to find beyond a reasonable doubt that at least one of ten aggravating circumstances had been met. Mitigating circumstances were also to be considered, and all death sentences were subject to mandatory appeal. Thus, a death penalty regime based on guided jury discretion now passed constitutional muster. The decision for a companion case, *Woodson v. North Carolina* (1976), specifically banned mandatory death sentences.

It is not at all clear that the death penalty regime approved in *Gregg* is able to meet the objections of jury discretion and arbitrary application of capital punishment that underlie *Furman*. Although subsequent litigation struck down jury guidelines that were deemed too vague, juries were still called on to consider unique circumstances pertaining to each case. Further inconsistency was introduced into the application of the death penalty through such practices as prosecutorial charging discretion, plea bargaining, and executive clemency. It thus appeared that *Gregg* marked a changed political sentiment on the part of the Court, perhaps even, as a practical matter, overruling *Furman*. With the decision in *Gregg*, the Court signaled a green light to executions. The death penalty moratorium came to an end in January of 1977, when the state of Utah executed Gary Gilmore by firing squad.

**Race and the Death Penalty.** The interest of the LDF in capital punishment should have surprised no one. It was long known that the death penalty was applied most frequently to society's outcast groups, especially the poor and members of minority groups. Over half of the convicts executed for all capital crimes between 1930 and 1995 were African Americans, far exceeding their proportion of the nation's population. Even more striking, of the 450 executions for rape between 1930 and 1965, more than 90 percent involved African American convicts. Criminologist Marvin Wolfgang, in a 1966 study, found that of 119 convicted rapists executed in twelve southern states between 1945 and 1965, 110 were black. The question remained as to whether these discrepancies could be explained by nonracial factors, such as a propensity to commit more heinous crimes.

## EXECUTIONS IN THE UNITED STATES, 1930-1995

| Year or Period | Total | White | Black |
| --- | --- | --- | --- |
| 1930 to 1939 | 1667 | 827 | 816 |
| 1940 to 1949 | 1284 | 490 | 781 |
| 1950 to 1959 | 717 | 336 | 376 |
| 1960 to 1967 | 191 | 98 | 93 |
| 1968 to 1976 | 0 | 0 | 0 |
| 1977 to 1982 | 6 | 5 | 1 |
| 1983 | 5 | 4 | 1 |
| 1984 | 21 | 13 | 8 |
| 1985 | 18 | 11 | 7 |
| 1986 | 18 | 11 | 7 |
| 1987 | 25 | 13 | 12 |
| 1988 | 11 | 6 | 5 |
| 1989 | 16 | 8 | 8 |
| 1990 | 23 | 16 | 7 |
| 1991 | 14 | 7 | 7 |
| 1992 | 31 | 19 | 11 |
| 1993 | 38 | 23 | 14 |
| 1994 | 31 | 20 | 11 |
| 1995 | 56 | 33 | 22 |
| **All years** | **4172** | **1940** | **2187** |

*Source:* U.S. Bureau of the Census, *Statistical Abstract of the United States: 1997.* 117th ed. Washington, D.C.: U.S. Government Printing Office, 1997.

*Note:* Excludes executions by military authorities. Figures in "total" column include races other than white and black.

A research team lead by David Baldus studied more than 2,400 criminal homicide cases in Georgia, from 1973 to 1980, tried under the death penalty regime approved in *Gregg.* Taking account of more than 230 separate characteristics of each case, they employed sophisticated statistical analysis to weigh the effect of each in producing death sentences. Their results found that, when adjusted for legitimate nonracial factors, the race of the *defendant* did not result in a strikingly disproportionate application of the death penalty. However, a strong correlation was uncovered between the race of the *victim* and the passing of a capital sentence.

In raw numbers, white or black killers of white victims were eleven times more likely to receive the death penalty than were killers of African American victims. Even when nonracial variables were factored in, killers of white victims were executed 4.3 times as often as were killers of blacks. The discrepancy was inexplicable, except by the inference that race prejudice continued to affect the death penalty regime, even after *Gregg*. In fact, the race of the victim proved to be a stronger predictor of a capital sentence than such factors as the defendant's prior history of violence, that the victim was a police officer, or that the killing occurred during an armed robbery. The supposition drawn from these results was that prosecutors, when faced with the killer of an African American victim, were less likely to seek the death penalty or more likely to accept a plea bargain eliminating death. Alternatively, juries, even guided statutorily by nonracial aggravating and mitigating circumstances, were less likely to impose death for the killing of a black victim, perhaps valuing the life of a black person less highly than that of a white victim.

These data formed the basis for the LDF's next challenge to capital punishment, in *McCleskey v. Kemp* (1987), as violating both the Eighth Amendment and the equal protection clause of the Fourteenth Amendment. Such a disparate racial impact would seem to call into question the effectiveness of *Gregg* in eliminating the arbitrary or discriminatory factors in applying the death penalty that had informed *Furman*. However, writing for the Court, Justice Powell held that to make an equal protection claim, McCleskey had to demonstrate that either the Georgia legislature or the jury in his particular case was motivated by racial animus or a discriminatory purpose. The social background data revealed in the Baldus study were insufficient to make even a prima facie case that McCleskey had personally suffered from racial discrimination and, in any event, were more appropriately considered in a legislative forum. Similarly the discrepancy revealed in the Baldus study was insufficient to demonstrate a violation of the Eighth Amendment because it did not offend society's evolving standards of decency. Justices Brennan, Marshall, Stevens, and Blackmun dissented.

In *Furman* and *Gregg*, the Court had sought to remove arbitrary and capricious factors, presumably including racial prejudice, from the application of the death penalty in the United States. However, with *McCleskey*, the Court appeared to be turning its back on that promise by foreclosing the last avenue for arguing for the per se unconstitutionality of capital punishment. It did find in the Eighth Amendment limits to the kinds of crimes that could be deemed capital offenses. In *Coker v. Georgia* (1977), the Court found a capital sentence disproportionate to the crime of rape and therefore barred by the Eighth Amendment. Similarly, *Enmund v. Florida* (1982) barred the death penalty for a felony murder in which the defendant did not commit, nor intend or contemplate, the killing. However, this ruling was modified in *Tison v. Arizona* (1987) to permit sentencing to death of a codefendant in a felony murder in which there was major participation in the felony combined with reckless indifference to human life. These rulings indicate that the Court views the Eighth Amendment as imposing substantive limits on the death penalty, at least concerning the issue of proportionality.

At the end of the twentieth century, thirty-eight states authorized the death penalty for first-degree murder. The federal government also authorized death for certain homicides, as well as for espionage, treason, or running a large-scale drug enterprise, but has not carried out a single capital sentence since 1963. As of April, 1999, 3,565 prisoners were on death row in the United States, while only 580 prisoners had been executed since 1977. Death row inmates are overwhelmingly poor and uneducated and disproportionately African American and southern. Many have suffered from inadequate assistance of counsel at trial. The most significant innovation by the Court toward the end of the twentieth century was increasing restrictions on the availability of federal *habeas corpus* review of state death penalty convictions and sentences. The apparent goal of the Court is to permit the states to apply post-*Gregg* death penalty law, largely absent federal judicial supervision.

## Further Reading

Bedau, Hugo Adam, ed. *The Death Penalty in America: Current Controversies.* New York: Oxford University Press, 1997.

Cole, David. *No Equal Justice: Race and Class in the American Criminal Justice System.* New York: New Press, 1998.

Constanzo, Mark. *Just Revenge: Costs and Consequences of the Death Penalty.* New York: St. Martin's Press, 1997.

Haines, Herbert H. *Against Capital Punishment: The Anti-Death Penalty Movement in America, 1972-1994.* New York: Oxford University Press, 1999.

Hanks, Gardner C. *Against the Death Penalty: Christian and Secular Arguments Against Capital Punishment.* Scottsdale, Pa.: Herald Press, 1977.

Latzer, Barry. *Death Penalty Cases: Leading U.S. Supreme Court Cases on Capital Punishment.* Boston: Butterworth-Heinemann, 1998.

Mello, Michael A. *Dead Wrong: A Death Row Lawyer Speaks Out Against Capital Punishment.* Madison: University of Wisconsin Press, 1997.

Protess, David. *A Promise of Justice: The Eighteen-Year Fight to Save Four Innocent Men.* New York: Hyperion, 1998.

*John C. Hughes*

# CENSORSHIP

***Description:*** The examination of any material in advance of publication, performance, or broadcast with the aim of preventing "objectionable" materials from being distributed

***Relevant amendment:*** First

***Significance:*** Censorship is commonly used by dictators to prevent the spread of ideas hostile to their rule, but modern democracies abhor censorship of nearly all expression except obscenity, where prior restraints are sometimes allowed

Repressive governments such as dictatorships have given censorship, or "prior restraint" (the suppression of materials before publication, performance, or broadcast), a very bad name. It is easy to understand why prior restraint is so important in a dictatorship. If a dictator waits until after publication, the dangerous ideas are already widespread, and extreme penalties may not deter some critics from voicing their opposition to a regime. In modern democracies, on the other hand, censorship is generally shunned. In the United States, censorship is allowed by the federal or state governments (or their agents) only if such prior restraint can be made compatible with the free expression portions of the First Amendment to the U.S. Constitution, which read: "Congress shall make no law . . . abridging the freedom of speech, or of the press; or the right of the people peaceably to assemble."

The First Amendment divides the free expression of ideas into two major categories: freedom of speech and the press, and freedom of peaceable assembly. Neither speech nor press is to be restrained, but the presence of the word "peaceably" in connection with assemblies indicates that assemblies can be, and routinely are, subject to prior restraint or censorship. Yet even in the case of assembly, prior restraints are allowed only for a reason such as allowing the "free movement of traffic in public areas." They must not be used to block the presentation of ideas simply because they are objectionable to the authorities.

Freedom of speech and the press is different from freedom of assembly because of its more passive character, although the U.S. Supreme Court has not always consistently and officially said so. The press, in particular, is regarded as a less dangerous medium for the expression of ideas, since reading is a far more passive activity than speaking to an audience. While it is possible to imagine someone making a speech that would incite a riot, it is very difficult to imagine a crowd reading a newspaper and then rioting. Because speech is frequently given before an assembly, speech falls partially under the First Amendment's requirement that assembly must be peaceable to avoid being restrained. This requirement rests on a distinction between ideas and actions. Pure ideas, as expressed in the press or in speeches to peaceable assemblies, are fully protected, but the requirement that an assembly must be peaceable may lead to some restraints on speech, even if there are no prior restraints on the press.

The essence of freedom of speech and the press is that there shall be no prior restraint—no censorship of any material in advance of its distribution. This requirement clearly implies that there may be punishments or restraints applied afterward, a view that is part of a long Anglo-Saxon legal tradition. In an age when censorship laws were focused against "blasphemy," John Milton argued in his *Areopagitica* (1644) against such laws: "Let [Truth] and falshood grapple; who ever knew truth put to the worse in free and open encounter?" By the eighteenth century, the battle against censorship had been sufficiently successful that the great jurist William Blackstone could write in book four of his *Commentaries on the Laws of England*: "The liberty of the press is indeed essential to the nature of a free state; but this consists of laying no *previous* restraints upon publications."

This tradition carried over into the colonies and led to the adoption of the First Amendment in 1791. Freedom of the press became an issue only a few years after the passage of the Bill of Rights when the Federalists passed the Alien and Sedition Acts in 1798 to punish their political opponents. Despite considerable controversy, the Federalists justified the acts by saying they did not impose a prior restraint. The political outcry was so great that Federalist John Adams lost the 1800 election to Thomas Jefferson, who pardoned all who had been convicted under the acts. Shortly thereafter the Federalists ceased to be a cohesive political party, and the Alien and Sedition Acts were considered such a black mark that no attempt was made to pass anything like them for more than a hundred years.

Throughout the 1800's, the common understanding of the First Amendment was that the federal government could not pass a law that restricted freedom of the press. Since the Bill of Rights was interpreted as applying only to the national government, however, sedition laws existed in various states. After the Fourteenth Amendment was passed following the Civil War, a basis for applying the principles of the Bill of Rights to the states was established, although the U.S. Supreme Court did not immediately accept this interpretation. During World War I, Congress passed two acts, the Sedition Act and the Espionage Act, which produced the first "free speech" cases, but no restraints on the press in advance of publication were enacted.

**Prior Restraint Cases.** The first U.S. Supreme Court decision on prior restraint was *Near v. Minnesota* (1931). Near published an anti-Semitic newsletter in Minneapolis, Minnesota, which charged that local government officials were Jewish-influenced and corrupt. Authorities sought to use a state statute to prevent Near from publishing, but the U.S. Supreme Court held that this was an impermissible prior restraint. Also, for the first time, it applied the free press portion of the First Amendment to state governments, utilizing the due process clause of the Fourteenth Amendment "selectively incorporating" part of the Bill of Rights.

The second Supreme Court prior restraint case, *New York Times Co. v. United States* (1971, the "Pentagon papers" case), involved hundreds of top-secret government documents that were photocopied by Daniel Ellsberg, knowing he was in violation of the security clearance laws. The documents were printed by *The New York Times* and other newspapers. The documents disclosed U.S. violations of international law and other matters damaging to the government. The Pentagon papers were clearly stolen government property, but the legal question was whether the newspapers could be restrained in advance from publishing them. The Supreme Court ruled against the government by a 6-3 vote. All nine justices upheld the "no prior restraint" concept, but they disagreed whether the restraint was justified by the extraordinary issues in this case. While each judge wrote a separate opinion, three major groups can be distinguished. The first group (justices Hugo Black, William O. Douglas, William Brennan, and Thurgood Marshall) maintained that no circumstances justified any prior restraint. Justices Warren Burger, Harry

Blackmun, and John Harlan upheld prior restraint but requested more time to examine the documents before deciding whether a permanent restraining order should be issued.

Justices Potter Stewart and Byron White, the swing votes who voted with the first four justices to allow publication of the Pentagon papers, believed that the "no prior restraint" presumption was too strong to overrule in this case but held open the idea mentioned in *Near* that there might be extreme circumstances in which prior restraint would be justified—such as a newspaper's attempt in wartime to publish the secret route of a naval convoy through submarine-infested waters. Given the Court's disregard of the U.S. government's anger and embarrassment at publication of the Pentagon papers, it is hard to imagine circumstances which would justify prior restraint. In two hundred years, the Supreme Court has never found a case that justified prior restraint and, since 1931, has never allowed any state or local government to exercise prior restraint, even when the expression of ideas is embarrassing to the government.

**Obscenity.** Not all ideas are political ideas, and the question of whether censorship can be justified also includes the artistic and scientific arenas. In particular, the Supreme Court has found it necessary to confront obscenity and pornography, particularly when applying the First Amendment to the states, many of which long had restrictive statutes on such subjects.

Despite the clear language of the First Amendment that "Congress shall make no law" abridging freedom of the press or speech, there have long been other rights which the Court has counterbalanced against the right of free expression. For example, there is a right of the adult population to avoid being assaulted in public by widespread display of materials that they might regard as offensive. There is an even more important need to protect children from pornographic materials which might damage their growth and development as human beings. Prior restraint is allowable for any pornography involving sexual acts by children, as the Court made clear in *New York v. Ferber* (1982). Sex acts involving children are against the law in every jurisdiction within the United States.

Regarding the publication of pornographic materials depicting adults for the use of other adults in the privacy of their own homes, the Supreme Court has found grounds to provide prior restraint of some materials. It has had great difficulty in doing so in practice, however, principally because of the strong constitutional opposition to prior restraint. Also, although the Supreme Court has consistently held that obscene materials are not protected under the First Amendment, it has had serious problems defining obscenity.

**Roth v. United States.** In *Roth v. United States* (1957), the Supreme Court attempted to define obscenity for the first time in the modern era. The first premise of the Court's *Roth* decision was that "all ideas having even the slightest redeeming social importance—unorthodox ideas, controversial ideas, even ideas hateful to the prevailing climate of opinion—have the full protection of the [First Amendment] guarantees." Because the First Amendment has been interpreted to protect virtually all ideas against prior restraint except obscene ones, the definition of obscenity was crucial, but it proved very difficult. Earl Warren, U.S. Chief Justice from 1953 to 1969, once said that defining obscenity presented the Court with its "most difficult" area of adjudication. In *Roth*, the Court said that to be obscene, expression had to be "utterly without redeeming social importance." Obscenity was fully defined by the following phrase: "Whether to the average person applying contemporary community standards, the dominant theme of the material taken as a whole appeals to prurient interests."

"Prurient" was defined as "material having a tendency to excite lustful thoughts." The Court asserted that "sex and obscenity are not synonymous," however, because the Court could not equate sex and obscenity without legitimizing the banning of a wide range of artistic, medical, and scientific materials. While there is a certain logic to the Supreme Court's decision in the *Roth* case, the decision itself involves a number of words which are not easy to define. Obscenity is difficult to define, but so are the words "lustful" and "prurient." A number of questions quickly became apparent. How can one decide that something is "utterly without redeeming social importance"? What "community standards" should be followed? Is the community a particular town, a particular state, or the nation as a whole? Moreover, exactly who is an "average person"? Lower courts quickly found that reaching judicial determinations on whether particular works fit within a definition that includes so many vague words was extremely daunting.

Ideally, the Supreme Court should provide clear definitions that can serve as workable guidelines for legislators, courts, and attorneys all across the nation. When the Court does not do so, it invites a flood of litigation, because only the Court can determine what its own vague guidelines mean. Since it did not do so in *Roth*, it found a huge number of obscenity cases being presented to it. Furthermore, the Court's own agreement on the *Roth* definition was short-lived.

**Per Curiam Rulings.** By 1967, several distinct positions were evident. Justices Black and Douglas maintained that the principle of "no prior restraint" is so strong that neither federal, state, nor local governments have any power to regulate any sexually oriented matter on the ground of obscenity. Justice Harlan took the opposing view that the federal government could control the distribution of "hard-core" pornography by using its enumerated powers and that states were entitled to even greater freedom to ban any materials which state courts had reasonably found to treat sex in a fundamentally offensive manner. A variety of other views were held by the other justices.

From 1967 until 1973, the Court followed the practice, established in *Redrup v. New York* (1967), of issuing *per curiam* reversals of convictions for the dissemination of obscene materials if at least five members of the Court, applying their separate tests, deemed them not to be obscene. *Per curiam* decisions are generally unsatisfactory in that they do not include any accompanying opinions as guidance for lower courts. As with vague guidelines, they invite endless litigation. At one point in the struggle to define hard-core pornography, Justice Stewart, with evident frustration, said of obscenity, "I can't define it, but I know it when I see it." While this statement became the punch line of many jokes, it was essentially an accurate description of the Court's approach from 1967 to 1973. The Court was deciding obscenity cases on an individual and retroactive basis, which was unsatisfactory for lower courts, prosecuting attorneys, police officers, defense attorneys, the producers of the materials, and the public.

**Miller v. California.** Sixteen years after *Roth* a new definition of obscenity was offered in the case *Miller v. California* (1973) and the companion case *Paris Adult Theatre v. Slaton*. Since five justices voted for the definition, it became the new definitive holding (or leading case) on the subject, but it proved little better than its predecessor.

The new definition made two major changes. First, it specifically rejected the standard "utterly without redeeming social value," which had been established in *Memoirs v. Massachusetts* (1966), in favor of a broader standard. The obscenity label can be applied only to a work which, "taken as a whole, appeals to the prurient interest," which depicts or describes sexual conduct in a "patently offensive way," and which, "taken as a whole, lacks serious literary, artistic, political, or scientific value." Second, the Court rejected the notion of national community standards in favor of local community standards. The Court explained that the United States "is simply too big and too diverse for this Court to reasonably expect that such standards could be articulated for all 50 States in a single formulation, even assuming the prerequisite consensus exists."

Promptly some communities began defining obscenity very restrictively. A Georgia community banned the 1971 film *Carnal Knowledge.* The case reached the Supreme Court, and once again, in *Jenkins v. Georgia* (1974), it was faced with making a decision on a case-by-case basis. The Court held that the film could not be found to appeal to the prurient interest or be found patently offensive under Georgia community standards, thus setting a guideline for the limits of allowable differences in local community standards.

Censorship and prior restraint are so alien to the American system that the Supreme Court has found it virtually impossible to apply censorship in any area. On the one hand, the Court acknowledges that adults have a right to be protected from unwanted public obscenity and that children must be protected. On the other, the Court is uncomfortable with any form of prior restraint. It may be that there is no way to write a clear obscenity law, but the Court's failure to provide clear standards has led to considerable litigation: There have been only two Supreme Court cases concerning prior restraint of political ideas, but there have been hundreds of obscenity cases.

**The Broadcast Media.** The issue of obscenity becomes still more complicated when one addresses the issue of electronic broadcasting. While the freedom to express political ideas is well protected, this protection is not as great for the broadcast media as it is for print media. The reason is that radio and television must use broadcast or microwave frequencies which are considered public property. Therefore the owners of radio and television stations must receive a license from the Federal Communications Commission (FCC). The licensing requirement can be viewed as a form of prior restraint. The government does not seek to control news broadcasts, however, generally granting them the same freedom as the print media; similarly, there is no government control of individual broadcasts of artistic, scientific, or medical materials.

Yet broadcasters, knowing that their licenses (which may be extremely lucrative) can be revoked or denied renewal, engage in considerable self-censorship, which also occurs in the film industry. Generally, self-censorship has been sufficiently effective that only a few cases of license nonrenewal exist. Some conservative commentators and politicians have argued that this self-censorship does not go far enough. In fact, a fairly sizeable minority of citizens are concerned by what they describe as a climate of permissiveness with regard to sex and violence, particularly on television. In mid-1995, for example, Congress heatedly debated whether to require manufacturers of television sets to include a "V-chip" that would allow parents to block their children's viewing of programs with violent or sexual content.

**Public Live Presentations.** Public live presentations fall into the category of assemblies and are therefore subject to the restriction that they must be "peaceable." Since the question of riots or violent behavior is not often at stake, an issue more often debated is the extent to which governments (primarily local but occasionally state) can restrain public live presentations of a sexual nature. Public displays in areas of public traffic, where such presentations might assault the sensibilities of some adults or be viewed by children, are widely prohibited by indecent exposure laws.

The problem is more complex for public live presentations in private businesses or in publicly or privately owned and operated theaters. Those who favor censorship of sexually explicit materials have been most successful in restricting sexually explicit presentations in establishments that sell alcoholic beverages or those in which activities that come close to prostitution can be documented. For other privately owned establishments open exclusively to adults, local governments have generally found it difficult to write statutes or ordinances which are specific enough to avoid being declared unconstitutionally vague without at the same time being declared unconstitutional for restraining freedom of expression. Even publicly owned and operated theaters have been forced to permit their use by productions that include nudity. Officials in Chattanooga, Tennessee, discovered this in the 1970's when they attempted to bar the presentation of the musical *Hair* from being performed in a publicly owned and operated theater (*Southeastern Promotions, Ltd. v. Conrad,* 1975).

### Further Reading
The best book of general scholarship on the subject is Henry J. Abraham and Barbara A. Perry's *Freedom and the Court* (6th ed. New York: Oxford

University Press, 1994). For a concise, thoughtful summary of the reasons it is so difficult to fashion a rule or definition of pornography, see Kent Greenwalt's "Pornography," in his *Speech, Crime, and the Uses of Language* (New York: Oxford University Press, 1989). Wallace Mendelson's *The American Constitution and Civil Liberties* (Homewood, Ill.: Dorsey Press, 1981) contains useful excerpts from important Supreme Court cases on censorship. For a detailed history of the free speech clause, see Stephen A. Smith's "The Origins of the Free Speech Clause," in Raymond S. Rodgers, *Free Speech Yearbook: The Meaning of the First Amendment, 1791-1991* (Carbondale, Ill.: Southern Illinois University Press, 1991).

*Richard L. Wilson*

# CHILLING EFFECT

*Description:* Indirect negative effect on protected speech resulting from certain laws or government policies

*Relevant amendment:* First

*Significance:* Otherwise unobjectionable laws and policies are sometimes invalidated by U.S. courts because they might "chill," or discourage, speech protected by the First Amendment

The U.S. Supreme Court has often repeated that freedom of speech needs "breathing room." Laws that serve appropriate ends may nevertheless creep so close to a regulation of protected speech that they discourage people from speaking for fear of adverse legal consequences. The concern for chilling effects on speech therefore surfaces in a variety of First Amendment contexts. For example, the Court has frequently overturned vague regulations of speech which—if written more clearly—would probably have survived constitutional challenge. Vague speech regulations have an "in terrorem" effect. Because they do not distinguish crisply between permissible and impermissible speech, such regulations risk deterring or chilling speech protected by the First Amendment as well as speech that government might otherwise be free to limit. Fearful of exposing themselves to government sanction, individuals might refrain from engaging in speech that falls within the First Amendment's umbrella of protection. To preserve First Amendment values, the Court routinely overturns such chillingly vague statutes. In *Smith v. Goguen*

(1974), for example, the Court held unconstitutional a statute making it a criminal offense to treat the United States flag "contemptuously." The statute, according to the Court, was impermissibly vague, since what is "contemptuous to one man may be a work of art to another."

A concern for possible chilling effects on protected speech also lies at the core of the overbreadth doctrine. An overbroad statute is one that is designed to restrict or punish speech that is not constitutionally protected. As it is drafted, however, an overbroad statute reaches not only unprotected speech but speech that is guarded by the First Amendment. The overbreadth doctrine allows individuals to complain of a statute's overreaching even if the speech of these individuals is otherwise unprotected. The doctrine essentially allows such individuals to champion the cause of unnamed speakers whose protected speech might be subject to sanction under an overly broad statute. For example, in *Houston v. Hill* (1987), the Supreme Court invalidated as substantially overbroad a Houston, Texas, ordinance making it a crime to "assault, strike or in any manner oppose, molest, abuse or interrupt any policeman in the execution of his duty." The Court acknowledged that some speech directed against police officers might be punished. However, it ruled that the statute reached too broadly, since "the First Amendment protects a significant amount of verbal criticism and challenge directed at police officers." By overreaching, therefore, the local ordinance would inevitably have the effect of stifling such protected criticism. As such, the ordinance was overturned as substantially overbroad.

*Richard L. Wilson*

# CIVIL RIGHTS AND LIBERTIES

*Description:* The phrase "civil liberties" refers to the personal freedoms that are guaranteed against government infringement. In contrast, "civil rights" denotes those individual and group rights that require governmental action for enforcement.

*Relevant amendments:* First through Ninth, Fourteenth

*Significance:* The words "liberty" and "right" can be used interchangeably to some extent, without doing violence to the meaning they have acquired over the ages. The "Bill of Rights" in the U.S. Constitution is, in fact, a list of liberties. However, the phrases "civil liberties" and "civil rights" have now acquired sufficiently distinctive meanings, each with a history of its own. They should be treated as discrete concepts.

"Congress shall make no law respecting an establishment of religion." So begins the First Amendment. The Bill of Rights is a repository of people's liberties in that it defines the areas where people are to be left alone to live their lives free of impediments. The word "Congress" is never again mentioned in this document, but neither is there any reference to any other legislative power. Writing in *Barron v. Baltimore* in 1833, Chief Justice John Marshall observed that there was a unity of purpose in these amendments, for they were proposed and ratified at the same time. As such, the rights guaranteed in these amendments were all to be "understood as restraining the power of the general government, not as applicable to the States." In short, these freedoms did not provide any protection against state and local abuses.

The person who gave us the Bill of Rights had warned us that the principal source of mischief against personal liberties would be the states and their local communities, and not the national majority. If James Madison could have had his way, the Bill of Rights would have applied to the states as well. His original draft had an amendment that had the following words: "No state shall infringe the equal rights of conscience, nor the freedom of speech, or of the press, nor of the right of trial by jury in criminal cases." Madison conceived this paragraph to be "the most valuable amendment on the whole list." However, the conservatives in the Senate were afraid of what the new central government might do someday to undermine the sovereignty of the states which they represented. Madison's favorite amendment was rejected decisively.

Eventually, the nation came around to embracing Madison's vision, though more out of desperation in the wake of the Civil War than as a concession to his argument. Not only did the Fourteenth Amendment define U.S. citizenship, with a view to protecting the rights of individuals from abuse by local majorities, it also contained this critical language, which would have pleased the Father of the Bill of Rights: "No State shall make or enforce any law which shall abridge . . ." Nevertheless, the actual use of the Bill of Rights against state and local abuses was not to materialize until 1925, when, in *Gitlow v. New York*, the Supreme Court began to read, in earnest, certain provisions of that document into the due process clause of the Fourteenth Amendment in a series of actions which would come to be known as "selective incorporation."

*Contemporary magazine illustration of people celebrating the passage of the Civil Rights Act of 1866 outside the gallery of the House of Representatives.* (Associated Publishers)

The Fourteenth Amendment, ratified in 1868, did more than pave the way for the "nationalization of the Bill of Rights." Like the other two Civil War amendments—the Thirteenth (1865), banning slavery, and the Fifteenth (1870), prohibiting the denial of the right to vote for reasons of "race, color, or previous condition of servitude"—the Fourteenth called the nation's attention to a whole new problem known as "civil rights." The blacks were no longer slaves, but they were not yet free, certainly not equal with the whites. They were entitled to their rights. However, who was to deliver to them those rights?

Congress responded to this challenge with a series of legislative enactments, all under the fitting name of "Civil Rights Act," beginning with the bold, sweeping and highly controversial Civil Rights Act of 1866, which defined citizenship and guaranteed rights related to contracts and property ownership. The fierce debate over the constitutionality of this law did not end until Congress passed a constitutional amendment which included some of these controversial provisions. The Fourteenth Amendment became the basis for Congress's second major assault upon racial injustice.

Enacted in the name of the amendment's equal protection clause, the Civil Rights Act banned all discrimination in public facilities and accommodations owned and operated by corporations and private individuals. However, the Supreme Court declared the law unconstitutional in the

*Civil Rights Cases* of 1883, on the grounds that the amendment's prohibitions were aimed at the states, not corporations and private individuals. Congress had no power to prescribe criminal penalties for private acts of discrimination under this amendment, said the Court, against a bitter dissent from Justice John Harlan, who read the three Civil War amendments far more broadly than his brethren.

Congress did not enact another civil rights law until 1957. The 1957 and 1960 Civil Rights Acts made the Justice Department the command post in the war on racial discrimination. Then came the historic Civil Rights Act of 1964, by far the most comprehensive civil rights law in the nation's history. Although it was intended on the whole as an enforcement of the Fourteenth Amendment's equal protection mandate, its sweeping public accommodations provisions in Title II had to be given some other justification so as not to repeat the mistake of 1875. Congress this time decided to rely on the commerce clause, and later that year, in two separate cases, Title II of the 1964 Civil Rights Act was handily upheld by the Supreme Court as an exercise of Congress's commerce power. With that ruling, the Supreme Court left the 1883 precedent undisturbed, merely noting that it was not "apposite" here. The 1964 Civil Rights Act was followed a year later by another monumental statute, the

*President Dwight D. Eisenhower (second from right) at the swearing-in ceremony of the President's Commission on Civil Rights, which was authorized by the Civil Rights Act of 1957. (Library of Congress)*

Voting Rights Act, whose contested provisions, dealing with literacy devices and federal examiners, were upheld by the Supreme Court in 1966, in *South Carolina v. Katzenbach,* as a "valid" exercise of the federal government's power under the Fifteenth Amendment.

**Further Reading**

Curtis, Michael Kent. *No State Shall Abridge: The Fourteenth Amendment and the Bill of Rights.* Durham, N.C.: Duke University Press, 1986.

Hall, Kermit L., et al. *American Legal History: Cases and Materials.* New York: Oxford University Press, 1991.

Karst, Kenneth. *Belonging to America: Equal Citizenship and the Constitution.* New Haven, Conn.: Yale University Press, 1989.

Veit, Helen E., et al., eds. *Creating the Bill of Rights: The Documentary Record from the First Federal Congress.* Baltimore, Md.: Johns Hopkins University Press, 1991.

*Sugwon Kang*

# CLEAR AND PRESENT DANGER TEST

*Description:* First legal standard established by the Supreme Court in 1919 to determine whether speech posed such a direct and imminent threat to society that it could be punished without violating the free speech guarantees of the First Amendment to the U.S. Constitution.

*Relevant amendment:* First

*Significance:* Originally adopted to uphold the convictions of radicals during World War I, the clear and present danger test was transformed into a standard protecting a wide spectrum of controversial, offensive, and even hateful speech.

Although the First Amendment was ratified in 1791, thereby guaranteeing that Congress could make no law abridging freedom of speech, freedom of the press, or other personal rights, it was not until 1919 that the Supreme Court squarely addressed the limits of free speech.

Fearing the impact of disloyal speeches, leaflets, and newspaper articles during World War I, Congress passed the Espionage Act of 1917, which prohibited obstruction of the war effort. By 1919 three separate cases had reached the Court in which Eugene Debs, leader of the Socialist Party; Charles Schenck, an official of the Socialist Party; and Jacob Frohwerk, the publisher of a socialist newspaper, had all been convicted of violating the Espionage Act and sentenced to jail. In each case, the Court voted unanimously to uphold the convictions, despite arguments that the antiwar activists' statements and publications were constitutionally protected under the First Amendment.

The task fell to Justice Oliver Wendell Holmes to write the opinions explaining the Court's decisions. By 1919, Holmes, at age seventy-six, had served on the Court for seventeen years and had acquired a reputation as one of the finest legal minds in the country. In *Schenck v. United States,* Holmes wrote that the "question in every case is whether the words are used in such circumstances and are of such a nature as to create a clear and present danger that they will bring about the substantive evils that Congress has a right to prevent." Without using the words "clear and present danger," the companion opinions in *Debs v. United States* and *Frohwerk v. United States,* also written by Holmes, upheld the convictions.

**A Reconsideration.** In the coming months, however, Holmes and his friend and colleague, Justice Louis D. Brandeis, seriously reconsidered the importance of free speech in a democratic society, even in times of war. In *Abrams v. United States* (1919), while the majority of the Court upheld the convictions of a group of Russian immigrants for distributing pamphlets condemning President Woodrow Wilson for sending U.S. troops to fight against the Bolshevik Revolution in Russia, Holmes and Brandeis joined in a vigorous dissent.

Speaking for the Court, Justice John H. Clarke relied on Holmes's own clear and present danger test. The leaflets violated the law because they had been distributed "at the supreme crisis of the war" and amounted to "an attempt to defeat the war plans of the Government." Moreover, the general strike advocated by the *Abrams* defendants would have necessarily hampered prosecution of the war with Germany.

In dissent, Holmes did not repudiate his earlier opinions. Instead, he denied that "the surreptitious publishing of a silly leaflet by an unknown man" created "a clear and imminent danger that will bring about forthwith certain substantial evils that the United States constitutionally may seek to prevent." Tilting the clear and present danger test away from an instrument in service of restricting speech and toward a shield protecting

*In his opinion on Abrams v. United States, Justice John H. Clarke drew on Oliver Wendell Holmes's definition of "clear and present danger."* (Collection of the Supreme Court of the United States)

speech, Holmes argued that the First Amendment protected the expression of all opinions "unless they so imminently threatened immediate interference with the lawful and pressing purposes of the law that an immediate check is required to save the country."

**A Tool for Protection.** The clear and present danger test fell out of favor until the late 1930's when for more than a decade the Court used it to protect speech in a wide array of situations. However, in the midst of the Cold War and the mounting fear of communism, in *Dennis v. United States* (1951), the Court ignored the immediacy requirement of the clear and present danger test and upheld the convictions of eleven Communist Party leaders for conspiring to advocate the violent overthrow of the government.

In 1969 the Supreme Court adopted the Holmes-Brandeis dissent in *Abrams*. In *Brandenburg v. Ohio*, the Court reversed the conviction of a Ku Klux Klan leader under a state statute prohibiting criminal syndicalism. Consequently, a half century after it was first articulated, the clear and present danger test matured into a modern barrier to censorship, setting a high threshold protecting a wide spectrum of diverse and controversial speech. The Court held that the guarantees of the First Amendment "do not permit a State to forbid or proscribe advocacy of the use of force or of law violation except where such advocacy is directed to inciting or producing imminent lawless action and is likely to incite or produce such action." In words reminiscent of Holmes's prescient dissent in *Abrams*, the Court significantly strengthened constitutional protection for freedom of expression.

*Stephen F. Rohde*

# COMMERCE CLAUSE

*Description:* The clause in the U.S. Constitution giving Congress the power to regulate trade among the states

*Relevant amendment:* Tenth

*Significance:* The Supreme Court has upheld congressional use of the commerce clause as justification for a broad range of federal legislation

Article I, section 8 of the U.S. Constitution states that Congress "shall have the power . . . to regulate commerce with foreign nations, and among the several states, and with the Indian tribes." The part of this clause dealing with the states was extremely important in enabling the United States to develop an effective, integrated economic system, but its influence reaches far beyond the realm of a narrow definition of commerce. The first Supreme Court case involving the commerce clause, *Gibbons v. Ogden* (1824), established that it applies to interstate commerce but not to commerce within one state. Chief Justice John Marshall's opinion in the case broadly defined commerce to include all commercial "intercourse," not only the traffic of goods. In the late nineteenth century, the commerce clause was cited as justification for congressional establishment of the Interstate Commerce Commission and for the Sherman Antitrust Act (1890).

In the early twentieth century the federal government began using the commerce clause as the basis for national legislation involving crime, public safety, and morality, as in the Mann Act (1910) and the Automobile Theft Act of 1915. Until the 1930's, the Supreme Court maintained a distinction between manufacturing and commerce, but in 1937 it began to interpret the commerce clause broadly enough to allow regulating the manufacture of goods intended for interstate transportation and sale. In the years since World War II, there has been considerable federal legislation based on the commerce clause. One of its most remarkable uses was in justifying civil rights legislation in the 1960's. In cases such as *Heart of Atlanta Motel v. United States* (1964), the Supreme Court held that, because racial discrimination has a harmful effect on interstate commerce, Congress can pass and enforce antidiscrimination laws.

# COMMERCIAL SPEECH

*Description:* Ideas expressed in advertising
*Relevant amendment:* First
*Significance:* Commercial speech historically has been among the least protected forms of expression

In the twentieth century the trend changed somewhat to offer increased protection to commercial speech. Canadian courts, for example, consider commercial speech within the constitutional protection afforded all speech, and seek to balance the interest in free speech against the reasons offered for the limitation on the speech. American courts apply a more complex three-step analysis to commercial speech restrictions.

After *Central Hudson Gas and Electric Corp. v. Public Service Commission* (1980), a court must first determine whether the speech is protected by the First Amendment of the U.S. Constitution. To be protected, the speech must promote lawful activity and must not be misleading. States may ban altogether commercial speech promoting illegal activities (such as illegal drug use) and advertising that is inherently misleading. But states may not completely ban advertising that is only potentially misleading.

In the second step, a court examines whether the asserted governmental interest in regulation is substantial. This requires some important state interest, and courts have acknowledged that protection of citizens and preservation of community aesthetics are both suitable interests. In the final step of the analysis, the court examines whether the regulation directly advances the governmental interest asserted and whether it is not more extensive than is necessary to serve the asserted interest. A court will apply an intermediate standard of review, inquiring whether the "fit" between the asserted governmental interest and the regulation of speech is reasonable. A state need not employ the least restrictive means to accomplish its interests, but it must select a means narrowly tailored to achieve the desired objective without unreasonable burdens on commercial speech.

# COMSTOCK ACT

***Description:*** A law amending postal legislation to enforce the prohibition against using the mails to send sexually suggestive material

***Relevant amendment:*** First

***Significance:*** The most restrictive obscenity statute ever passed by Congress, the Comstock Act limited the availability of even mild forms of pornography until the courts expanded First Amendment protection in the 1950's

In 1865, Congress passed the Postal Act, making it a crime to use the mails for sending any "publication of a vulgar or indecent character." Anthony Comstock, a tireless crusader against pornography, successfully lobbied Congress to make the postal regulations more restrictive. The re-

*Anthony Comstock.*
(Library of Congress)

sulting 1873 legislation created special agents with wide discretion to seize obscene matter and provided for criminal penalties of up to five years' imprisonment for the first offense. Books and magazines, including serious novels such as Theodore Dreiser's *Sister Carrie* (1900), were proscribed if they contained any sexual references considered "lewd" or "lascivious" by Victorian standards.

By the 1930's, the Comstock Act had been amended to become less restrictive, but much of its language, while reinterpreted, continued into the 1990's. The Supreme Court affirmed the constitutionality of the law's principles in numerous cases after 1877, but beginning with the landmark case *Roth v. United States* (1957), the Court liberalized the law by insisting on a narrow definition of obscenity.

*Thomas T. Lewis*

# CONSCIENTIOUS OBJECTION

*Description:* Claim of exemption from compulsory military service, or at least from combat, based on ethical, moral, or religious grounds. Only claims based on religious principles raise constitutional issues.

*Relevant amendment:* First

*Significance:* Controversies surrounding conscientious objection are most likely to occur when the nation is at war and begins conscription, especially during an unpopular war. The Supreme Court struggled with controversies over how conscientious objector status is to be defined and who is exempted from military obligation.

Conscription to raise an armed force dates to the American Revolution, when some states imposed requirements of military service on their male citizens. Both North and South resorted to a military draft during the Civil War. In the twentieth century, conscription became well established as an efficient means for Congress to carry out its Article I authority "to raise and support armies." Thus far, the requirement to answer the call to arms was confined to men, and the decision to exempt from obligatory military service on religious grounds was left to the political discretion of Congress. However, when Congress has adopted policies respecting conscientious objection, the constitutional problems that have resulted have been many and complex.

**Religious Objectors.** Controversies over conscientious objection arise from the unprecedented religious diversity of the American population, including a number of pacifist sects whose adherents avoid all participation in warfare and others permitting their adherents to participate only in "just wars." Quite apart from the practical observation that pacifists make ineffectual soldiers, it might be thought that the First Amendment's free exercise of religion clause would require Congress to exempt religious pacifists from military service, rather than force citizens to act contrary to religious conscience. However, the Supreme Court, in the *Selective Draft Law Cases* (1918), rejected such a claim, calling "its unsoundness . . . too apparent to require us to do more." Even so, it had historically been the practice to grant exemptions to members of specific sects, at least when the latter were sufficiently prominent to secure the respect of the surrounding community. For example, New York's first constitution, adopted in 1777, exempted Quakers from service, although it also authorized the legislature to impose special fees in lieu of service. The Draft Act of 1864 and that of 1917 offered exemptions for members of pacifist sects, although the latter authorized their conscription into noncombat roles.

This deference to religious principle generates its own constitutional problems, however. When membership in a pacifist sect becomes the basis for granting exemption from the draft, Congress would seem to violate the establishment of religion clause. Although the precise meaning of this clause is uncertain, all agree that it requires Congress to avoid discriminating among sects. Identifying Quakers, or any other specific sects, as recipients of conscientious objector status might be viewed as creating a privilege on the basis of religious belief. Even without naming specific sects, Congress faces a dilemma in finding a religiously neutral way of limiting the exemption, lest it become universal. Thus, the crux of the problem is to define a category of persons who might claim exemption from conscription in a way that violates neither the free exercise nor the establishment of religion clauses of the First Amendment. Any attempt to do so exposes the potential conflict between these two clauses.

**A Careful Approach.** Perhaps in recognition of this dilemma, the Court usually avoided constitutional rulings in conscientious objector cases, purporting to resolve them by statutory interpretation. However, despite its ruling in the 1918 draft law cases, in the twentieth century, the Court clearly attempted to interpret draft statutes in a way that makes them conform to the complex demands of the First Amendment. It is equally clear that Congress struggled with this issue but was less sensitive to the requirements of the establishment of religion clause than the Court.

The Draft Act of 1917, for example, extended conscription to all able-bodied men, exempting members of any "well-recognized religious sect or organization" that forbade its "members to participate in war in any form." This formulation privileged adherents of well-recognized religions, compared with religions lacking such organization or doctrinal clarity, thereby conferring conscientious objector status on Quakers but denying it to equally sincere objectors who did not belong to any such organization. It also denied conscientious objector status to those whose religious principles included distinctions between just and unjust wars, such as Roman Catholics.

The Selective Training and Service Act of 1940 sought to avoid the problem of sectarian discrimination by dropping the requirement that the conscientious objector be a member of a well-recognized sect. An individual had only to object to war in any form based on "religious training and belief." This standard was refined in 1948, when Congress defined religious training and belief to include "an individual's belief in a relation to a Supreme Being involving duties superior to those arising from any human relation, but [excluding] essentially political, sociological, or philosophical views or a merely personal moral code." Even with these enhancements, however, the definition of conscientious objection failed to achieve religious neutrality because it excluded religions that did not include a supreme being (such as Buddhism) and religions that were not monotheistic (such as Hinduism).

In *United States v. Seeger* (1965), the Court sought to remedy this problem by interpreting this definition of religious training and belief as including any "sincere and meaningful belief which occupies in the life of its possessor a place parallel to that filled by the God of those admittedly qualifying for the exemption." Although this interpretation sought to eliminate the problem of discrimination among sects, it did so by extending conscientious objector status to many persons holding "political, sociological or philosophical views or merely a personal moral code," people to whom Congress had specifically denied such an exemption, as the Court recognized in *Welsh v. United States* (1970). However, in *Gillette v. United States* (1971), the Court held that exemption from service could still be denied to those whose religiously based objection did not include war in all forms. Thus, those who believed in fighting only just wars still could not qualify for conscientious objector status.

In *Clay v. United States* (1971), the Court established a three-part test by which conscientious objector claims were to be evaluated, requiring that the claim be based on a religious belief as defined in *Seeger*, that the objection is to war in all forms, and that the claim is sincere.

**Further Reading**

Choper, Jesse H. *Securing Religious Liberty: Principles for Judicial Interpretation of the Religion Clauses.* Chicago: University of Chicago Press, 1995.

Morgan, Richard E. *The Supreme Court and Religion.* New York: Free Press, 1972.

Moskos, Charles C., and Whiteslay, eds. *The New Conscientious Objection: From Sacred to Secular Resistance.* New York: Oxford University Press, 1993.

Pfeffer, Leo. *Church, State, and Freedom.* Boston: Beacon Press, 1967.

Tribe, Lawrence. *American Constitutional Law.* 2d ed. Westbury, N.Y.: The Foundation Press, 1990.

*John C. Hughes*

# CONTRACT, FREEDOM OF

*Description:* Also known as "liberty of contract," the doctrine that individual persons and business firms should be free to enter into contracts without undue interference from government.

*Relevant amendments:* Fifth, Fourteenth

*Significance:* From 1897 to 1937, a probusiness Supreme Court used the freedom of contract doctrine to overturn numerous economic regulations designed to protect the interests of workers and the general public.

The Supreme Court recognized that the Fifth Amendment's due process clause protected some substantive rights to property and liberty as early as *Scott v. Sandford* (1857). The drafters of the Fourteenth Amendment, among other goals, wanted to protect the liberty and equality of African Americans to enter into legally binding contracts involving property and employment. With the growth of state regulations in the late nineteenth century, therefore, it was not surprising that proponents of laissez-faire capitalism seized on the Fourteenth Amendment's due process clause as a means of promoting substantive liberties in matters of business and economics. Justice Stephen J. Field and jurist Thomas M. Cooley were among the most influential proponents of this substantive due process approach, which was soon accepted by several state courts.

After debating the concept on numerous occasions, a majority of the Court finally accepted the idea that the Fourteenth Amendment protected a substantive freedom of contract in *Allgeyer v. Louisiana* (1897). In this case, the Court invalidated a Louisiana law that made it illegal for residents of the state to enter into insurance contracts by mail with out-of-state companies. Writing for the majority, Justice Rufus W. Peckham declared that U.S. citizens enjoyed the freedom to make contracts relevant to the pursuit of their economic interests.

**The *Lochner* Era.** Through the four decades following *Allgeyer*, the Court looked on freedom of contract as a normative ideal and required states to assume a high burden for proving that any restraint on the liberty was justified on the basis of accepted police powers, such as protecting the public's safety, health, or morality. The most prominent cases usually involved legislation regulating terms of employment, such as maximum working hours and minimum wages. In *Lochner v. New York* (1905), for example, a five-member majority overturned a labor law limiting the number of hours that bakers could work each week, and the majority insisted that employees should have the freedom to work as many hours as they wished. In *Adair v. United States* (1908) and *Coppage v. Kansas* (1915), the Court struck down federal and state laws that outlawed yellow dog contracts (employment contracts in which workers agree not to join unions). The majority of the Court was not impressed with the inequality in bargaining positions between employers and workers. Justice Oliver Wendell Holmes wrote vigorous dissents in such cases.

Nevertheless, the freedom of contract doctrine was used in ways that would later be considered progressive. In *Buchanan v. Warley* (1917), for example, the concept was a major reason for the Court's overturning of a St. Louis segregation ordinance that prohibited whites from selling residential housing to African Americans.

The Court often accepted the constitutionality of restraints on the freedom of contract, but only when a majority concluded that a restraint was a reasonable means for enforcing legitimate police powers. For example, the Court in *Holden v. Hardy* (1898) upheld a Utah law that made it illegal for miners to work more than eight hours a day because of the manifest dangers of underground mining. Likewise, in *Muller v. Oregon* (1908), the Court determined that the special health needs of women provided justification for limiting their industrial workday to ten hours. Yet, in *Adkins v. Children's Hospital* (1923), a bare majority overturned a District of Columbia's minimum wage for women. The obvious inconsistency between *Muller* and *Children's Hospital* reflected the inherent subjectivity in all decisions grounded in substantive due process.

**Judicial Revolution of 1937.** The Court began to moderate its position on freedom of contract after Charles Evans Hughes became chief justice in 1930. During President Franklin D. Roosevelt's first term, nevertheless, four conservative justices—dubbed the "Four Horsemen"—remained firmly committed to the *Lochner/Adair* line of thinking. In *Morehead v. New York ex rel. Tipaldo* (1936), Owen J. Roberts joined the four to overturn New York's minimum-wage law. During the 1936 election, *Morehead* was widely denounced and was one of several cases that led to Roosevelt's Court-packing plan. For several reasons, Roberts abandoned the Four

*Chief Justice Charles Evans Hughes.* (Collection of the Supreme Court of the United States)

Horsemen in *West Coast Hotel Co. v. Parrish* (1937), which upheld Washington State's minimum-wage law. Speaking for a majority of five, Hughes acknowledged that the Constitution protected liberty, but he defined liberty as the absence of arbitrary restraints. Two weeks later, the Court abandoned its *Adair* precedent in *National Labor Relations Board v. Jones and Laughlin Steel Corp.*, upholding the Wagner Act protections of labor's right to organize and join unions.

After the Court reversed itself in 1937, it never again struck down a public policy based on the freedom of contract doctrine. In effect, it almost entirely abandoned any judicial supervision based on the doctrine—a development that is part of its movement toward exercising only minimal scrutiny of all economic regulations. Since then, the Court has upheld economic regulations only when they have appeared to be rationally related to legitimate governmental interests. The Court might resurrect the freedom of contract doctrine if it were to find some governmental regulation of contracts totally unreasonable or arbitrary. Although the Court lost interest in freedom of contract after 1937, it did not entirely stop reading substantive due process guarantees into the Fifth and Fourteenth Amendments.

### Further Reading

Corwin, Edward. *Liberty Against Government: The Rise, Flowering, and Decline of a Famous Judicial Concept.* Reprint. Westport, Conn.: Greenwood Press, 1978.

Ely, James, Jr. *The Guardian of Every Other Right: A Constitutional History of Property Rights.* New York: Oxford University Press, 1992.

Seigan, Bernard. *Economic Liberties and the Constitution.* Chicago: University of Chicago Press, 1980.

*Thomas T. Lewis*

# COUNSEL, RIGHT TO

*Description:* The opportunity for defendants in federal criminal proceedings to be represented by lawyers.

*Relevant amendment:* Sixth

*Significance:* The right to legal counsel gives people accused of crimes access to expert help in defending themselves in the complex arena of a criminal trial. In 1963 the Supreme Court interpreted the Fourteenth Amendment as extending this element of due process to defendants in state trials.

Although the Sixth Amendment of the U.S. Constitution appeared to contain the right to legal counsel, the exact meaning of that provision was unclear until interpreted by Congress and the Supreme Court. In 1790, while the Sixth Amendment was still being ratified, Congress passed the Federal Crimes Act, which required that defendants in federal capital cases be provided with legal representation. The Court extended this same protection to all federal criminal cases, regardless of whether they involved the death penalty, in *Johnson v. Zerbst* (1938).

**Special Circumstances Doctrine.** Although some states required the appointment of lawyers even before the Sixth Amendment was ratified, there was no national code of due process that obligated the states to provide legal help for people accused of crimes. It was not until 1932 that the Court imposed even a limited requirement on state courts to provide legal counsel, and as late as 1963, some states still refused to pay for lawyers for poor defendants.

In *Powell v. Alabama* (1932), the first Scottsboro case, the Court, by a 7-2 majority, overturned Alabama's convictions of nine African American youths for raping two white women. The young men had been given a *pro forma* trial and sentenced to death. Although they had received court-appointed lawyers, the attorneys provided a weak defense. The trial judge behaved in an overtly biased fashion toward the defendants, and evidence that might have cast doubt on Alabama's case was never presented by the young men's lawyers. In his majority opinion, Justice George Sutherland did not extend the right to counsel to all state criminal cases, but he did establish the "special circumstances" doctrine. The Court ruled that in state capital cases where there were special circumstances, such as the illiteracy of the defendant, state trial judges were obligated to appoint competent lawyers to represent the accused. For more than thirty years, the special circumstances doctrine would be the law of the land, requiring state courts to appoint legal counsel in only the most obvious and serious situations of defendant need.

**A Reconsideration.** Although the Court had the opportunity to apply the right to counsel to all state criminal cases in *Betts v. Brady* (1942), it declined to do so, sticking to the case-by-case scheme it had prescribed in the *Powell* case. It was not until the 1963 case of *Gideon v. Wainwright* that the Court finally retired the special circumstances doctrine. Clarence Gideon was a drifter with a history of committing petty crimes. He was accused of breaking into a pool hall and stealing some money and liquor. Although Gideon asked the trial judge to appoint him a lawyer, the judge, relying on *Betts*, refused to do so. After a failed attempt at defending himself, Gideon was sentenced to a long term in prison. Gideon appealed his conviction on Sixth and Fourteenth Amendment grounds to the Supreme Court.

The Court had been looking for just the right case to overrule what most of them considered a flawed decision in *Betts v. Brady*. To reverse *Betts*, the Court needed a case in which an intelligent person, denied a lawyer, had been unable to successfully defend himself. Because Gideon was an intelligent man, there could be no question that the trial judge might have improperly denied him special circumstances status. Likewise, because Gideon was white, there could be no question of possible racial discrimination to muddy the waters. The charges against Gideon were not complicated. Gideon was an intelligent man, with a sympathetic, even helpful trial judge, who failed miserably to defend himself against noncomplex charges. This made *Gideon* the perfect case to overrule the special circumstances doctrine, and on March 18, 1963, a unanimous Supreme Court, speaking through Justice Hugo L. Black, applied the right to counsel to all state criminal proceedings.

In *Argersinger v. Hamlin* (1972) and *Scott v. Illinois* (1979), the Court extended the right to counsel to misdemeanor trials that resulted in jail sentences but not to those that resulted in fines or lesser punishment.

**The Pretrial Period.** *Gideon* left many important questions unanswered, including at what point in the criminal investigation a suspect who requested a lawyer had to be provided with one. In *Escobedo v. Illinois* (1964), the Court ruled that a suspect asking for counsel during a police interrogation had to be granted representation.

In *Miranda v. Arizona* (1966), the Court went a step further, requiring the police to advise suspects of their right to a lawyer even if they did not ask to speak with an attorney. According to the Court, a person suspected of committing a crime should be provided with a lawyer at the moment that individual ceases being one of several possible suspects and becomes the principal focus of the criminal investigation. The decisions in these two cases showed that, in the Court's collective mind, the Sixth Amendment right to counsel was firmly connected to the Fifth Amendment's protection from compulsory self-incrimination.

**Further Reading**

Garcia, Alfredo. *The Sixth Amendment in Modern American Jurisprudence.* Westport, Conn.: Greenwood, 1992.

Horne, Gerald. *"Powell v. Alabama": The Scottsboro Boys and American Justice.* New York: Franklin Watts, 1997.

Lewis, Anthony. *Gideon's Trumpet.* New York: Vintage, 1989.

Wice, Paul B. *"Miranda v. Arizona": "You Have the Right to Remain Silent . . ."* New York: Franklin Watts, 1996.

*Marshall R. King*

# CRUEL AND UNUSUAL PUNISHMENT

*Description:* A key provision of the Eighth Amendment to the U.S. Constitution prohibiting the most shockingly barbarous punishments and conditions of incarceration.

*Relevant amendment:* Eighth

*Significance:* Although elusive and elastic, the concept of cruel and unusual punishment has enabled the Supreme Court to adjust criminal punishments according to varying standards of decency and proportionality.

Borrowing from the English Bill of Rights of 1688, the framers of the U.S. Bill of Rights (1791) included in the Eighth Amendment to the U.S. Constitution a prohibition against "cruel and unusual punishment." Like so much else in the Constitution, and particularly in the Bill of Rights, the meaning, scope, and limitations of these figurative words were left to be determined by the Supreme Court. The results have been inconsistent, conflicting, and enigmatic.

The Court has struggled over whether the prohibition sets absolute and immutable standards that persist over time or instead expresses a goal of proportionality that varies depending on the circumstances. Consequently, the body of Court decisions interpreting the prohibition suffers from a lack of cohesion, allowing succeeding justices to fill the words with their own values and sensibilities.

During its first century, the Court paid scant attention to the prohibition on cruel and unusual punishment. In 1910 the Court held, in *Weems v. United States,* that the crime of being an accessory to the falsification of a public document could not justify a sentence of twelve to twenty years at hard labor in chains and a permanent deprivation of civil rights.

It was not until the 1970's that the Court dwelt seriously on the prohibition, most prominently in the context of the death penalty. In *Furman v. Georgia* (1972), a fractured Court, with all nine justices writing separate opinions, struck down capital punishment with a 5-4 vote. Only Justices William J. Brennan, Jr., and Thurgood Marshall found that the death penalty was categorically unconstitutional based on the prohibition against cruel and unusual punishment, which the two justices construed as a flexible device reflecting "evolving standards of decency" based on public opinion, jury verdicts, and legislative enactments.

However, four years later in *Gregg v. Georgia* (1976), a plurality of the Court found that the prohibition did not invariably preclude capital punishment but only prohibited torture, gratuitously painful methods of execution, or punishments not officially authorized by law.

In noncapital cases, the Court has sent mixed signals. In *Rummel v. Estelle* (1980), a 5-4 majority held that sentencing a man to a life sentence for three felonies committed over nine years for crimes totaling $229.11 was not cruel and unusual. However, in *Solem v. Helm* (1983), again on a 5-4 vote, the Court invalidated a life sentence for a man, with prior nonviolent felony convictions, found guilty of passing a hundred-dollar check on a nonexistent account.

Inevitably, the Court will continue to grapple with the dilemma of giving meaning to one of the most opaque provisions in the Bill of Rights.

*Stephen F. Rohde*

# DOUBLE JEOPARDY

**Description:** Guarantee, stated in the Fifth Amendment, that if a person has been acquitted or convicted of an offense, he or she cannot be prosecuted a second time for that same offense.

*Relevant amendment:* Fifth

*Significance:* For nearly two centuries the Supreme Court decided very few double jeopardy cases, but in the last three decades of the twentieth century, it decided many.

The second clause of the Fifth Amendment, part of the Bill of Rights, states "nor shall any person be subject for the same offense to be twice put in jeopardy of life or limb." For the first part of the existence of the United States, federal criminal cases were not appealed to the Supreme Court, so it had no federal double jeopardy cases. In addition, in *Barron v. Baltimore* (1833), the Court said that the provisions of the Bill of Rights limited the power of only the federal government and were inapplicable to the states. Consequently, there were no state court double jeopardy cases for the Court to review. Not until *Benton v. Maryland* (1969) did the Court conclude that the double jeopardy clause was applicable to the states, relying on the selective incorporation doctrine of the due process clause of the Fourteenth Amendment. Since that time, so many, and sometimes contradictory, double jeopardy cases came before the Court that Chief Justice William H. Rehnquist referred to this area of the law as a Sargasso Sea—one in which even a skillful navigator could become entangled and lost.

**The Basic Protection.** Jeopardy—the immediate threat of conviction and punishment—attaches in a criminal case when a jury is sworn in or, if there is no jury, when a judge begins to hear evidence. Whether jeopardy has attached is important because events occurring before that time, such as dismissal of the charges, will not preclude a subsequent prosecution; a dismissal of the charges after jeopardy has attached would preclude their being brought again.

A defendant who has been acquitted cannot be reprosecuted for that offense. Even with a relatively weak case, a prosecutor who could try the case multiple times might be able to perfect the presentation of witnesses and evidence so that eventually a jury would agree to convict. The Court found that such a result would be fundamentally unfair and would violate double jeopardy in *Ashe v. Swenson* (1970). After an acquittal, no matter how strong the state's evidence may have been, the defendant may not be forced to undergo the stress and expense of another prosecution for that crime, regardless of whether the verdict in the second case is a conviction or an acquittal.

Similarly, the Court ruled that a person cannot be tried again after having previously been convicted of the same offense in *Brown v. Ohio* (1977). However, in *United States v. Ball* (1896), the Court found that a necessary exception to this rule does allow the reprosecution of an individual whose conviction was reversed on appeal. There are many reasons why a conviction might be reversed, such as the improper admission of prejudicial evidence or inaccurate instructions to the jury. In these situations, after the reversal of the first conviction, the case could be retried without using the inadmissible evidence and with proper instructions to the jury, and the retrial would not be double jeopardy.

**Exceptions.** The doctrine protects against only successive criminal prosecutions or punishments; it does not prohibit a criminal prosecution after a civil action or a civil action after a criminal action. For example, property used in the commission of certain crimes, such as houses, cars, and other vehicles used in the manufacture and distribution of illegal drugs, is subject to forfeiture to the government. Such forfeiture actions usually are deemed to be civil rather than criminal punishments. Therefore, in *United States v. Ursery* (1996), the Court ruled that a person's having to forfeit his or her house and car to the government because they were used in a drug transaction is not the imposition of double jeopardy, although the individual had previously been criminally convicted and sentenced for the same drug transaction.

Similarly, those who have served the entire sentence for conviction of a sexual offense, such as rape or child molestation, may subsequently be adjudicated as sexually violent predators and ordered confined and treated until it is safe for them to be released. Because the subsequent adjudication is deemed civil and not criminal, the Court, in *Kansas v. Hendricks* (1997), found there is no double jeopardy, even if such sexual offenders might end up being confined for the rest of their lives.

The dual sovereignty doctrine is another major exception to the protection against double jeopardy. The basic guarantee is that the same sovereign, or government, will not prosecute or punish an individual twice for the same offense. There is no double jeopardy violation, however, if different sovereigns prosecute an individual for the same offense. For these purposes, the federal government of the United States and the government of a given state, such as California, are deemed to be separate sovereigns.

Cities and counties derive their governmental authority from that of the state in which they are located, so that neither a city nor a county is considered a separate sovereign from the state. Consequently, prosecutions for the same offense in, for example, Chicago municipal court and Illinois state courts would violate double jeopardy. In *Heath v. Alabama* (1985), the Court ruled that because the states are separate sovereigns from one another, prosecutions for the same offense by two separate states do not violate double jeopardy. With traditional crimes, such as murder or rape, it would be unusual for two states to have sufficient contact with the crime to have jurisdiction to prosecute it, but many conspiracies, especially those involving illegal drugs, have sufficient contacts with several states to confer jurisdiction on more than one. Nonetheless, dual sovereignty prosecutions involving two or more states are relatively rare.

**Further Reading**

Lafave, Wayne, and Jerold Israel. *Criminal Procedure.* St. Paul: West Publishing, 1985.

McAninch, William. "Unfolding the Law of Double Jeopardy." *South Carolina Law Review* 44 (1993): 411.

Miller, Lenord. *Double Jeopardy and the Federal System.* Chicago: University of Chicago Press, 1968.

*William Shepard McAninch*

# DUE PROCESS, PROCEDURAL

*Description:* Right not to be deprived by government of life, liberty, or property without notice and an opportunity to be heard according to fair procedures.

*Relevant amendment:* Fifth

*Significance:* The Supreme Court considers procedural due process to be one of the most fundamental constitutional rights.

The Supreme Court recognized that the constitutional right to procedural due process derives historically from the Magna Carta (1215), which prohibited the English monarch from depriving a certain class of subjects of their rights except by lawful judgment of their peers or by the law of the land. When the United States gained its independence, language modeled on the Magna Carta provision was included in some of the state constitutions. Soon after the ratification of the U.S. Constitution, the Fifth Amendment was adopted as part of the Bill of Rights. This amendment, applicable to the federal government, provided in part that "no person shall . . . be deprived of life, liberty, or property, without due process of law." In 1868 the Fourteenth Amendment formulated the same prohibition with regard to state—and, by implication, local—governments.

The due process clauses apply to criminal as well as civil procedures. However, because other constitutional protections are triggered in criminal matters by specific provisions of the Fourth, Fifth, Sixth, and Eighth Amendments, the Court has often invoked these more specific constitutional provisions in criminal procedure cases when it is unnecessary to address the more general requirements of the due process clauses.

**Basic Principles.** The Court ruled, in *Collins v. City of Harker Heights* (1992), that due process clauses provide a guarantee of fair procedure in connection with governmental deprivations of life, liberty, or property. In *Florida Prepaid Postsecondary Education Expense Board v. College Savings Bank* (1999), it held that procedural due process does not prevent governmental deprivation of life, liberty, or property; it merely prevents such deprivation without due process of law. Furthermore, the governmental deprivation must be deliberate. According to its finding in *Daniels v. Williams* (1986), a civil action against a governmental entity cannot be predicated on a due process theory if the governmental conduct at issue was merely negligent.

The two major components of fair procedure are notice and an opportunity to be heard. A primary purpose of the notice requirement is to ensure that the opportunity for a hearing is meaningful, as the Court determined in *West Covina v. Perkins* (1999). In both judicial and quasi-judicial proceedings, the Court determined that due process requires a neutral and detached judge in the first instance in *Concrete Pipe and Products of California v. Construction Laborers Pension Trust* (1993). However, where an initial determination is made by a party acting in an enforcement capacity, it found that due process may be satisfied by providing for a neutral adjudicator to conduct a *de novo* review (complete rehearing) of all factual and legal issues in *Marshall v. Jerrico* (1980).

The Court often (but not always) evaluates procedural due process issues by considering the three factors brought out in *Mathews v. Eldridge* (1976): the private interest affected by the official action; the risk of erroneous deprivation of such interest through the procedures used and the probable value, if any, of other procedural safeguards; and the relevant governmental interest.

**Criminal Procedure.** The Court applied the due process clauses in the criminal law area in cases in which other constitutional provisions do not apply. For example, the Court held that the adjudication of a contested criminal case in a mayor's court violates due process where the mayor's executive responsibilities may create a desire to maintain a high flow of revenue from the mayor's court in *Ward v. Village of Monroeville* (1972). It also held that a child in delinquency proceedings must be provided various procedural due process protections in *In re Gault* (1967).

The Court also made two rulings regarding placement in mental institutions. In *Vitek v. Jones* (1980), it held that a convicted felon serving a sentence in prison may not be transferred to a mental institution without appropriate procedures to determine whether he or she is mentally ill, and in *Foucha v. Louisiana* (1992), it determined that a person found not guilty of a crime by reason of insanity who is accordingly confined in a mental hospital is entitled to constitutionally adequate procedures to establish the grounds for continued confinement when the original basis for the confinement no longer exists.

**Other Applications.** The Court applied the procedural component of the due process clause in many other contexts. For example, in *United States v. James Daniel Good Real Property* (1993), it held that, absent exigent circumstances, due process requires notice and a meaningful opportunity to be heard before the government can seize real property subject to civil forfeiture. In *Goldberg v. Kelly* (1970), the Court held that welfare recipients could not be deprived of their benefits without procedural due process protections. Similarly, in *Memphis Light, Gas and Water Division v. Craft* (1978), the Court established federal due process procedures for termination of public utility service to customers in states that have a just cause requirement for such termination.

In *Cleveland Board of Education v. Loudermill* (1985), the Court determined that tenured classified civil servants were entitled to at least some procedural due process before termination, such as notice of allegations and opportunity to respond, coupled with a full posttermination hearing. However, it found that defamatory statements by governmental officials, in the absence of other governmental action, do not trigger due process analysis in *Paul v. Davis* (1976).

**Further Reading**

American Bar Association. *Due Process Protection for Juveniles in Civil Commitment Proceedings.* Chicago: American Bar Association, 1991.

Decker, John F. *Revolution to the Right: Criminal Procedure Jurisprudence During the Burger-Rehnquist Court Era.* New York: Garland, 1993.

Galligan, Denis J. *Due Process and Fair Procedures: A Study of Administrative Procedures.* New York: Oxford University Press, 1996.

Roach, Kent. *Due Process and Victims' Rights: The New Law and Politics of Criminal Justice.* Toronto: Toronto University Press, 1999.

*Alan E. Johnson*

# DUE PROCESS, SUBSTANTIVE

*Description:* The doctrine that the liberty protected by the due process clauses of the Fifth and Fourteenth Amendments encompasses more than the procedural rights owed by the government when it seeks to punish someone for a crime.

*Relevant amendment:* Fifth

*Significance:* Substantive due process has become the chief means by which the Supreme Court defines and extends the constitutional rights enjoyed by people in the United States.

One of the intents of the framers of the Fourteenth Amendment was to protect the property and contract rights of newly freed slaves from state law. The amendment states that the state shall not take away any person's life, liberty, or property without "due process of law." The phrase "due process" usually meant proper legal procedure, especially in criminal law. However, in *Allgeyer v. Louisiana* (1897), the Supreme Court, most of whose members believed strongly in laissez-faire capitalism, decided that part of the "fundamental liberty" protected by the due process clause was a substantive right to make contracts. This new right was frequently used by the Court to strike down state economic regulations with which the justices disagreed. For example, in *Lochner v. New York* (1905), the Court declared unconstitutional a New York law restricting the number of hours per day that bakers could work because it interfered with the right of the bakers to contract with their employers for their services. Justice Oliver Wendell Holmes filed a powerful dissenting opinion in the case. The

Court also found a few other fundamental rights applicable to the states.
In *Gitlow v. New York* (1925), for example, it held that freedom of speech, a
First Amendment right, limited state
governments. However, Holmes's reasoning in the *Lochner* dissent eventually prevailed. In 1936 the Court upheld a Washington state minimum-
wage law in *Morehead v. New York ex rel.
Tipaldo.* Soon after *Morehead,* several
older, more conservative justices retired from the court. President Franklin D. Roosevelt appointed progressive justices, and a new era of judicial
self-restraint began. To many observers, it appeared unlikely that substantive due process guarantees would surface again.

*While Justice George Shiras, Jr., was
serving on the Supreme Court from
1892 to 1903, he frequently used the
substantive due process doctrine to
overturn economic regulations.*
(Library of Congress)

**Substantive Due Process Reborn.** The Court's interest in substantive liberty was rekindled in the 1960's. On November 1, 1961, the Planned Parenthood League of Connecticut opened a center in New Haven. On November 10, its executive director, Estelle Griswold, and its medical
director, Dr. Harold Buxton, were arrested for violating the Connecticut
birth control statute. This law, which had been on the state's books since
1879, prohibited the use of birth control devices and the provision of
birth control information. Griswold and Buxton were the first people
ever to have been charged under the statute. An earlier attempt to challenge the law had been defeated when the Court refused to take jurisdiction because no one had ever been prosecuted. Griswold and Buxton
were convicted and appealed to the Court.

The Court's opinion in *Griswold v. Connecticut,* written by Associate Justice William O. Douglas for a 7-2 majority, struck down the Connecticut
statute. Douglas reasoned that many constitutional provisions as well as
many of the Court's cases had established a zone of privacy into which
states are forbidden to intrude. The First Amendment, which protects
speech and religion, also protects privacy in associations; the Third
Amendment prevents the government from forcing the populace to

house soldiers; and the Fourth Amendment limits "unreasonable" warrantless intrusions into the home. The Fifth Amendment includes some substantive liberties. Finally, the Ninth Amendment establishes that there may be constitutional rights that are not explicitly set forth in the Constitution. Taken together, Douglas argued, these provisions establish a constitutional marital privacy right that the Connecticut birth control statute infringed.

The two dissenters in the case, Associate Justices Hugo L. Black and Potter Stewart, argued that the decision would return the Court to the discredited era of substantive due process in which the justices had written their policy preferences into the Constitution. Black and Stewart pointed out that there was no explicit textual support in the Constitution for the new right of marital privacy. They were particularly perturbed by the majority's use of the Ninth Amendment, which seemed completely open ended to them and would give the Court limitless authority to define rights beyond the text of the Constitution.

The same right to receive and use contraceptive devices was extended to unmarried persons in *Eisenstadt v. Baird* (1972). In this case a Massachusetts statute was declared unconstitutional by the Court on two grounds: It unconstitutionally discriminated against unmarried people, and it collided with "a fundamental human right" to control conception.

**Abortion.** The following year, conception and privacy rights were further extended by the Court in *Roe v. Wade* (1973). This famous case established that a pregnant woman has a constitutional right to an abortion on demand during the first trimester of pregnancy. Justice Harry A. Blackmun, writing for the seven-justice majority, argued that the Court's substantive due process cases had established a right of privacy that "is broad enough to encompass a woman's decision whether or not to terminate her pregnancy" and that outweighs the state's interest in protecting prenatal life, at least during the first trimester of pregnancy. Blackmun turned to historical medical and legal thinking about pregnancy and abortion to help define the extent of abortion rights. Some state regulation of abortions is permitted in the second trimester, and abortion may be prohibited altogether in the third.

The two dissenters, Justices William H. Rehnquist and Byron R. White, maintained that there is no "fundamental" right to an abortion on demand and referred to the historical tradition in England and the United States of prohibiting abortion. They argued that the Court should defer to the wishes of the majority, at least in the absence of a traditional fundamental right. *Roe v. Wade* is perhaps the boldest assertion of substantive due process rights by the Court. It has been immensely controversial and has resulted in a great deal of political action in opposition to the Court's decision and in occasional violence directed at abortion clinics, physicians, and patients. In the years since *Roe*, the Court has revisited the case often. Although the decree has been modified somewhat, the central holding—that a pregnant woman has a right to an abortion on demand in the first trimester—remains intact.

**Limit on New Rights.** At the end of the twentieth century, *Roe v. Wade* represented the high-water mark of the Court's protection of substantive liberties. The Court declined to extend the concept to protect homosexual sodomy in *Bowers v. Hardwick* (1986). A Georgia statute that prohibited anal or oral sex was challenged by Michael Hardwick, a gay man who had been threatened with prosecution under the law after he was found in bed with another man in the course of a police drug raid. In his opinion for the majority, Justice Byron R. White wrote that

> Sodomy was a criminal offense at common law and was forbidden by the laws of the original 13 States when they ratified the Bill of Rights. In 1868 when the Fourteenth Amendment . . . was ratified, all but 5 of the 37 States in the Union had criminal sodomy laws. In fact, until 1961, all 50 States outlawed sodomy, and today, 24 States and the District of Columbia continue to provide criminal penalties for sodomy performed in private and between consenting adults. . . . Against this background, to claim that a right to engage in such conduct is "deeply rooted in this Nation's history and tradition" or "implicit in the concept of ordered liberty" is, at best, facetious.

White also pointed out that *Griswold, Eisenstadt,* and *Roe* had all spoken to the right to decide whether or not to bear children. This crucial element is absent in *Bowers.* Four justices—Harry A. Blackmun, William J. Brennan, Jr., Thurgood Marshall, and John Paul Stevens—argued that the case was really about a "fundamental right to be let alone," and that the Court's earlier privacy decisions established just that. Although *Bowers* is a 5-4 decision, the issue did not appear again before the Court. The Georgia supreme court struck down the statute in question on independent state constitutional grounds in 1999.

The Court resisted attempts to get it to establish substantive rights to die or to assisted suicide. In *Cruzan v. Director, Missouri Department of Health* (1990), the Court refused to order the removal of life-support equipment from Nancy Cruzan, a young woman in a "persistent vegetative state" as a result of injuries suffered in an automobile accident. The majority, perhaps unwilling to further politicize the Court's work in the wake of the controversy surrounding *Roe v. Wade,* made it clear that it preferred to allow state governments to resolve these newly arising life and death questions. Similarly, in 1997 the court refused to hear a claim that an Oregon assisted-suicide law is unconstitutional.

The "new" substantive due process has allowed the Supreme Court to define new individual constitutional rights. So far these have been limited to substantive rights already found in the First Amendment and additional reproductive privacy rights. The doctrine is very controversial because every time the Court limits state power, it is acting in an antimajoritarian way. It is not clear to the public why the right to an abortion is somehow "fundamental" while the "bedroom privacy" argued for in the Georgia sodomy case is not. Nothing appears to illuminate these decisions besides the wishes of the justices. The Constitution itself neither explicitly establishes these rights nor implies them with any clarity. The absence of textual support for these decisions puts perception of the Court's legitimacy at risk.

**Further Reading**
The property law and contract clause background of substantive due process is well discussed in *The Guardian of Every Other Right: A Constitutional History of Property Rights* by James Ely, Jr. (New York: Oxford University Press, 1992). *Private Property and the Limits of American Constitutionalism: The Madisonian Framework and Its Legacy* by Jennifer Nedelsky (Chicago: University of Chicago Press, 1990) provides less technical coverage of some of the same topics. There is a vast literature on the "true" meaning of the Fourteenth Amendment and whether it does or does not "incorporate" the Bill of Rights. The classic argument for the incorporationist position is *The Supreme Court in United States History* by Charles Warren (Boston: Little, Brown, 1937), while the opposition is best represented by Charles Fairman's *The Fourteenth Amendment and the Bill of Rights: The Incorporation Theory* (New York: Da Capo Press, 1970). A more recent work suggesting curtailing the judiciary's role is *The Fourteenth Amendment and the Bill of Rights* by Raoul Berger (Norman: University of Oklahoma Press,

1989). An argument supporting the Court's activities may be found in *Freedom and the Court: Civil Rights and Liberties in the United States* by Henry J. Abraham and Barbara A. Perry (6th ed., New York: Oxford University Press, 1994). Similarly the legitimacy of the privacy decisions and the natural law threads of thought that produced them have engendered enormous comment. One balanced work is *The Supreme Court and the Second Bill of Rights: The Fourteenth Amendment and the Nationalization of Civil Liberties* by Richard C. Cortner (Madison: University of Wisconsin Press, 1981).

*Robert Jacobs*


# ELASTIC CLAUSE

**Description:** Last clause of Article I, section 8, of the U.S. Constitution, authorizing Congress to make all laws necessary and proper for exercising its enumerated powers and any other power granted by the Constitution to the national government.

**Relevant amendment:** Tenth

**Significance:** After an 1819 Supreme Court decision, the elastic clause provided the basis for the doctrine of implied powers, stretching the powers of the national government beyond those specifically granted by the Constitution.

In 1791, when advising President George Washington on the constitutionality of establishing a national bank, Thomas Jefferson and others opposed to a strong national government maintained that Congress was limited to exercising those powers expressly granted by the Constitution, for example, the power to coin money. All other powers were reserved for the states. Jefferson argued that the necessary and proper clause imposed additional limits on the powers of Congress. The clause limited any use of powers not expressly granted by the Constitution except when such powers were absolutely necessary or indispensable to the exercise of an enumerated power. A national bank, for example, was unconstitutional both because the Constitution did not expressly delegate the power to create corporations to Congress and because a bank was not an indispensable means for achieving Congress's legitimate ends. A broader interpretation of the clause, Jefferson argued, would effectively create a national government with unlimited power.

*Alexander Hamilton.*
(National Portrait
Gallery, Smithsonian
Institution)

   Alexander Hamilton and others opposed Jefferson's strict construction of the clause, maintaining that the Constitution established an independent national government that, although exercising limited powers, was fully sovereign within the scope of its powers. Hamilton argued that the elastic clause had to be broadly interpreted as granting whatever additional powers would assist Congress in carrying out its enumerated powers. The clause allowed Congress to do not just what was indispensable but also whatever was convenient or helpful to achieving its ends. The incorporation of a bank, for example, was constitutional because it was a useful means for Congress to carry out its delegated power to collect taxes.

   When the controversy over the incorporation of the Second Bank of the United States reached the Supreme Court in *McCulloch v. Maryland* (1819), Chief Justice John Marshall transformed Hamilton's loose construction of the clause into constitutional law. In his opinion, he stated that if the ends were legitimate and within the scope of the Constitution, all means that were appropriate and not prohibited, as well as consistent with "the letter and spirit" of the Constitution, were constitutional. His decision meant that the Constitution did not limit the federal government's powers to those expressly delegated, but included powers implied by Congress's freedom to choose the means by which it would carry out its responsibilities.

**Further Reading**

Fisher, Louis. *The Politics of Shared Power: Congress and the Executive.* College Station: Texas A&M University Press, 1998.

Gunther, Gerald. *John Marshall's Defense of "McCulloch v. Maryland."* Stanford, Calif.: Stanford University Press, 1969.

*Joseph V. Brogan*

# ESPIONAGE ACTS

*Description:* Laws passed during World War I outlawing the unauthorized transmission of information that might injure the nation's defense and banning a wide range of expressions of opinion critical of governmental policies or symbols during wartime.

*Relevant amendment:* First

*Significance:* Espionage Act prosecutions led to the first significant attempts by the Supreme Court to interpret the free speech provisions of the First Amendment, including the original espousal of the clear and present danger test.

On June 15, 1917, two months after the United States entered World War I, Congress passed the Espionage Act. In addition to outlawing a wide variety of acts that fit the commonsense definition of "espionage," including the gathering, transmission, or negligent handling of information that might harm U.S. defense efforts, the law forbade, during wartime, the willful making or conveying of false information with intent to interfere with the nation's armed forces or to promote the success of its enemies, as well as willful attempts to cause insubordination, disloyalty, mutiny, or refusal of duty within the military or the obstruction of military recruitment or enlistment. In practice, this law was used as the springboard for massive prosecutions of antiwar speeches and publications of all kinds across the United States, based on the theory that many such viewpoints were false and, in any case, aimed at undermining recruitment or other aspects of the war effort.

Despite the sweeping language and even more sweeping prosecutions associated with the 1917 law, a far more draconian amendment to the Espionage Act, sometimes known as the Sedition Act, was enacted in 1918 in response to complaints that the original law was not stringent enough to suppress antiwar sentiment. The 1918 amendments outlawed virtually all conceivable criticism of the war, including any expressions of support for "any country with which the United State is at war" or that opposed "the cause of the United States therein." Also banned was the oral or printed dissemination of all "disloyal, profane, scurrilous, or abusive language" about the "form of government" of the country, the Constitution, the flag, the military, and military uniforms, as well as any language intended to bring any of the above into "contempt, scorn, contumely, or disrepute."

Under these laws, more than two thousand people were indicted for written or verbal criticism of the war and more than one thousand were convicted, resulting in more than one hundred jail terms of ten years or more. No one was convicted under the espionage acts during World War I for spying activities. The 1918 amendments to the Espionage Act were repealed in 1920. Although the original 1917 law remains in effect, it was virtually never used after World War I to prosecute expressions of opinion (partly because the 1940 Smith Act included more updated sedition provisions); it has, however, been used in cases involving alleged theft of information, including in the prosecutions of Julius Rosenberg and Ethel Rosenberg during the Cold War and the Vietnam War-era prosecution of Daniel Ellsberg for dissemination of the Pentagon Papers.

**Court Rulings.** The Supreme Court handed down six rulings concerning the constitutionality of Espionage Act prosecutions in 1919-1920, during a severe "red scare." In every case, it upheld lower court convictions. Although the Court's rulings no doubt reflected the anticommunist climate, they had long-term significance because they were the first cases in which the Court sought to interpret the free speech clauses of the First Amendment and thus helped shape decades of subsequent debate and interpretation of this subject. In *Schenck v. United States* (1919), the Court upheld the conviction (under the original 1917 law) of a group accused of seeking to obstruct enlistment in the armed forces by mailing antidraft leaflets. Despite the lack of evidence that Schenck's mailings had any effect whatsoever, the Court, in a famous ruling penned by Justice Oliver Wendell Holmes, rejected Schenck's First Amendment claims. Holmes wrote that although the defendants would have been within their constitutional rights in saying what they did in ordinary times, the character of "every act depends upon the circumstances in which it is done." Just as "the most stringent protection of free speech would not protect a man in falsely shouting fire in a theater and causing a panic," the question was always whether the expression was used in such circumstances and was of such a nature as to create a "clear and present danger " that it would cause the "substantive evils" that Congress has the right to prevent.

In *Abrams v. United States* (1919), a second landmark case (based on the 1918 amendment), the Court upheld the conviction of a group of defendants who had thrown from a New York City rooftop leaflets critical of U.S. military intervention against the new Bolshevik government in Russia. This case became known especially because of a dissent by Holmes, who essentially maintained that no clear and present danger had been demonstrated and that Congress could not constitutionally forbid "all effort to change the mind of the country." In words that became famous both for their eloquence and because, after 1937, most Court rulings in First Amendment cases reflected their sentiment more than the those of the majorities in either *Abrams* or *Schenck*, Holmes declared that U.S. constitutional democracy was based on giving all thought an opportunity to compete in the free trade in ideas, and as long as that experiment remained part of the Constitution, Americans should be "eternally vigilant against attempts to check the expression of opinions that we loathe and believe to be fraught with death, unless they so imminently threaten interference with the lawful and pressing purposes of the law that an immediate check is required to save the country."

In the only significant Espionage Act case involving First Amendment claims to be decided by the Court after 1920, a Court majority reflected Holmes's *Abrams* dissent. In *Hartzel v. United States* (1944), involving a man who had mailed articles attacking U.S. policies during World War II to Army officers and draft registrants (circumstances almost identical to *Schenck*), the Court reversed Hartzel's conviction on the grounds that there was no proof he had willfully sought to obstruct the activities of the armed forces.

**Further Reading**

Chafee, Zechariah. *Free Speech in the United States.* New York: Atheneum, 1969.

Goldstein, Robert Justin. *Political Repression in Modern America: 1870 to the Present.* Boston: G. K. Hall, 1978.

Polenberg, Richard. *Fighting Faiths: The Abrams Case, the Supreme Court, and Free Speech.* New York: Viking Penguin, 1987.

*Robert Justin Goldstein*

# EXCLUSIONARY RULE

*Description:* Judicially created doctrine proscribing the admissibility at trial of evidence obtained illegally through violation of a defendant's constitutional rights.

*Relevant amendments:* Fourth, Fifth

*Significance:* The Supreme Court ruling in 1914 excluded the use of physical evidence gathered through unreasonable search or seizure, and later rulings prohibited any evidence obtained in violation of the Fifth Amendment right against self-incrimination, the Sixth Amendment right to counsel, and Fifth and Fourteenth Amendment rights to due process of law.

The exclusionary rule, as applied to Fourth Amendment search and seizure provisions, originated with the Supreme Court's 1914 decision in *Weeks v. United States.* Although no emergency conditions existed, police officers had twice conducted nonconsensual, warrantless searches of Freemont Weeks's home, obtaining letters and documents that were later used as evidence against him over his objections at trial. Weeks was ultimately convicted, and the Supreme Court addressed his appeal. In a unanimous opinion, the Court noted that the Framers of the Constitution intended through the passage of the Bill of Rights to protect the American people from the general warrants that had been issued under the authority of the British government in colonial times.

The Court declared that the courts, which are charged with the support of the Constitution, should not sanction the tendency of those who enforce the criminal laws of the country to obtain conviction by means of unlawful seizures. The Court concluded that if letters and private documents can be seized illegally and used in evidence against a citizen accused of an offense, the protection of the Fourth Amendment against unreasonable searches and seizures is of no value.

This newly minted rule was strengthened by *Silverthorne Lumber Co. v. United States* (1920), and *Agnello v. United States* (1925), which made clear that illegally acquired evidence could not be used by the government, regardless of the nature of the evidence. However, the mandatory exclusion of illegally obtained evidence pertained only to federal law enforcement and trials. Although the Court eventually agreed in *Wolf v. Colorado* (1949) that the due process clause of the Fourteenth Amendment prohibited illegal state governmental searches and seizures, it initially maintained that the states did not necessarily have to use the exclusionary rule as a method of enforcing that right. The states were allowed to come up with other safeguards to protect the constitutional rights of their citizens.

**Silver Platter Doctrine.** The incorporation of the prohibitions of the Fourth Amendment into the due process clause of the Fourteenth Amendment did not secure compliance by state law enforcement officers. In fact, because no real means of regulating unlawful state law enforcement behavior existed, state law enforcement agents cooperated with federal agents by providing them with illegally seized evidence, which was admissible in federal court because it was not obtained by federal agents. This practice became known as the "silver platter doctrine" because federal agents were being served up evidence much like food on a platter.

The silver platter doctrine was denounced by the Court in *Elkins v. United States* (1960), which disallowed the admission of evidence obtained by state officers during a search that, if conducted by federal officers, would have violated a defendant's Fourth Amendment rights. The Court decided that it hardly mattered to victims of illegal searches whether their rights had been abridged by federal agents or by state officers, and that if the fruits of an illegal search conducted by state officers could no longer be admitted in federal trials, no incentive would exist for federal and state agents to cooperate in such abhorrent schemes.

Partially because of state law enforcement officers' disregard for the Fourth Amendment's proscriptions, in *Mapp v. Ohio* (1961), the Court reconsidered its stance on extending the exclusionary rule to state action.

*Mapp v. Ohio.* In 1957 Cleveland, Ohio, police officers went to Dollree Mapp's home with the goal of finding and questioning a bombing suspect. When the officers requested entry, Mapp refused to let them in without a search warrant. The officers returned a few hours later and forcibly entered Mapp's house. A struggle ensued; officers handcuffed Mapp and carried her upstairs, then searched her entire house, including the basement. They found obscene materials during their search, and she was charged and convicted of possessing them. During her trial, no warrant was introduced into evidence. The Ohio supreme court upheld Mapp's conviction, although it acknowledged that the methods used to obtain the evidence offended a sense of justice.

In the *Mapp* majority opinion, the Court deplored the futility of protecting Fourth Amendment rights through remedies such as civil or criminal sanctions. It noted the failure of these remedies and the consequent constitutional abuses and suggested nothing could destroy a government more quickly than its failure to observe its own laws. The Court declared that if the Fourteenth Amendment did not bar improperly seized evidence, the Constitution would consist of nothing more than empty words. In addition, more than half of the states had already adopted the exclusionary rule through either statutory or case law. Therefore, the Court ruled that the exclusionary rule applied to the states as well as the federal government. This avoided the incongruity between state and federal use of illegally seized evidence. Through *Mapp*, the Court altered state criminal trial procedures and investigatory procedures by requiring local officials to follow constitutional standards of search and seizure or suffer exclusion of evidence at trial.

**Rationale for the Rule.** Some legal experts theorize that the exclusionary rule is a natural outgrowth of the Constitution. The government cannot provide individual rights without protecting them, and the exclusionary rule provides this function. Therefore, the rule is an implicit part of the substantive guarantees of the Fourth Amendment prohibition against unreasonable search and seizure, the Fifth Amendment right against self-incrimination, the Sixth Amendment right to counsel, and the Fifth and Fourteenth Amendment rights to due process. The exclusionary rule also involves the concept of maintaining judicial integrity. The introduction into evidence of illegally gathered materials must be proscribed to maintain judicial integrity and deter police misconduct.

The most common reason invoked for assertion of the exclusionary rule is that it effectively deters constitutional violations and that this deterrent effect is crucial to the vitality of the constitutional amendments. Beginning with *United States v. Calandra* (1974), the Court viewed the rule as primarily a judicial creation designed to deter police misconduct. Therefore, the Court felt free to balance the costs of excluding evidence against the benefits of the rule's effect as a deterrent and produced an ever-expanding list of judicially acknowledged exceptions to the exclusionary rule.

**Exceptions to the Rule.** After 1961, when the Court held that the states must apply the exclusionary rule to state investigatory and trial procedures, the rule came under increasing attack by those who argued that it exacts too great a price from society by allowing guilty people to either go free or to receive reduced sentences.

The Court, reflecting societal division over the exclusionary rule, fashioned a number of exceptions to it. For example, in *Calandra*, the Court refused to allow a grand jury witness the privilege of invoking the exclusionary rule in refusing to answer questions that were based on illegally seized evidence, as any deterrent effect that might be achieved through application of the rule was too uncertain. For the same reason, the Court also held that illegally seized evidence may be admitted at trial in civil cases (*United States v. Janis*, 1976) and when it would "inevitably" have been discovered through other legal means (*Nix v. Williams*, 1984) as well as used to impeach a witness's credibility (*United States v. Havens*, 1978) and against third persons (*United States v. Paynor*, 1980).

However, what most eroded the exclusionary rule was the good faith exception, first approved for criminal cases by the Court in *United States v. Leon* (1984). The good faith exception permitted the use of illegally acquired evidence if the officers who seized it did so in good faith. In *Leon*, the Court found no reason to apply the exclusionary rule to a situation in which an officer relied on a search warrant issued by a neutral magistrate that later was found not to be supported by probable cause. The Court reasoned that in such a case, the exclusion of evidence would have no deterrent effect on police officers and would exact too great a price from society. In *Illinois v. Krull* (1987), the Court ruled that the exclusionary rule did not bar the admissibility of evidence seized in good faith reliance on a statute, subsequently found to be unconstitutional, which authorized warrantless administrative searches.

In 1995 the Court again extended the good faith exception when it held in *Arizona v. Evans* that the exclusionary rule does not require suppression of evidence seized in violation of the Fourth Amendment because of inaccurate information based on a court employee's clerical errors. In *Evans*, a police officer made an arrest following a routine traffic stop when his patrol car computer erroneously indicated there was an outstanding misdemeanor warrant for Evans's arrest. When the issue of suppression reached the Court, it again applied the rationale of *Leon*. There was neither any evidence that court employees were inclined to ignore or subvert the Fourth Amendment nor any basis for believing that application of the rule would have an effect on the future behavior of court employees. Therefore, the Court decided that it would not serve the purposes of justice to apply the exclusionary rule in *Evans*.

**Further Reading**

Joel Samaha discusses the history of the exclusionary rule, rationales that justify it, and its social costs and deterrent effects in *Criminal Procedure* (4th ed., St. Paul, Minn.: West Publishing, 1999). For basic information regarding the exclusionary rule and its exceptions, see Louis Fisher's *Constitutional Rights: Civil Rights and Civil Liberties* (2d ed., New York: McGraw-Hill, 1995), Lee Epstein and Thomas G. Walker's *Constitutional Law for a Changing America: Rights, Liberties, and Justice* (3d ed., Washington, D.C.: Congressional Quarterly, 1998), Craig Ducat and Harold Chases's *Constitutional Interpretation: Rights of the Individual* (6th ed., St. Paul, Minn.: West Publishing, 1996), and Joan Biskupic's *The Supreme Court and Individual Rights* (3d ed., Washington, D.C.: Congressional Quarterly, 1997).

*Rebecca Davis*

# FIRST AMENDMENT ABSOLUTISM

*Description:* Position that protections given by the First Amendment to the U.S. Constitution are absolute, not subject to qualification or abridgement in any way.

*Relevant amendment:* First

*Significance:* Very few First Amendment absolutists sat on the Supreme Court, and the Court never made a First Amendment decision based on the absolutist approach.

Among the Supreme Court justices who could be called First Amendment absolutists is Justice Hugo L. Black. He argued that when the First Amendment said "Congress shall make no law" it meant that Congress should make absolutely no laws abridging First Amendment rights. Almost all other justices have taken that with a grain of salt, opining that "no law" meant something other than absolutely no laws.

Justice William O. Douglas joined Black in most of his absolutist decisions, and he wrote that the government should take an enabling position regarding First Amendment issues, especially freedom of the press, creating opportunities for citizens to publish opinions. However, the Court majority never took an absolutist approach to First Amendment issues.

The First Amendment can be separated into three divisions: the religion clauses (establishment and freedom), the speech and press clauses, and the clauses guaranteeing peaceable assembly and the right to petition. Most of the Court's First Amendment decisions relate to speech and press, and a substantial number of cases relate to religion. Only a handful are about assembly and petition rights.

**Speech and Press.** The Court clearly stated that no absolute freedom of speech or the press exists. It found in *Cohen v. California* (1971) that there is no absolute freedom to speak wherever or whenever one chooses and in *Dennis v. United States* (1951) that the "societal value of speech must on occasion be subordinated to other values and considerations." It should be noted that *Dennis,* a case involving the trial of people charged with preaching the violent overthrow of the government by the Communist Party, is not unanimously considered good law today. Neither is *Schenck v. United States* (1919), a case involving people convicted of distributing leaflets urging draftees not to bear arms; this violated the Espionage Act of 1917. Their conviction was unanimously upheld by the Court. In his opinion, Justice Oliver Wendell Holmes wrote that freedom of speech does not give one the right to shout a false "fire" warning in a crowded theater. Holmes's words served as the foundation of the clear and present danger test. The Court used the clear and present danger test as well as a balancing test (which examines the gravity of the danger to see if it justifies suppressing freedom of speech) in numerous decisions to determine when First Amendment freedom of speech and press rights could be abridged.

When Justice Joseph Story, a friend and colleague of Chief Justice John Marshall, wrote his commentaries on the law, he argued that the government has a right to protect its survival, and

*In his commentaries on the law, Justice Joseph Story argued that the government has a right to protect its survival.* (Courtesy of Art & Visual Materials, Special Collections Department, Harvard Law School)

the Court upheld that line of reasoning in *American Communications Association v. Douds* (1950). The free speech and free press clauses must be balanced against compelling public interests, the Court ruled, and it appears that every effort to challenge that ruling has been denied certiorari. The Court ruled that regulation of speech and the press must not be content-based, must bear a reasonable relationship to a significant government interest, and must allow for other channels of communication.

**Religion.** The Court comes closest to the absolutist position when it rules on religion cases. The religion clauses are absolute "as far as they go," the Court ruled, but they do not require complete separation of church and state. What they do require is that the government avoid regulating religious beliefs, establishing a state religion, and showing any preferences among religions or between religion and irreligion. When religious belief is translated into action, the state can intervene to regulate or prevent the action. Any legislation, the Court ruled in *Larkin v. Grendel's Den* (1982), must meet three rules: First, it must meet a secular legislative purpose; second, it must neither advance nor inhibit religion; and third, it must not entangle the government with religion.

**Assembly and Association.** Neither the right to assemble nor that to associate was judged to be absolute. For example, in *Cox v. New Hampshire* (1941), the Court upheld a license requirement for public parades and processions. In various cases, it endeavored to establish where and how people could assemble. The Court also examined association issues, trying to determine whether membership in certain clubs or organizations could be denied to members of various groups and whether those institutions were public or private.

### Further Reading
Alderman, Ellen, and Caroline Kennedy. *In Our Defense: The Bill of Rights in Action.* New York: Morrow, 1991.

Black, Hugo LaFayette. *One Man's Stand for Freedom: Mr. Justice Black and the Bill of Rights.* New York: Alfred A. Knopf, 1971.

Dennis, Everett, Donald M. Gillmore, and David L. Grey, eds. *Justice Hugo Black and the First Amendment: "No Law" Means "No Law."* Ames: Iowa State University Press, 1978.

Duran, James C. *Justice William O. Douglas.* Boston: Twayne, 1981.

Fellman, David. *The Constitutional Rights of Association.* Chicago: University of Chicago Press, 1963.

Hocking, William Ernest. *Freedom of the Press: A Framework of Principle.* New York: Da Capo Press, 1972.

Levy, Beth, and Denise M. Bonilla. *The Power of the Press.* Bronx, N.Y.: H. W. Wilson, 1999.

Miller, William Lee. *The First Liberty: Religion and the American Republic.* New York: Alfred A. Knopf, 1986.

St. John, Jeffrey. *Forge of Union, Anvil of Liberty: A Correspondent's Report on the First Federal Elections, the First Federal Congress, and the Bill of Rights.* Ottawa, Ill.: Jameson Books, 1992.

Smolla, Rodney A. *Free Speech in an Open Society.* New York: Alfred A. Knopf, 1992.

*Dwight Jensen*

# FIRST AMENDMENT BALANCING

**Description:** Weighing of different interests involved in cases raising First Amendment claims, typically the free speech rights of an individual versus the potential harm posed to society as a whole.

**Relevant amendment:** First

**Significance:** Although all Supreme Court First Amendment rulings involve the balancing of different claims and interests, the Court explicitly or implicitly invoked the balancing test most consistently during the 1947-1957 period. It almost invariably placed a higher value on social than individual claims in free speech cases, thus often upholding convictions.

The Supreme Court's First Amendment jurisprudence gradually evolved after World War I. Earlier, the Court had invoked various tests for resolving First Amendment conflicts, including the well-known clear and present danger test first invoked in *Schenck v. United States* (1919). During the 1947-1957 period, the Court, usually implicitly but sometimes explicitly, appears to have been guided by a balancing test, through which the Court sought to weigh competing interests and claims against each other.

**Ten Years of Balancing.** All legal cases, by definition, involve competing considerations, and therefore any jurisprudence involves balancing, as indeed does virtually all private decision making. However, the concept of First Amendment balancing is particularly apparent in the Court's First Amendment jurisprudence during the 1947-1957 period because of the manner and outcome of its rulings. When the Court seems to have invoked balancing during this period, it invariably gave more weight to perceived societal interests over First Amendment claims of individuals and organizations. Therefore, in the view of its critics, the Court claimed to be impartially balancing competing interests while in fact placing a thumb on the social side of the scales. After 1957, the Court largely abandoned the balancing test in First Amendment cases, instead generally relying on other tests such as the preferred freedoms doctrine, which tended to yield results favoring individual rights.

*American Communications Association v. Douds* (1950) is one of the relatively few cases in which the Court explicitly elaborated balancing considerations. At issue was a provision of the 1947 Taft-Hartley (Labor-

*Chief Justice Fred M. Vinson believed that the Supreme Court had a duty to determine which interests needed greater protection in cases in which constitutional principles conflict.* (Collection of the Supreme Court of the United States)

Management Relations) Act that required all union officials to sign noncommunist affidavits in order to maintain their offices and for their unions to qualify for various benefits under existing federal labor laws. Chief Justice Fred M. Vinson's majority opinion upholding the validity of the contested provision declared that the clear and present danger standard of *Schenck* was not intended to create an absolutist test. He stated that when a statute's effect on a person's ability to exercise First Amendment rights was relatively small but the public interest to be protected was significant, a rigid test that necessitated the demonstration of imminent danger to the nation's security was an "absurdity." Instead, Vinson said, the Court's duty was to determine which interest needed greater protection under the particular circumstances of the case. He weighed the likely effects of the statute on the free exercise of First Amendment rights against the "congressional determination that political strikes are evils of conduct which cause substantial harm to interstate commerce" and that communists "pose continuing threats to the public interest when in positions of union leadership."

In *Dennis v. United States* (1951), the Court upheld the conviction of top U.S. Communist Party leaders for conspiracy to advocate and organize the overthrow of the government. In his concurring opinion, Justice Felix Frankfurter, a leading advocate of balancing, stated, "The demands of free speech in a democratic society as well as the interest in national security are better served by candid and informed weighing of the competing interests, within the confines of the judicial process, than by announcing dogmas too inflexible for the non-Euclidean problem to be solved."

**Criticisms.** Frankfurter's reference to inflexible "dogmas" was a response to critics of balancing, who claimed that it was consistently invoked in a manner that overlooked or watered down compelling free speech claims. Among the critics of balancing was Justice Hugo L. Black, who was associated with the absolutist view that held that absolutely no law should be passed that abridged First Amendment rights. In *Barenblatt v. United States* (1959), Black declared that the Court's application of balancing amounted to amending the First Amendment to read, "Congress shall pass no law abridging freedom of speech, press, assembly, and petition unless Congress and the Supreme Court reach the joint conclusion that on balance the interest of the government in stifling these freedoms is greater than the interest of the people in having them exercised."

Similarly, in *Smith v. California* (1959), Black argued that because the

First Amendment said Congress could pass "no law abridging" free speech rights, this meant that the Constitution placed these rights above any competing claims, and therefore no federal agency, including the Court, had the power or authority to subordinate speech and press to what they think are more important interests.

**Further Reading**

Abernathy, M. Glenn, and Barbara Perry. *Civil Liberties Under the Constitution.* Columbia: University of South Carolina Press, 1993.

Barker, Lucius, and Twiley W. Barker, Jr. *Civil Liberties and the Constitution.* Englewood Cliffs, N.J.: Prentice-Hall, 1994.

Emerson, Thomas. *The System of Freedom of Expression.* New York: Vintage Books, 1970.

*Robert Justin Goldstein*

# FIRST AMENDMENT SPEECH TESTS

*Description:* Rules set forth in several twentieth century Supreme Court decisions by which the Court judged later claims of protected speech.

*Relevant amendment:* First

*Significance:* To First Amendment absolutists and civil libertarians, the speech tests employed by the Supreme Court severely weakened individuals' constitutional rights to free speech. To others, the tests balanced the rights of government and society with those of individuals.

Beginning in the early twentieth century, the Supreme Court adopted tests by which to decide claims of First Amendment protection. The first and most frequently applied test is that of clear and present danger and its subsequent modifications. Developed by Justices Oliver Wendell Holmes and Louis D. Brandeis, this test weighs an individual's First Amendment rights against the government's right to protect itself and its citizens.

The clear and present danger test was set forth by Justice Holmes in *Schenck v. United States* (1919). Charles Schenck and his codefendants were convicted under the 1917 Espionage Act for disrupting military recruiting by distributing antiwar leaflets. Schenck appealed, citing First Amendment protection, but the Court unanimously upheld the conviction. In the opinion for the Court, Holmes wrote, "The question in every case is whether the words used are used in such circumstances and are of such a nature as to create a clear and present danger that they will bring about the substantive evils that Congress has a right to prevent. It is a question of proximity and degree." The clear and present danger at the time was World War I, and the substantive evil was the hindering of national defense.

**Changing Applications.** However, just as free speech is not absolute, according to the Court, speech tests also are not absolute. Chief Justice Fred M. Vinson, in the majority opinion in *Dennis v. United States* (1951), wrote, "Neither Justice Holmes nor Justice Brandeis ever envisioned that a shorthand phrase should be crystallized into a rigid rule to be applied inflexibly without regard to the circumstances of each case. . . . Nothing is more certain in modern society than the principle that there are no absolutes, that a name, a phrase, a standard has meaning only when associated with the considerations which gave birth to the nomenclature." Therefore, the Court continuously modified and reinterpreted the clear and present danger test.

For example, in *Gitlow v. New York* (1925), the test was further qualified. Despite a lack of clear and present danger, the Court upheld Benjamin Gitlow's conviction for publishing the *Left-wing Manifesto*, which urged a violent government overthrow. The majority opinion of Justice Edward T. Sanford put forth that speech is not protected "if its natural tendency and probable effect was to bring about the substantive evil which the legislative body might prevent." The Court applied this new bad tendency test again in *Whitney v. California* (1927) to uphold the conviction of Charlotte Anita Whitney, a communist. She was guilty under California's criminal syndicalism law because the organization in which she participated promoted violent political action. In upholding the conviction, the Court cited a state's right to protect itself from organizations advocating criminal acts.

In addition to changing the definitions for tests, the Court also inconsistently applied them. For example, in *Terminiello v. Chicago* (1949), Father Arthur Terminiello's conviction was narrowly overturned, despite a riot by protestors during his inflammatory speech. In writing the majority opinion, Justice William O. Douglas modified the clear and present danger test by adding that it must be "of a serious substantive evil that rises far above public inconvenience, annoyance, or unrest." This particular

Court was of the opinion that speech is necessarily provocative and that the ensuing disturbance was mild enough to be quelled by police.

In *Dennis,* the Court again modified the definition of clear and present danger. In upholding the convictions of communists under the Smith Act (1940), Chief Justice Fred M. Vinson restated Chief Judge Learned Hand's lower court ruling: "In each case [courts] must ask whether the gravity of the 'evil,' discounted by its improbability, justifies such invasion of free speech as is necessary to avoid the danger." The Court thus created the grave and probable danger test, which removed the burden of the state to prove the existence of an immediate danger to itself. Consequently, civil liberties were severely weakened.

**Dissenting Views.** First Amendment speech tests are not without criticism, as Justice Hugo L. Black's dissenting opinion in *Dennis* illustrates: "I cannot agree that the First Amendment permits us to sustain laws suppressing freedom of speech and press on the basis of Congress' or our own notions of mere 'reasonableness.' Such a doctrine waters down the First Amendment so that it amounts to little more than an admonition to Congress." Black's dissent is important because the Court seemed to favor the side of government in the First Amendment cases brought to it.

By *Brandenburg v. Ohio* (1969), however, the Court redefined clear and present danger, and in so doing, began to favor civil liberties. Ku Klux Klan leader Clarence Brandenburg was convicted under Ohio's criminal syndicalism law, which was modeled on the California statute under which Whitney was convicted decades earlier. The Court overturned the conviction and established the incitement test. In its unsigned majority opinion, the Court distinguished between speech and action. It stated that speech advocating force or lawlessness is protected; however, speech "directed to inciting or producing imminent lawless action" or "likely to incite or produce such action" is unprotected. The Court referred to this ruling in subsequent cases.

### Further Reading

Killian, Johnny H., ed. *The Constitution of the United States of America: Analysis and Interpretation.* Washington, D.C.: Government Printing Office, 1987.

Rabban, David M. *Free Speech in Its Forgotten Years.* New York: Cambridge University Press, 1997.

*Beau David Case*

# FLAG DESECRATION

*Description:* Act of physically "harming" the U.S. flag, usually through
such means as burning or tearing; at times the term was also applied to
verbal criticism of the flag or what it represents.

***Relevant amendment:*** First

***Significance:*** The Supreme Court upheld the right, under the First
Amendment, of people to both verbally and physically assault the flag
and, in so doing, helped define and extend the meaning of constitutionally protected symbolic speech.

The U.S. flag, a symbol of the nation, is displayed widely in front of government buildings, private homes, and commercial enterprises and used
extensively as a design springboard for clothing, advertising, and a wide
variety of other products. However, it attracted little interest and received
little public display for more than eighty years after its original adoption
as a symbol of the nation by the Continental Congress on June 14, 1777.
Only the outbreak of the Civil War (1861-1865) transformed the flag into
an object of public adoration—although only, of course, in the North.

The newly found Northern love for the flag continued after the Civil
War, but the flag's growing popularity was not accompanied by any sense
that it should be regarded as a sacred object or relic. During the nation's
rapid postwar industrialization, as the modern advertising industry developed, the flag became increasingly popular as a decorative accompani-
ment in the commercialization of a wide range of products. Gradually, after 1890, Union veterans and members of patriotic-hereditary groups
such as the Sons of the American Revolution began to protest alleged
commercial debasement of the flag, which they declared would ultimately cause the significance of both the flag and patriotism to degrade
among the general public. After about 1900 the supposed threat to the
flag shifted from commercialization to that allegedly posed by its use as a
means of expressing political protest by political radicals, trade union
members, and immigrants (who were often indiscriminately lumped together).

Between 1897 and 1932 veterans and hereditary-patriotic groups lobbied for stringent laws to "protect" the flag from all forms of alleged "desecration" (the harming of sacred religious objects) and succeeded in obtaining passage of flag desecration laws in all forty-eight states, with thirty-

one states acting between 1897 and 1905 alone. The laws generally outlawed attaching anything to or placing any marks on the flag, using the flag in any manner for advertising purposes, and physically or verbally "harming" flags in any way, including, typically, publicly mutilating, trampling, defacing, defiling, defying, or casting contempt on the flag. The term "flag" was generally defined to mean any object of any form, size, or material that resembled the U.S. flag.

**Early Court Rulings.** The earliest state flag desecration laws were quickly and, at first, successfully challenged in local and state courts as illegally restricting property rights by adversely affecting commercial interests. However, in *Halter v. Nebraska* (1907), the Supreme Court upheld Nebraska's law in sweeping terms that made clear the futility of any further legal challenges for the foreseeable future. In a case involving sales of Stars and Stripes beer, which had pictures of flags on the bottle labels, the Court declared that the state was entitled to restrict property rights for the valid and worthy purpose of fostering nationalism. In a ruling that did not address free speech rights, the Court declared that "love both of the common country and of the State will diminish in proportion as respect for the flag is weakened," that advertising usage of the flag tended to "degrade and cheapen it in the estimation of the people," and that the state was entitled to "exert its power to strengthen the bonds of the Union and therefore, to that end, may encourage patriotism and love of country among its people."

The Court did not consider another flag desecration case until 1969, and during the interim period, the constitutionality of flag desecration laws was essentially considered beyond review by the lower courts. The Court revisited the issue during the Vietnam War, when flags were widely burned or used in other unorthodox ways to express political dissent (resulting in hundreds of flag desecration prosecutions).

In *Street v. New York* (1969), the Court relied heavily on its rulings in *Stromberg v. California* (1931) and *West Virginia State Board of Education v. Barnette* (1943) to strike down flag desecration provisions that outlawed *verbal* disrespect for the flag as violating the First Amendment. The Court, by a 5-4 vote, overturned Street's flag desecration conviction on the grounds that because he had been charged under a provision of New York's law outlawing casting contempt on the flag by words or acts and evidence concerning his statements had been introduced at trial, he might have been convicted for his words alone. Any such conviction, in the absence of any evident threat to the peace or incitement to violence, was held to violate the First Amendment because "it is firmly settled that under our Constitution the public expression of ideas may not be prohibited merely because the ideas are themselves offensive to some of their hearers," even opinions about the flag "which are defiant or contemptuous." The Court completely avoided addressing the constitutionality of laws that banned *physical* flag desecration on the grounds that there was no need to decide the case "on a broader basis than the record before us imperatively requires." Aside from *Street,* the Court in 1974 overturned convictions in two other Vietnam-era flag desecration cases, *Goguen v. Smith* and *Spence v. Washington,* which were both decided on narrow grounds that again avoided directly addressing the validity of state interests in protecting the physical integrity of the flag in light of First Amendment questions.

**A Texas Flag Burning.** In *Texas v. Johnson* (1989), which arose from a 1984 Dallas flag-burning incident, the Court directly faced the question of physical desecration of the flag, ruling by a 5-4 vote that Texas's venerated objects law had been unconstitutionally applied to Johnson. Texas advanced two interests as overriding Johnson's First Amendment rights, but the Court dismissed them. First, it found that the state's interest in maintaining order was not implicated because no disturbance of the peace occurred or threatened to occur because of Johnson's act. Second, regarding a need to preserve the flag as a national symbol, the Court held that because Johnson's guilt depended on the communicative nature of his conduct, the Texas statute violated the main principle behind the First Amendment, that the government cannot ban the expression of an idea because society finds that idea offensive or disagreeable. Citing its holding in *Street* that a state cannot criminally punish a person for speech critical of the flag, the Court declared flatly that Texas's attempt to distinguish between written or spoken words and nonverbal conduct "is of no moment where the nonverbal conduct is expressive, as is here, and where the regulation of that conduct is related to expression, as it is here."

Furthermore, the Court declared that the government cannot ban expression of ideas that it does not like because the expression takes a particular form; therefore, the state cannot criminally punish a person for burning a flag in political protest on the grounds that other means of expressing the same idea were available. The Court concluded that the principles of freedom reflected in the flag would be reaffirmed by its decision: "We do not consecrate the flag by punishing its desecration, for in doing so we dilute the freedom that this cherished emblem represents."

*Johnson* touched off an intense and massive uproar across the United States. Virtually every member of Congress endorsed resolutions condemning the ruling. To circumvent the ruling, most Democrats maintained that an ordinary law would suffice, but President George Bush and most Republicans maintained that a constitutional amendment would be required. The Democratic congressional leadership noted that *Johnson* struck down a Texas statute that forbade flag desecration likely to cause "serious offense" to observers, rather than, as the Court noted at one point, "protecting the physical integrity of the flag in all circumstances" and argued that the court might uphold such a "content neutral" law.

**The 1989 Flag Protection Act.** Whether due to a perceived cooling of public sentiment, to increasing signs of growing opposition to a constitutional amendment, or to increased acceptance of the argument that trying a statute first was preferable to a constitutional change, by October, 1989, the drive for a constitutional amendment, seemingly unstoppable in late June after President Bush endorsed it, was sputtering. On October 19, the constitutional amendment failed to reach the two-thirds majority it required in the Senate. However, both houses of Congress passed the proposed statutory alternative, the Flag Protection Act of 1989.

The Flag Protection Act provided penalties of up to one year in jail and a one thousand dollar fine for anyone who "knowingly mutilates, physically defiles, burns, maintains on the floor or ground, or tramples upon any flag of the United States" with "flag" defined as "any flag of the United States, or any part thereof, made of any substance, of any size, in a form that is commonly displayed." Although the stated purpose of the act was to end flag burnings, its immediate impact was to spur perhaps the largest single wave of such incidents in U.S. history, as flags were burned in about a dozen cities shortly after the law took effect in late October.

Acting under an extraordinary expedited review procedure mandated by the act, the Court struck down the Flag Protection Act by a 5-4 vote in *United States v. Eichman* on June 11, 1990. The *Eichman* ruling essentially underlined *Johnson*, finding that the government's interest in protecting the flag's position as a symbol of the United States and certain ideals did not justify the infringement on First Amendment rights. Although conceding that the new law, unlike the Texas statute in *Johnson,* did not explicitly place content-based limits on the scope of prohibited conduct, the Court held that the Flag Protection Act still suffered from the same fundamental flaw as the Texas law, namely that it could not be justified without reference to the content of the regulated speech. The Court added, "Punishing desecration of the flag dilutes the very freedom that makes this emblem so revered, and worthy of revering."

The *Eichman* decision sparked an immediate renewal of calls by President Bush and others for a constitutional amendment. However, the proposed amendment was defeated in both houses of Congress in 1990. After Republicans gained control of both houses of Congress in 1994, the amendment was passed by the required two-thirds majority in the House in 1995, 1997, and 1999. However, in the Senate, it failed to gain a two-thirds majority by three votes in 1995 and by four votes in 2001.

**Further Reading**

Curtis, Michael, ed. *The Flag Burning Cases.* Vol. 2 in *The Constitution and the Flag.* New York: Garland, 1993.

Goldstein, Robert Justin. *Burning the Flag: The Great 1989-1990 American Flag Desecration Controversy.* Kent, Ohio: Kent State University Press, 1996.

_____, ed. *Desecrating the American Flag: Key Documents of the Controversy from the Civil War to 1995.* Syracuse, N.Y.: Syracuse University Press, 1996.

_____. *Saving "Old Glory": The History of the American Flag Desecration Controversy.* Boulder, Colo.: Westview Press, 1995.

Miller, J. Anthony. *"Texas v. Johnson": The Flag Burning Case.* Springfield, N.J.: Enslow, 1997.

*Robert Justin Goldstein*

# GAG ORDER

*Description:* A trial judge's order requiring attorneys, police, and parties involved in a criminal proceeding not speak to the news media concerning the proceeding

*Relevant amendment:* First

*Significance:* A gag order, or rule, is designed to protect a defendant's right to a fair trial while at the same time providing for a press free from more extreme censorship

Since the U.S. Supreme Court overturned Samuel H. Sheppard's murder conviction in 1965 because a trial judge had permitted a media circus to deny him a fair trial, judges have sequestered juries during trials and issued gag orders, or rules, to the parties, attorneys, police, and potential witnesses barring them from talking to the press outside court before the trials begin. Such gag orders, while a form of censorship, minimize excessive pretrial publicity that might damage a court's ability to find a jury untainted by prejudicial remarks, while avoiding a direct prior restraint or censorship of the press.

In *Nebraska Press Association v. Stuart* (1976) the trial judge, believing that pretrial hearings, as trials, were required to be open to the press and public under the Sixth Amendment, allowed the press in a pretrial hearing without realizing how damaging information in a dramatic murder case would be. The judge then imposed a gag order banning members of the press from printing what they had learned. However, the Supreme Court ruled that this was an impermissible prior restraint on the press. The Court balanced press freedom against the defendant's right to a fair trial by allowing judges to issue gag orders to keep material secret, but it did not permit them to impose gag orders on the press even if they acquire prejudicial information on the defendant. Similarly, the Court has allowed military secrecy, but has forbidden prior restraints after secrets have reached the press.

*Richard L. Wilson*

# GAY AND LESBIAN RIGHTS

*Description:* Claims of constitutional protections against legal disabilities imposed on the basis of homosexual orientation.

*Relevant amendments:* Fifth, Ninth, Fourteenth

*Significance:* Despite efforts to secure Supreme Court rulings that would protect gay or lesbian individuals' sexual privacy or that would protect them from discriminatory treatment by the law, the Supreme Court has tended to avoid the issue of gay rights through denials of certiorari, ruling on the issue only twice.

The U.S. Constitution does not expressly assign rights to persons based on their sexual orientation. However, the due process clauses of the Fifth and Fourteenth Amendments promise fair treatment by the legal system. The equal protection clause of the Fourteenth Amendment guarantees equality before the states, and the Supreme Court has construed the due process clause of the Fifth Amendment as imposing a similar require-ment on the federal government. These clauses would seem to offer ho-mosexual individuals considerable protection from the kinds of legal dis-crimination and disability that has long been their lot.

In *Griswold v. Connecticut* (1965) and *Eisenstadt v. Baird* (1972), the Court found a right of privacy that encompassed the decision to use con-traceptives. These cases, combined with rulings creating reproductive rights, suggested to some a broad due process right of privacy over inti-mate choices, possibly including the choice of sexual partner. The Court was invited to rule on this issue on several occasions, an invitation that was declined through denials of certiorari until 1986. In *Bowers v. Hardwick* (1986), a sharply divided Court held that this right of privacy did not en-compass consensual homosexual sodomy. The right of privacy pertained to matters of reproduction, marriage, and family, and the Court viewed homosexual activity as unrelated to any of these. Dissenters construed the issue presented in prior cases and in *Bowers* differently, as invoking a broad right to be left alone. Twenty-four states then had sodomy statutes, enforced nearly exclusively against homosexuals. Many have since re-pealed these laws.

Discrimination against gay, lesbian, or bisexual persons in employ-ment housing, public accommodations, and elsewhere has fueled de-mands for legislative relief, and some jurisdictions, mostly on the munici-pal level, have responded. A backlash against such ordinances produced Colorado's Amendment 2, an amendment to the state constitution adopted by popular referendum, prohibiting legislation protecting ho-mosexuals from discrimination. In *Romer v. Evans* (1996), the Court ruled that Amendment 2 violated the equal protection clause of the Four-teenth Amendment. The equal protection clause did not obligate the states to enact legislative protections. However, Colorado's constitutional preclusion of legislative protection was found "inexplicable by anything but animus" against homosexuals and did not further any proper state policy but only inequality for its own sake. "A state cannot so deem a class of persons strangers to its laws," the Court stated.

Some gay and lesbian activists have argued that the Constitution grants them a right to civil marriage. They point to *Loving v. Virginia* (1967), in which the Court held the equal protection clause barred the states from outlawing interracial marriage. By the end of the twentieth century, the issue had been litigated only before the supreme courts of Vermont and Hawaii, where the state supreme court upheld a law banning same-sex marriages. However, many Supreme Court watchers believed the issue likely to come before the Court in the early 2000's.

**Further Reading**

Gertsmann, Evan. *The Constitutional Underclass: Gays, Lesbians, and the Failure of Class-Based Equal Protection.* Chicago: University of Chicago Press, 1999.

Miller, Diane Helen. *Freedom to Differ: The Shaping of the Gay and Lesbian Struggle for Civil Rights.* New York: New York University Press, 1998.

Nava, Michael, and Robert Dawidoff. *Created Equal: Why Gay Rights Matter in America.* New York: St. Martin's Press, 1995.

*John C. Hughes*

# GRAND JURY

*Description:* Panel of ordinary citizens having the authority to view evidence of criminal activity, presented by a prosecutor, solely to determine if sufficient evidence exists to warrant submitting the accused to trial.

*Relevant amendment:* Fifth

*Significance:* Although long celebrated as a protection against the abuse of prosecutorial power, the Supreme Court imposed few procedural limits on the grand jury's own sweeping investigatory powers. Thus, the contemporary grand jury may have actually become an instrument to expand prosecutorial power.

The grand jury is descended from English common law dating to the twelfth century. It originally performed an investigatory function, as citizens were assembled to report local crimes to an itinerant judge so that appropriate trials could be held. By the seventeenth century, the grand jury also demonstrated that it could, by its refusal to indict, protect the citizen against arbitrary, vindictive, or politically motivated prosecutions. In the North American colonies, the grand jury became a bastion of home rule, resisting prosecutions under oppressive British colonial policies. So esteemed was the grand jury in America that the Fifth Amendment of the U.S. Constitution provided that "No person shall be held to answer for a capital, or otherwise infamous crime, unless on a presentment or indictment of a Grand Jury." This provision continues to govern all federal felony prosecutions, crimes that could result in a year or more of incarceration. However, the grand jury is today in decline, used in fewer than half the states. It was abolished in Great Britain in 1933, after having fallen into disuse there for many years.

The federal grand jury has followed the common law model of twenty-three citizens, with a quorum of sixteen. The grand jury is chosen from a cross section of the citizenry, without regard to race, national origin, religion, sex, or economic circumstances. A vote of twelve is sufficient to approve an indictment, or a formal accusation of criminal activity. Therefore, the grand jury is distinct from the petit, or trial, jury. The latter hears evidence at a public trial, including evidence presented by the defense, and may convict by unanimous vote only if convinced of guilt beyond a reasonable doubt. The grand jury convenes in secret to hear evidence presented by the prosecutor, solely to determine if there is sufficient cause to proceed to trial. The very permissive standard of evidence employed for this determination is merely that a crime has been committed and that there is "probable cause" to believe the subject of the investigation has committed it. A refusal to indict will block the prosecution. However, a disappointed prosecutor may present evidence to a subsequent grand jury, in hopes for an indictment, without the impediment of the Fifth Amendment's double jeopardy provision.

Given its historical veneration and inclusion in the Bill of Rights, the grand jury could be expected to be a more universal presence in U.S. criminal justice. Most prosecutions are conducted under state authority, however, and in *Hurtado v. California* (1884), the Supreme Court held that the grand jury indictment was not an essential part of due process protected against abuse by the states by the Fourteenth Amendment. This ruling remains in effect today, even as most other provisions of the Bill of Rights have since been applied to the states through the incorporation doctrine of the Fourteenth Amendment. Most states authorize an alternative procedure called an "information," whereby a prosecutor presents evidence to a judge, who performs an equivalent screening function. Many of those states that use grand juries have altered their size, quorum, or the majority necessary to indict, all in the interest of streamlining an expensive and, in the eyes of many, a dated procedure.

**Procedural Rights.** Despite its celebrated status as a protection against prosecutorial overreaching, the Court has extended few procedural safeguards to the federal grand jury. It has been given wide latitude to conduct its secret investigations, compelling the appearance of witnesses and the production of documents. Prosecutors dominate the proceedings of the grand jury and are not obligated to present exculpatory evidence. The subject of a grand jury investigation has no right to appear or to confront and cross-examine witnesses. Indeed, unless already under arrest, the subject may not know that he or she is being investigated. Few evidentiary rules are observed, therefore, for example, hearsay evidence may be introduced. In *United States v. Calandra* (1974), the Court declined to apply the Fourth Amendment exclusionary rule to bar evidence from the grand jury that would be inadmissible at trial. Indeed, by granting access to its subpoena power, the grand jury may offer prosecutors an avenue toward evidence the Fourth Amendment would otherwise place beyond reach.

Because the proceedings are secret, witnesses appear without an attorney present. They may, only on their own motion, step outside the grand jury room to consult with their attorney. Indigent witnesses have no right to court-appointed counsel. Witnesses may invoke their Fifth Amendment immunity against self-incrimination to resist having to testify, but the prosecutor is under no obligation to warn them of this right. The right against compulsory self-incrimination can also be circumvented by a grant of immunity, even against the wishes of the witness. This immunity can be "transactional," which bars all future prosecution for matters on which the witness has testified, or the more limited "use" immunity, which permits future prosecution for matters that were the subject of grand jury testimony if based on independent evidence.

The practical significance of the grand jury in contemporary criminal law is controversial. Its original investigatory function has been taken over by professional police bureaucracies. Generally compliant and dominated by prosecutors, the ability of the grand jury to serve as a bulwark against arbitrary prosecution is realized only sporadically. Critics point to occasional abuse of the grand jury to support their contention that it is today more of a threat to liberty than a foundation for liberty's protection.

**Further Reading**

Clark, Leroy D. *The Grand Jury: The Use and Abuse of Political Power.* New York: Quadrangle, 1975.

Frankel, Marvin E., and Gary P. Naftalis. *The Grand Jury: An Institution on Trial.* New York: Hill & Wang, 1977.

Katzmann, Gary S. *Inside the Criminal Process.* New York: W.W. Norton, 1991.

*John C. Hughes*

# HATCH ACT

*Description:* An act that became law in 1939 that restricted the political activities of federal employees

*Relevant amendment:* First

*Significance:* The Hatch Act prohibited employees of the federal government from using their official authority to affect an election or to engage in political management or campaigns

The Hatch Act was enacted in response to a special Senate investigation showing that government officials had coerced federal workers to contribute to the reelection campaign of a U.S. senator in 1938. A second, and possibly more important reason for its passage was a fear that President Franklin D. Roosevelt would use the growing number of federal workers as a formidable political machine. In March of 1939, Senator Carl Hatch of New Mexico introduced legislation incorporating the recommendations of the special Senate committee prohibiting the involvement of federal employees in any political organization. They retained the right to vote and could privately express their political opinions. Political appointees and policy-making employees were not included in the act. By restricting the political activity of federal workers, the act addressed three objectives: It precluded the use of the federal workforce for political purposes; it prevented the bureaucracy from becoming a powerful political actor; and it reduced the influence of partisan politics in the hiring, promotion, and firing of federal employees. The Hatch Act was amended in 1993 to allow federal employees, acting as private citizens, to engage in any legal political activity while not on the job.

# HATE CRIMES

*Description:* Criminal acts motivated by hatred of and directed against
members of a particular group
*Relevant amendment:* First
*Significance:* Hate crimes injure the victim and society in ways that other
crimes do not; it has been argued that, because of their nature, they
generate more injury, distress, and suffering than do other crimes

In 1984, Alan Berg, a Jewish talk show host on a Denver radio station, was
fatally shot on his way home by several members of a neo-Nazi hate
group. In 1986, three white teenagers attacked three black men in
Howard Beach, New York, for no other reason than the fact that they
were black. Both these actions were hate crimes—crimes motivated by
the hatred of a certain group, such as a certain race, ethnic group, religion, gender, or sexual orientation. Since the mid-1980's, hate crimes
have been on the rise.

Hate crimes are typically excessively brutal, and quite often they are
carried out in a random fashion against strangers, as with the incidents
involving the Howard Beach black men. Authors Jack Levin and Jack
McDevitt have given several explanations as to why these crimes occur:
the perpetrator's negative and stereotypic view of other people, the possibility that bigotry is becoming more widely tolerated, the resentment that
one group feels toward another because it has been left out of the mainstream of society, a perpetrator's desire for the thrill of the action, a perpetrator's reaction to a perceived or imagined injury such as the loss of a
job promotion or a benefit, and finally, a perpetrator's wish to rid the
world of evil.

**Federal Laws Against Hate Crimes.** There are a number of different types
of laws which victims of hate crimes can use against perpetrators. In the
last years of the twentieth century, most states enacted laws to deal specifically with these types of crimes. Several statutes also address these crimes
on a federal level. There are federal laws prohibiting conspiracies against
the rights of citizens, prohibiting a deprivation of rights under color of
law, and prohibiting damage to religious property and obstruction of
persons in the free exercise of their religious beliefs. In addition, there
are federal statutes that prohibit forcible interference with civil rights

and willful interference with civil rights under the fair housing laws. These federal statutes have rarely been applied to hate crimes for several reasons. First, if a president does not emphasize civil rights, the attorney general in that administration will not be likely to prosecute these crimes. Second, since most of these statutes require that the victim be engaged in an activity involving a federally protected right, such as buying a house or eating in a restaurant, they do not apply to many victims. Third, the remedies under the federal statutes are limited. Fourth, only certain groups, such as racial and religious groups, are protected under these statutes. Sexual orientation is not. Thus, the most active prosecution of hate crimes has been at the state level.

**State Laws Prohibiting Expressive Conduct.** On June 21, 1990, two young white men burned a cross on the property of a black family in St. Paul, Minnesota. One of the men, designated by his initials, R.A.V., because he was only seventeen at the time, was charged in accordance with a new city "bias-motivated" disorderly conduct ordinance which read, "Whoever places on public or private property, a symbol, appellation, characterization, or graffiti, including, but not limited to, a burning cross or Nazi swastika, which one knows or has reasonable grounds to know arouses anger, alarm or resentment in others on the basis of race, color, creed, religion, or gender commits disorderly conduct and shall be guilty of a misdemeanor." R.A.V. could have been charged with simple trespass, disorderly conduct, breach of the peace, or even a more severe crime such as terroristic threats. Instead, in what was to become a test case of the statute and others similar to it, the prosecutor decided to invoke this law, which punished the expression of a viewpoint.

R.A.V.'s attorney, Edward J. Cleary, decided to challenge the constitutionality of the law under the First Amendment to the Constitution. A Minnesota district court agreed that the ordinance was unconstitutional. The prosecutor decided to appeal the decision to the Minnesota Supreme Court. This court overturned the lower court ruling. R.A.V. appealed to the Supreme Court of the United States for a review of the case. On June 22, 1992, the Court issued a unanimous opinion in *R.A.V. v. City of St. Paul* declaring that the ordinance was unconstitutional. Five of the justices held that the ordinance was unconstitutional because it prohibited the expression of subject matter protected by the First Amendment.

Four of the justices said that the ordinance was overbroad in that it included in its proscriptions expression which was protected by the First Amendment. The entire Court thought that the city had other means by which to prosecute R.A.V. Thus, the Court concluded that, offensive as the action in which R.A.V. had engaged was, the action was protected under the Constitution to the extent that it was expressive conduct.

**State Hate Laws Prohibiting Conduct.** In 1991, a nineteen-year-old black man, Todd Mitchell, and his friends came out of a theater showing the film *Mississippi Burning* so enraged that, upon seeing a fourteen-year-old white youth (Gregory Riddick) on the street, they assaulted him. Coming out of the film, Mitchell said to others in his group, "Do you all feel hyped up to move on some white people?" Then, when Mitchell saw Riddick walking by, he added, "There goes a white boy—go get him." The group kicked and beat the boy for five minutes.

Riddick remained in a coma for four days before he returned to consciousness with probably permanent brain damage. Mitchell was convicted of aggravated battery, normally punishable by a maximum sentence of two years. Because the jury found that the crime was motivated by racial animus, however, the sentence was increased to seven years in accordance with a state statute which read, "If a person commits the crime of aggravated battery and intentionally selects the victim 'in whole or in part because of the actor's belief or perception regarding the race, religion, color, disability, sexual orientation or ancestry of that person,' the maximum sentence may be increased by not more than five years."

Within hours after the Supreme Court announced its opinion in *R.A.V.*, the Wisconsin Supreme Court struck down this law as unconstitutional. The state appealed the decision to the Supreme Court of the United States, and on June 11, 1993, in a unanimous opinion less than half the length of *R.A.V.*, the Supreme Court reversed the decision and held that "enhancement" laws such as this which punish hate-motivated conduct are constitutional. The Court, in *Wisconsin v. Mitchell*, distinguished this case from *R.A.V.* by stating that *R.A.V.* dealt with expression and this case with conduct.

The Court went on to state that with criminal acts, the more purposeful the conduct, the more severe is the punishment. Thus, when a defendant's beliefs add to a crime and motivate the defendant into action, the motive behind the conduct is relevant to the sentencing and punishment. Second, the Court stated that these enhancement laws are similar in aim to civil antidiscrimination laws and that they are justified because the conduct involved inflicts greater individual and societal harm than do other crimes.

Some commentators, such as Edward J. Cleary, who argued *R.A.V.* before the Supreme Court, view *Mitchell* with alarm and sense that these enhancement statutes come dangerously close to punishing a person's thoughts and thereby infringing upon First Amendment rights. He would question why those who attack a person of another race should, because they hate that race and express it, be subject to stricter laws than those who attack in silence. By upholding the enhancement laws, Cleary suggests, the Supreme Court blurred the lines between speech and action. Others believe that, because of the Court's emphasis on the analogy between these enhancement-type laws and antidiscrimination laws, these laws are constitutional. In sum, if a statute infringes upon expression, as in *R.A.V.*, it will be held unconstitutional; if a statute prohibits conduct, it will be upheld.

By 1991, thirty-five states had adopted some form of law to deter hate crimes. These laws, if they pass constitutional scrutiny, are not without practical problems. First, in many instances (as was the case in *R.A.V.*), prosecutors may wait to find the perfect case to fit the statute. The usefulness of the statute is thereby limited. Second, if there is a successful prosecution under the statute, there may be problems in carrying out a severe punishment. Most hate crime offenders are under twenty-one and do not have prior criminal records. Jails are overcrowded, and it seldom makes sense to jail the entire group involved in the crime. If only leaders are jailed, there is ample evidence that prison will make them worse.

*Jennifer Eastman*

# HICKLIN RULE

*Date:* 1868
*Issue:* Obscenity and pornography
*Relevant amendment:* First
*Significance:* The decision of the Court of Queen's Bench in *Regina v. Hicklin* established a test for obscenity known as the Hicklin rule that was long used not only in Great Britain, but in Canada and the United States

In 1857 Great Britain's Parliament passed Lord Campbell's Act, which gave magistrates the power to seize and destroy obscene material. The Hicklin case of 1868 tested that act. Henry Scott, a fervent Protestant, published a pamphlet, *The Confessional Unmasked*, that was an exposé of alleged depraved practices within the Roman Catholic church. Government magistrates seized 252 copies of the pamphlet and ordered their destruction. When Scott appealed, a court recorder named Hicklin revoked the order. When the government appealed Hicklin's decision, Chief Justice Alexander Cockburn of the Court of Queen's Bench reinstated the order for the pamphlets' destruction. In so doing he defined what was meant by obscenity:

> whether the tendency of the matter charged as obscenity is to deprave and corrupt those whose minds are open to such immoral influences and into whose hands a publication of this sort may fall.

This definition became known as the "Hicklin rule," or "Hicklin test." Though British in origin, it was used in U.S. courts until 1957. Because of the breadth of the Hicklin rule, obscenity prosecutions were easy to achieve in the United States for seventy-five years. Because it required only a "tendency" to deprave or corrupt, it swept broadly. Anyone could come under its scope. Furthermore, by merely hypothesizing into whose hands the material might fall, the rule extended its scope. The Hicklin rule expressly stated that it wanted to protect children. Thus, children who might tend to be depraved or corrupted, or into whose hands obscene materials might fall, were the main beneficiaries of the rule.

Such reasoning was, however, entirely hypothetical. Adult tastes and interests were simply not considered. Therefore under the Hicklin rule, the adult public could be reduced to reading what was deemed fit only for children, or the most susceptible persons. Furthermore, even if only a part of the material were considered obscene, the whole work could be pronounced obscene and thereby censored. Examples of works banned under this rule during its seventy-five year tenure in the United States include such popular novels as Ernest Hemingway's *For Whom the Bell Tolls* (1940) and James Jones's *From Here to Eternity*. In the 1957 American cases *Butler v. Michigan* and *Roth v. United States*, the U.S. Supreme Court changed the standard to preclude only that material so obscene that it might have a negative influence on the average person.

# INDIAN BILL OF RIGHTS

***Description:*** Popular name for the Indian Civil Rights Act of 1968 (ICRA), which extended most of the guarantees in the U.S. Bill of Rights, as well as other constitutional rights, to the tribal governments and courts of Native American societies.

***Relevant amendments:*** First through Tenth

***Significance:*** During the decade following passage of the Indian Bill of Rights, members of Indian tribes complained that the federal courts were applying the legislation in ways inconsistent with Native American cultural traditions. However, in 1978 the U.S. Supreme Court authorized the tribal courts to exercise final authority over its interpretation and enforcement.

In *Talton v. Meyers* (1896), the Supreme Court held that Native American tribes, in view of their quasi-sovereign status, were not bound by the Bill of Rights and other provisions of the U.S. Constitution, unless specified

*President Harry S. Truman meeting with Indian leaders at the signing of the Indian Claims Commission Act in 1946.* (Library of Congress)

otherwise by federal legislation. The Court recognized that Congress had plenary power to decide which constitutional rights, if any, were applicable to the tribal governments. Over the years, many people accused the tribal governments and tribal courts of arbitrary and despotic actions. Responding to these complaints, the Senate Judiciary Committee, under the leadership of Senator Sam Erwin, held extensive hearings and investigations, resulting in the enactment of the Indian Bill of Rights (IBR) under Title II of the Civil Rights Act of 1968.

The ten articles of the IBR contain most of the provisions enumerated in the first eight amendments of the U.S. Bill of Rights. Congress deliberately excluded a number of items in order not to interfere with the unique characteristics of the Indian tribes and their governmentss. The three most important excluded items are the First Amendment's disallowance of religious establishments, the Second Amendment's right to keep and bear arms, and the Seventh Amendment's right of jury trials in civil suits. The IBR recognizes the right of counsel before tribal courts but only at the defendant's "own expense." Although the IBR requires the tribes to provide "equal protection of the laws," it exempts the tribes from the Fifteenth Amendment's prohibition of using race as a qualification for voting. In addition, the IBR includes the original Constitution's ban on bills of attainder and ex post facto laws.

For ten years, a significant number of people went to the federal courts accusing tribal authorities of ignoring provisions of the IBR. Tribal lawyers often complained that federal judges were conditioned by Anglo-American views on individualism that were inconsistent with Native American culture. They also argued that the federal courts tended to disrespect established principles of tribal sovereignty.

In a gender-discrimination suit, *Santa Clara Pueblo v. Martinez* (1978), the U.S. Supreme Court held that the IBR did not authorize individuals to sue the tribes in federal courts because the Congress had not explicitly authorized such suits. The Court reasoned that the tribes, as "semi-sovereign nations," retained their rights to sovereign immunity unless "unequivocally" removed by federal legislation. The decision strengthened tribal self-determination, but at the cost of allowing tribal courts, if so inclined, to ignore most provisions of the IBR. As a result of the decision, the power of the federal courts to enforce the IBR was subsequently limited to *habeas corpus* relief for persons held in tribal custody. Advocates of women's rights have been especially unhappy with the outcome of the *Martinez* ruling.

**Further Reading**
Wunder, John. *"Retained by the People": A History of the Indian Bill of Rights.*
New York: Oxfore Univ. Press, 1994.

*Thomas T. Lewis*


# INDIGENT CRIMINAL DEFENDANTS

*Description:* Persons accused of crimes who, due to their poverty, are not
   able to adequately provide for their own defense.
*Relevant amendments:* Fifth, Sixth
*Significance:* In an adversary trial system, defendants who are not able to
   obtain legal representation, or pay other costs for their defense, will
   not receive a fair trial. The Supreme Court ruled in favor of appointment of counsel for these defendants in the 1960's.


Although social scientists have long debated the causes of crime, it is beyond dispute that the impact of the criminal justice system is felt most
heavily among the most economically disadvantaged members of society.
In city after city, young, unemployed men dominate the criminal dockets.
Nearly two out of three incarcerated individuals lack a high school di-
ploma, and less than 8 percent have ever attended college. Controversy
concerns whether poverty causes crime or merely funnels deviants into
relatively unremunerative and highly risky kinds of criminal activity,
where they are more likely to be apprehended. Another theory is that
these crime statistics reflect institutional class biases in the criminal justice system, such as the inability of the impoverished defendant to mount
an adequate defense. The commitment to equal justice under law is severely tested by a criminal justice system that imposes further disabilities
on the most disadvantaged members of the community.
   The Supreme Court noted in *Griffin v. Illinois* (1956), "There can be no
equal justice where the kind of trial a man gets depends on the amount of
money he has." This egalitarian impulse was most completely manifest in
right-to-counsel cases and seemed to peak during the late 1950's and
1960's. It was, however, tempered by considerations of federalism and
the realization that public aid to all indigent defendants would be expen-

*Scottsboro defendant Haywood Patterson, who escaped from prison fifteen years after he and his fellow defendants were convicted.* (National Archives)

sive and unpopular. In *Powell v. Alabama* (1932), also known as the Scottsboro case, the Court overturned rape convictions of seven itinerant African American youths. The youths were sentenced to death after one-day trials conducted in an atmosphere of racial hostility and at which they had been casually represented by an attorney unfamiliar with Alabama law who volunteered for the case on the morning of the trial. The Court found the trial to be fundamentally unfair. Adequate representation for such vulnerable defendants required the appointment, at public expense, of effective counsel with ample skill and time to prepare a credible defense. However, in *Betts v. Brady* (1942), the Court confined the right to appointed counsel in state prosecutions to cases in which special circumstances, not including mere poverty, rendered the defendant particularly vulnerable.

**The Right to Counsel.** In *Johnson v. Zerbst* (1938), the Court found that the Sixth Amendment required the appointment of counsel for all federal felony trials, a right not extended to state legal systems until *Gideon v. Wainwright* (1963). *Gideon* well illustrated the issues presented by the indigent defendant. An unemployed drifter with a poor education and a record of petty crimes, Gideon was denied appointed counsel at his trial for breaking and entering a pool hall and stealing change from a cigarette machine. Forced to defend himself, Gideon failed to explore several credible defenses or to adequately cross-examine the state's single—and dubious—witness. After the Court overturned his conviction, Gideon was tried a second time. At last represented by an attorney, he was acquitted.

The principle of *Gideon* was extended to other areas of the criminal process but not comprehensively. *Escobedo v. Illinois* (1964) and *Miranda v. Arizona* (1966) extended the right to appointed counsel into the pre-trial stages of the criminal process. *Griffin* required states to waive costs for filing appeals, in this case the expensive production of a trial transcript. The right to counsel was also extended to sentencing but only to the initial appeal. In *Ross v. Moffitt* (1974), the Court held that the state need not supply appointed counsel for discretionary appeals to the state supreme court. Presumably, no such right exists for appeals to the U.S. Supreme Court, although the Court has appointed counsel once a case is accepted for review. In *Gagnon v. Scarpelli* (1973), the "special circumstances" rule of *Betts* was revived for probation revocation hearings, requiring the appointment of counsel only for probationers who were unusually disadvantaged beyond their poverty.

Perhaps the clearest example of the Court's lessened favor of the appointment of counsel is *Argersinger v. Hamlin* (1972), in which the Court declined to extend the *Gideon* precedent to all misdemeanor cases. It ruled that the trial court needs to provide assistance of counsel only in cases in which the contemplated punishment is incarceration. Misdemeanor courts are known for their summary procedures, in which the mere presence of counsel often results in dismissal of charges. Because even conscientious judges operate under bureaucratic pressure to keep up with heavy caseloads, *Argersinger* is widely ignored in practice. Most misdemeanor defendants are unlikely to be incarcerated and are anxious to pay their fines and be done with it. For the indigent, however, even a modest fine can have a significant impact on his or her living standard.

**Questions of Fairness.** An issue yet to be effectively addressed involves the adequacy of counsel for poor defendants, whether appointed or retained. Many defendants are represented by court-appointed public defenders. Despite their talent and good intentions, public defenders tend to operate under the pressure of unrealistic caseloads and inadequate funding. Defendants who, like the Scottsboro men, first encounter their attorney just before trial are not unusual. Without time or resources to conduct a thorough investigation of the case, public defenders are often reduced to arranging a plea bargain. The economics of criminal defense work often place the private attorney in a similar position.

If access to judicial process is fundamental to the fair administration of criminal justice, it would be expected that the Court would facilitate the indigent's access to its own forum. The Court permits petitioners for certiorari to file *in forma pauperis*, or as a pauper. The resulting waiver of the Court's modest filing fees may be more symbolic than substantive, since less than 1 percent of such petitions are accepted for review. In the 1990's the numbers of *in forma pauperis* petitioners was the fastest growing segment of the Court's caseload, which came to account for more than half of all petitioners. Many of these are filed by prisoners alleging deficiencies in their convictions. Most are frivolous, although an occasional *in forma pauperis* petition, like that in *Gideon*, results in a significant decision. The Court now requires a person filing *in forma pauperis* to provide documentation of his or her impecunious circumstances.

### Further Reading

Casper, Jonathan. *American Criminal Justice: The Defendant's Perspective.* Englewood Cliffs, N.J.: Prentice-Hall, 1972.

Cole, David. *No Equal Justice: Race and Class in the American Criminal Justice System.* New York: New Press, 1999.

Feeley, Malcome. *The Process Is the Punishment: Handling Cases in Lower Criminal Court.* New York: Russell Sage, 1992.

Lewis, Anthony. *Gideon's Trumpet.* New York: Random House, 1989.

Reiman, Jeffrey H. *The Rich Get Richer and the Poor Get Prison: Ideology, Class, and Criminal Justice.* Needham, Mass.: Allyn & Bacon, 1997.

*John C. Hughes*


# JAPANESE AMERICAN RELOCATION

*Description:* The removal of more than 112,000 Japanese immigrants and their children, most of whom were U.S. citizens, to detention camps as a result of President Franklin D. Roosevelt's Executive Order 9066 in 1942.

*Relevant amendment:* Fifth

*Significance:* The removal of tens of thousands of U.S. citizens to detention camps and the restrictions placed on the movement of thousands
of others, purely on the basis of national origin, were found to be unconstitutional acts by the Supreme Court, though most of these wartime restrictions were not actually lifted until 1945.

In 1790 the Nationality Act established the standards to be used for U.S.
citizenship and naturalization. The law stated that only free white persons were eligible to become U.S. citizens. The primary intent of this law
was to create a legal distinction between people of African descent and
European immigrants. Although the law did not specifically address
Asian immigrants, whose numbers were almost insignificant at the time,
in practice those who entered were categorized as nonwhites and therefore denied citizenship.

After the Civil War, the Fourteenth Amendment (ratified in 1868) proclaimed that anyone born in, and subject to, the jurisdiction of the
United States would be a U.S. citizen. The intent of this amendment was
to grant citizenship to the black former slaves in the South. However, in
1870 Congress passed legislation to amend the naturalization law, effectively retaining the prohibition of citizenship for nonwhite immigrants.
The result was that only white people or people of African descent already in the United States could become naturalized citizens. Neither
Asian immigrants nor their U.S.-born children were granted these rights.

In 1898 the Supreme Court ruled in the *United States v. Wong Kim Ark*
that anyone born in the United States could became a citizen. This decision was the result of a three-year lawsuit by an American-born Chinese
man, Wong Kim Ark, who was detained and prevented from reentering
the United States after returning from a trip to China. Although this decision upheld birthright citizenship for all U.S.-born Asians, the Supreme
Court still acknowledged the power of Congress to restrict naturalization.
In *Ozawa v. United States* (1922), the Court rejected the application for citizenship of Takao Ozawa, who had been raised and educated in the
United States but was born in Japan, judging him ineligible for naturalization because he was nonwhite.

Also in 1922, Congress passed the Cable Act. This law provided that
"any woman citizen who marries an alien ineligible to citizenship shall
cease to be a citizen of the United States." The justification for this act was
that civil law generally recognized a husband's citizenship over the wife's.

An Asian American or white woman with U.S. citizenship who married an Asian immigrant lost her citizenship. If the marriage terminated by divorce or death, the white woman was eligible to reapply for citizenship, but the Asian American woman could not. The law was amended in 1931 to permit Asian American women married to Asian immigrants to retain or regain their U.S. citizenship, but it was repealed in 1936.

**The Seeds of Relocation.** After the first Japanese arrived in Hawaii in 1868, many workers immigrated to the island. Immigration to the U.S. mainland, however, largely remained limited to wealthier, more highly educated Japanese. After Hawaii became an American possession in 1898, the number of laborers who reached the mainland increased significantly. In 1899, 2,844 Japanese arrived on the mainland, but two years later, in 1900, 12,635 Japanese entered the continental United States. Many white Americans viewed the influx of Japanese and Chinese immigrants as an economic and cultural threat, and racial tensions grew, especially on the West Coast where most Asian immigrants had settled. Pressure from the western states forced the federal government to restrict Japanese immigration by means such as the Gentlemen's Agreement with Japan (1908).

The Gentlemen's Agreement prohibited immigration by Japanese men; however, it permitted the wives of immigrants already in the country to enter. Ironically, the agreement actually increased immigration because immigrant men believed that they must immediately send for their wives in Japan or risk permanent separation. Many single men hurriedly sent pictures of themselves to Japan to find wives or asked relatives and friends to send pictures of prospective brides willing to come to the United States. Thus, many Japanese women, while still in Japan, married Japanese men living in the United States without ever seeing more than a photo; these "picture brides" crossed the ocean by themselves with visas sent by their husbands in the United States. To stem this great influx, Congress passed the Immigration Exclusion Act of 1924, virtually barring any further Japanese immigration.

**World War II.** Immediately after Japan bombed Pearl Harbor in 1941, Lieutenant General John L. DeWitt (military commander of the western defense zone) suggested removal of all persons of Japanese ancestry—citizens or aliens—from all West Coast states. Many Japanese Americans' homes were searched by Federal Bureau of Investigation agents, and

*Internee resting in a typical barracks room at the government's Manzanar camp in California's eastern Sierras.* (National Archives)

within four days, 1,370 Japanese immigrants had been taken from their homes and places of business with no warning. Less than a month after Pearl Harbor, the Treasury Department froze the financial assets of Japanese nationals and bank accounts registered under Japanese-sounding names. Although the Treasury Department soon eased these restrictions, Japanese Americans were not allowed to withdraw more than one hundred dollars per month from the bank. The federal government also seized money from Japanese American clubs and organizations; for example, in 1942 the government took seventy thousand dollars from the Japanese Association of New York, returning fifty thousand of it in 1953.

In February, 1942, just one week after DeWitt submitted the final recommendation for relocation, President Franklin D. Roosevelt signed Executive Order 9066, which sent 112,350 people of Japanese descent to detention camps, describing them as either "enemy aliens" or "strangers from a distant shore." This order applied only to the mainland; in Hawaii, where one-third of the population was of Japanese ancestry, no restrictions were ever enacted. In March of 1942, the draft status of Japanese Americans was reclassified, and men of military age were exempted under a 4-F classification, which implied that being of Japanese ancestry was a physical defect, eliminating the possibility of military service. In 1943, however, the government changed this policy, making Japanese American men subject to the draft. By the end of the war in 1945, almost 40,000 Japanese Americans served in the U.S. armed services, several thousand of them coming from the detention camps.

**Supreme Court Decisions.** Japanese Americans soon questioned the legality of the executive order and other government policies. Some objected to the loss of property on the grounds of due process; some questioned the right of the government to restrict the liberty and movement of U.S. citizens; and others disputed the moral authority of the government to force men in detention centers to join the military. Most of these challenges were eventually heard by the Supreme Court, though the Court itself avoided acting on the constitutionality of exclusion and actual detention until near the war's end.

Min (Minoru) Yasui, a Japanese American lawyer and U.S. citizen, doubted the legality of the curfews for Japanese Americans that were imposed soon after the start of the war. He deliberately violated a curfew in Portland in 1942 to force the courts to hear this issue. After he was arrested, his U.S. citizenship was taken away because he had studied in a Japanese language school and had worked for the Japanese consulate. Though a lower court found the curfew unconstitutional, the Supreme Court in *Yasui v. the United States* (1943) reversed this finding, claiming that the government possessed extraordinary powers in time of war, especially in the light of Japanese Americans' "continued attachment" to Japan. The same year, Gordon Hirabayashi, also a U.S. citizen of Japanese descent, was arrested for violating curfew. Hirabayashi turned himself in to the Seattle office of the Federal Bureau of Investigation for failing to report for imprisonment. After Hirabayashi had spent five months in jail, the Supreme Court, in *Hirabayashi v. United States* (1943), unanimously upheld the constitutionality of the curfew. He was ordered to serve another ninety days of work on a government road crew.

In October, 1944, in *Korematsu v. United States*, the Court upheld the constitutionality of the exclusion order by a 6-3 vote. Fred Korematsu, a U.S. citizen of Japanese descent, was arrested for trying to avoid incarceration in a detention camp. He had plastic surgery done on his nose and eyelids to look less Japanese and changed his name to Clyde Sarah, a Spanish-Hawaiian sounding name. Unlike Yasui and Hirabayashi, Korematsu did not wish to create a test case; he just wanted to stay with his fiancé who was not of Japanese ancestry.

In July, 1942, attorney James Purcell filed a writ of *habeas corpus* with the federal court in San Francisco on behalf of Mitsuye Endo, an American-born civil service employee. Although the cases of Yasui, Hirabayashi, and Korematsu challenged the curfews and exclusion orders, Endo's case challenged the legality of the detention camps themselves. At first, lower courts found against Endo. However, after a two-year struggle, in December, 1944, in *Ex parte Endo*, the Supreme Court set her free, saying that because she had been found to be a loyal citizen, the War Relocation Authority could not detain her against her will. The Court, thus, ruled that detention of citizens was unconstitutional and loyal U.S. citizens of Japanese descent were free to move anywhere in the United States.

In spite of the federal government's discriminatory treatment of Japanese Americans, the Court's decisions showed progress toward protecting this group's rights. For example, Fred Oyama, a U.S. citizen of Japanese descent became the titleholder of land in California that his immigrant parents were prohibited from owning because of the California Alien Land Act of 1913. While the Oyama family was in the detention camps, the state government attempted to seize the land, and Fred Oyama sued under the equal protection clause. The Supreme Court's 6-3 decision in *Oyama v. California* (1948) supported Oyama, stating that "the rights of a citizen may not be subordinated merely because of his father's country of origin."

These various wartime Supreme Court decisions were instrumental in establishing equal rights for Japanese Americans. By the early 1950's most state and local alien land acts and other discriminatory ordinances against Japanese had been repealed. However, these decisions also represent a substantial cost to all Americans' constitutional liberties. As was evident in the Yasui, Hirabayashi, and Korematsu decisions, the guarantees of due process in the Constitution are not unambiguous. If the government can claim military necessity, the Court may uphold the restriction of individual liberties.

**The Legacy of Evacuation.** One-third of the people interned by the War Relocation Authority were not American citizens. This lack of citizenship does not necessarily indicate a lack of allegiance to or intent to remain in the United States, however, because Japan-born immigrants were not eligible to naturalize regardless of their wishes. Although Chinese immigrants were allowed to naturalize in 1943, and Indians and Filipinos in 1946, Japanese were not permitted to gain citizenship until the McCarran-Walter Act in 1952.

In the late 1960's, Japanese American groups in San Francisco, Southern California, and Seattle began to agitate for compensation for the detention and subsequent losses suffered during World War II. After much legal paperwork and protest, in 1988 Japanese Americans were recognized as being guilty of nothing but being of the wrong ancestry at the wrong time. Abe Fortas, who had overseen the War Relocation Authority while undersecretary of the interior, called the evacuation "a tragic error." By 1993 some sixty thousand surviving Japanese American former detainees received compensation in the amount of twenty thousand dollars per person.

**Further Reading**

Perhaps the best place to begin the study of the legal aspects of the Japanese American incarceration is Angelo N. Ancheta's *Race, Rights, and The Asian American Experience* (New Brunswick: Rutgers University Press, 1998). Ancheta, a civil rights attorney, covers legal issues historically, looking at both Japanese Americans and other Asian Americans in the United States. Masako Herman's *The Japanese in America 1843-1973* (New York: Oceania Publications, 1974) is highly recommended for its chronology of Japanese American lawsuits and documentation on the various laws, acts, and orders. *Democracy on Trial: The Japanese American Evacuation and Relocation in World War II* (New York: Simon & Schuster, 1995) by Page Smith helps link military, political, economic, racial, and personal motivations of the relocation. Paul R. Spickard's *Japanese Americans: The Formation and Transformations of an Ethnic Group* (New York: Twayne, 1996) reports in detail demographic data historically for each state. Roger Daniels has made a good connection between Chinese and Japanese experiences in the United States in his *Asian America: Chinese and Japanese in the United States Since 1850* (Seattle: University of Washington Press, 1988), as does Sucheng Chan in *Asian Americans: An Interpretive History* (New York: Twayne, 1991).

*Nobuko Adachi*

# JUDICIAL SCRUTINY

*Description:* Standard by which the Supreme Court evaluates the constitutionality of certain governmental actions. The three levels of judicial
scrutiny are strict scrutiny, intermediate (or heightened) scrutiny, and
ordinary (or minimum) scrutiny.
*Relevant amendments:* First through Tenth
*Significance:* These levels of judicial scrutiny and their consistent usage by
the Court enable institutions and citizens alike to feel comfortable
that similar cases will be adjudicated in similar ways.

The Supreme Court employs tests, or standards of review, with the aim of
giving parties to a specific case some reasonable expectation as to the outcome of their particular constitutional claims. The use of standards permits each party to know, prior to the actual hearing, how the judiciary will
probably approach the case and how the judiciary is likely to resolve any
single issue. Variations in levels of review also signify the Court's willingness to provide (through more rigorous tests) increased judicial protection for "discreet and insular minorities," as it did in *United States v.
Carolene Products Co.* (1938). These tests can take many forms and can be
used in many different constitutional inquiries, but the most common
tests are those that involve the Court's scrutinizing governmental activity.

**The Three Levels.** The Court uses three levels of judicial scrutiny. The
lowest standard of review is defined as ordinary, or minimal, scrutiny.
Here, the burden to demonstrate a violation of the Constitution falls on
the individual, as the Court presumes the governmental action in question is constitutional. When applying an ordinary level of scrutiny, the
Court employs the rational basis test, which asks the government to demonstrate that the action is reasonably related to a legitimate governmental objective. If the government can do so, then the Court will reject the
argument of the petitioner and the action will be deemed constitutional.
The Court regularly uses ordinary scrutiny in cases involving economic
regulation, such as *Williamson v. Lee Optical Co.* (1955), and ones in which
the legislative classification does not warrant increased judicial protection, such as *Massachusetts Board of Retirement v. Murgia* (1976).

An intermediate, or heightened, level of scrutiny is applied by the
Court when a government action potentially discriminates on the basis of

gender or illegitimacy and therefore violates the equal protection clause of the Fourteenth Amendment. The impetus for applying a more rigorous test in the areas of gender and illegitimacy stems from the perception that these groups require additional—or heightened—judicial protection due to their status as (numerical or de facto) minorities. Because of the heightened nature of the review, the Court does not adopt the presumption of constitutionality standard found in the ordinary level of scrutiny but instead mandates that the government demonstrate more than simply a reasonable purpose for the law. Intermediate review requires that the government identify an important governmental objective that is substantially furthered by that particular action.

*Craig v. Boren* (1976) is the principal case that formally introduced an intermediate level of scrutiny. In *Craig*, the Court addressed the issue of gender discrimination by reviewing an Oklahoma statute that prohibited the sale of 3.2 percent beer to women under the age of eighteen and men under the age of twenty-one. In an opinion written by Justice William J. Brennan, Jr., the Court ruled that under the newly instituted intermediate standard of review, the Oklahoma legislature could not satisfy the requirements set up by the test. The law treating men differently from women, Brennan argued, "did not serve important governmental objectives and [was not] substantially related to [the] achievement of those objectives."

The third level of judicial scrutiny is the most difficult for the government to satisfy. Strict scrutiny refers to the standard used by the Court when assessing the constitutionality of governmental actions that may interfere with fundamental rights or potentially discriminate on racial grounds. In the area of racial discrimination, the Court, in *Korematsu v. United States* (1944), noted that "all legal restrictions which curtail the civil rights of a single racial group are immediately suspect. That is not to say that all such restrictions are unconstitutional. It is to say that courts must subject them to the most rigid scrutiny." As such, the Court adopts a presumption of unconstitutionality when applying this most rigorous test; it asks the government to articulate a compelling reason for discriminating based on race or impinging on a fundamental right. Additionally, the Court insists that the government action be closely related to the state's compelling objective. If the government is going to discriminate based on racial classifications or regulate one of the most fundamental freedoms, the Court demands that it have an extraordinarily important reason for doing so. Needless to say, very few governmental actions have ever satisfied the strict scrutiny test.

**Some Guidelines.** Distinctions between differing levels of review—and the subsequent application of the actual tests—are not always easy to define. The difference between an important governmental objective and a legitimate one or between means that are closely related and ones that are merely substantially related are not always clear. However, the Court has provided some guidelines for the application of the various tests. A compelling governmental interest is one that is of paramount importance, and a close relationship is one in which the Court is satisfied that there is no alternative, that the government has no option but to interfere with a fundamental right or discriminate based on race.

*Korematsu v. United States* (1944) provides the most cited example. The case involved the Court's review of the constitutionality of President Franklin D. Roosevelt's executive order mandating that people of Japanese ancestry on the West Coast adhere to certain restrictions on their freedom (including curfews, detentions, and relocations) during the early part of World War II. In upholding the order, the Court claimed that a "pressing public necessity" may justify the violation of certain freedoms and discrimination against certain groups. Although the Court applied the strict scrutiny test, the government cited national security as a

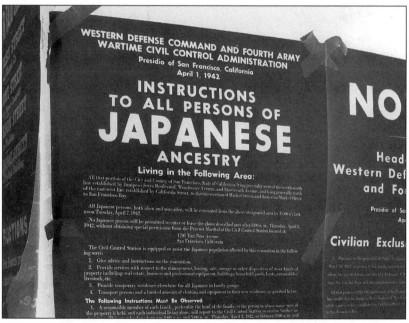

*Relocation order posted in San Francisco in April, 1942.* (National Archives)

compelling reason for detaining Japanese Americans. Additionally, the government claimed that in order to maintain national security during such a major conflict, it had no alternative but to restrict the extension of some basic freedoms to a group of Americans. *Korematsu* is the only case in which the Court applied the strict scrutiny test to a racially based restriction and upheld the law.

### Further Reading

Chemerinsky, Erwin. "Breakdown in the Levels of Scrutiny." *Trial* 33 (March, 1997): 70-71.

Coffin, Elizabeth Buroker. "Constitutional Law: Content-based Regulations on Speech, a Comparison of the Categorization and Balancing Approaches to Judicial Scrutiny." *University of Dayton Law Review* 18 (Winter, 1993): 593-633.

Levinson, Sanford. "Tiers of Scrutiny—from Strict Through Rational Bases—and the Future of Interests: Commentary on Fiss and Linde. *Albany Law Review* 55 (1992): 745-761.

Shaman, Jeffrey M. "Cracks in the Structure: The Coming Breakdown of the Levels of Scrutiny." *Ohio State Law Journal.* 45 (1984): 161-183.

Wexler, Jay D. "Defending the Middle Way: Intermediate Scrutiny as Judicial Minimalism." *George Washington Law Review* 66 (January, 1998): 298-352.

*Beau Breslin*

# JURY, TRIAL BY

*Description:* Legal process in which a group of citizens sworn as jurors hears evidence presented at trial and then collectively decides on the accused's culpability for a crime or civil offense.

*Relevant amendments:* Sixth, Seventh

*Significance:* Supreme Court rulings affirm the importance of trial by jury as a protection against government oppression of the accused and as an avenue for citizen participation in the democratic process.

Article III, section 2, of the U.S. Constitution provides the right to trial by jury for all crimes except impeachment, and the Seventh Amendment grants this right in civil cases involving twenty dollars or more. The Sixth

Amendment provides the right to be tried by an impartial jury.

In *Palko v. Connecticut* (1937), the Supreme Court interpreted these constitutional provisions as applicable only in federal trials, reasoning that trial by jury was not a fundamental right and therefore was not applicable to the states through the Fourteenth Amendment's due process clause. This meant states were not required to provide jury trials but could choose to do so.

The Court reversed its position in *Duncan v. Louisiana* (1968), ruling that trial by jury in criminal cases is a fundamental right applicable to the states. The Court's reasoning in *Duncan* emphasized the importance of jury trials as part of due process and as a significant aspect of participatory democracy. In subsequent cases, the Court clarified the scope of the right to trial by jury, finding it applicable in any case involving a minimum possible sentence of six months of incarceration and in some cases with a shorter penalty. However, the Court did not extend the Seventh Amendment requirement of trial by jury in civil cases to the states, instead leaving state governments to decide this.

Despite the Court's recognition of the importance of trial by jury, minors in the juvenile justice system lack this right. The Court, in the case *In re Gault* (1967), reasoned that because juvenile court proceedings are not adversarial (in contrast to adult courts), jury trials are not necessary. However, juveniles tried in adult court gain the right to trial by jury.

Historically, jurors had the right to decide questions of both law and fact, but in *Sparf and Hansen v. United States* (1899), the Court restricted jurors to deciding issues of fact. In their capacity as fact finders, jurors in criminal trials decide whether the prosecution has proven beyond a reasonable doubt that the defendant is guilty as charged, a requirement the Court noted in *In re Winship* (1970) that is intended to protect against erroneous convictions. Jurors in most civil cases use the less stringent "preponderance of the evidence" standard. In *Witherspoon v. Illinois* (1968), the Court emphasized the role of jurors as the conscience of the community.

**Further Reading**

Abramson, Jeffrey. *We, the Jury*. New York: Basic Books, 1994.

Finkel, Norman J. *Commonsense Justice: Jurors' Notions of the Law*. Cambridge, Mass.: Harvard University Press, 1995.

Kalven, Harry, Jr., and Hans Zeisel. *The American Jury*. Chicago: University of Chicago Press, 1970.

Litan, Robert E., ed. *Verdict: Assessing the Civil Jury System*. Washington, D.C.: Brookings Institution, 1993.

*Diana R. Grant*

# JURY COMPOSITION AND SIZE

*Description:* Composition and number of members in a jury, a group of citizens brought together to hear testimony and determine a verdict in a trial.

*Relevant amendment:* Sixth

*Significance:* The Supreme Court shapes how the right to trial by jury occurs in practice, addressing key issues such as jury selection procedures, composition, size, and decision rule.

The right to trial by jury is guaranteed by Article III of the U.S. Constitution as well as by the Sixth, Seventh, and Fourteenth Amendments. Although the right to jury trial is largely immune to legislation, the particulars, including jury size, selection, and composition, are not as firmly fixed, and therefore, have been the subject of legislation and challenges in the Supreme Court.

A common method of jury selection before 1968 was the "key man" system, relying on prominent citizens in the community to serve. This meant many citizens were excluded from jury duty, despite being legally eligible. As early as 1880 in *Strauder v. West Virginia*, the Court had struck down a state law excluding African American men from jury duty as a violation of equal protection. Nonetheless, the practice of excluding minorities from jury service continued unacknowledged by the Court, as illustrated by its decision in *Swain v. Alabama* (1965) allowing exclusion of potential jurors on the basis of race. Similarly, although women became eligible for jury duty between 1870 and 1940 (depending on locale), most states continued to exclude women from jury pools (the groups from which jurors are drawn). The Court addressed this in *Taylor v. Louisiana* (1975), striking down the practice of including women in jury pools only if they volunteered.

In 1968 Congress enacted the Jury Selection and Service Act, requiring that federal jury pools be made up of citizens drawn at random "from a representative cross section of the community." In *Taylor*, the Court extended this requirement to states. The random selection requirement substantially changed the methods used to create jury pools but did not address how individual jurors were selected during jury questioning.

However, the new focus on inclusiveness raised new jury selection and composition questions for the Court, leading it to revise its earlier position in *Swain* on the use of peremptory challenges. In a series of cases, the Court ruled that peremptories cannot be used to exclude potential jurors solely on the basis of race (*Batson v. Kentucky*, 1986) or gender (*J. E. B. v. Alabama ex rel. T. B.*, 1994). In *Holland v. Illinois* (1990), the Court clarified that it is the process of selecting the jury pool that must be representative rather than the juries themselves.

The Court noted that the use of twelve-person juries and the unanimous decision rule are simply historical customs rather than legal requirements. Nonetheless, it supported the tradition of jury unanimity until 1972, when it allowed majority verdicts in state criminal trials (*Apodaca v. Oregon*; *Johnson v. Louisiana*). States can also use majority decision rules in civil cases; however, federal criminal and civil cases retain a unanimity requirement.

In *Williams v. Florida* (1970), the Court allowed six-person juries in state criminal cases, provided they use a unanimous decision rule. The Court's reasoning noted the lower costs of smaller juries but misconstrued the implications of research examining the influence of jury size on deliberations. The Court set the minimum jury size by rejecting five-person juries in *Ballew v. Georgia* (1978).

**Further Reading**

Abramson, Jeffrey. *We, the Jury*. New York: Basic Books, 1994.
Fukurai, Hiroshi, E. Butler, and R. Krooth. *Race and the Jury*. New York: Plenum, 1993.
Hans, Valerie, and Neil Vidmar. *Judging the Jury*. New York: Plenum, 1987.

*Diana R. Grant*

# LIBEL

*Description:* Printed or broadcast defamation, which entails false statements holding an individual up to ridicule, contempt, or hatred, or causing an individual to be avoided by others.
*Relevant amendment:* First

***Significance:*** Libel law is an attempt to balance individuals' interest in reputation against the media's freedom of the press. In 1964 the Supreme Court began to shift from favoring individuals to favoring the media in cases involving libel.

Victims of libel, or defamatory false statements, sue the media for damages. Courts award monetary compensation to victims for the injury they suffered and stipulate punitive measures to chastise the press and thereby deter it and media companies from libeling others. The Supreme Court long considered defamatory statements irrelevant to the First Amendment because the statements did not contribute to the exposition of ideas and search for truth envisioned by those who wrote the amendment. The limited value of the statements was outweighed by the need to protect individuals' reputation. Therefore, the Court allowed states to fashion libel law as they saw fit, and it rarely heard libel cases. One exception was *Beauharnais v. Illinois* (1952), which involved "group libel" (later called "hate speech"). The Court upheld the law.

**Actual Malice.** In *New York Times Co. v. Sullivan* (1964), the Court, under Chief Justice Earl Warren, began to shift the balance in libel doctrine toward the media. In the early 1960's, the police commissioner of Montgomery, Alabama, sued *The New York Times* for printing an ad, with minor inaccuracies, bought by black clergymen protesting the treatment of civil rights demonstrators in the city. Although the ad did not mention the police commissioner by name or title, he claimed that it attacked him implicitly. Although he did not claim that it caused him any injury, he did not have to under state law, and the jury awarded him half a million dollars. Another county commissioner sued *The New York Times* for the same ad and was also awarded half a million dollars. By the time the case reached the Court, eleven more libel suits had been brought by local or state officials in Alabama against *The New York Times* or the Columbia Broadcasting Service for seven million dollars. There was nothing unusual about Alabama's law, which resembled other states' laws. The justices, then, could see that libel laws could be used by public officials to punish the press for criticism—in this case, a northern newspaper for coverage of southern race relations—even if the inaccuracies were minor and the officials suffered no real injury.

The Court's ruling made it harder for plaintiffs who were public officials to win libel suits. It established the actual malice test, which requires plaintiffs to prove that the defamatory statements were made with knowledge of their falsity or with reckless disregard for their truth or falsity. This standard is somewhat ambiguous, but the Court made clear that recklessness is beyond carelessness, which is the usual basis for establishing negligence in lawsuits. Despite its name, the test does not revolve around the everyday meaning of the word "malice." The plaintiff does not have to show maliciousness; and even if the plaintiff does show maliciousness, this showing by itself does not meet the test. A reporter can be "out to get" an official, publish defamatory statements, and still not be found guilty of actual malice. Maliciousness is relevant only if it helps the official prove that the reporter knew the statements were false or published them with reckless disregard for their truth or falsity.

The Court recognized that this test would allow the press to publish more false statements but insisted that this result was necessary to allow breathing room so the press can enjoy its full rights under the First Amendment.

**Application of the Test.** The Court solidified its ruling by applying the actual malice test to an array of public officials, including judges (*Garrison v. Louisiana,* 1964); county attorneys (*Henry v. Collins,* 1965), court clerks (*Beckley Newspapers v. Hanks,* 1967), and law enforcement officers, including police on the beat (*St. Amant v. Thompson,* 1968, and *Time v. Pape,* 1971). In applying the test to the manager of a small county-owned and operated ski area, the Court showed how far down the ranks of public employees its definition of public officials would extend. The Court also solidified its ruling by indicating that reckless disregard meant having serious doubts about the truth of the statements in *St. Amant.* Even being extremely sloppy would not be considered reckless.

At the same time, the Warren Court extended its ruling by applying the actual malice test to public figures in 1967 in *Curtis Publishing Co. v. Butts* and *Associated Press v. Walker.* Public figures are people who are well known or who have sought public attention. The Court's justifications were that the distinction between the public and private sectors has blurred and that public figures, like public officials, often play an influential role in society and also have sufficient access to the media to rebut any false accusations against them. This ruling made it harder for public figures to win libel suits.

The Warren Court classified as public figures a university athletic director, who was not paid by the state and therefore not a public official

(*Curtis*) and a retired air force general (*Associated Press*). The Court, under Chief Justice Warren E. Burger, classified as public figures a real estate developer who was engaged in a controversy with the local school board (*Greenbelt Cooperative Publishing v. Bresler*, 1970) and candidates for public office (*Monitor Patriot Co. v. Roy*, 1971, and *Ocala Star-Banner v. Damron*, 1971).

A plurality of the early Burger Court sought to extend *The New York Times* doctrine by applying the actual malice test to private persons embroiled in public issues (*Rosenbloom v. Metromedia*, 1971). They maintained that people are all public persons to some degree and that public officials and public figures are private persons in some ways. The key was whether public issues were involved. If so, the press should feel free to report on these issues for the public's benefit. The plurality's views, if adopted by a majority of the justices, would have made it harder for private persons to win libel suits.

As more holdovers from the Warren Court retired from the Burger Court, the new majority concluded that the balance had tipped too far toward the First Amendment and away from guarding the reputations of private persons. In 1974 a majority ruled that private persons, even if embroiled in public controversies, would not have to meet the actual malice test to win compensatory damages. (States could set the exact standard, but plaintiffs would have to show at least negligence by the press.) However, they would still have to prove actual malice to win punitive damages (*Gertz v. Robert Welch*, 1974). The justices sympathized with private persons' desires to be compensated for any injuries they suffered but not their efforts to be awarded additional, punitive damages, which often were sizable and unrelated to the severity of the injuries.

With this ruling, the Burger Court completed the process of nationalizing and constitutionalizing libel law—making the law conform to certain national constitutional standards, rather than allowing it to develop through the process of state common law—that the Warren Court began in *The New York Times*.

The Burger Court also began to define the public figure category narrowly. The Court held that plaintiffs could be considered public figures if they have general fame or notoriety to the people exposed to the defamatory statements. In *Gertz*, a lawyer who was well known in legal and civic circles in Chicago was not known by the general population of the city, so he was not deemed a public figure. A socialite in Palm Beach, Florida, who was so prominent that she subscribed to a local clipping service, was not known outside of her community, so she was not deemed a public figure in a lawsuit against a national publication (*Time v. Firestone*, 1976). Alternatively, the Court held that plaintiffs could be considered public figures if they thrust themselves into a public controversy. However, a lawyer who represented a family who sued a police officer in a controversial case (*Gertz*) and a scientist who applied for federal funds for research (*Hutchinson v. Proxmire*, 1979) were not classified as public figures. The Court ruled that they were doing their jobs rather than thrusting themselves into public controversies. Thus, these plaintiffs, as private persons, did not need to meet the actual malice test to win compensatory damages.

The Burger Court also clarified the point that public issues must be involved before the constitutional standards developed in libel cases could be invoked by the defendants in libel suits. Dun and Bradstreet, which had issued an inaccurate credit report, argued that as a widely known company, it should be considered a public figure (and, therefore, the plaintiff would be forced to prove actual malice). However, the Court insisted that this was a private dispute, rather than a public issue, and as such Dun and Bradstreet was not entitled to any First Amendment protection in *Dun and Bradstreet v. Greenmoss Builders* (1985).

**The Rehnquist Court.** Under the guidance of Chief Justice William H. Rehnquist, the Court held that companies can be considered public figures if the dispute involves a public issue. Bose Corporation sued *Consumer Reports* for a magazine article critical of the sound of Bose speakers. The article addressed a subject of interest to the public, so it was considered a public issue and Bose Corporation was deemed a public figure (*Bose Corp. v. Consumers Union of the United States*, 1984).

Although the Rehnquist Court reversed or eroded many rulings made by the Warren and Burger Courts, it maintained protection for media defendants in decisions involving the burden of proof in libel suits in *Philadelphia Newspapers v. Hepps* (1986) and *Anderson v. Liberty Lobby* (1986) and the attempt to circumvent libel law by suing for torts that have easier standards for plaintiffs in *Hustler Magazine v. Falwell* (1988). In *Masson v. New Yorker Magazine* (1991) the Court gave leeway to reporters, when quoting individuals, to clarify or condense direct quotations as long as reporters do not materially alter the meaning of the statements.

For statements to be considered defamatory, they must be capable of being proven false. The Rehnquist Court found that they must have been asserted as facts, rather than mere opinions in *Milkovich v. Lorain Journal Co.* (1990). Accordingly, it found that parodies cannot be defamatory, even if they humiliate their subjects in *Hustler Magazine v. Falwell.*

The Supreme Court's doctrinal changes beginning in 1964 reduced the total number of libel suits filed and also the success rate for plaintiffs who are public officials or figures. Only one out of ten of these plaintiffs wins his or her suit.

**Further Reading**

Anthony Lewis's *Make No Law* (New York: Random House, 1991) is a readable case study of *New York Times Co. v. Sullivan.* Harry Kalven, one of the foremost First Amendment scholars at the time, analyzed the landmark case in "The *New York Times* Case: A Note on 'The Central Meaning of the First Amendment,'" *Supreme Court Review* (1964): 191. James Kirby's *Fumble* (New York: Dell, 1986) is a fascinating case study of *Curtis Publishing Co. v. Butts.* Kirby, a lawyer hired by the Southeastern Conference to investigate the allegations that gave rise to the suit—that two college coaches conspired to fix a football game between their teams—reports his conclusions. Renata Adler's *Reckless Disregard* (New York: Alfred A. Knopf, 1986) examines a pair of prominent cases that never reached the Supreme Court—the libel suits of U.S. general William Westmoreland against the Columbia Broadcasting Service and Israeli general Ariel Sharon against *Time* magazine. The decisions of juries in these and other libel suits are examined in *Trial by Jury* (New York: Simon & Schuster, 1990), edited by Stephen Brill, which shows the difficulty jurors have when asked to apply the actual malice test. The impact of the Court's decisions involving public officials and figures is analyzed in Randall Bezanson, Gilbert Cranberg, and John Soloski's *Libel Law and the Press* (New York: Free Press, 1987). Proposed reforms in libel law are addressed in Lois Forer's *A Chilling Effect* (New York: Norton, 1988).

*John Gruhl*

# LOYALTY OATHS

*Description:* Sworn promises not to be disloyal to the government

*Relevant amendment:* First

*Significance:* During the 1940's, 1950's, and 1960's loyalty oaths served as a form of censorship to suppress "subversive" speech by public employees, teachers, and union leaders

In the late 1940's, when many U.S. government officials and other public employees were suspected of harboring communist sympathies, the federal government and many state governments began requiring loyalty oaths to be administered to those working on the public payroll. These oaths were first used by the administration of President Harry S. Truman, who issued Executive Order 9835 on March 21, 1947, creating the Loyalty Review Board to coordinate loyalty policies. The board was empowered to dismiss workers or refuse to hire anyone who might be disloyal to the government.

Initially, Congress allowed only dismissals from limited numbers of executive departments, such as State and Defense (and, later, Treasury, Commerce, and Justice). Under Truman's successor, President Dwight D. Eisenhower, the policy extended to all executive branch departments. Eisenhower also tightened the loyalty program through Executive Order 10540, under which anyone suspected of disloyalty was required to prove otherwise.

**Decisions Upholding Loyalty Oaths.** The first instance in which such an oath was challenged in court occurred in 1950 in *American Communications Association v. Douds.* The challenge arose from a section of the Labor Management Relations Act of 1947 mandating that in order for a labor union to benefit from national labor laws, all officers had to sign affidavits stating that they were not Communist Party members and did not believe in the party's goals. The U.S. Supreme Court, in an opinion written by Chief Justice Fred M. Vinson, ruled 5-1 that the law was in the purview of Congress through its power to regulate interstate commerce. Only Justice Hugo L. Black dissented, stating that the law violated the First Amendment's bans on regulation of speech and assembly.

The next year three more cases came before the Court challenging loyalty oaths. In April, in *Joint Anti-Fascist Refugee Committee v. McGrath* (1951), the authority of the U.S. attorney general to list organizations that were deemed subversive was declared constitutional. The Court, however, also decided that the attorney general had exceeded his bounds in including three groups, the Joint Anti-Fascist Refugee Committee, the National Council of American-Soviet Friendship, and the International Workers Order, on the list without allowing them a hearing. The Court recognized this as a due-process case and avoided ruling on any First Amendment issue.

The Court also rendered 1951 decisions in *Gerende v. Board of Supervi-*

sors of Elections and *Garner v. Public Works of the City of Los Angeles.* The former concerned a Maryland law that required candidates running for public office to sign affidavits affirming that they had no intention of plotting a government overthrow. The law was upheld by the Court in a 7-2 decision, with only Black and William O. Douglas dissenting. In the majority opinion, Justice Tom C. Clark wrote that the law did not constitute a bill of attainder, as had been charged by the plaintiffs, but was merely a qualification for running.

Clark also spoke for the majority in *Garner,* again concluding that the loyalty oath required of public employees did not constitute a bill of attainder; nor was it an *ex post facto* law, since it involved a type of activity that had been previously proscribed for public employees. Black and Douglas, this time joined by Felix Frankfurter and Harold H. Burton, again dissented, holding that the law did indeed constitute a bill of attainder. Again, there was no discussion of First Amendment rights of speech or assembly in either case.

In 1952 the Court again upheld a state loyalty requirement. Unlike in previous instances, however, the case addressed First Amendment concerns of free speech and assembly. A teacher had been fired under New

*In a 1952 Court decision, Justice Sherman Minton supported loyalty oaths, arguing that individuals could choose between public employment and organization membership.* (Collection of the Supreme Court of the United States)

York State's Feinberg Law, which stated that membership in any organization that advocated overthrow of the government was grounds for dismissal of anyone employed by the public. A list of such organizations was kept by the New York Board of Regents. The Supreme Court decided, 6-3, in *Adler v. Board of Education, City of New York,* that it was the duty of the state to screen its employees in order to ensure that they maintained the integrity of public office. In the majority opinion, Justice Sherman Minton also held that freedom of speech and assembly were not violated because it was the prerogative of the individual to choose between public employment and organization membership. Two of the dissenters, Black and Douglas, disagreed vigorously, arguing that the law amounted to little more than guilt by association, thereby violating the First Amendment.

**Decisions Striking Down Loyalty Oaths.** In 1952 the Court for the first time struck down a loyalty oath. In *Wieman v. Epdegraff,* the Court considered an Oklahoma law that required all public officials to take a loyalty oath and that also stated that anyone involved either knowingly or unknowingly in a subversive organization would be dismissed or denied employment. Justice Clark wrote that association alone could not be used as grounds for dismissal; rather, such association had to be coupled with a complicity in an organization's beliefs and goals.

By the mid-1960's, the Court began to look at loyalty oaths less favorably. In *United States v. Brown* (1965), it ruled the provision of the Labor Management Relations Act upheld in *Douds* to be unconstitutional. In 1959 Congress had eliminated the affidavit requirement and replaced it with a provision forbidding Communist Party members from holding union offices. The law was challenged by Communist Party member Archie Brown, who had been denied a seat on the executive board of a local branch of the International Longshoremen's and Warehousemen's Union. The Court, in an opinion by Chief Justice Earl Warren, ruled in Brown's favor. Stating that while Congress does have the authority under the Constitution's commerce clause to regulate the activities of unions and to weed out dangerous members of the labor movement, Congress must do so in a more general way. According to Warren, the revised law did not meet that requirement, thus violating the Constitutional prohibition of bills of attainder.

In 1966 another loyalty-oath statute was struck down. In *Elfbrandt v. Russell,* an Arizona law requiring state employees to take an oath that they had no affiliation with the Communist Party or any other organization with intent to overthrow the government was ruled unconstitutional. In contrast to the law struck down in *Wieman,* the Arizona law stated that only those who were knowingly involved in such an organization could be prosecuted; however, such individuals could still be punished even if they did not agree with the organization's subversive beliefs. In his opinion for the Court, Justice Douglas concluded that the oath was in violation of the First Amendment's right of association.

The *Adler* decision was the next to be reversed. In *Keyishian v. Board of Regents of the University of the State of New York* (1967), Justice William J. Brennan, Jr., declared the New York law that had been upheld in *Adler* unconstitutionally vague and overbroad, an issue that had not been considered in the earlier case. Brennan reasoned that it would prove impossible for a teacher, for example, always to know if all statements made about abstract doctrines could be considered either treasonable or seditious.

*John B. Peoples*

# MIRANDA RIGHTS

*Description:* A requirement that the police inform suspects of their right against self-incrimination and their right to counsel during custodial interrogation.

*Relevant amendments:* Fifth, Sixth

*Significance:* A 1966 Supreme Court ruling created the Miranda rights. In a number of cases after its initial ruling, the Court clarified and refined its decision.

The Miranda rights were created by the Supreme Court's 5-4 decision in *Miranda v. Arizona* (1966). Miranda, a suspect in a kidnaping and rape case, confessed after being interrogated for two hours. The confession was admitted in trial, and Miranda was convicted. The Court overturned his conviction, ruling that the confession was inadmissible because the police failed to inform Miranda of his constitutional right to avoid self-incrimination and to obtain counsel before questioning him during a custodial investigation. The Court established guidelines, known as the Miranda rights, for informing suspects of their Fifth Amendment rights.

The *Miranda* ruling has been continually reexamined since its inclusion in the U.S. justice system. It left a number of unanswered questions, including how to determine whether the accused was in fact in custody (and therefore needed to be read his or her rights), whether the suspect's statements were spontaneous or the product of an investigation (and needed to be preceded by the reading of rights), and whether the individual effectively waived his or her rights. Subsequent cases helped answer these questions and define when the practice of reading suspects their rights can be suspended, which is usually if the questioning is being conducted in certain contexts and if larger issues—notably public safety—are concerned.

**A Question of Time and Place.** In *Orozco v. Texas* (1969), the Court upheld a lower court's ruling that four police officers should have read the Miranda rights to a suspect before questioning began in the suspect's bedroom at four o'clock in the morning. However, in *Beckwith v. United States* (1976), the Court held that statements received by Internal Revenue Service agents during a noncoercive and noncustodial interview of a taxpayer under a criminal tax investigation conducted in a private residence did not require a reading of the Miranda rights, provided that the taxpayer was informed that he was free to leave the interview at any time.

In its 1966 ruling, the Court stated that the reading of the rights is necessary only if the suspect is in custody or deprived of freedom in a significant way. In the case of *Oregon v. Mathiason* (1977), the suspect entered the police station after an officer told him that he would "like to discuss something with him." It was made clear to the suspect that he was not under arrest. During his visit to the police station, the suspect confessed, and his confession was ruled admissible, despite the suspect not having been read his Miranda rights. The Court, in *North Carolina v. Butler* (1979), stated that "the trial court must look at all the circumstances to determine if a valid waiver has been made. Although an express waiver is easier to establish, it is not a requirement."

Still many questions remained unanswered, and further interpretations of *Miranda* followed. In *Smith v. Illinois* (1984), the Court declared that suspects taken into custody could invoke their Miranda rights very early in the process, even during the interrogator's reading of their rights, effectively ending their questioning before it starts. In *Berkemer v. McCarty* (1984), the Court determined that the Miranda rights must be read any time "in-custody" interrogation regarding a felony, misdemeanor, or minor offense takes place. However, it stated that routine questioning during traffic stops did not place enough pressure on detained people to necessitate officers' warning them of their constitutional rights.

**Some Exceptions.** In *New York v. Quarles* (1984), the Court ruled six to three that there is a "public safety" exception to the requirement that Miranda rights be read. In *Quarles*, police officers arrested a man they believed had just committed a rape. They asked the man where he had discarded a gun. The arrest took place in a supermarket, and the suspect was thought to have concealed the gun somewhere inside the supermarket. The gun was found and used as evidence. In such circumstances, the Court declared, "The need for answers to questions in a situation posing a threat to the public safety outweighs the need for the prophylactic rule protecting the Fifth Amendment's privilege against self-incrimination." *Quarles* was a significant ruling, eroding *Miranda*'s influence.

Subsequent cases challenged the Court's interpretation of *Miranda*. In *Oregon v. Elstead* (1985), police officers received a voluntary admission of guilt from a suspect who had not yet been informed of his constitutional rights. The suspect made a second confession after he had been read his Miranda rights and had signed a waiver. Regarding the second confession, the Court ruled that "the self-incrimination clause of the Fifth Amendment does not require it to be suppressed solely because of the earlier voluntary but unwarned admission." Furthermore, in *Pennsylvania v. Muniz* (1990), the Court decided that the routine questioning and videotaping of drivers suspected of driving under the influence was permissible even if the Miranda rights had not been recited.

In addition, the Court held that reciting the Miranda rights is not required when the suspect gives a voluntary statement and is unaware that he or she is speaking to a law enforcement officer. In *Illinois v. Perkins* (1990), an undercover government agent was placed in a cell with Perkins, who was incarcerated on charges unrelated to the subject of the agent's investigation. Perkins made statements that implicated him in the crime that the agent sought to solve, but he later claimed that the statements should have been inadmissable because he was not read his Miranda rights. However, even though Perkins was unaware that his cell mate was a government agent, his statements—which led to his arrest— were deemed admissible.

**Further Reading**
Carmen, Rolando Videl. *Criminal Procedure*. West Publishing, 1998.
Weinreb, Lloyd L. *Leading Constitutional Cases on Criminal Justice*. Foundation Press, 1996.

*Dean Van Bibber*

# MISCEGENATION LAWS

*Description:* Laws that prohibited interracial marriages and/or attached
criminal penalties to sexual relations and cohabitation between whites
and nonwhites
*Relevant amendments:* Fifth, Fourteenth
*Significance:* State miscegenation laws were examples of explicit racial discrimination in U.S. statutory law; they criminalized and penalized the
unions of persons of differing racial heritages and denied legal legitimacy to mixed-race children born to such interracial couples

Thirty-eight of the states at one time had miscegenation laws in force;
seven of those thirty-eight repealed their laws before 1900. All southern
states (not including the District of Columbia) had miscegenation statutes. Many western states (including Arizona, California, Montana, Nevada, Oregon, Utah, and Wyoming), in addition to forbidding intermarriage between blacks and whites, also specifically prohibited unions
between whites and Native Americans or whites and Asian Americans.
Penalties upon conviction varied from a maximum imprisonment of
more than two years in most of the South and some other states (ten years
in Florida, Indiana, Maryland, Mississippi, and North Carolina) to sentences ranging between a few months and two years in other states. Enforcement of the laws was random and irregular.

The key case in ending miscegenation laws was *Loving v. Virginia*
(1967). At the time that the U.S. Supreme Court heard the *Loving* case,
sixteen states still had miscegenation laws in force. Virginia's laws dealing
with racial intermarriage were among the nation's oldest. They stemmed
from statutes formulated in the colonial period (1691) and had been
strengthened by more stringent miscegenation legislation passed in the
mid-1920's in which whiteness was very narrowly defined. The codes that
became law in 1924 were aimed primarily at discriminating against peo-

ple of mixed African American and white heritage and/or of American Indian background.

In the *Loving* case, Richard Perry Loving, who was white, had married Mildred Delores Jester, who was African American, in Washington, D.C., in June, 1958. The Lovings made their home between Fredericksburg and Richmond in Caroline County, Virginia. They were issued warrants of arrest in July, 1958, and in January, 1959, they were convicted before the Caroline County court of violating Virginia's antimiscegenation statute. Their minimum sentences (of one year imprisonment each) were suspended on agreement that they would leave the state. They moved to Washington, D.C., until 1963,

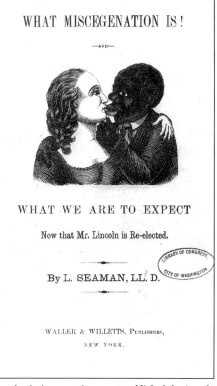

WHAT MISCEGENATION IS!

—AND—

WHAT WE ARE TO EXPECT

Now that Mr. Lincoln is Re-elected.

By L. SEAMAN, LL. D.

WALLER & WILLETTS, PUBLISHERS,
NEW YORK.

*Antimiscegenation tract published during the early 1860's.* (Library of Congress)

when they returned to their farm in Virginia and worked with attorneys Bernard Cohen and Philip Hirschkop of the American Civil Liberties Union (ACLU), who placed their case under appeal. The miscegenation law and the Lovings' convictions were upheld by the Virginia Supreme Court of Appeals in March, 1966, but in June, 1967, the U.S. Supreme Court overruled the appellate finding. The Supreme Court ruled that use of race as a basis for prohibiting marriage rights was unconstitutional under the Fourteenth Amendment's equal protection and due process provisions. The ruling nullified all remaining laws forbidding interracial marriage. Previous to the unanimous 1967 ruling, the U.S. Supreme Court had taken a conservative approach to this civil rights issue. It had repeatedly avoided reviewing lower court convictions based on state antimiscegenation laws (*Jackson v. Alabama*, 1954; *Naim v. Naim*, 1955; *McLaughlin v. Florida*, 1964).

# NATURAL LAW

*Description:* A "higher law" that, according to some political philosophers, applies to all human beings everywhere, is discoverable by reason alone, and is a standard by which to evaluate the laws made by human beings.

*Relevant amendment:* Ninth

*Significance:* Considerable debate continues regarding whether a "higher law" exists and whether the Supreme Court should rely on it in interpreting the U.S. Constitution.

Natural law is best understood in contrast to positive law and to divine law. Positive law is that made by human beings; it may differ widely from one society to the next. Divine law is that set down in religious teachings; it often strongly influences the laws made by human beings and is said to be knowable only through revelation.

According to philosophers, natural law, unlike divine law, is knowable through the use of reason alone, via the human ability to reflect on the nature of the world and on other people. Because nature is universal, natural law is universal. It therefore stands as a body of "higher law" in relation to the laws made by human beings. According to the doctrine of natural law, positive law is just or morally right to the extent that it reflects the natural law.

**Locke and Hobbes.** Although the idea of natural law was first elaborated by the ancient Greeks and Romans and given its fullest premodern expression in the philosophy of the medieval philosopher Saint Thomas Aquinas, the concept of natural law that most affected U.S. jurisprudence derives primarily from the political philosophy of John Locke. Together with other Enlightenment

*British philosopher John Locke.*
(Library of Congress)

philosophers such as Thomas Hobbes, Samuel von Pufendorf, and Hugo Grotius, Locke transformed the classical and medieval understandings of natural law. This transformation was made possible on the basis of a fundamentally new conception of nature and its relationship to the human world of politics.

Ancient and medieval political philosophy shared the view that human beings are by nature political animals. Modern political philosophy, beginning with Niccolò Machiavelli and Hobbes, broke with this view, arguing that human beings are not naturally political. According to Hobbes, for example, life in the state of nature is "solitary, poor, nasty, brutish, and short." In the state of nature, no sovereign exists; each person must compete against all others. Competition, scarcity, the desire for glory, and fear for one's life make existence in the natural state terrifying. Although people are free in the state of nature to do what they desire, they cannot possibly enjoy this unlimited freedom. They have rights—natural rights—in the state of nature, but they cannot enjoy them. Therefore, they consent to form a "social compact"; they give up their unlimited freedom to be ruled in civil society so that they might enjoy a prosperous peace and comfortable self-preservation. People's natural desire to preserve themselves is thus fulfilled in the most rational manner possible by following what Locke termed the "first and fundamental natural law." This law commands the preservation of the society and everyone in it. Even the sovereign power that makes human laws is governed by this natural law.

**Natural Law and U.S. Law.** The concept of natural law finds expression in the opening sentence of the Declaration of Independence (1776), which justifies the American Revolution in terms of an appeal to "the laws of nature and of nature's God." Following the philosophy of Locke, the laws of nature are transformed into natural rights: All human beings are endowed with the inalienable rights to life, liberty, property, and the pursuit of happiness, and all are equal insofar as they possess these inalienable rights. The purpose of government is to protect people's rights, and all legitimate government is based on the consent of the governed.

The idea of a body of "higher law," whether it takes the form of natural laws or natural rights, has been powerfully influential in U.S. jurisprudence, particularly in the context of interpreting the vague due process and equal protection clauses of the Fourteenth Amendment. In a number of famous cases, particularly *Calder v. Bull* (1798) and *Adamson v. Cali-*

*fornia* (1947), the Supreme Court debated whether there is any "higher law" or are any "principles of natural justice" that should determine how the Constitution is to be interpreted. The issue was also hotly debated in the 1991 Senate hearings to confirm Court nominee Clarence Thomas. The issue of the existence of a "higher law" raises the question of how much latitude the Court has to read substantive moral values into the Constitution. Critics of the idea of a "higher law" interpretation of the Constitution fear that such a doctrine would allow justices to read their own moral values into the Constitution and would make the judiciary too powerful in its ability to override the will of the people as expressed by their national and state governments.

**Further Reading**

Arkes, Hadley. *Beyond the Constitution.* Princeton, N.J.: Princeton University Press, 1990.

Berns, Walter. "Judicial Review and the Rights and Laws of Nature." In *The Supreme Court Review 1982,* edited by Phillip Kurland, Gerhard Casper, and Dennis Hutchinson. Chicago: University of Chicago Press, 1983.

Corwin, Edward S. *The "Higher Law" Background of American Constitutional Law.* Ithaca, N.Y.: Cornell University Press, 1955.

Gerber, Scott. *To Secure These Rights: The Declaration of Independence and Constitutional Interpretation.* New York: New York University Press, 1995.

Grey, Thomas. "Do We Have an Unwritten Constitution?" *Stanford Law Review* 27 (1975): 703.

Locke, John. *Essays on the Law of Nature.* Oxford: Clarendon Press, 1954.

*Patrick Malcolmson*

# NEWSROOM SEARCHES

*Description:* Inspection of a news organization's offices by law enforcement officers to find evidence of crimes believed to be in the possession of the news agency.

*Relevant amendments:* First, Fourth

*Significance:* The Supreme Court did not recognize that news organizations were protected from searches under the First Amendment freedoms of speech and press. However, federal and state legislatures subsequently enacted statutes giving news organizations such enhanced protections.

In a series of cases in the 1970's, the press asserted that a fundamental aspect of the freedoms of speech and press protected by the First Amendment was the right to gather news without unreasonable restraint from the government. The press argued that the right to publish information was meaningless without some recognition of a right to gather information.

One of the issues pursued by the press was enhanced protection from newsroom searches by law enforcement officials seeking to discover evidence of crimes committed by someone other than the news organization or its employees. The press argued that if law enforcement agents were allowed to search news organizations' files for evidence of wrongdoing collected in the course of reporting, the press's efforts at newsgathering would be hampered. In particular, potential confidential sources would be less willing to confide in journalists because newsroom searches might uncover their names, and the press would engage in self-censorship to conceal its possession of information that might potentially interest law enforcement. Additionally, internal editorial deliberations would be inhibited by the prospect that a search would disclose the details of those deliberations, and reporters would be deterred from preserving information for future use for fear that it would be seized by the police. Lastly, the news organization's operations would be disrupted during such searches.

In *Zurcher v. The Stanford Daily* (1978), the Supreme Court held that the Constitution did not prohibit searches of newsrooms and that the standard Fourth Amendment rules, including the warrant requirement, applied to newsroom searches. When the materials sought in a search were protected by the First Amendment, the Court said, the Fourth Amendment requirements limiting law enforcement officials must be applied with "scrupulous exactitude."

After *Zurcher*, Congress and several state legislatures enacted statutes providing news organizations with greater protections against searches. The Privacy Protection Act of 1980 bars searches of notes, drafts, or similar material prepared by journalists. Other material, including, for example, documents or other items given to a journalist, are subject to seizure in limited circumstances, such as when necessary to prevent serious physical injury or help a party obtain documents after the news organization has disobeyed a subpoena. Some state laws offer news organizations greater protection than the federal statute provides.

**Further Reading**

Dienes, C. Thomas, Lee Levine, and Robert C. Lind. *Newsgathering and the Law.* Charlottesville, Va.: Michie Law, 1997.

Teeter, Dwight L., Jr., and Don R. Le Duc. *Law of Mass Communications.* Westbury: The Foundation Press, 1992.

*Bernard W. Bell*

# NUREMBERG FILES

*Description:* In 1999, Planned Parenthood won a large civil judgment against an antiabortion organization because of its provocative listings of specific names and addresses of abortion providers over the Internet, but a federal appeals court overruled the judgment as a violation of the freedom of expression protected by First Amendment.

*Relevant amendment:* First

*Significance:* The controversial ruling of the appellate court, *Planned Parenthood v. American Coalition of Life Activists* (2001), held that the First Amendment protected a right to encourage violence against specific individuals unless the message was both intended and likely to produce imminent lawless action.

In the early 1990's, an organization of antiabortion activists called the American Coalition of Life Advocates (ACLA) published the names and addresses of doctors and staff providing abortion services. The lists encouraged a few fanatics within the group's audience to use violence against particular individuals. In 1997, the ACLA began sponsoring sites on the Worldwide Web, including the "Nuremberg Files," which invoked the name of the German city where Nazi criminals had been tried for crimes against humanity after World War II. The sites, which were designed by Neil Horsley, did not explicitly advocate harm to the 225 listed providers, but they included lurid illustrations of dead fetuses and suggested that concerned citizens might have to resort to extra-legal means to stop the "baby butchers." Although Horsley denied that the sites were intended to be "hit lists," he declared approvingly that providers should know that pro-life activists were ready to "blow their brains out." When listed providers were killed, the Web site of the Nuremberg Files lined out their names, and if when providers were wounded, their names were grayed out. During the 1990's, at least seven murders and seventeen attempted murders of providers occurred, as well as at least five bombings and thirty cases of arson at abortion clinics.

In 1995, before the ACLA site was established, Planned Parenthood and other abortion providers brought a civil suit against the ACLA under a federal statute, the Freedom of Access to Clinic Entrances Act. In 1999, a jury trial took place in Portland, Oregon, and the plaintiffs won a judgment of $109 million. Because of the judgment, the Nuremberg Files and similar Web sites were temporarily removed from the Internet. The ACLA appealed the case to the Ninth Circuit Court of Appeals, which hears federal appeals in nine western states.

On March 28, 2001, a three-judge panel unanimously vacated the judgment as an unconstitutional restraint on the ACLA's freedom of expression. Speaking for the panel, Circuit Judge Alex Kozinski explained: "Political speech may not be punished just because it makes it more likely that someone will be harmed at some unknown time in the future by an unrelated third party." Kozinski noted that the Supreme Court in *Brandenburg v. Ohio* (1969) had ruled that communications with a political message were protected unless a speaker intended to incite imminent lawless behavior and the speech was likely to produce such an outcome. He also quoted extensively from *National Association for the Advancement of Colored People v. Caliborn Hardware Co.* (1982), in which the Supreme Court had overturned a judgment against NAACP leaders for threatening violence against African Americans not participating in an economic boycott. Even though violence against nonparticipants had occurred, it did not take place immediately after the provocative communications.

Many observers—both liberal and conservative—were outraged by the three-judge panel's ruling. Senator Charles Schumer and other authors of the relevant federal statute requested a review of the ruling by all eleven judges on the appeals court. On October 4, 2001, the court announced that the eleven judges would hear the case, but did not announce a date. Whatever the outcome of the review, it was entirely possible that the controversial case would have to be decided by the Supreme Court. Meanwhile, the Nuremberg Files, in modified form, reappeared on the Internet.

*Thomas T. Lewis*

# OBSCENITY AND PORNOGRAPHY

*Description:* An obscenity is an utterance or act that is morally or ethically
   offensive; pornography is the depiction of erotic behavior intended to
   arouse sexual excitement.
*Relevant amendment:* First
*Significance:* The Supreme Court held obscenity to be a category of
   speech not protected by the First Amendment. The justices had difficulty agreeing on a definition of obscenity, not forming a standard until a 1973 ruling.

Obscenity is one of several categories of speech deemed unprotected by
the First Amendment in *Chaplinsky v. New Hampshire* (1942). In this case,
the Supreme Court argued that obscenity and lewdness are analogous to
libel (knowingly false speech that injures a person's reputation) and
fighting words (speech that may incite the individual to whom the speech
is addressed to attack the speaker). The Court reasoned that such speech
is not essential to the rational exchange of ideas cherished by the First
Amendment and is of little value to society. Any harm arising from suppression is outweighed by society's interest in maintaining order and morality.

**Defining Obscenity.** The Court did not directly address the question of
obscenity's constitutional status until *Roth v. United States* and *Alberts v.
California* (1957). Writing for a 6-3 majority, Justice William Joseph
Brennan, Jr., held that obscenity is unprotected by the First Amendment
because it is "utterly without redeeming social importance." Brennan
stressed that "sex and obscenity are not synonymous" and distinguished
between them by explaining that obscene material deals with sex in a
manner appealing to "the prurient interest." Brennan defined prurient
as "having a tendency to excite lustful thoughts" or appealing to a
"shameful and morbid interest in sex." What became known as the Roth-
Alberts test for obscenity was formulated by Brennan in this way: Material
was obscene if "to the average person, applying contemporary community standards, the dominant theme of the material taken as a whole appeals to the prurient interest."
   In subsequent years, the Court found it difficult to define more precisely each element of the Roth-Alberts test. In *Jacobellis v. Ohio* (1964),

Justice Potter Stewart questioned whether he could "intelligibly" define obscene material, though he averred that "I know it when I see it" and went on to find that the material involved was not obscene. Three years later, in *Redrup v. New York* (1967), the Court overturned an obscenity conviction in a *per curiam* decision (an opinion "by the court" that briefly expresses the decision but identifies no author), and for the next six years in more than thirty obscenity cases, the Court decided each *per curiam*, the individual justices applying their own understanding of the definition of obscenity. (Justice Hugo L. Black, true to his absolutist approach to First Amendment interpretation, refused to view any of the movies or publications involved in these cases.)

These Warren Court decisions were criticized for failing to provide clear guidelines to law enforcement officials charged with applying federal, state, and local antiobscenity statutes. There was also concern that nonobscene sexually explicit speech might be stifled if speakers feared that speech they thought protected might later be found punishable. However, others found the Warren Court's standards too permissive, and these decisions, among others, were issues in the 1968 presidential election.

In *Miller v. California* and *Paris Adult Theatre v. Slaton* (1973), the Burger Court reaffirmed *Roth's* finding that obscenity is not protected by the First Amendment and expounded the current test for obscenity. Writing for a 5-4 majority, Chief Justice Warren E. Burger held that three requirements must be met to find material obscene. First, the average person, applying contemporary community standards, must find the material appealing to his or her prurient interest. Second, the material must depict sexual conduct in a patently offensive way ("patently offensive representations . . . of ultimate sexual acts" and "patently offensive representations . . . of masturbation, excretory functions, and lewd exhibition of the genitals"). Third, material is obscene if, taken as a whole—not simply focusing on isolated passages or pictures in, for example, a book or magazine—it "lacks serious literary, artistic, political, or scientific value." In short, obscenity is "hard core" pornography.

In *Paris Adult Theatre v. Slaton*, decided the same day as *Miller*, Justice Brennan, who authored the majority opinion in *Roth*, questioned whether this new approach would bring stability to the law of obscenity and suggested that fundamental First Amendment values were jeopardized. He argued that government's interest in regulating sexually explicit materials was confined to distribution to minors or unwilling adults and that regulation of the distribution of such materials to consenting adults was inconsistent with the First Amendment. Obscenity opponents praised the Court for achieving a majority opinion defining obscenity and rejecting an earlier approach—used by the Court in the 1966 Fanny Hill case (*A Book Named "John Cleland's Memoirs of a Woman of Pleasure" v. Attorney General of Massachusetts*)—that a work is obscene if it is "utterly without redeeming social value." This minimal social value test placed a heavy burden on prosecutors, in essence requiring them to prove a negative. Under *Miller*, prosecutors merely have to show that a work lacks "serious" literary, artistic, political, or scientific value.

In *New York v. Ferber* (1982), the Court created an important exception to the principle that nonobscene sexually explicit material is entitled to First Amendment protection. The *Ferber* case involved a New York State law prohibiting the knowing production, exhibition, or distribution of any material depicting a "sexual performance" by a child under sixteen. Ferber was convicted for selling two films showing young boys masturbating. The Court upheld the conviction, even though this material did not meet the *Miller* test for obscenity. The Court reasoned that the state had a "compelling interest" in protecting the physiological, emotional, and mental health of children, citing the close relationship between child pornography and child abuse.

In *Osborne v. Ohio* (1990), the Court held that the government may regulate private possession of child pornography. The Court reasoned that an earlier case, *Stanley v. Georgia* (1969), was not applicable here. In *Stanley*, the Court overturned a conviction for possession of obscenity. Justice Thurgood Marshall's opinion for the Court stressed the freedom of individuals to read or watch what they choose in the privacy of their own home. (*Stanley* has never been overruled but neither has it been extended. In *United States v. Reidel* [1971], for example, the justices rejected the argument that a right to possess obscene materials entails a right to receive them despite a governmental ban on shipment of such materials.) In *Osborne*, over a dissent by Justice Brennan in which he argued that the controlling precedent was *Stanley*, the Court reasoned that the privacy interest was outweighed by the state's need to protect children by attacking the "market for the exploitative use of children."

**Sexually Oriented Nonobscene Speech.** Some types of sexual speech, while not meeting the definition of obscenity, are treated by the Court as low value speech. The government has more room to regulate such speech than it would if it were targeting a political speech or a newspaper editorial. The Court has used the metaphor of a ladder. Obscenity, libel, or fighting words are at the bottom of the ladder, while a speech at a political rally or a newspaper editorial are at the top. Sexually oriented nonobscene speech is somewhere in between and, in the eyes of some justices, closer to the bottom.

The Court has never given a detailed definition of this category but it is clear that sexually explicit nonobscene material is included. One example involves movie theaters specializing in "adult" entertainment—material involving "specified sexual activities" or "specified anatomical areas." In *Young v. American Mini Theatres* (1976), the Court said cities could limit how many adult theaters could be on any block and exclude them from residential neighborhoods. The Court stressed that attempts to place complete bans on such establishments would raise First Amendment problems. Subsequently in *City of Renton v. Playtime Theaters* (1986), the Court approved a zoning ordinance that banned adult theaters located within one thousand feet of any residential zone, church, park, or school. The practical effect of Renton's law was to exclude such establishments from 95 percent of the land in the city. The remaining 5 percent was unsuitable for such establishments, but the Court, relying on *Young*, upheld the ordinance.

Also near the bottom of the ladder is nude dancing. In *Barnes v. Glen Theatre* (1991), the Court held that the government may completely ban nude dancing. At issue in *Barnes* was an Indiana statute prohibiting public nudity. The Court split five to four, and there was no majority opinion. The plurality opinion by Chief Justice William H. Rehnquist described nude dancing as "within the outer perimeters of the First Amendment, though . . . only marginally so." Rehnquist argued that the ban on nude dancing was needed to protect "societal order and morality." In the chief justice's view, Indiana was not proscribing erotic dancing but rather targeting public nudity. Justice Byron R. White's dissenting opinion argued that nudity is an expressive component of the dance rather than "merely incidental 'conduct.'"

Whatever the exact definition of sexually oriented nonobscene speech, the Court has indicated that nudity per se is not enough to place the communication near the bottom of the ladder. In *Erznoznik v. Jacksonville* (1975), the Court overturned a Jacksonville, Florida, ordinance prohibiting a drive-in movie theater from showing films including nude scenes if the screen was visible from a public street or any other public place. The

Court stressed that nudity alone is not obscene and not enough to curtail First Amendment protections.

**Profane and Indecent Language.** Profane and indecent language, the familiar Anglo-Saxon four-letter word being the prototypical example, does not meet the *Miller* definition of obscenity, and the Court has found such language protected by the First Amendment. The notion that the government may not punish speech simply because some find it offensive, a bedrock principle of First Amendment interpretation, found classic expression in *Cohen v. California* (1971). In *Cohen*, the Court overturned the conviction of an anti-Vietnam War protester charged with disturbing the peace by wearing in the corridor of a courthouse a jacket with the words "Fuck the Draft" emblazoned on its back. Justice John Marshall Harlan II's majority opinion rejected the notion that the state can prohibit offensive language. Harlan was concerned that, under the guise of prohibiting particular words, the government might seek to ban the expression of unpopular views. Additionally, Harlan endorsed Cohen's argument that words are often used as much for their emotive as their cognitive impact. Cohen could not have conveyed the intensity of his feeling if the jacket said "I Don't Like the Draft." In *Sable Communications v. Federal Communications Commission* (1989), the Court reiterated that government may prohibit obscene but not indecent speech.

However, the Court has also recognized situations in which the government can ban profane or indecent language. One such situation is broadcasting. In *Federal Communications Commission v. Pacifica Foundation* (1978), the Court allowed the Federal Communications Commission (FCC) to punish indecent language broadcast over an FM radio station. The station aired a portion of a monologue on "seven dirty words" by comedian George Carlin. Chief Justice Burger's opinion emphasized that broadcast media are unique in their pervasiveness and in their ability to intrude into the home. Burger also expressed concern about the accessibility of such broadcasts to children.

Applying *Pacifica* to another pervasive and intrusive medium—cable television—in 1996, the Court considered several provisions of a federal law regulating the broadcast of "patently offensive" sexually oriented material on cable. The Court held in *Denver Area Educational Consortium v. Federal Communications Commission,* that cable operators could refuse to carry sexually explicit broadcasting. The Court again stressed the need to protect children. At the same time, the Court found unconstitutional a requirement that sexually oriented programs be confined to a single channel that could not be viewed unless the cable subscriber requested access in writing. Although concerned about the availability of such material to children, the Court believed that the law could have chosen less restrictive alternatives, such as facilitating parental blockage of such channels.

In *Reno v. American Civil Liberties Union* (1996), the Court overturned a 1996 federal law, the Communications Decency Act, which attempted to protect minors by criminalizing "indecency" on the Internet. Justice John Paul Stevens's 7-2 majority opinion found that the act placed too heavy a burden on protected speech and threatened "to torch a large segment of the Internet community." The Court said the Internet is analogous to the print rather than broadcast medium and therefore entitled to full First Amendment protections. The Court voiced concern that the law would threaten legitimate discussion of sexual topics posted online by the plaintiffs, for example, groups such as Stop Prisoner Rape or Critical Path AIDS Project.

Another exception to the Court's protection of profane and indecent language arises in the context of schools. The Court upheld the right of public school officials to punish a student for indecent speech. In *Bethel School District No. 403 v. Fraser* (1986), the Court found that Fraser's school assembly speech, containing no profanity but numerous sexual innuendoes, was "wholly inconsistent with the 'fundamental value' of public school education." *Bethel* exemplifies the Court's tendency to defer to school authorities and to emphasize an orderly educational process over student free speech rights.

**Further Reading**

For a comprehensive overview of the Court's approach to civil rights and liberties issues, consult Henry J. Abraham and Barbara A. Perry's *Freedom and the Court* (7th ed., New York: Oxford University Press, 1998). Chapter 5, "The Precious Freedom of Expression," is an excellent introduction to the Court's First Amendment jurisprudence and includes a thorough and balanced discussion of pornography and obscenity. In general, the literature on freedom of expression is voluminous. Readers might start with two classics by a towering figure, Alexander Meiklejohn: *Free Speech and Its Relation to Self-Government* (Port Washington, N.Y.: Kennikat Press, 1972) and *Political Freedom: The Constitutional Powers of the People* (New York: Oxford University Press, 1965). More recent studies that are also valuable include Lee Bollinger's *The Tolerant Society* (New York: Oxford University Press, 1986), Rodney A. Smolla's *Free Speech in an Open Society* (New York: Alfred A. Knopf, 1992), Nat Hentoff's *Free Speech for Me—But Not for Thee* (New York: HarperCollins, 1993), and Kent Greenwalt's *Fighting Words* (Princeton, N.J.: Princeton University Press, 1995). A variety of works deal specifically with obscenity or pornography. For a conservative approach, see Harry M. Clor's *Obscenity and Public Morality* (Chicago: University of Chicago Press, 1969) or Walter Berns's *The First Amendment and the Future of American Democracy* (New York: Basic Books, 1976). For a radical feminist approach to pornography, see two works by Catharine MacKinnon: *Only Words* (Cambridge, Mass.: Harvard University Press, 1993) and *Feminism Unmodified* (Cambridge, Mass.: Harvard University Press, 1987). For a response to MacKinnon and Clor, see Nadine Strossen's *Defending Pornography* (New York: Scribner, 1995). A balanced overview of these and other positions can be found in a collection of essays edited by Robert M. Baird and Stuart E. Rosenbaum, *Pornography: Private Right or Public Menace?* (Buffalo, N.Y.: Prometheus Books, 1991).

*Philip A. Dynia*

# PETITION, RIGHT OF

*Description:* Right of the people to ask their government to redress their grievances.

*Relevant amendment:* First

*Significance:* Freedom to petition, one of the First Amendment rights, is relatively well accepted; however, the Supreme Court placed some minor limitations on the way or place in which the petitioning occurred.

The First Amendment to the Constitution states: "Congress shall make no law abridging the freedom of the people to petition the government for a redress of grievances." As is true of most of the rights enumerated in the Bill of Rights, this right has its origins in English common law. Section 61 of the Magna Carta (1215), for example, describes how barons may exercise their right to petition the Crown for redress of grievances. Under the English Bill of Rights (1689), the fifth item on a list of rights of the people is a right to petition the king. The right is also listed in the Declarations and Resolves of the Continental Congress, and in the Declaration of Independence one of the reasons given for rebellion against the king is that "our repeated petitions have been answered only by repeated injury." Of the rights listed in the First Amendment (the other are separation of church and state, freedom of religion, freedom of speech, freedom of the press, and right of assembly), freedom to petition is the least controversial and the most taken for granted, perhaps because the exercise of the right to petition is less likely to affect the exercise of other rights.

The people have readily and consistently employed their right to petition. Some petitions are formally audited and widely disseminated, with highly sophisticated methods used to gather signatures. In various states, petitions can be used to place initiatives on the ballot in statewide elections. If the initiative receives a sufficient number of votes in the election, it becomes law. Petitions can also be simple, from handwritten personal letters to a small group of homeowners asking a city council member to address a traffic issue on a particular street. A telephone call can also be considered a petition. The Supreme Court has a less onerous task in defining what a petition is than what obscenity or unprotected speech is, given that a petition is clearly a plea that a government or official take some specified action.

**Cases.** Often the right to petition has been considered together with other rights, such as that of assembly. In *Thornhill v. Alabama* (1940), the Court held that orderly union picketing was a protected form of assembly and petition, and thus the state law constraining it was unconstitutional. On the other hand, in *United States v. Harriss* (1954), the Court upheld a federal law requiring certain lobbyist to register themselves. In *Edwards v. South Carolina* (1963), the Court overturned the convictions of 180 African American students who had marched peaceably in protest of racial discrimination. The police claimed that because a hostile crowd was waiting for the students at the end of their march, it was necessary to arrest them to prevent a riot. The Court held that even a disorderly crowd, let alone the fear of one, does not trump the right of petition.

In *United States v. Grace* (1983), the Court overturned a federal law against picketing and handing out leaflets on the steps of the Supreme Court's building. However, the Court has shown less tolerance toward the right to petition when it touches on military issues. In *Brown v. Gilnes* (1980), it held that base commanders could prevent military personnel from sending a petition to Congress, and in *Walters v. National Association of Radiation Survivors* (1985), the Court upheld a $10 limit on the amount a veteran could pay an attorney to pursue claims with the Veterans Administration, arguing that the limit was not a constraint on the right to petition.

In *Burson v. Freeman* (1992), a Tennessee law forbidding campaign-related speech within one hundred feet of the entrance to a polling place was overturned. The Court noted that the law was a "content-based restriction on political speech in a public forum." In *McIntyre v. Ohio Elections Commission* (1995) the Court invalidated an Ohio law that prohibited the distribution of campaign literature that did not contain the name and address of the person or campaign official issuing the literature, and in *Talley v. California* (1960) the Court invalidated an ordinance prohibiting all anonymous leafleting. More recently, in *Buckley v. American Constitutional Law Foundation* (1999), the Court overturned a Colorado statute that imposed a requirement that petition circulators wear identification badges and organizations initiating petition drives meet strict reporting requirements.

**Controversy.** People, corporations, and interest groups have the right to pay lobbyists, public relations firms, and advertisers to advocate their causes before the government and in the media. This fact has led to complaints that equal access for all effectively results in greater access for the wealthy. The Court generally has taken a dim view of limitations, even those motivated by "fairness," upon the right to petition.

The right has met with some controversy regarding prisoners. Generally, conservatives have cited frivolous complaints by prisoners and have argued that prisoners should not have unlimited access to the ears of government officials. Liberals, in turn, have cited cases seeking redress for the gross mistreatment of prisoners to argue that they should not lose their right to petition the government. This controversy is often subsumed in the larger issue of the rights of prisoners to pursue more formal legal claims.

### Further Reading

BeVier, Lillian R. *Campaign Finance "Reform" Proposals: A First Amendment Analysis.* Washington, D.C.: Cato Institute, 1997.

Farber, Daniel A. *The First Amendment.* New York: Foundation Press, 1998.

Murphy, Paul L. *The Shaping of the First Amendment, 1791 to the Present.* New York: Oxford University Press, 1992.

Shiffrin, Steven H., and Jesse H. Choper. *The First Amendment: Cases, Comments, Questions.* St. Paul, Minn.: West Publishing, 1996.

*Eric Howard*


# PREFERRED FREEDOMS DOCTRINE

*Description:* An attempted ranking of constitutional rights so that some, notably those of the First Amendment, are deemed fundamental to a free society and consequently are given enhanced judicial protection.

*Relevant amendment:* First

*Significance:* Through the 1940's the preferred freedoms doctrine was used to explain the Supreme Court's continued invalidation of laws restricting First Amendment freedoms of speech, press, and religion, even as it ceased to interfere with laws that regulated economic relations.

In the 1930's the Supreme Court abandoned the doctrine of freedom of contract that had been used since *Lochner v. New York* (1905) to invalidate economic regulations by states and the federal government. At the same time, the Court seemed to increase its vigilance when freedoms of speech, press, or religion were at issue. In *Palko v. Connecticut* (1937), the Court distinguished fundamental rights, those that represented "the very essence of a scheme of ordered liberty," and so would be protected against state abridgment by the due process clause of the Fourteenth Amendment.

In *United States v. Carolene Products Co.* (1938), the Court proposed enhanced judicial scrutiny of laws restricting the political process or laws aimed at "discrete and insular minorities." This provided the Court with a rationale for greater activism in First Amendment and equal protection clause cases. However, in *Kovacs v. Cooper* (1949), Justice Felix Frankfurter criticized any such ranking of rights as not guided by the text of the Constitution and therefore reflecting only the political values of the justices. The preferred freedoms doctrine has continued to influence equal protection and fundamental rights theories. An unstated ranking of freedoms seems to animate the selection of cases through the writ of certiorari.

*John C. Hughes*

# INNOCENCE, PRESUMPTION OF

*Description:* The idea that a person accused of a crime does not need to
    prove innocence; rather, the prosecution must prove the person guilty
*Relevant amendment:* Fifth
*Significance:* The presumption that an accused person is innocent until
    proven guilty is an essential element of the American criminal justice
    system

The presumption of innocence traces its roots to Roman law. Its role in
the early common law of England is obscure, but it was clearly established
by 1802. In England and the United States it is viewed as the source of the
"proof beyond a reasonable doubt" requirement in criminal trials.

The presumption of innocence is not explicitly provided for in the
Constitution. It is inferred from the due process clauses of the Fifth and
Fourteenth Amendments (as held in the Supreme Court cases *Coffin v.
United States,* 1895, and *Taylor v. Kentucky,* 1978, respectively). The presumption of innocence describes the right of a defendant to offer no
proof of innocence in a criminal case. It also describes the duty of the
prosecution to offer evidence that the defendant committed the crime
charged and to convince the jury beyond a reasonable doubt that, in the
light of the offered evidence, the defendant is guilty of the crime
charged. The fact that a jury is instructed to presume that a defendant is
innocent until proven guilty assists the jury in understanding the limited
circumstances under which it should vote to convict a defendant. It also
cautions a jury to not convict based on the fact the defendant was arrested
and is being tried or on mere suspicion that the defendant committed
the crime charged. In this sense the presumption of innocence aids the
jury in understanding the requirement that the prosecution prove its
case beyond a reasonable doubt, a concept which can be difficult for a
jury to understand.

A defendant charged with a federal crime is entitled to receive a presumption of innocence jury instruction if he or she requests it, as established in *Coffin v. United States.* This is not the rule in state crime trials. Despite the long history of its importance and function, the Supreme Court
has held that a presumption of innocence instruction need not be given
to every jury in state criminal trials. The Supreme Court has interpreted
the due process clause of the Fourteenth Amendment as requiring it only

when the failure to give such an instruction in the case would deprive a defendant of a fair trial in the light of the totality of the circumstances. Many states, however, have held that the presumption of innocence charge to a jury is required by their state constitutions or statutes.

If a defendant is presumed innocent, then what is the justification for holding a criminal defendant in jail pending trial? Holding the defendant in jail prior to trial certainly seems to be imposing punishment before the defendant has been found guilty, which would appear to be logically inconsistent with the ideal of the presumption of innocence. In *Bell v. Wolfish* (1979), the Supreme Court explained why the presumption of innocence does not apply to pretrial proceedings. The Court held that the role of the presumption of innocence is limited to the guilt-determining process at the defendant's trial. Before trial, the defendant's right to freedom is defined by the Fourth, Fifth, and Eighth Amendments. The government may need to hold a defendant in jail prior to trial to ensure that he or she appears for the trial or to protect the community from possible criminal conduct by the defendant prior to trial. In many, but not all, circumstances, the Eighth Amendment provides that a defendant has a right to bail before trial.

# PREVENTIVE DETENTION

*Description:* Confinement of a criminal defendant before final conviction and sentencing

*Relevant amendment:* Fifth

*Significance:* Federal and state statutes permit preconviction detention upon finding that the accused is likely to flee or is a threat to the safety of the community

Under the English system at the time of the American Revolution, some criminal defendants were released on bail while those accused of the most serious felony offenses, especially crimes subject to capital punishment, were detained pending trial. Although some legal writers suggest that this pretrial detention was to protect the community from the dangerous propensities of the accused, case law indicates that detention was to make sure the defendant was present at trial. Current American practice, which evolved from English law, allows defendants to remain free on bail or on personal recognizance except in capital offenses with abundant evidence of guilt, when the defendant is likely to flee, or when the accused poses a danger to the community or to witnesses.

Preventive detention statutes call into question three important principles of American law: the presumption of innocence, the right to due process, and the prohibition against excessive bail. Indispensable to the American criminal justice system is the proposition that one who is accused of a crime is presumed innocent until proven guilty. Opponents of preventive detention contend that an accused person has no less of a right to freedom than any other member of society and that the only proper basis for preconviction confinement is the risk of flight. Nevertheless, other grounds for detention are recognized by federal and state law. The Fifth Amendment prohibits the deprivation "of life, liberty, or property, without due process of law." However, due process is satisfied by a hearing before a judicial officer in which the person to be detained has the right to be present and to contest the evidence favoring detention. The mandate of the Eighth Amendment, that "[e]xcessive bail shall not be required," is also frequently cited by those who condemn preventive detention. They argue that this implies a right to be released on bail in all cases, except perhaps capital cases for which bail was not available under English common law. The courts, however, have consistently held that this amendment only limits the discretion of judges to set high bail in cases for which Congress or a state legislative body has authorized that bail be granted. The right to bail is fundamental but not absolute. It is not a constitutional violation to provide bail in some cases and deny it in others. The requirement is only that courts must act reasonably and conform to the Constitution and statutes.

The Bail Reform Act gives judicial officers the discretion to detain defendants in federal criminal cases upon finding that no condition or combination of conditions will reasonably assure the appearance of the accused to stand trial or protect the safety of others in the community. Preventive detention may be ordered for those accused of crimes of violence, of offenses which may be punishable by life imprisonment or death, or of certain drug-related offenses. It also may be ordered for defendants with two or more previous felony convictions, for those who pose a serious risk of flight, and for those who the court finds will obstruct justice or intimidate witnesses or jurors.

State courts also have the power to deny bail in order to assure the presence of the accused at trial and to protect the community unless such powers are limited by the Constitution or by statute. Typical statutes permit criminal defendants to be released on bail except in capital cases where the facts are evident or the presumption of guilt is great. Some statutes also allow preventive detention for felony offenses involving acts of violence in which guilt is obvious or when the defendant would be likely to harm another if released.

# PRIOR RESTRAINT

*Description:* Government restraint of objectionable material before its publication, distribution, performance, or broadcast
*Relevant amendment:* First
*Significance:* Prior restraint has long been the essence of censorship because it has been one of the most effective tools used by governments to prevent the spread of offending ideas

Government leaders and other authorities have given prior restraint of free expression a bad name, but it is easy to understand why prior restraint is important to them. If authorities wait until after offensive ideas are expressed to punish offenders, the damage has already been done. Even extreme retroactive penalties, including death, may not deter some critics from voicing their opposition. In the Soviet Union, in which prior restraint and severe penalties for expressing ideas were commonplace, there were always holders of dissident views, such as Aleksandr Solzhenitsyn and Andrei Sakharov, willing to write or speak out, in spite of what the regime could do to them after their ideas came to light.

In modern democracies, prior restraint has long been proscribed as one of the best ways to encourage free expression. As early as the mid-eighteenth century, the great British jurist William Blackstone wrote in his *Commentaries* (1765-1769) that "liberty of the press is indeed essential to the nature of a free state; but this consists of laying no *previous* restraints upon publications." Blackstone's *Commentaries* was one of the major sources of law for the American colonists and the early leaders of the United States. Abundant evidence demonstrates that the nation's Founders shared a common understanding that freedom of the press meant at minimum no prior restraint. At the same time, prior restraint has been recognized as a necessary part of those forms of expression in

*British jurist William Blackstone, whose* Commentaries *have helped shape both British and American legal traditions.* (Courtesy of Art & Visual Materials, Special Collections Department, Harvard Law School)

which assembly is involved. The U.S. Bill of Rights guarantees only that Congress shall not abridge the right "peaceably to assemble," implying a right to restrain assemblies in advance.

**Prior Restraint in the United States.** Although the absence of prior restraint is the starting point, free expression has come to encompass a great deal more. Shortly after passage of the Bill of Rights in 1791, laws restricting press freedom became a major issue with the passage of the Sedition Act of 1798. The ruling Federalist Party feared losing the 1800 presidential election to its Democratic-Republican opponents and sought to restrain opposition newspapers by making it a criminal offense to write false, malicious stories about the government or its officials, including the president. The Federalists justified the law by arguing that it did not impose a prior restraint. When adopted, the Sedition Act was used to convict several Democratic-Republican publishers who attacked its reputation for fairness. The ensuing political outcry was so great that the Federalists lost the presidency and never regained it. Thomas Jefferson, after winning, pardoned those convicted. The experience kept the national government from attempting similar acts for more than a hundred years, and added the recognition that restraints after the fact can also limit free expression by what later came to be known as the chilling effect.

Definition of the First Amendment limits was left to the twentieth century U.S. Supreme Court. The first example of an attempted prior restraint on the press came in *Near v. Minnesota* (1931). A man named Near published a newspaper in Minneapolis, Minnesota, that denounced local "Jewish" government officials for graft and corruption. Minnesota authorities sought to use state statutes to stop Near from publishing his anti-Semitic newsletter, since no federal statute existed. After the case reached the U.S. Supreme Court, the Court initially decided that the First Amendment's free press clause applied to the states as well as the federal government by using the Fourteenth Amendment's due process clause to rule that all persons were entitled to equal protection of the laws under their state governments. The Court then ruled that despite the despicable character of Near's views, no state could exercise a prior restraint on a newspaper.

A later case of attempted prior restraint on the press involved a set of purloined documents known as the Pentagon Papers that raised serious national security issues in 1971. Nevertheless, the Supreme Court declined to allow a prior restraint to stop their publication in *The New York Times*. After this case, it became difficult to see what circumstance would justify a prior restraint on the press in the United States.

**Prior Restraint and Freedom of Assembly.** The First Amendment divides the free expression of ideas into three categories: press, speech, and peaceable assembly. Neither speech nor press is to be restrained as a free expression of ideas, but the amendment's use of the word "peaceably" in connection with the right to assembly means that assemblies can be—and routinely are—subject to prior restraint. Even in cases of assembly, however, prior restraints are only allowed for reasons of time, place, or manner and cannot be used to block expression of ideas.

Freedom of press and freedom of speech differ from freedom of assembly because of their more passive character, although the U.S. Supreme Court has not always consistently and officially said so. Press, in particular, is regarded as a less dangerous medium for the expression of ideas since reading is a more passive activity than speaking to an audience. While speakers have often been known—intentionally or unintentionally—to incite audiences to riot, it is difficult to imagine people reading a newspaper to riot spontaneously.

Because speech is frequently expressed before assemblages, it falls partially under the First Amendment's requirement that unless an assembly is peaceable, it may be restrained. This point rests on a distinction between ideas and actions. Pure ideas as expressed in the press or in speeches to peaceable assemblies are fully protected, but the requirement that an assembly must be peaceable may lead to restraints on speech, even if there are no prior restraints on the press. The essence of freedom of the press is no prior restraint of any protected material before its distribution, but it clearly implies that restraints may be applied afterward.

By the late twentieth century, concern about chilling effect had led the proponents of free expression to oppose the use of libel laws as postrestraints. The cost of litigation meant that many who would otherwise speak out would be restrained. The Supreme Court recognized this by limiting the grounds by which newspapers could be held accountable in libel cases, thereby limiting the extent to which postrestraints apply to newspapers. However, the essence of freedom of expression still rests on no prior restraint or no censorship.

*Richard L. Wilson*

# PRIVACY, RIGHT OF

*Description:* The right of individuals to be free from unwarranted publicity or uninvited intrusions into their personal affairs

*Relevant amendments:* Fifth, Ninth, Fourteenth

*Significance:* Although the U.S. Constitution does not use the word "privacy," the Bill of Rights secures specific kinds of privacy interests, and the Supreme Court has interpreted the Constitution to protect a general right to privacy which includes personal autonomy and intimate relationships

Many of the provisions of the U.S. Constitution protect values which people commonly include under the multifaceted label "privacy." The First Amendment means that people should be allowed privacy in their beliefs and expressions of beliefs. The Third Amendment permits individuals to refuse to take soldiers into their homes in peacetime. The Fourth Amendment protects against unreasonable searches of persons, homes, and property. The Ninth Amendment recognizes that rights exist that are not enumerated in the Constitution. Both the Fifth and Fourteenth Amendments appear to give some substantive rights to liberty and property, concepts at the core of an individual's private interests.

**Publicity and Invasions of Privacy.** The modern notion of a legal, expansive right to general privacy really began in 1890, when lawyers Louis Brandeis and Charles Warren published a famous article in the *Harvard Law Review* entitled "The Right to Privacy," arguing that "the right to be let alone" was "the most comprehensive of rights and the right most valued by civilized man." Brandeis and Warren advocated the use of tort law to deter invasions of privacy by the press and others. Beginning with New York in 1903, most states gradually allowed civil suits for the unauthorized use of one's name, the public disclosure of private affairs, and publicity presenting one in a false light.

Any legal restraint on publicity eventually comes in conflict with the First Amendment guarantee of a free press. For this reason, in *Time, Inc. v. Hill* (1967), the Supreme Court applied its standards for libel of public persons to unwanted publicity about private individuals if the publicity relates to a "newsworthy" story. Thus, a private individual described in a story of public interest is able to collect damages only if the writer or publisher resorts to "deliberate falsity or a reckless disregard for the truth."

The Court extended this test in *Cox Broadcasting Corporation v. Cohn* (1975), in which it overturned a civil award arising under a Georgia privacy statute that made it illegal to publicize the name of a rape victim. The Court declared it unconstitutional to punish the news media for providing "truthful information available in the public record." If the state wished to protect the privacy of victims, it could delete the relevant information from public court documents. In a subsequent case, *Florida Star v. B.J.F.* (1989), the Court again emphasized press freedom over privacy when it overturned a civil award against a newspaper for illegally reporting the full name of a rape victim, the name coming from police records. A minority of three justices argued that more weight should be given to the privacy of innocent victims.

**Privacy and the Fourth Amendment.** Because of the British colonial experience, the framers of the Fourth Amendment wanted to deny the government the power to conduct general searches of buildings with writs of assistance. In the famous Massachusetts trial of 1761, *Paxton's Case*, James

*George Orwell's 1949 novel*
Nineteen Eighty-Four *depicted*
*a grim future world in which*
*civil liberties do not exist and*
*privacy is unknown.* (Museum
of Modern Art, Film Stills
Archive)

Otis had argued against the use of general writs, declaring that an individual in his house should be "as secure as a prince in his castle."

The Supreme Court only gradually tried to prevent the police from violating the Fourth Amendment. In one of the first important cases, *Boyd v. United States* (1886), Justice Joseph Bradley insisted that the courts had the duty to uphold the spirit of the amendment, writing that it applied "to all invasions on the part of the government and its employees of the sanctity of a man's home and the privacies of life." In *Weeks v. United States* (1914), the Court began a rigorous assault on unreasonable searches by mandating the "exclusionary rule," which disallows any use of illegally obtained evidence in criminal trials.

In his famous dissent in *Olmstead v. United States* (1928), Justice Brandeis interpreted the Fourth Amendment broadly to prohibit "every unjustifiable intrusion on the privacy of the individual." Most of Brandeis's ideas were accepted in *Katz v. United States* (1967), a case in which the Court interpreted the amendment to require a valid search warrant whenever the police enter into a zone in which a person has a "reasonable expectation of privacy." The Court has reaffirmed the *Katz* principle on numerous occasions. In *Terry v. Ohio* (1968), for example, the Court allowed the police to stop and frisk based on reasonable suspicion but insisted that whenever individuals harbor a reasonable expectation of privacy they are "entitled to be free from unreasonable governmental intrusion."

One controversial question is whether mandatory drug testing is contrary to Fourth Amendment rights, especially when there is no basis for individualized suspicion. When the U.S. Customs Service began to require drug tests of employees entering sensitive positions in the service, the Court in *National Treasury Employees Union v. Van Raab* (1989) voted 5 to 4 that the government's compelling interest in law enforcement outweighs the "privacy interests" of the employees. The Court, however, insisted that only the special demands of the positions justified this "diminished expectation of privacy."

**Privacy of Association.** The Constitution does not explicitly mention a freedom of association, but First Amendment rights for free expression and peaceful assembly logically imply the privilege to meet with others to establish organizations for the advancement of ideas and opinions. The Supreme Court recognized this expansive view in *National Association for the Advancement of Colored People v. Alabama* (1958), with Justice John Harlan speaking of constitutional protection for "privacy in group association."

In general, private associations may decide to include or exclude people for any reason, even prejudices based on race or gender. In *Rotary International v. Rotary Club of Duarte* (1987), however, the Court upheld a California statute that required large business clubs to include women. Insisting that the club was not a small, intimate organization and that its mission would not be changed by admitting women, the Court was careful to acknowledge that "the freedom to enter into and to carry on certain intimate or private relationships is a fundamental element of liberty protected by the Bill of Rights."

**Substantive Due Process and Privacy.** The period from 1897 to 1937 is often called the "Lochner age." During these years the Supreme Court insisted that the due process clauses of the Fifth and Fourteenth Amendments protected substantive rights to liberty and property. This approach meant that any restraint on these substantive rights would be judged unconstitutional unless justified by a legitimate objective of law enforcement. The conservative Court emphasized the right of persons to make private contracts without governmental interference; this "liberty of contract" almost invariably supported laissez-faire economic policies, as in *Lochner v. New York* (1905).

During the Lochner age, however, there were at least two substantive due process decisions recognizing liberties which would later be incorporated into a generic right to privacy. In the first case, *Meyer v. Nebraska* (1923), the Court struck down a state law making it illegal to teach non-English languages in all schools. The rationale was a broad conception of liberty which included family relationships, education, and the "orderly pursuits of happiness by free men." Second, the Court in *Pierce v. Society of Sisters* (1925) overturned a state law which prohibited parents from sending their children to private schools. The ruling affirmed "the liberty of parents and guardians to direct the upbringing and education of children under their control." Although the Court in 1937 stopped striking down economic regulations based on the application of substantive due process, it never overturned the *Meyer* and *Pierce* precedents, and years later these cases would often be quoted to defend the libertarian notion that government may not intrude into a zone of private family life and personal autonomy.

**Privacy and Reproductive Freedom.** In gradually developing an explicit right of general privacy, the Supreme Court dealt with issues of sexuality and reproduction. In the watershed case *Skinner v. Oklahoma* (1942), the Court unanimously overturned Oklahoma's Habitual Criminal Sterilization Act, which allowed the sterilization of "habitual criminals." Justice William O. Douglas, a partisan of Brandeis's views on privacy, utilized the argument that the individual's right to procreate was "a basic liberty." Later, in *Loving v. Virginia* (1967), the Court declared that a state miscegenation law was unconstitutional because it violated the right of individuals to choose their own marriage partners.

The most influential case that specifically proclaimed reproductive privacy rights was *Griswold v. Connecticut* (1965). Overturning a state statute that prohibited the use of contraceptives, Justice Douglas argued for the majority that there were penumbras (partial shadows) to the Bill of Rights that created "zones of privacy" not specifically mentioned in the Constitution and that one such zone was the right of a married couple to practice family planning. Marriage and procreation, he wrote, were associated with "a right to privacy older than the Bill of Rights—older than our political parties, older than our school system." While six other justices agreed with the outcome in *Griswold*, at least one justice wanted to find the right of privacy in the Ninth Amendment, and others wanted to find it in a substantive due process reading of the due process clause.

A few years later, the Court in *Eisenstadt v. Baird* (1972) expanded the right of privacy somewhat by overturning a Massachusetts law which prohibited the distribution of contraceptives to unmarried people. The *Eisenstadt* decision recognized that the right of privacy inhered in the individual rather than the marital relationship, and it explicitly declared that the right included freedom from governmental intrusion into one's personal choice about whether to give birth to a child.

**Privacy and Abortion Rights.** The Court's decisions proclaiming the right to use birth control were in the background to *Roe v. Wade* (1973), the controversial case in which the Court ruled that laws outlawing abortion violated a woman's right to privacy. Justice Harry Blackmun, writing for the majority, found the right of privacy primarily in the "concept of personal liberty" guaranteed by the Fourteenth Amendment. He declared that this right "is broad enough to encompass a woman's decision whether or not to terminate her pregnancy." Whatever the rights of a fetus, he argued, they are secondary to the woman's right of privacy, at least until the fetus becomes viable.

During the subsequent two decades, the Court approved of many restrictions on a woman's right to have an abortion, but it continued to guarantee the basic right. In these later cases, the Court increasingly emphasized that the underlying right to privacy was an aspect of liberty based on a substantive due process reading of the Fourteenth Amendment. Thus the term "liberty interest" tended to replace the term "right to privacy."

**Privacy and Personal Autonomy.** One problem with building privacy rights on the concept of substantive due process is that subjective judgments inevitably determine which rights are protected and which are not. Thus, in *Kelly v. Johnson* (1976), the Court upheld a regulation which limited the length of policemen's hair, but in *Moore v. East Cleveland* (1977) the Court overturned a city ordinance limiting the occupancy of any dwelling to a narrow definition of a family, prohibiting a grandmother from living with her grandchildren. In *Moore*, Justice Lewis Powell referred to the string of privacy cases and concluded that "freedom of personal choice in matters of marriage and family life is one of the liberties protected by the due process clause." The most controversial aspect of

Powell's opinion was his suggestion that protections of substantive due process should be limited to institutions and practices "deeply rooted in this Nation's history and tradition."

In the controversial case *Bowers v. Hardwick* (1986), the Court considered the nation's history and tradition when it concluded that the right of privacy gave no protection for the right to engage in homosexual practices, even in a private bedroom. Writing for the majority, Justice Byron White accepted that the due process clause protected many substantive liberties, but he insisted that the Court should show "great resistance to expand the substantive reach of those Clauses." In *Cruzan v. Director, Missouri Department of Health* (1990), on the other hand, the Court found enough history and tradition to conclude that competent adults possess the constitutional right to refuse unwanted medical intervention, even when death is the result of such a refusal.

**Informational Privacy.** In contrast to the Court's recognition of claims for personal autonomy in regard to one's body and relationships in the traditional family, it has found little occasion to expand protection for "informational privacy." In its major decision dealing with the issue, *Whalen v. Roe* (1977), the Court upheld a state law which required the keeping of computer files on all patients obtaining dangerous but legal drugs. While acknowledging an individual's interest in maintaining autonomy over some personal information, the Court considered that the law did not "pose a sufficiently grievous threat" to establish a constitutional violation. As *Whalen* illustrates, courts have generally allowed legislative bodies to decide on appropriate means to safeguard interests in informational privacy. Congress has recognized the public's concern for the issue, as seen in the Privacy Act of 1947, which allows individuals to have access to personal information in files of federal agencies, except for law enforcement and national security files.

*Thomas T. Lewis*

# PRIVILEGES AND IMMUNITIES

*Description:* Special rights and exemptions provided by law, which are protected from state government abridgment by Article IV of the U.S. Constitution and the Fourteenth Amendment.

*Relevant amendments:* First through Eighth

*Significance:* The Court made only limited use of these clauses; its reluctance to protect rights with them is a reflection more of the Court's political concerns than of the provisions' substance.

The Supreme Court has given the privileges and immunities clauses varying interpretations according to what it considered the nation's exigent political and economic needs. Opinions addressing these provisions illustrate the political nature of the Court's decision making. Both clauses arise from intergovernmental concerns within the federal system and require that state governments treat citizens with basic equality; litigation about them has also examined the federal courts' role in guaranteeing "fundamental rights."

Article IV, section 2, of the U.S. Constitution provides that "the Citizens of each State shall be entitled to all Privileges and Immunities of Citizens of the other states." In *The Federalist* (1788) No. 80, Alexander Hamilton maintained that this clause was "the basis of the Union." Along with the full faith and credit clause and fugitive felons and fugitive slaves provisions, this clause was designed to ensure interstate comity. Its obvious purpose was to protect citizens of one state from being treated as aliens while in another state. Evidently, the clause did not literally mean what it said. A Georgian has the right to conduct trade in Maryland but not to vote in Maryland's elections. The earliest standard to distinguish between these activities was propounded by Justice Bushrod Washington. Sitting on circuit court, he held that this clause pro-

*Bushrod Washington—a nephew of President George Washington—was the first justice to articulate the principle of the fundamental rights of citizens traveling or doing business in other states.* (Collection of the Supreme Court of the United States)

tected out-of-state citizens' fundamental rights, those that "belong, of right, to citizens of all free governments" in *Corfield v. Coryell* (1823).

**Substantial Reason Test.** The Court never fully embraced Washington's interpretation. It rarely used the clause to protect fundamental rights, except to ensure some measure of equal treatment by state governments for citizens of other states. Its concern was primarily with the political fallout of interstate relations rather than the rights of individual citizens. The nineteenth century Court limited its use of the clause to protecting the professional, property, and business rights of out-of-state citizens and to providing them access to state courts. The Court's major twentieth century development of the Article IV clause held that lawful state discrimination against citizens of other states must exhibit a "substantial reason for discrimination" beyond their out-of-state citizenship in *Toomer v. Witsell* (1948). The most notable use of the *Toomer* standard was *Doe v. Bolton* (1973), in which the court struck down a statute that allowed only state residents to obtain abortions in Georgia.

After it adopted the *Toomer* "substantial reason" test, the Court returned to the fundamental rights standard in one significant case. It upheld a Montana law that required a higher fee for the hunting licenses of nonresidents than for those for residents. It ruled that equal access to hunting licenses for nonresidents was "not basic to the maintenance of well-being of the Union" in *Baldwin v. Fish and Game Commission* (1978). In all cases, the Court applied the Article IV clause only to unequal treatment of out-of-state citizens, and in most of them, it also based its holdings on the commerce clause.

**The Fourteenth Amendment.** The Fourteenth Amendment includes the injunction that "No state shall make or enforce any law which shall abridge the privileges or immunities of the citizens of the United States." This clause's primary author, John Bingham, contended that the privileges and immunities referred to "are chiefly defined in the first eight amendments to the Constitution," which he maintained, "were never limitations upon the power of the States, until made so by the Fourteenth Amendment."

The *Slaughterhouse Cases* (1873) presented the first significant litigation concerning the meaning of the Fourteenth Amendment. In that decision, the Court rendered the privileges or immunities clause ineffective as the basis for federal protection of individual rights. The appellants claimed that their right to labor was violated by a Louisiana law that required New Orleans butchers to use a central slaughterhouse. Writing for a 5-4 majority, Justice Samuel F. Miller ruled that the privileges or immunities clause did not protect a right to labor. He maintained that the clause protected only the privileges or immunities granted by the United States and that regulation of the right to labor fell within the authority of the states.

The next day, the Court applied *Slaughterhouse*'s narrow interpretation to hold that the clause did not prevent Illinois from denying women licenses to practice law in *Bradwell v. Illinois* (1873), thus confirming the view of the clause held by the Court ever since. The political and cultural basis of the decision was indicated by Justice Joseph P. Bradley's concurrence, "Women are to fulfill the noble and benign offices of wife and mother." This, he maintained, "is the law of the Creator." A century later, when the Court turned to the Fourteenth Amendment to protect women from discriminatory state laws, it relied on the equal protection clause.

In both *Slaughterhouse* and *Bradwell,* the Court responded to political considerations. It recognized that all citizens' fundamental rights should be secured against infringement. It was also committed to the federal system and determined that the states should retain primary responsibility for governing and protecting the rights of the people. To rule otherwise, the *Slaughterhouse* majority argued, would make "this court a perpetual censor upon all legislation of the states."

Justice Stephen J. Field decried *Slaughterhouse* for reducing the privileges and immunities clause to "a vain and idle enactment, which accomplished nothing." His dissent contained the seeds of the doctrines of freedom of contract and substantive due process that dominated the Court's economic rulings for half a century. Because *Slaughterhouse* emasculated the privileges or immunities clause, when the Court espoused these doctrines, it based them on the Fourteenth Amendment's due process clause. To this day, when the Court chooses to protect individual rights, it turns to the due process, equal protection, or commerce clauses rather than the weakened privileges or immunities clause.

In 1999 the Supreme Court resurrected the privileges and immunities clause in *Saenz v. Roe.* In that case it struck down California's durational residency requirement for welfare benefits. Justice John Paul Stevens declared that newly arrived residents of a state must be provided the same privileges and immunities as the state's citizens. The *Saenz* holding raised the possibility that the Court in the future might rely on the privileges and immunities clause, rather than substantive due process.

**Further Reading**

Olsen, Trisha. "The Natural Law Foundation of the Privileges or Immunities Clause of the Fourteenth Amendment." *Arkansas Law Review* 48 (1995): 347-438.

Rosen, Jeffery. "Translating the Privileges or Immunities Clause." *George Washington Law Review* 66 (1998): 1241-1268.

Scarborough, Jane L. "What If the Butcher in the *Slaughterhouse Cases* Had Won?: An Exercise in 'Counterfactual' Doctrine." *Maine Law Review* 50 (1998): 211-224.

Simson, Gary J. "Discrimination Against Nonresidents and the Privileges and Immunities Clause of Article IV." *University of Pennsylvania Law Review* 128 (1979): 379-401.

*Chuck Smith*

# PROBABLE CAUSE

*Description:* The likelihood that a search or seizure warrant is justified; the Fourth Amendment states that no search or arrest warrants "shall issue, but upon probable cause"

*Relevant amendment:* Fourth

*Significance:* The probable cause requirement, an important concept in search and seizure law, protects individuals against government abuse of its power to seize evidence and arrest people suspected of a crime

In Great Britain a series of statutes beginning in the fourteenth century authorized government officials and, in some cases, private individuals to search for and seize certain items. The power to search and seize was not effectively limited, and many abuses occurred in terms of indiscriminate searches and seizures. For example, the Licensing Act of 1662 authorized almost unlimited searches and seizures by the king's secretaries of state in their efforts to seek out any seditious or unlicensed publication of books and pamphlets. General warrants and writs of assistance, some of the most obnoxious forms of unlimited search and seizure power, were used extensively by England to enforce its mercantile taxation policies and to investigate illegal smuggling activities in the American colonies.

The Fourth Amendment to the U.S. Constitution was designed to prevent the federal government from using the much-hated general warrants and writs of assistance. The requirement of probable cause ensured that warrants for searches and seizures would not be issued based on only vague claims that they were necessary for the protection of the state or its citizens.

The Fourth Amendment's probable cause requirement was never intended to prevent or frustrate law enforcement. The Supreme Court has consistently emphasized that the determination of probable cause is pragmatic inquiry, the outcome of which is dependent on the specific facts in each case. In each case, probable cause should be determined using a practical, nontechnical approach in examining the facts. Whether probable cause exists in a case involving a warrant turns on the question of whether, based on the totality of the circumstances disclosed in the warrant application, a magistrate using common sense could conclude that there was a fair probability that evidence sought would be found in the place to be searched or that the person sought committed the alleged crime. According to the U.S. Supreme Court in *Illinois v. Gates* (1983), when a warrant is used, an appellate court should give great deference to the magistrate's determination of probable cause so long as it has a substantial basis in facts disclosed in the affidavits supporting the request for a warrant.

In some cases probable cause is also the standard used by judges in determining whether action taken by the police without a warrant was an unreasonable search or seizure. In a warrantless circumstance, the determination of probable cause turns on the question of whether trustworthy facts and circumstances within a police officer's knowledge at the time he or she acted would lead a person of reasonable caution to conclude that a crime was being or had been committed or that the evidence sought may be found in the place searched (*Draper v. United States*, 1959). In *Terry v. Ohio* (1968), the Supreme Court authorized brief warrantless detention and, in some circumstances, a limited search of individuals based on reasonable suspicion. Subsequently, the Supreme Court has reemphasized that in most cases when a finding of probable cause is required, the facts must establish the presence of more than a reasonable suspicion.

# PROPERTY RIGHTS

*Description:* The recognition from the perspective of natural, constitutional, statutory, or common law of the extent to which individuals,

business entities, or organizations may acquire, keep, use, and dispose of tangible or intangible things free from interference by others.
*Relevant amendment:* Fourth
*Significance:* The Supreme Court's various and changing pronouncements regarding the meaning and constitutional status of property rights, the result of conflicting theories, provoke great controversy.

The Supreme Court's involvement with property rights issues derives mainly from the Fifth Amendment, applicable to the federal government, and the Fourteenth Amendment, applicable to the states. Both amendments prohibit the deprivation of property without due process of law. Much controversy has attended the Court's interpretation and application of the due process clause in the context of property rights. During the late nineteenth and early twentieth centuries, a concept of substantive due process evolved whereby the Court invalidated federal and state economic legislation on the basis of the due process clause. However, a reaction to what was called "economic due process" occurred during the middle and late 1930's, when the Court reversed course and began to apply only a "rational basis" test to economic legislation. By the end of the twentieth century, the use of a substantive due process concept to protect property rights continued to be held in judicial disrepute.

The protection of property rights under the procedural rather than the substantive component of the due process clause was less controversial. However, during and after the 1970's the concept of property used in procedural due process discussions came to include positive legal rights created by regulatory legislation. Thus, the Court formulated procedures that must be followed when the government deprives a person of such modern legislative entitlements as welfare benefits and civil service employment.

The Fifth Amendment also contains the takings clause, which forbids the taking of private property for public use without "just compensation." The takings clause is applied to state and local government by way of the Fourteenth Amendment. During the final decades of the twentieth century, the Court's increasing use of the takings clause to protect property rights evoked controversy both inside and outside the Court.

**The Court's Early Understanding.** The early justices on the Court shared the view of the Founders of the nation that government was instituted to protect the life, liberty, and property of each person. Thus, in *Calder v.*

*Justice Samuel Chase regarded laws that take property from one person and give it to another to be contrary to the first principles of the social compact.* (Collection of the Supreme Court of the United States)

Bull (1798), Justice Samuel Chase observed that a law that took property from one person and gave it to another would be contrary to the great first principles of the social compact. However, the compromise over slavery embodied in the original Constitution resulted in slaves being recognized as property by the Court. In 1857 the Court went so far as to hold, in *Scott v. Sandford*, that a free African American whose ancestors had been slaves could not be a "citizen" within the meaning of the Constitution.

The slavery question was resolved by the Civil War. The Thirteenth Amendment abolished slavery in 1865, and three years later, the Fourteenth Amendment granted citizenship to all persons born or naturalized in the United States and prohibited the states from abridging the privileges or immunities of such citizens and from denying to any person due process and equal protection of the laws.

**Divergence in Property Rights Theory.** The adoption of the Fourteenth Amendment left open the question of the extent to which the Court would apply the due process clause of that amendment to protect private property rights from encroachment by state and local governments. In the *Slaughterhouse Cases* (1873), a 5-4 majority held that the Fourteenth

Amendment due process clause did not prevent the state of Louisiana from granting a monopoly on slaughtering livestock to a particular private company.

In *Munn v. Illinois* (1877), the Court held that the state of Illinois could control the prices charged by grain elevators in Chicago. Chief Justice Morrison R. Waite wrote for the majority that state governments may regulate property that becomes clothed with a public interest, and that property becomes clothed with a public interest when it is used in a manner that affects the public at large.

In dissent, Justice Stephen J. Field articulated a classic statement on property rights and their enforcement under the Fourteenth Amendment. Field pointed out that under the principle adopted by the majority, state government could regulate virtually all businesses, thus depriving property owners of the important right of free use of their property. He thought the majority view subverted the rights of private property and necessarily resulted in all property being held at the mercy of state legislatures. The common law doctrine that government could regulate property affected with a public interest referred only to property that had been specifically dedicated by its owner to public uses or to property that was affected by special governmental privileges. The majority had, in Field's opinion, twisted this doctrine into a license for unlimited governmental infringement on property rights.

In the closing decades of the nineteenth century, Field's views regarding the Fourteenth Amendment and property rights became the majority view of the Court. In several decisions, the Court held that state legislation affecting property rights violated the Fourteenth Amendment due process clause. This notion of substantive due process protection of property rights continued until the mid-1930's. Many of these cases invoked the liberty component of the due process clause to protect freedom of contract. For example, in *Allgeyer v. Louisiana* (1897), the Court invoked a freedom of contract concept in the context of out-of-state insurance contracts, and in *Lochner v. New York* (1905), the Court used the same concept to invalidate state-imposed daily maximums placed on working hours.

**The New Issue of Zoning.** An early exception to the substantive due process protection of property rights emerged in the context of zoning. At the beginning of the twentieth century, the question arose whether municipal zoning regulations were unconstitutional deprivations of property rights. The Court addressed this issue in *Euclid v. Ambler Realty Co.*

(1926). In that case, a municipal zoning ordinance limited a portion of the property owner's land to residential use. The property owner and its *amicus curiae* argued that the zoning ordinance violated the fundamental nature of property ownership, confiscated and destroyed a great part of the land's value, constituted a cloud on the title of the land, and accordingly deprived the property owner of liberty and property without due process of law in derogation of the Fourteenth Amendment.

The Court disagreed with the position of the property owner, holding instead that general zoning regulations satisfy the requirements of the Fourteenth Amendment due process clause unless they are clearly arbitrary and unreasonable, having no substantial relation to the public health, safety, morals, or general welfare of the community. Although the precise holding of *Euclid* was limited to the context of injunctive relief, the practical effect of this decision was to make it almost impossible to challenge zoning regulations under a due process theory for many decades. Accordingly, when the resurgence of Court recognition of property rights in zoning cases finally came, it arrived under the rubric of the Fifth Amendment takings clause (as applied to states and their political subdivisions by the Fourteenth Amendment), not under a due process theory.

**The New Deal Cases.** The stock market crash of 1929 and the ensuing Great Depression led to President Franklin D. Roosevelt's New Deal policies of the middle and late 1930's. To try to revive the economy, the New Deal proposed a vast new role for the federal government in the economy. Many state governments also commenced what were then considered to be radical interventions in economic matters. The Court's initial reaction to the new governmental programs was to hold several of them unconstitutional under substantive due process concepts.

President Roosevelt's attempt to increase the number of justices sitting on the Court (in order to allow him to appoint justices favorably disposed toward New Deal legislation) led to a revolution in Court jurisprudence in economic matters. For example, in *United States v. Carolene Products Co.* (1938), the Court held that legislation affecting ordinary commercial transactions would henceforth enjoy the presumption that it rested on some rational basis within the knowledge and experience of the legislators. In contrast, the presumption of constitutionality was narrower when legislation appeared on its face to be within a specific prohibition of the Constitution, for example, specific prohibitions in the Bill of Rights. Through the remainder of the twentieth century, the Court was reluctant

*President Franklin D. Roosevelt.*
(White House Historical
Society)

to invalidate economic legislation under the Fifth Amendment and Four-teenth Amendment due process clauses, and substantive protection of property rights was largely confined to the takings clause.

**Renewed Interest in Property Rights.** After decades of quiescence, the constitutional protection of property rights began a long journey toward renewed recognition in the late twentieth century. In *Lynch v. Household Finance Corp.* (1972), Justice Potter Stewart authored a plurality opinion that expressed a rationale for constitutional recognition of property rights in the context of a jurisdictional issue. Although Justice Byron R. White, joined by Chief Justice Warren E. Burger and Justice Harry A. Blackmun, dissented on the basis of a jurisdictional issue not linked to the property rights question, the dissenters expressed agreement with the plurality's statements regarding property rights.

The plurality opinion observed that it is difficult to draw a line between personal liberties and property rights with any consistency or principled objectivity. Accordingly, the dichotomy between personal liberties and property rights is a false one. The right to enjoy property without unlaw-ful deprivation is as much a "personal" right as is the right to speak or the right to travel. A fundamental interdependence exists between the per-sonal right to liberty and the personal right in property. In articulating this position, the plurality opinion cited such classic statements of prop-erty rights as John Locke's *Of Civil Government* (1690) and Sir William Blackstone's *Commentaries* (1765-1769).

Although *Lynch* appeared to presage the possible rehabilitation of substantive due process to protect property rights, no such reprise of economic due process occurred. Rather, the Court confined its renewed interest in property rights to the takings clause.

**The Takings Clause Cases.** In *Pennsylvania Coal Co. v. Mahon* (1922), the Court held that the takings clause could be invoked in the context of governmental regulation. Writing for the Court, Justice Oliver Wendell Holmes made the well-known statement that although property may be regulated to a certain extent, if regulation goes too far it will be recognized as a taking. Holmes observed that a strong public desire to improve the public condition is not enough to warrant achieving the desire by a circumventing the constitutional way of paying for the change.

The Court has recognized a variety of property interests as being "private property" within the meaning of the takings clause, for example, contracts (*Lynch v. United States*, 1934), leaseholds (*United States v. General Motors Corp.*, 1945), air space (*United States v. Causby*, 1946), an interpleader fund and the interest accruing thereon (*Webb's Fabulous Pharmacies v. Beckwith*, 1980), trade secrets (*Ruckelshaus v. Monsanto Co.*, 1984), fractional interests in land (*Babbit v. Youpee*, 1997), and interest earned on state-mandated attorney trust accounts (*Phillips v. Washington Legal Fund*, 1998). In *Phillips*, the Court restated its well-established principle that property is more than economic value, also consisting of the group of rights that an owner exercises over a thing, such as the right to possess, use, and dispose of it.

During and after 1987 the Court used the takings clause to foster greater protection of property rights in land. In *First English Evangelical Lutheran Church of Glendale v. County of Los Angeles* (1987), the Court adopted the doctrine that a temporary governmental regulation prohibiting all development of land results in a temporary taking for which just compensation is due to the landowner for the period of the taking. In *Nollan v. California Coastal Commission* (1987), the Court held that a state requirement of a public easement as a prerequisite of a development permit violated the takings clause under the circumstances of that case. The Court held in *Lucas v. South Carolina Coastal Council* (1992) that a governmental deprivation of all economically beneficial or productive use of land is a taking of that land within the meaning of the Fifth Amendment.

In *Dolan v. City of Tigard* (1994), the Court held that certain municipal exactions associated with building permits would be subject to a stricter test than the traditional rational basis test for due process evaluation of economic legislation. Writing for the Court, Chief Justice William H. Rehnquist reflected the increasing concern for property rights when he stated that the takings clause was as much a part of the Bill of Rights as the First or Fourth Amendments and should therefore not be relegated to the status of a poor relation.

**Legislative Entitlements as Property Rights.** The Court has sometimes recognized legislative entitlements as property interests sufficient to trigger procedural due process. In *Goldberg v. Kelly* (1970), the Court observed that welfare entitlements were more in the nature of property than a gratuity and that such property interests created by governmental programs are entitled to certain procedural due process protections. Similarly, in *Board of Regents v. Roth* (1972) and *Perry v. Sindermann* (1972), the Court determined that a person's interest in a governmental benefit is a property interest if there are rules or mutually explicit understandings that support the person's claim of entitlement to the benefit. Where state entitlements are concerned, the property interests are created and their dimensions are defined by state law. If, for example, a state creates a tenure system for governmental employees whereby the employee may be discharged only for good cause, then federal procedural due process protections are implicated.

Therefore, in *Cleveland Board of Education v. Loudermill* (1985), the Court held that Ohio's statutory system of classified civil service employees triggered the procedural component of the Fourteenth Amendment due process clause and that such due process required Ohio to afford tenured employees pretermination proceedings before they could be discharged, even though Ohio law provided no such pretermination procedure. In *Memphis Light, Gas and Water Division v. Craft* (1978), the Court held that a customer of a utility service had a property interest in such service for procedural due process purposes where a state law provided that such utility service could not be terminated except for cause.

**Reticence About Economic Due Process.** During the 1990's the Court continued to apply only a rational basis test to property rights cases brought under the substantive component of the due process clauses. For example, in *United States v. Carlton* (1994), the Court applied the rational basis test to a retroactive amendment to the Internal Revenue Code that cost the relying taxpayer $631,000. The majority opinion, authored by Justice Blackmun, reiterated the Court's long-standing disregard of the pre-New Deal precedents that required exacting review of economic legislation. In an opinion concurring in the judgment, Justice Antonin Scalia (joined by Justice Clarence Thomas) restated his position that the very concept of substantive due process is an oxymoron and that the due process clause should be applied only to procedural matters.

In *Eastern Enterprises v. Apfel* (1998), the Court considered the imposition by Congress of retroactive and substantial financial liabilities under the Coal Industry Retiree Health Benefit Act of 1992 (Coal Act). A plurality opinion of four justices considered it a violation of the takings clause for Congress to impose financial liability on a company in which such liability was based on the company's conduct far in the past and was unrelated to any commitment that the company made or to any injury it caused. However, five justices rejected a takings clause analysis, arguing that the term "private property" in that clause referred only to specific property, not general financial resources. Justice Anthony M. Kennedy, applying a substantive due process analysis to the retroactivity question, joined the four justices supporting a takings theory to invalidate the provision. The other four justices, applying a fundamental fairness test to the retroactivity issue, concluded that the provision did not offend substantive due process.

Thus, the Court continued its decades-long refusal to invoke substantive due process to invalidate economic legislation. However, the Court showed increasing willingness to consider the protection of property rights under the Fifth Amendment takings clause.

## Further Reading

James W. Ely, Jr.'s *The Guardian of Every Other Right: A Constitutional History of Property Rights* (2d ed., New York: Oxford University Press, 1998) contains an overview of the constitutional history of property rights. The Framers' view of property rights is set forth in *The Federalist* (1788), especially in essay No. 10 by James Madison. However, Charles A. Beard claimed in *An Economic Interpretation of the Constitution of the United States* (New York: Free Press, 1913) that the Framers were motivated by their own personal economic interests. Beard's view was challenged by Robert E. Brown in his *Charles Beard and the Constitution: A Critical Analysis of "An Economic Interpretation of the Constitution"* (New York: W. W. Norton, 1956) and Forrest McDonald in *We the People: The Economic Origins of the Constitu-*

*tion* (Chicago: University of Chicago Press, 1958). Richard A. Epstein's *Takings: Private Property and the Power of Eminent Domain* (Cambridge, Mass.: Harvard University Press, 1985) was influential in the growing movement to use the takings clause for protection of property rights. Epstein elaborated a more comprehensive position in *Principles for a Free Society: Reconciling Individual Liberty with the Common Good* (Reading, Mass.: Perseus Books, 1998). Bernard H. Siegan's *Property and Freedom: The Constitution, the Courts, and Land-Use Regulations* (New Brunswick, N.J.: Transaction, 1997) discussed the Court's takings decisions from a pro-property rights perspective. Cass R. Sunstein's *After the Rights Revolution: Reconceiving the Regulatory State* (Cambridge, Mass.: Harvard University Press, 1990) attempted to set forth constitutional principles favorable to a regulatory state, and Bernard Schwartz directly opposed the resurgence of property rights protection in *The New Right and the Constitution: Turning Back the Legal Clock* (Boston: Northeastern University Press, 1990).

*Alan E. Johnson*

# PUBLIC FORUM DOCTRINE

*Description:* Constitutional doctrine relating to attempts by government bodies to control speech activities on public property.

*Relevant amendment:* First

*Significance:* Though the Supreme Court initially held that government bodies have the same power to control the use of public properties as private owners, during the twentieth century the Court expanded the rights of citizens to engage in expressive activities in public venues.

Government bodies in the United States own and manage a variety of property, including streets, parks, and public buildings. In their role as property owners, government bodies often seek to exercise control over the activities that occur on government property, including expressive activities. Early in the twentieth century, the Supreme Court interpreted the First Amendment's free speech clause to permit government the same broad discretion to control activities on its property as enjoyed by most private property owners. Over the course of the twentieth century, however, the Court eventually crafted distinctions among *types* of government property that dictated the kinds of control government might exercise over speech-related activities on public property. The Court's elaboration of these distinctions is commonly referred to as the public forum doctrine.

**Traditional Public Forums.** The core of the public forum doctrine was the Court's determination that some forms of government property were held by government in trust for its citizens for speech-related purposes. Public streets and parks, for example, have, according to the Court, "immemorially been held in trust for the use of the public and, time out of mind, have been used for purposes of assembly, communications of thought between citizens, and discussing public questions." The Court designated public properties traditionally held for speech-related properties as "public forums."

Within these public forums, the Court sharply limited government power to regulate speech-related activities. In particular, the public forum doctrine prevents the government from attempting to exclude speech from such forums out of hostility to the views expressed or the subject matters addressed in the speech. Government, however, is not without all power to regulate speech in public forums. It may regulate the timing, placement, or manner of speech in such forums. These kind of regulations—commonly referred to as time, place, and manner restrictions—allow government to control the volume of concerts in public parks, for example, or to schedule appropriate times for parades on public streets. In public forums, then, government may coordinate expressive activities, but it may not censor particular views or subjects. Although government may enforce reasonable time, place, and manner restrictions on speech in these forums, it may discriminate against speech with a particular content only if it demonstrates a compelling justification. This kind of demonstration is rare, but occasionally government will proffer a weighty enough justification, as, for example, in *Frisby v. Schultz* (1988), when the Court upheld a ban on focused picketing on the public streets in front of a particular resident, such as a picket by abortion protestors of the home of a doctor who performed abortions.

**Designated Public Forums and Nonpublic Forums.** Eventually, the Court had to consider whether other types of public property were subject to the same rules as those it had applied to classic public forums such as public streets and parks. In *Perry Education Association v. Perry Local Educators' Association* (1983), the Court described three categories of public property and the measure of protection to the accorded speech in each of these three types of property. In the first place, the Court reiterated the protection given to speech in "traditional" public forums such as streets or parks. In the second place, the Court identified some types of public property as "designated" public forums. These exist when government opens particular property for a wide range of expressive purposes. In these cases, government must abide by the same rules that apply to traditional public forums. In particular it may not attempt to prevent particular subjects or viewpoints from gaining access to the forum. Thus, in *Widmar v. Vincent* (1981), the Court held that a university could not prevent a Christian student group from meeting in university facilities that had been made generally available to other student groups for speech-related activities.

Finally, the Court ruled in *Perry Education Association* that certain types of public property might be reserved by government for particular purposes and not made available to the public for general expressive activities. Within these "nonpublic forums," government may exercise considerable control over speech, even to the extent of choosing what subjects may be addressed in these forums. Government may not, however, attempt to suppress the expression of particular viewpoints. Furthermore, at a minimum, any regulations of speech in nonpublic forums must be reasonable. Within these broad parameters government may designate particular uses for its nonpublic forums, including particular expressive uses. Thus, for example, in *United States Postal Service v. Greenburgh Civic Associations* (1981), the Court held that mailboxes are nonpublic forums and that federal law may restrict access to mailboxes to postal material. Similarly, in *Greer v. Spock* (1976), the Court determined that military bases were not public forums and that demonstrations in this venue could be prohibited.

### Further Reading

Hentoff, Nat. *Free Speech for Me—But Not for Thee: How the American Left and Right Relentlessly Censor Each Other.* New York: HarperCollins, 1993.

Kalven, Harry. *A Worthy Tradition: Freedom of Speech in America.* New York: Harper & Row, 1988.

O'Neil, Robert M. *Free Speech in the College Community.* Bloomington: Indiana University Press, 1997.

Smolla, Rodney A. *Free Speech in an Open Society.* New York: Alfred A. Knopf, 1992.

Tedford, Thomas L. *Freedom of Speech in the United States.* New York: Random House, 1985.

*Timothy L. Hall*

# PUBLIC USE DOCTRINE

***Description:*** Right of the general public to use property in a way that contributes to the general welfare. In eminent domain cases, this right is superior to any individual's right. Specific definitions of public use are often a function of economic theory and political philosophy.

***Relevant amendment:*** Fifth

***Significance:*** This doctrine, rooted in the takings clause of the Fifth Amendment of the U.S. Constitution, allows public authorities to acquire or use land. Typically, the Supreme Court allows the legislative branch to determine whether the use serves a public purpose.

The Supreme Court broadly interpreted the public use doctrine to mean that land seized under the takings clause of the Fifth Amendment of the U.S. Constitution must be used for the public interest or in some way serve a legitimate public purpose. The Court typically defers to the legislative branch in defining the extent to which a "public purpose" is achieved. For example, in *Berman v. Parker* (1954), a unanimous Court stated that the judiciary's role in determining whether government's power to take lands and convert them to public use was being exercised for a public purpose was "extremely narrow." Moreover, in *Hawaii Housing Authority v. Midkiff* (1984), the Court sustained Hawaii's Land Reform Act of 1967, which sought to break up large estates and give families the ability to buy property from the state. Writing for the Court, Justice Sandra Day O'Connor argued that when "the legislature's purpose is legitimate and its means are not irrational, our cases make clear that empirical debates over the wisdom of takings [are] not to be carried out in federal courts."

In terms of patent law, public use signifies that an inventor has permitted his or her invention to be used by the general public either with or without compensation. The invention is thus said to be in public use. Patent law declares a patent to be invalid if the invention has been in public use for more than one year before patent application.

*P. J. Brendese III and Matthew Lindstrom*

# RELEASED TIME

*Description:* Practice of permitting public school students to attend classes
in religious instruction offered by community volunteers during regular school hours.

*Relevant amendment:* First

*Significance:* The effort to inculcate religious values into public school students through released time was declared unconstitutional by the Supreme Court in 1948. It was the first time an activity was found to violate the establishment clause of the First Amendment.

Under a 1943 state law, a Champaign, Illinois, school board undertook a
program whereby local clergy came into public school buildings to offer
religious instruction for one class period each week to those students
whose parents consented to the exercise. For others, study hall was available. Justice Hugo L. Black, writing for the Supreme Court in *Illinois ex rel.
McCollum v. Board of Education* (1948), ruled that the practice violated the
establishment clause because tax-supported property was used for religious purposes and because the state's compulsory attendance law assisted in a fundamental way the program of religious instruction.

Wishing to avoid the same constitutional infirmity, New York State permitted its public school students to attend religious instruction classes *off*
school grounds. Challenged in *Zorach v. Clauson* (1952), the practice was
upheld. Justice William O. Douglas, writing for the Court, ruled that the
change in locale constituted a sufficient separation of church and state.
Adopting a more accommodating position than the Court had in
*McCollum,* Douglas said, "We are a religious people whose institutions
presuppose a Supreme Being."

*Kenneth F. Mott*

# RELIGION, ESTABLISHMENT OF

*Description:* An alliance or entanglement between government and religion prohibited by the First Amendment to the U.S. Constitution.

*Relevant amendment:* First

*Significance:* In the mid-twentieth century, the Supreme Court settled on a view of the establishment clause that erected a formidable wall between religious and governmental affairs. However, later cases permitted religious symbols and activities in some public contexts and sometimes gave religious groups equal access to government facilities and benefits.

The Supreme Court made a relatively late entrance into the long debate about the appropriate relation between religion and government in the United States, not adding its voice until the 1940's, more than one hundred and fifty years after the writing of the First Amendment, which restrains Congress from making any laws "respecting an establishment of religion." In 1868 in the wake of the Civil War, the Reconstruction Congress proposed and the states ratified the Fourteenth Amendment to the Constitution. This amendment's due process clause protects citizens from deprivation of life, liberty, or property without due process of law. In the 1940's, the Court ruled that this clause made the provisions of the First Amendment applicable to the states, thus making state and local governments subject to the Constitution's prohibition against establishment of religion.

**Aid to Religious Institutions.** In its earliest significant interpretation of the establishment clause, the Court addressed the contentious issue of whether and to what extent the establishment clause limited government aid to private religious schools. In *Everson v. Board of Education of Ewing Township* (1947), the Court considered the constitutionality of state reimbursements to parochial school parents for the expense of transporting their children to the schools. A closely divided Court eventually upheld these reimbursements, characterizing them as only incidentally aiding religious schools in a limited measure comparable to that entailed in police and fire protection for religious institutions. More important, though, in an opinion by Justice Hugo L. Black, the Court set forth the formulation of the establishment clause that would guide its various encounters with church-state problems in the future. At the very least, the Court insisted, the establishment clause means that government can neither establish a particular state or national church, prefer one religion over another, nor aid religion.

Finding principles to transform the sparse words of the establishment clause into a guide for the various intersections between government and religion in modern society was no easy task. Although *Everson* outlined in broad strokes the general contours of the establishment prohibition, it did not settle the many issues that still lay before the Court. The Court made its most enduring attempt to craft a more precise statement in 1971, when it eventually settled on what would thereafter be referred to as the *Lemon* test. *Lemon v. Kurtzman* (1971) involved state laws that directly subsidized the salaries of teachers who taught secular subjects in parochial and other nonpublic schools. The Court found these laws unconstitutional on the basis of its conclusion that they offended a three-pronged test of compliance with the establishment clause. To satisfy the clause, a law must have a secular legislative purpose, have a primary effect that neither advances nor hinders religion, and not foster an excessive entanglement between government and religion. The state laws at issue in *Lemon* created an excessive entanglement between government and religious institutions, the Court concluded, since teachers—even of secular subjects—in parochial schools would be inextricably intertwined with the religious mission and activities of those schools. Any surveillance of teachers in parochial schools intended to prevent such an intertwining would itself constitute an impermissible entanglement.

Sustained criticism of the *Lemon* test proliferated in the following years, both on and off the Court. Critics argued that the test was in principle hostile to religion and that in practice it had produced inexplicable results. Under the test, for example, the Court had approved loans of secular textbooks to parochial schools but not loans of maps. Similarly, the Court in *Everson* had approved reimbursements of expenses of parents to transport their children to parochial schools, but it subsequently invalidated state programs that attempted to subsidize the cost of field trips taken by parochial school children. Notwithstanding this criticism, the Court declined to overrule *Lemon* explicitly, although during the 1980's and 1990's it increasingly formulated the establishment prohibition in terms other than those adopted in *Lemon*. Furthermore, a majority of the Court continued to construe the establishment clause as placing significant limits on direct aid to religious institutions.

**Free Speech and the Establishment Clause.** In early establishment cases, the Court insisted that any significant aid to religion was forbidden by the First Amendment. However, in some contexts, this prohibition against aiding religion collided with notions of fairness and equality. Under the doctrine of free speech, for example, the Court has generally frowned on government laws and policies that discriminate against speech on the basis of its content. Suppose, then, that a university allows a wide assortment of student groups to use university classrooms after hours for meetings and that a group of religious students seeks to use a classroom. Allowing the religious students to use university facilities might be characterized as "aiding" religion; nevertheless, refusing to allow this use would clearly constitute discrimination against the religious speech of the students. In *Widmar v. Vincent* (1981), the Court resolved this apparent conflict between the principles of free speech and the establishment clause by ruling in favor of the religious students. The establishment clause, according to the Court, did not prevent the use of university facilities by religious groups on equal terms with other groups. Accordingly, any discrimination against the religious groups in the access to generally available facilities was an impermissible discrimination against them.

The *Widmar* principle was regularly invoked by the Court during the 1980's and 1990's to uphold claims brought by religious believers alleging that they had been discriminated against in the name of the establishment clause. In *Lamb's Chapel v. Center Moriches Union Free School District* (1993), the Court declared unconstitutional a school's discriminatory treatment of a religious group that sought to use school facilities after hours. The Court held that the school's practice of allowing outside groups to use its facilities after hours for social or civic meetings prevented it from barring religious groups from similar uses. Moreover, in *Rosenberger v. University of Virginia* (1995), the Court expanded the antidiscrimination principle of *Widmar* to include discrimination in the allocation of student fees. In *Rosenberger*, a Christian student group at the University of Virginia sought to take advantage of the university's practice of paying the printing costs of student organizations who published printed materials. When the Christian student group sought payment for the costs of printing a proselytizing newsletter, the university refused, claiming that the establishment clause prohibited this kind of assistance to a religious organization. A majority of the Court disagreed, however, and concluded that the establishment clause did not bar the payments at issue and that the free speech clause prohibited the university's discriminatory treatment of the religious group.

**Religion and Public Schools.** The Court's late twentieth century enthusiasm for equality concerns has partially breached the so-called "wall of separation" between church and state that once characterized the Court's pronouncements concerning the establishment clause. However, in one area, at least, this wall of separation remains formidable. Beginning with the school prayer decisions in the 1960's, the Court has been especially vigilant in policing alliances between government and religion in the public schools. In *Engel v. Vitale* (1962), the Court invalidated the practice of having public school children recite a prayer composed by state education officials. A year later, in *Abington School District v. Schempp* (1963), the Court extended this holding to prohibit recitations of the Lord's Prayer and devotional Bible readings in public school classrooms. Eventually, the Court would reach a similar conclusion regarding prayers offered at graduation ceremonies, finding in *Lee v. Weisman* (1992) that they also violated the establishment clause.

After the first decisions in the school prayer cases, the Court developed the three-part *Lemon* test, which required that laws and official government policies have secular purposes and effects and not excessively entangle government and religion. When the Court entertained a new series of cases involving religion and public schools in the 1980's, it focused especially on the secular purpose requirement. In the first case, *Stone v. Graham* (1980), the Court held unconstitutional the posting of copies of the Ten Commandments in public school classrooms. The school district in question argued that it had a legitimate secular purpose in calling attention to an important source of Western law. A majority of the Court concluded, however, that the principal justification behind the display of the Ten Commandments was a religious one and that this purpose offended the establishment clause. In the second case, *Wallace v. Jaffree* (1985), the Court considered an Alabama statute that had authorized moments of silence in school classrooms for meditation and prayer. Although in separate opinions, a majority of the members of the Court suggested that moment of silence statutes might be constitutional in principle, the Court nevertheless concluded that the Alabama statute had been supported by an unconstitutional religious purpose of returning prayer to public schools. Finally, in *Edwards v. Aguillard* (1987), the Court turned to the secular purpose requirement once again to invalidate a Louisiana statute that had mandated the teaching of creationism in schools that taught the theory of evolution.

**Public Religious Ceremonies and Symbols.** The vigilance with which the Court patrolled the boundaries of church and state in the public schools did not always manifest itself in other public contexts. The Court wrestled with the long-standing presence in American life of a measure of religiousness in public contexts and sought to harmonize this presence with its establishment doctrine. For example, in *Marsh v. Chambers* (1983), the Court acknowledged that prayers in certain public contexts had been commonplace in U.S. history since its earliest days. The First Congress had appointed chaplains to its sessions with prayers, and Court sessions themselves began with the invocation, "God save the United States and this Honorable Court." Faced with this historical precedent, a majority of the Court—in an opinion by Chief Justice Warren E. Burger—concluded that the Nebraska legislature's practice of beginning its sessions with a prayer offered by a chaplain paid to do so did not offend the establishment clause. Even more controversial was the Court's decision in *Lynch v. Donnelly* (1984), which upheld a city's display of the traditional Christian nativity scene during the Christmas season. Chief Justice Burger again announced the Court's opinion and declared that the city had a secular purpose in sponsoring the nativity scene—to celebrate the Christmas holiday and to depict the origins of the holiday. The decision was closely divided, however, and Justice Sandra Day O'Connor provided the crucial fifth vote needed to reach this result. Although she agreed with the result articulated by the chief justice, in her opinion, the presence along with the nativity scene of other holiday symbols inoculated the nativity scene from an establishment violation. Because the nativity scene was set among such items as a Santa Claus house, reindeer and a sleigh, candy-striped poles, a Christmas tree, carolers, and lights, it could not be seen as an endorsement of a particular religious faith, according to Justice O'Connor. Five years later, in *Allegheny County v. American Civil Liberties Union Greater Pittsburgh Chapter* (1989), the Court would reach a different result concerning a nativity scene displayed alone on public property during the Christmas season. Set in this context, the nativity scene amounted to an endorsement of Christianity according to a majority of the Court and therefore violated the establishment clause.

**The Meaning of the Establishment of Religion.** The last two decades of the twentieth century saw increasing dissatisfaction on the Court with its establishment doctrine. The three-part *Lemon* test that had governed the Court's resolution of establishment issues for a time seemed less capable of continuing to command assent among a majority of justices. In this state of disarray, individual members of the Court attempted to articulate new understandings of the antiestablishment principle. Justice William H. Rehnquist, for example, suggested in his dissent to the Court's decision in *Wallace v. Jaffree* that the establishment clause should be understood only to prevent government preference for one religion over another. So long as government endorsed or aided religion in general, he contended, rather than endorsing or aiding a particular religion, then the establishment clause was not violated.

Justice Anthony M. Kennedy, in the early 1990's, seemed to propose his own key to understanding the establishment clause. In *Lee v. Weisman,* for example, his opinion for the Court focused on the coerciveness of a graduation prayer on those who did not share the religious tenets expressed in the prayer. This emphasis seemed to suggest that noncoercive government alliances with religion might survive an establishment clause challenge. Finally, and most important, in the mid-1980's Justice Sandra Day O'Connor proposed that the hallmark of an establishment clause violation was its purpose or effect in endorsing religion generally over nonreligion or in endorsing a particular religion over others. She first elaborated this no-endorsement vision of the establishment clause in a series of concurring opinions, beginning with the first nativity scene case, *Lynch v. Donnelly.* By the end of the 1980's, however, her no-endorsement test seemed to have captured a majority view on the Court because the Court applied her test to resolve another nativity scene issue in *Allegheny County v. American Civil Liberties Union, Greater Pittsburgh Chapter.* However, during the 1990's, Justice O'Connor's vision of the establishment clause was not featured again in opinions for the Court. All during this decade, no majority ever coalesced to overrule the three-part test of *Lemon.* Instead, the justices were fragmented in their views of the establishment clause, agreeing sometimes on the result in particular cases but seldom agreeing on the broader principles that explained these results.

**Further Reading**

The most comprehensive collection of Court decisions relating to the First Amendment's religion clauses is *Toward Benevolent Neutrality: Church, State, and the Supreme Court,* edited by Ronald B. Flowers and Robert T. Miller (Waco, Tex.: Baylor University Press, 1998). Similar, though less inclusive collections of Court cases may be found in *The Believer and the Powers That Are: Cases, History, and Other Data Bearing on the Relation of Religion and Government,* by John Thomas Noonan, Jr. (New York: Macmillan, 1987), and *Religious Liberty in the Supreme Court: The Cases That Define the Debate over Church and State,* edited by Terry Eastland (Grand Rapids, Mich.: Wm. B. Eerdmans, 1995). The Court has regularly consulted the history of church-state relations in colonial and revolutionary America to inform its interpretation of the establishment clause. Thomas Curry's *The First Freedoms: Church and State in America to the Passage of the First Amendment* (New York: Oxford University Press, 1986) contains an excellent treatment of these periods. *A Nation Dedicated to Religious Liberty: The Constitutional Heritage of the Religion Clauses,* by Arlin M. Adams and Charles J. Emmerich (Philadelphia: University of Pennsylvania Press, 1990), combines both coverage of the historical background of the religion clauses and their current interpretation by the Court.

For an influential argument that the Court has given too prominent a place to religious skepticism in its interpretation of the religion clauses, see Mark DeWolfe Howe's *The Garden and the Wilderness: Religion and Government in American Constitutional History* (Chicago: University of Chicago Press, 1965). An opposing viewpoint may be found in *The Godless Constitution: The Case Against Religious Correctness,* by Isaac Kramnick and R. Laurence Moore (New York: W. W. Norton, 1996). *Everson Revisited: Religion, Education, and Law at the Crossroads,* edited by Jo Renee Formicola and Hubert Morken (Lanham, Md.: Rowman & Littlefield, 1997), explores the significance and future of the Court's seminal establishment clause decision in *Everson v. Board of Education.* Robert S. Alley's *School Prayer: The Court, the Congress, and the First Amendment* (Buffalo, N.Y.: Prometheus Books, 1994) provides an evenhanded treatment of one of the most contentious areas of the Court's establishment clause law. The increasing prominence of the principle of equality over that of separation is explored and supported in *Equal Treatment of Religion in a Pluralistic Society,* edited by Stephen V. Monsma and J. Christopher Soper (Grand Rapids, Mich.: Wm. B. Eerdmans, 1998). This movement is contrasted with the case for nearly total separation of government and religion made by Marvin E. Frankel, a former New York federal judge, in *Faith and Freedom: Religious Liberty in America* (New York: Hill & Wang, 1994).

*Timothy L. Hall*

# RELIGION, FREEDOM OF

**Description:** Freedom of religious belief and practice protected, in significant part, by the free exercise clause of the First Amendment.

**Relevant amendment:** First

*Significance:* The Supreme Court has generally interpreted the free exercise clause of the First Amendment to protect citizens from unfavorable government treatment on account of their religious beliefs or lack thereof, but the Court has not typically protected religious adherents from conflicts between their conscientious practices and the requirements of generally applicable laws.

The Supreme Court's attention to religious freedom has focused primarily on the meaning of the First Amendment's free exercise clause, though from time to time it has also considered other federal and state laws regarding religious liberty. The First Amendment prevents Congress from making laws prohibiting the free exercise of religion. Although the text of the clause limits its application to congressional infringements on religious liberty, the Court, beginning in the 1940's, declared this liberty to be one of the fundamental rights of free citizens made applicable to state and local governments through the due process clause of the Fourteenth Amendment. Therefore, as currently interpreted by the Court, the constitutional protection of the free exercise of religion applies to government action at every level.

**The War Against Polygamy.** In modern times, government actions specifically targeting unpopular religions for unfavorable treatment have been relatively rare. Far more common are claims by religious believers for exemptions from the requirements of otherwise generally applicable laws. The first significant claim of this sort reached the Court in the last part of the nineteenth century. The Court's resolution of the issue in that context—although briefly repudiated for part of the twentieth century—continues to guide its treatment of free exercise claims.

The case that became *Reynolds v. United States* (1879) grew out of efforts by the administration of President Ulysses S. Grant to stamp out the practice of polygamy in the Utah territory. Relying on a federal antibigamy law that prohibited the marriage of one person to multiple spouses, the Grant administration prosecuted numerous members of the Church of Jesus Christ of Latter-day Saints (Mormons) who, as a matter of religious belief and practice, had consummated bigamous marriages. The Mormon Church attempted to challenge the federal law through a test case brought by George Reynolds, secretary to Mormon leader Brigham Young. After being convicted of bigamy in the Utah territorial district court and having his conviction affirmed in the Utah territorial supreme court, Reynolds appealed his case to the U.S. Supreme Court. The essence of his claim was that the First Amendment's free exercise clause, in guaranteeing religious liberty, prevented the application against him of the federal antibigamy law, since bigamous marriage practices were an essential component of his religion.

The Court unanimously rejected Reynolds's claim. In an opinion by Justice Morrison R. Waite, the Court distinguished between religious beliefs and religious actions, determining that beliefs were immune from legislative prescription but that actions fell within the proper provenance of the law. Reynolds, the Court opined, had been prosecuted not for his beliefs but for his bigamous actions. By the free exercise clause, "Congress was deprived of all legislative power over mere opinion, but was left free to reach actions which were in violation of social duties or subversive of good order." Moreover, the Court readily concluded that the practice of polygamy violated important social duties and was subversive of good order. Congress, then, had acted fully within its constitutional authority.

The Court also determined that the free exercise clause did not guarantee Reynolds an exemption from an otherwise valid exercise of lawmaking authority. Surely the believer in human sacrifice was not entitled to an exemption from the laws of murder nor was the widow who thought it her religious duty to burn herself on the funeral pyre of her husband entitled to an exemption from the laws forbidding suicide. In both cases, the law prohibited such acts, even when motivated by conscientious religious beliefs; and the free exercise clause did not secure any exemptions from these prohibitions. A contrary result was unthinkable to the Court. "To permit this would be to make the professed doctrines of religious belief superior to the law of the land, and in effect to permit every citizen to become a law unto himself."

Eleven years later, the Court lent its aid again to the war against polygamy. In *Davis v. Beason* (1890), the Court upheld an Idaho territorial statute that denied the vote to those who practiced or advocated the practice of polygamy or who belonged to an organization that did so. The Court demonstrated the frailty of the barrier between the absolute protection given to religious beliefs and the lawful regulation of religious practices. Under the statute at issue in the case, mere advocacy of polygamy or membership in an organization—such as the Mormon church—that engaged in such advocacy was sufficient to suffer loss of voting rights. Moreover, the Court adopted a tightly circumscribed notion of religion itself. Religion, the Court declared, had to do with one's relation to the Creator

and to the obligations that arose from such a relation. Under this definition, the Court stripped the Mormon practice of polygamy of its claimed
religiousness, thus finding additional reason to deny it protection under
the free exercise clause.

**Religion and the Political Process.** For almost a hundred years, the interpretation of the free exercise clause adopted in *Reynolds* meant that religious believers were protected against being deliberately targeted by the
government for hostile action but not from the burdens occasioned by
generally applicable laws. As governments at all levels increased the measure of their lawmaking activity in the twentieth century, inadvertent collisions between religious practice and lawmaking increased in frequency.

When legislative policies conflicted with the religious practices of influential segments of the population, lawmakers typically saw fit to craft
exemptions for the religious believers in question. For example, when
Congress implemented Prohibition's ban on consumption of alcoholic
beverages in the early part of the twentieth century, it took care to craft
an exemption for the sacramental uses of wine important to many Christian faiths. Similarly, when Congress provided for compulsory military
service at various junctures during the twentieth century, it made allow-
ance for certain religious objections to combat by placing the holders of
the requisite conscientious beliefs in noncombat positions.

At least in the case of conscientious objector status, the Court consistently took the position that the free exercise clause did not require this
accommodation, but the normal workings of the political process were
generally sufficient to shield influential religious practices from burden-
some encounters with the law. Minority faiths, however, could not be as-
sured of such solicitude from the political process, and the ruling in
*Reynolds* deprived them of any constitutional harbor.

**The Warren Court Revision.** For a brief interval during the second half of
the twentieth century, the Court appeared to reconsider *Reynolds* and
adopt an interpretation of the First Amendment far more protective of
religious practices. In *Sherbert v. Verner* (1963), the Warren Court turned
again to the question of whether a neutral law of general applicability
might nevertheless amount to an unconstitutional burden on the free exercise of religion. At issue in *Sherbert* was a state unemployment compensation scheme that refused to pay benefits to a Seventh-day Adventist
who, for religious reasons, refused to work on Saturday, the day of her

Sabbath. State officials judged that this refusal did not amount to the kind of "good cause" that would otherwise excuse a recipient of unemployment compensation benefits from accepting available work. A majority of the Court, however, in an opinion by Justice William J. Brennan, Jr., ruled that the state's failure to pay the Sabbatarian unemployment benefits amounted to a violation of the free exercise clause. To condition the claimant's receipt of unemployment benefits on her willingness to violate her conscientiously held religious beliefs required that the state demonstrate some overwhelming interest at stake in its legal requirement. Finding no such interest, the Court held that the state was required to pay the claimant the benefits.

The Court's opinion in *Sherbert* seemed to indicate that the free exercise clause protected religious believers from even the unintended effects of otherwise generally applicable laws. The Court's remedy in such cases was not to invalidate the law at issue in its entirety but simply to craft an exemption from the law's demands for the religious claimant. Nine years after the *Sherbert* decision, the Court revisited this issue and seemed to reaffirm its basic holding in *Sherbert*. In *Wisconsin v. Yoder* (1972), the Court considered whether a state compulsory attendance statute could be used to force Amish parents to send their children to school after age fourteen. First, the Court found that the statute imposed a burden on Amish religious beliefs and practices because the Amish insisted that their children would be unfavorably influenced by further schooling after the eighth grade. Second, the Court denied that the state had any compelling purpose for requiring further schooling of Amish children. Accordingly, a majority of the Court held, in an opinion by Chief Justice Warren E. Burger, that the Amish were exempted from the compulsory attendance statute, insofar as it required them to send their children to school beyond the eighth grade.

**Principle and Practice.** For roughly two decades after its decision in *Yoder*, the Court continued to adhere to the *Sherbert/Yoder* formulation of the free exercise clause: Religious believers were entitled to exemptions from laws that burdened their religious practices unless such laws were justified by some compelling governmental interest. Nevertheless, during these years, the Court routinely ruled *against* religious claimants who asserted free exercise claims. Sometimes, the Court found a significantly weighty public interest at stake, such as when it declined to exempt an Amish employer from the requirement of paying social securities taxes for his employees in *United States v. Lee* (1982). In other cases, the Court found that the government interests involved in particular environments such as prisons or the military warranted greater deference to the government policies. Therefore, in *Goldman v. Weinberger* (1986), the Court upheld an Air Force policy that prohibited an Orthodox Jewish officer from wearing a yarmulke, and in *O'Lone v. Estate of Shabazz* (1987), the Court found that reasonable prison regulations would be upheld even when they conflicted with the sincerely held religious beliefs of prisoners. Finally, in some cases, the Court determined that government decisions about how to conduct its own affairs did not amount to a burden on religious belief or practice. For example, in *Lyng v. Northwest Indian Cemetery Protective Association* (1988), a majority of the Court refused to interfere with government plans to allow the construction of a logging road on government property close to a sacred Native American religious site. Although the logging road would severely impair Native American religious practices, the Court held that the free exercise clause did not prevent the government from using its property as it saw fit.

**The Peyote Case.** Throughout the 1980's the Court continued to affirm in principle the rigorous standard of protection for religious liberty set forth in *Sherbert* and *Yoder*, but to find in practice any number of reasons for rejecting particular religious claims. In *Employment Division, Department of Human Resources v. Smith* (1990), the Court's principles finally caught up with its practice. At issue in the case were two Native Americans who had been fired from jobs as drug rehabilitation counselors because they had ingested peyote in connection with Native American religious rites. The state of Oregon, where the case arose, classified peyote as a controlled substance and made no exception for sacramental use by Native Americans. After being fired, the two Native Americans sought to obtain unemployment compensation benefits but were refused them on the grounds that they had been fired for job-related misconduct. They, in turn, contested this refusal, claiming that it violated their rights to free exercise of religion. The Court, however, rejected this claim.

An application of the *Sherbert/Yoder* test would have required the state of Oregon to demonstrate some compelling purpose for its peyote law. In fact, Justice Sandra Day O'Connor, agreeing with the result in the case but not in the reasoning of the majority opinion by Justice Antonin Scalia, argued that there was such a compelling purpose and that the Native Americans were thus entitled to no exemption for the Oregon controlled substance law. Nevertheless, a majority of the Court followed Justice Scalia in revisiting the rule in *Sherbert* and *Yoder*. According to Scalia, these cases announced no general rule but merely offered protection for religious believers in certain limited circumstances. The true rule, he declared, was that religious believers normally had no recourse under the free exercise clause against laws that were not targeted at suppressing their religious beliefs or practices but simply had the effect of burdening those beliefs or practices. Because Oregon's peyote law had not been created to target Native American religious practices but simply had the incidental effect of burdening that practice, the law was not subject to a successful free exercise challenge.

**The Religious Freedom Restoration Act.** Reactions to the Court's decision in *Smith* were immediate and stridently critical. Religious groups of all stripes combined with political leaders and legal scholars in denouncing the decision as a betrayal of the principles of religious liberty. In direct response to the *Smith* decision, Congress passed the Religious Freedom Restoration Act (1993) three years later. This law required exemptions for religious believers from federal, state, or local laws that burdened their religious practice unless some compelling reason justified the law and the law was the least restrictive means of furthering the interest. To enact the law, at least as it applied to state and local governments, Congress relied on the Fourteenth Amendment, which authorizes Congress to pass laws to enforce the provisions of this amendment. Congress reasoned that it had power to enforce the protection of religious liberty because this liberty was clearly among those subject to the Fourteenth Amendment's prohibition against depriving persons of "life, liberty, or property without due process of law."

Congress's attempt to invigorate the protections given religious conscience did not go unchallenged. As religious believers sought to wield the Religious Freedom Restoration Act in confrontations with state and local laws, government officials in these cases responded by arguing that Congress lacked the power to pass the Religious Freedom Restoration Act. In the last part of the 1990's one of these cases reached the Court. *Boerne v. Flores* (1997) involved a dispute between a Texas city and a Roman Catholic Church. The church wished to renovate its facilities to accommodate a swelling congregation. The city of Boerne, however, wished to preserve the historic ambiance of its downtown district, especially the mission-style Catholic sanctuary, and passed a historical preservation ordinance that blocked the church's plans.

When the church filed suit, claiming that the ordinance violated its rights under the Religious Freedom Restoration Act, the city responded by arguing that the federal law was unconstitutional. In a decision that surprised many observers, a majority of the Court agreed with the city and held that Congress's attempt to overrule the effect of the *Smith* decision invaded the Court's prerogatives. Championing its power to define the meaning of constitutional protections for liberty, the Court ruled that Congress lacked power to substitute its own view of free exercise for the view articulated by the Court's opinion in *Smith*.

**Further Reading**

*Toward Benevolent Neutrality: Church, State, and the Supreme Court*, edited by Ronald B. Flowers and Robert T. Miller (Waco, Tex.: Baylor University Press, 1998) is a comprehensive collection of Court decisions relating to the religion clauses in the First Amendment. Less inclusive collections include *The Believer and the Powers That Are: Cases, History, and Other Data Bearing on the Relation of Religion and Government*, by John Thomas Noonan, Jr. (New York: Macmillan, 1987), and *Religious Liberty in the Supreme Court: The Cases That Define the Debate over Church and State*, edited by Terry Eastland (Grand Rapids, Mich.: Wm. B. Eerdmans, 1995). *The Amish and the State*, edited by Donald B. Kraybill (Baltimore, Md.: Johns Hopkins University Press, 1993), provides useful background for the *Yoder* case and the ongoing conflicts between the Amish and government concerning matters of religious conscience. *Native American Cultural and Religious Freedoms*, edited by John R. Wunder (New York: Garland, 1996), offers similar background to the Court's encounters with Native American religious practices. Bette Novit Evans's *Interpreting the Free Exercise of Religion: The Constitution and American Pluralism* (Chapel Hill: University of North Carolina Press, 1997) examines the Court's decisions regarding religious liberty, focusing especially on the role of religious freedom in nurturing pluralism. The Catholic perspective of a respected federal appellate judge on religious liberty in the United States may be found in *The Lustre of Our Country: The American Experience of Religious Freedom*, by John T. Noonan, Jr. (Berkeley: University of California Press, 1998). In *The Culture of Disbelief: How American Law and Politics Trivialize Religious Devotion*, by Stephen L. Carter (New York: Basic Books, 1993), the author challenges the Court's religion cases as having undermined religious devotion.

*Timothy L. Hall*

# SCHOOL PRAYER

*Description:* Prayers and Bible readings sanctioned by school officials were efforts to promote religious beliefs and values in students in public educational institutions.

*Relevant amendment:* First

*Significance:* The practice of reciting officially sanctioned prayers or reading from the Bible in U.S. public schools was challenged as a violation of the doctrine of separation of church and state under the establishment clause of the First Amendment of the U.S. Constitution. Supreme Court rulings resulted in strong public criticism and in continuing efforts by Congress to reverse the Court's decision.

In 1962 the Supreme Court issued one of its most controversial decisions in *Engel v. Vitale.* At issue was a nondenominational prayer composed by the regents of the state of New York that was to be recited in public school classrooms by teachers on a voluntary basis. It read: "Almighty God we acknowledge our dependence upon Thee, and we beg Thy blessings upon us, our parents, our teachers, and our Country." Justice Hugo L. Black,

*After the Supreme Court banned school prayer, teachers found other ways to start the school day.* (Library of Congress)

writing the opinion for the Court, noted that the apparatus of the public school system was employed in the promotion of religion and thus resulted in a violation of the establishment clause. A year later, the Court struck down a state-mandated practice of reading passages from the Bible without commentary in *Abington School District v. Schempp*. In his opinion, Justice Tom C. Clark applied the same "strict separation" analysis.

In its decision in *Lemon v. Kurtzman* (1971), the Court developed the establishment clause test that remains in use and is applied in church-state cases. Chief Justice Warren E. Burger wrote, "First, the statute must have a secular legislative purpose; second, its principal or primary effect must be one that neither advances nor inhibits religion; finally, the statute must not foster 'an excessive government entanglement with religion.'" The first element of this three-prong test was invoked in *Wallace v. Jaffree* (1985) when the Court ruled unconstitutional an Alabama law requiring a daily moment of silence for prayer or meditation in public schools. The *Lemon* test was reaffirmed in *Lee v. Weisman* (1992), when the Court struck down Providence, Rhode Island, public school principals' use of members of the clergy to offer invocation and benediction prayers as part of the formal graduation ceremonies for middle and high schools.

In its efforts to define and apply the establishment clause, the Court developed several perspectives on how best to ensure that government refrain from endorsing a particular faith while at the same time protecting the religious freedom of liberty and conscience. The result often was a confusing line of precedents that offered no distinct or enduring first principles that work in all situations. Despite continuing and heavy criticism levied against the Court, however, its separationist stance on government-supported religion in public schools has remained firm.

*Kenneth F. Mott*

# SEARCH AND SEIZURE

*Description:* The law enforcement practice of searching people and places in order to seize evidence or suspects

*Relevant amendment:* Fourth

*Significance:* The Fourth Amendment requires an appropriate balance between criminal investigations and protection of people's privacy and possessions

Search and seizure law provides a focal point for the collision of competing objectives within the justice system. On the one hand, police must search for and seize evidence and suspects in order to enforce the criminal laws. On the other hand, the Fourth Amendment's prohibition on "unreasonable" searches and seizures aims to avoid granting too much power to police officials and to preserve people's privacy and liberty. The U.S. Supreme Court has regularly been presented with cases requiring the justices to interpret the Fourth Amendment in a way that satisfies the dual goals of protecting people's rights and simultaneously permitting police officers to conduct effective investigations.

**Historical Origins.** American search and seizure law can be traced to English origins. Although the roots of search and seizure in English common law are not clear, the English gradually developed the practice of using warrants to justify government intrusions into citizens' homes, usually in a search for stolen goods. Eventually, English kings began to use general warrants justifying unlimited searches. These warrants did not specify the places to be searched or the items being sought. In effect, law enforcement officers could use the general warrants to search as they pleased. For example, warrants came to be used to discover whether people possessed any books or pamphlets that criticized the king. Because of these abusive practices, in the mid-eighteenth century Parliament passed resolutions condemning general warrants, and English courts began to limit the government's use of such warrants.

In the American colonies, people felt victimized by "writs of assistance," general warrants used by British officials to conduct exploratory searches of people's homes and businesses. These searches were frequently used to determine whether all proper taxes and duties had been paid to the king for goods produced, bought, or sold. Disputes about such British tax policies and search and seizure methods contributed to the American Revolution.

After independence from Britain was achieved, the authors of the Bill of Rights had keen memories of their dissatisfaction with British search and seizure practices. As a result, they wrote the Fourth Amendment in order to set explicit limits on the government's ability to conduct searches and undertake seizures. According to the Fourth Amendment, "The right of the people to be secure in their persons, houses, papers, and effects, against unreasonable searches and seizures, shall not be violated, and no warrants shall issue, but upon probable cause, supported by oath or affirmation, and particularly describing the place to be searched, and the persons or things to be seized." The drafters of the Bill of Rights thus sought to prevent unreasonable searches by requiring the use of specific warrants that were to be issued by neutral judges after the presentation of evidence justifying the need for a search.

**Legal Doctrines.** For most of American history, the Fourth Amendment had little impact on police searches because the Supreme Court paid little attention to such issues. Moreover, the Fourth Amendment was initially applied only against federal law enforcement officials and not against state or local police. Some state judges interpreted their state constitutions to place limits on local enforcement activities, but police officers in many areas searched people and homes with impunity. Such searches were sometimes carried out for purposes of intimidation and harassment of the poor, members of racial minority groups, or political opponents of the local mayor or police chief.

The Supreme Court's development and enforcement of strong search and seizure rules began with the case of *Weeks v. United States* in 1914. Here the Court invalidated federal officers' warrantless search of a home by creating the "exclusionary rule." The Court declared that if any federal searches violate the Fourth Amendment, no evidence discovered during those searches can be used against a defendant in court, even if the evidence demonstrates the defendant's guilt. By making exclusion of evidence the remedy for improper searches and seizures, the Supreme Court effectively declared that it was more important to protect people's rights to privacy and liberty than to make sure that every criminal law was strictly enforced. Advocates of the exclusionary rule assumed that it would deter police from conducting improper searches.

In 1949, the Supreme Court declared that the Fourth Amendment's protections are also applicable against state and local police, although the justices declined to apply the exclusionary rule to such officers (*Wolf v. Colorado*). In 1961, however, the Court began to treat state and local police searches in the same manner as federal searches by applying the exclusionary rule to all law enforcement officers (*Mapp v. Ohio*). The Court's decision generated an outcry from local law enforcement officials, who claimed that the justices were preventing the police from catching guilty criminals. During the 1960's, many politicians criticized the Supreme Court's decisions on this and other cases having to do with the rights of criminal defendants.

One such critic was Richard Nixon, who, after winning the presidency in 1968, used his appointment powers to place on the Supreme Court new justices who believed that the search and seizure rules were too harsh on the police. One Nixon appointee, Chief Justice Warren Burger, wrote an opinion containing strident criticisms of the exclusionary rule and expressed the view that Fourth Amendment rights could be protected without excluding useful evidence found during improper searches (*Bivens v. Six Unknown Named Agents*, 1971). Eventually, the Supreme Court's composition changed to contain a majority of justices who shared Burger's view. Thus, during the 1980's in particular, the Supreme Court issued many new decisions making it easier for law enforcement officers to conduct searches and seize evidence without obtaining proper warrants.

For example, in *United States v. Leon* (1984), the Supreme Court created a "good-faith" exception to the exclusionary rule by permitting police to use evidence seized under a defective warrant that had been based on inadequate justification. Because the error had been made by the judge who issued the warrant rather than by the police officers who conducted the search, the Court permitted the evidence to be used. In another example of relaxed standards, the justices permitted police to search an apartment based on an erroneous belief that the suspect's girlfriend possessed the authority to consent to the search (*Illinois v. Rodriguez*, 1990).

The Supreme Court has identified a variety of situations in which police officers can search and seize people or evidence without any warrant. Such situations include automobile searches, stopping and frisking suspicious persons on the street, searches incident to an arrest, and searches conducted in emergency circumstances. In each of these circumstances, society's need to enforce laws and preserve criminal evidence could be defeated if officers were always required to obtain a warrant before conducting a search. Automobiles, for example, are mobile and could disappear with important evidence if the Supreme Court did not define some circumstances in which warrantless searches are permissible. In defining these circumstances, however, the justices seek to limit the conditions that justify a search in order to withhold from police officers the power to conduct searches on a whim.

**A Difficult Balance.** American search and seizure laws reflect changing decisions about the most appropriate balance between the need to investigate crimes and the Fourth Amendment's mandated goal of protecting people from governmental intrusions. During the 1960's, when many Americans became keenly aware of the concept of constitutional rights and the existence of harsh and discriminatory law enforcement practices, the Supreme Court gave great emphasis to the protection of rights, even if it meant that some guilty offenders would go free. In the 1970's and 1980's, however, fear of crime became a growing concern for many Americans. The greater attention given to issues of law and order by the public and politicians was reflected in changes in the Supreme Court's composition and, eventually, in changes in legal doctrines affecting search and seizure. By the mid-1990's, the Supreme Court had relaxed many of the restrictions placed on police officers' search and seizure methods during the 1960's.

Although the rearrangement of priorities gave police officers a freer hand in conducting searches and using improperly obtained evidence, the changes did not represent an abandonment of the Fourth Amendment's restrictions on search and seizure. Even the justices who believed that greater emphasis should be placed on crime control still identified some circumstances in which police officers' search and seizure activities went beyond constitutional boundaries. For example, in *Minnesota v. Dickerson* (1993), the Court invalidated the seizure of cocaine from a man's pocket, asserting that police engaged in a warrantless stop and frisk search of a suspicious person on the street had erred in extending their inquiry beyond a search for a weapon.

Another factor also helped to protect the Fourth Amendment. By the late twentieth century, police officers and judges had become better trained, more professional, and less connected to and controlled by local patronage politics. Thus these officials had greater legal knowledge and ethical sensitivity than their predecessors and sought on their own to respect citizens' Fourth Amendment rights.

Debates about search and seizure are likely to continue, because of the difficulties involved in achieving a consensus among policy makers, scholars, and judges about the appropriate interpretation of the Fourth Amendment. The inevitable collisions between the social goals of vigorously investigating crimes and protecting citizens from governmental intrusions virtually guarantee that courts will continually be presented with situations in which the Fourth Amendment must be interpreted to strike an appropriate balance between these goals. The most significant conflicts about search and seizure have generally focused on the exclusionary rule. Many scholars and judges believe that the Fourth Amendment is merely an empty promise if police officers are permitted to use improperly obtained evidence, yet the Supreme Court gradually permitted greater use of such evidence during the 1980's. As society's values change and new justices are appointed to the Supreme Court, there are likely to be further developments in search and seizure doctrine. Thus it is difficult to imagine that search and seizure issues will ever disappear from the nation's justice policy agenda.

*Christopher E. Smith*

# SEARCH WARRANT REQUIREMENT

*Description:* The necessity of obtaining a warrant from a judge, based on meeting certain criteria, before law enforcement personnel can conduct a search.

*Relevant amendment:* Fourth

*Significance:* The Supreme Court generally ruled against warrantless searches, which violate Fourth Amendment protections against unreasonable searches, but allowed some exceptions.

While under British rule, the thirteen North American colonies were subject to a system of law, one aspect of which was the writ of assistance, which allowed government officials to conduct general searches. The writ of assistance empowered local authories to search anywhere for contraband. British judges did not need to hear any facts regarding illegal activity before a writ was issued and a search conducted. A search could be conducted on mere suspicion and at any location. After the American Revolution, the citizens of the new country were interested in limiting government searches. The Bill of Rights, ratified in 1791, contained the Fourth Amendment, which protected people from unreasonable searches. The Fourth Amendment set out the requirements the government must meet before a search warrant can be issued. The amendment states a warrant cannot be issued "but upon probable cause, supported by Oath or affirmation, and particularly describing the place to be searched, and the persons or things to be seized."

**Requirements of a Search Warrant.** Through numerous cases, the Supreme Court has defined the exact requirement of the warrant clause.

The Court has repeatedly defined the "probable cause" needed for a search warrant to be issued. To obtain a search warrant, law enforcement officers must show they have reliable and sufficient facts that would cause a reasonable person to believe a criminal act has been committed and that items or a person subject to seizure are at the location to be searched. Probable cause for the warrant cannot be based on what the subsequent search uncovers, only on the facts known when the warrant was issued. The Court also ruled that the probable cause must have been obtained legally. If law enforcement obtains information through an illegal search, it cannot remove the unconstitutional taint on the evidence by later applying for a search warrant. The amount of time between the gathering of probable cause and the execution of the search warrant may make the warrant "stale." If an inordinate amount of time passes and doubt arises whether the object of the warrant is still at the location, then the warrant may become invalid because of outdated probable cause.

The warrant must particularly describe the place to be searched or the item or person to be seized. The place to be searched must be described in the warrant to the extent that it can be set apart from all other locations. The Court has ruled that if an officer can with reasonable effort ascertain and identify the place to be searched then the warrant will be valid. The warrant must also describe items to be seized well enough that an officer can exclude all other items. Failure of the description to be precise enough to exclude other locations or failure to adequately describe an item or person to be seized will make the warrant invalid and the search illegal.

Although the Fourth Amendment does not expressly state that a warrant will be issued by a neutral and detached magistrate, it is generally regarded to be inherent. One of the purposes of a warrant is to allow a neutral party to decide whether law enforcement has probable cause to conduct a search. It is an essential part of the search warrant process to have a detached party review the facts and issue a warrant only if probable cause is present. Failure to have a warrant issued by an impartial and unbiased party will invalidate the warrant and make the search illegal.

The final requirement of the search warrant clause requires the warrant to be supported by an oath or affirmation. The oath or affirmation must be administered by the party issuing the warrant before testimony about probable cause. The Court has held that if the person supplying the probable cause recklessly disregards the truth or knowingly gives false evidence, the search warrant is invalid.

**Exceptions.** The Supreme Court has found six instances in which a search is reasonable and valid without a warrant. When an officer arrests a suspect, the officer may conduct a search incident to an arrest. However, the Court ruled that only the person and the immediate area are subject to search in *Chimel v. California* (1969). The arrest must be lawful or the evidence may be deemed inadmissible under the exclusionary rule. Under the automobile exception established by *Carroll v. United States* (1925), if the police have probable cause to believe that an automobile contains evidence of a crime, fruit of a crime, or contraband, a search may be conducted without a warrant. If law enforcement observes evidence of a crime, and they have a legal right to be at the location, they may make a warrantless search under the plain view doctrine. The Court has recognized that a citizen may waive his or her Fourth Amendment rights by voluntarily and intelligently consenting to a search, allowing an officer to make a legal warrantless search. In *Terry v. Ohio* (1968), the Court concluded that officers may conduct a limited search of a person (by frisking him or her) for weapons if they have a reasonable suspicion that the person is armed and dangerous. The Court also held that when an officer is in hot pursuit, or where evidence may be destroyed or hidden away, or the evidence is a threat to public safety, an officer may make a warrantless search.

**Further Reading**

Ferdico, John N. *Criminal Procedure for the Criminal Justice Professional.* 3d ed. St. Paul, Minn.: West Publishing, 1985.

Klotter, John C. *Legal Guide for Police: Constitutional Issues.* 5th ed. Cincinnati, Ohio: Anderson, 1999.

O'Brien, David M. *Constitutional Law and Politics: Civil Rights and Liberties.* 3d ed. 2 vols. New York: W. W. Norton, 1997.

*Steven J. Dunker*

# SEDITION ACT OF 1798

*Description:* Federal statute enacted in 1798 that made interference or attempted interference with operations of the U.S. government a crime, criminalized oral and written utterances that tended to bring the government into disrepute, and liberalized the common law of seditious libel.

*Relevant amendment:* First

*Significance:* The Federalists intended the act to preserve control of the government and suppress the emerging Jeffersonian Republicans. Supreme Court justices, riding on circuit, upheld the act while it was in force, but twentieth century justices viewed the act as unconstitutional.

The Sedition Act of 1798 had three substantive sections. Section 1, the least controversial, provided that opposition to governmental operations or antigovernment conspiracies could be punished by fines up to five thousand dollars and confinement between six months to five years.

Section 2, the most controversial, codified the common law of seditious libel. It penalized certain kinds of political speech and permitted criminal prosecution for "knowingly and willingly" writing, publishing, or uttering statements that were "false, scandalous, and malicious" with the intent to defame the government, Congress, or president or to bring them into disrepute. Statements that turned people against the government or that promoted opposition to the nation's laws were likewise actionable. Conviction allowed imprisonment for up to two years and a maximum fine of two thousand dollars.

Section 3 liberalized seditious libel procedures. Under the common law, libel charges against the government were actionable if they tended to disturb the public peace or create animosities. Prosecutors had to prove publication and bad tendency to secure convictions. The common law allowed truth as a defense to private libel but not to libel aimed at the government or public officials. The reformed procedures provided that juries, not judges, decided issues of publication and bad tendency. Judges continued to charge juries and explain the law, but juries decided the facts and the law and judged a statement's truth or falsity. These procedural reforms shifted decision making from judges to juries.

**Early Views.** The Supreme Court never ruled directly on the Sedition Act, but from its enactment to its expiration in March, 1801, justices riding on circuit upheld the measure, some heartily. Chief Justice Oliver Ellsworth believed it limited the dangers that the national government confronted. Associate Justice Samuel Chase was the Court's most ardent defender of the measure. In cases against James T. Callendar and Thomas Cooper, prominent Antifederalist writers, Chase was, in essence, more a prosecutor than a neutral justice. Chase's overzealous involvement in Sedition

*The Supreme Court never ruled on the Sedition Act, but Chief Justice Oliver Ellsworth believed it served a useful purpose.* (Collection of the Supreme Court of the United States)

Act cases was reflected in several charges in the articles of impeachment brought against him in 1804 by the House of Representatives. Justices William Cushing, William Paterson, and Bushrod Washington all warmly endorsed the act. Like Chase, they informed juries that it was constitutional and encouraged convictions.

Jeffersonian Republicans (also known as Democratic-Republicans) opposed the act from the outset and fought vigorously for its repeal in 1799, but failed. They insisted that it violated the freedom of speech and press clauses of the First Amendment and secured resolutions to that effect from the legislatures of Virginia and Kentucky. After becoming president, Thomas Jefferson pardoned those who had been convicted under the act and remitted some fines, stating that the act was unconstitutional. In 1840 Congress agreed and repaid the remaining Federalist-imposed fines.

**Later Views.** In a well-known dissent to *Abrams v. United States* (1919), Associate Justice Oliver Wendell Holmes wrote, "I had conceived that the United States through many years had shown its repentance for the Sedition Act." Louis D. Brandeis joined his dissent. Some thirty years later, in a dissenting opinion in *Beauharnais v. Illinois* (1952), Associate Justice Robert H. Jackson, chief prosecutor in the Nuremberg War Crimes trial, observed that the enactment of the Sedition Act had come to be viewed as "a breach of the First Amendment." Continuing, he wrote that "even in the absence of judicial condemnation, the political disapproval of the Sedition Act was so emphatic and sustained that federal prosecution of the press ceased for a century."

The Sedition Act met considerable condemnation in the latter half of the twentieth century. In *New York Times Co. v. Sullivan* (1964), Justice William J. Brennan, Jr., noted that "although the Sedition Act was never tested in this Court, the attack upon its validity has carried the day in the court of history." Associate Justices Hugo L. Black and William O. Douglas concurred in Brennan's judgment that the court of history condemned the act. They noted that it had "an ignominious end and by common consent has generally been treated as having been a wholly unjustifiable and much to be regretted violation of the First Amendment." In a concurring opinion in *Garrison v. Louisiana* (1964), Douglas and Black quoted Holmes's 1919 observation that the nation had repented for having passed the act. A decade later, they reiterated their contempt for the 1798 measure in *Gertz v. Robert Welch* (1974), noting that it was a congressional attempt to "muzzle" the First Amendment, "a regrettable legislative exercise plainly in violation of the First Amendment."

**Freedom Versus Unity.** In *Sullivan,* Brennan summarized not only the modern view of the act but also the classic reason for conflicting views about its constitutionality. Brennan wrote, "Thus we consider this case against the background of a profound national commitment to the principle that debate on public issues should be uninhibited, robust and wide-open, and that it may well include vehement, caustic, and sometimes unpleasantly sharp attacks on government and public officials." Although Brennan severely criticized the act and praised Jefferson for pardoning those sentenced under it, his method of interpretation comports well with that of both the Federalists and Democratic-Republicans in the early national era. National commitments were central to Brennan and those who supported or opposed the act during its short life. Expressive freedoms were not ends in themselves but served broad national commitments. When those commitments changed, interpretations of the freedom of speech and press clauses changed.

The Federalists and Democratic-Republicans had different commitments and dramatically different notions about speech and press functions. Both parties had a keen pride of accomplishment in winning the American Revolution and securing the Constitution. However, each viewed itself as the true revolutionary heir, and in the 1790's, they accused each other of deliberately squandering dearly won freedoms embodied in the Constitution. Each came perilously close to thinking of the other as an illegitimate faction, animated by a party spirit that threatened to undermine the benefits that the Revolution had secured. It seemed clear that if the other party threatened the nation, it should be suppressed. They agreed that limitations on expressive freedoms were instrumental to preserving the Revolution and protecting the Constitution but split decisively over which level of government was responsible for protecting the nation from illegitimate factions.

The Federalists passed the politically inspired Sedition Act in an attempt to suppress the Democratic-Republicans. Federalist prosecutors targeted only Democratic-Republican editors, newspapers, and party leaders, enforcing the act most vigorously just before the election of 1800 in order to dampen attacks by the opposition party and to maintain control of the national government. In all, twenty-four or twenty-five individuals were arrested for violating the act. At least fifteen were indicted, and of the eleven who went to trial, ten were convicted. Because Supreme Court justices accepted the Federalist position, they upheld the act's constitutionality.

In the early nineteenth century, after Jefferson became president, Democratic-Republicans—sometimes with Jefferson's approval, if not urging—prosecuted Federalist editors. Like their Federalist counterparts, Democratic-Republican prosecutors targeted political speech. Neither party tried to curb completely the other's speech. Prosecutions were intermittent, inconsistent, and unpredictable. Each party used law to create a legal environment that forced the other to be self-censoring; if self-censorship was glaringly ineffective, prosecutors might spring into action.

**The Two-Party System.** Americans of the early national era believed they had good but fragile institutions, worthy of careful nurturing. Federalists and Democratic-Republicans felt obligated to shield the nation from unwarranted partisan attacks and to preserve revolutionary gains by limiting the other party's expressive freedom. In essence, the two parties bitterly contested the legitimacy of competing parties. They agreed that the other's licentious speech needed curbing but split over whether the national or state governments should impose the limits. In *Dennis v. United States* (1951), Associate Justice Felix Frankfurter noted that the central issue in the case was federalism rather than free speech or press. Jefferson, he wrote, had not condemned the Sedition Act because it limited political speech but because he thought states, not Congress, had "the right to enforce restrictions on speech."

By the end of the 1820's Americans believed that competing parties were a logical analog to the Constitution; parties gave an additional method of checking power. When one party put forth a program or set of policies, the competing party sponsored an alternative and thus acted as a check on the first party. As the party system gained legitimacy, the need for restraints on speech and press, such as those in the Sedition Act, disappeared. In the twentieth century, the Court consistently condemned the Sedition Act; however, it sustained restrictions on expressive freedoms when, as the Federalists believed in the 1790's, a good society with decent institutions was under unwarranted assault.

**Further Reading**

James M. Smith's *Freedom's Fetters: The Alien and Sedition Laws and American Civil Liberties* (Ithaca, N.Y.: Cornell University Press, 1956), which has extensive bibliographic notes, remains the standard treatment of the Sedition Act. For a somewhat simpler treatment, see John C. Miller's *Crisis in Freedom: The Alien and Sedition Acts* (Boston: Little, Brown, 1951). Leonard W. Levy's *Freedom of Speech and Press in Early American History* (Cambridge, Mass.: Harvard University Press, 1960) and *Emergence of a Free Press* (New York: Oxford University Press, 1985) put the Sedition Act in its broader constitutional and legal context. John D. Stevens's "Congressional History of the 1798 Sedition Law," *Journalism Quarterly* 13 (Summer, 1966): 247-256 provides a useful introduction to the congressional history of the act and Federalist prosecutions under it. Walter Berns's "Freedom of the Press and the Alien and Sedition Laws: A Reappraisal," *Supreme Court Review* (1970): 109-159 examines the relationship between the Sedition Act, Federalism, and slavery. Richard Hofstadter's *The Idea of a Party System: The Rise of Legitimate Opposition in the United States, 1780-1840* (Berkeley:

University of California Press, 1970) considers the broader political and ideological background from which the act emerged. Gregg Costa's "John Marshall, the Sedition Act, and Free Speech in the Early Republic," *Texas Law Review* 77 (1999): 1011-1047 analyzes the prominent Federalist and future chief justice who opposed the Sedition Act.

*Lester G. Lindley*

# SEDITIOUS LIBEL

*Description:* The criminal act of undermining government by publishing criticism of it or of public officials

*Relevant amendment:* First

*Significance:* Reaction against the concept of seditious libel contributed significantly to the growth of a broader concept of freedom of the press

Part of the common-law heritage of American justice, the crime of seditious libel gave way to a more libertarian view of the press's role in American politics.

**Origins and Early History.** The concept of seditious libel developed as part of English common law and was transplanted to the American colonies. Primarily concerned with the preservation of government, it viewed criticism that tended to lower the respect of the people for government as a criminal "assault." Under the doctrine of seditious libel, it did not matter if the offending words were true; indeed, since damaging words based on truth were likely to be more effective, the law held that "the greater the truth, the greater the libel." In seditious libel trials, the role of the jury was limited to determining the fact of publication. The judge determined whether the words were libelous.

Prosecutions for seditious libel were relatively rare in colonial America, though the concept did give rise to one of the eighteenth century's most famous trials. In 1735, John Peter Zenger, printer of the *New York Weekly Journal,* was charged with seditious libel for his criticisms of the colony's governor. Though Zenger admitted that he had published the offending material, he maintained that it was true and that truth was an adequate defense. Despite the judge's determination that his words were libelous, the jury refused to convict Zenger and found him not guilty. His resultant popularity may well have discouraged other prosecutions.

**Seditious Libel and Partisan Politics.** Seditious libel was still a crime when the Bill of Rights was adopted in 1791, and contemporary opinion seems to have held that the First Amendment's protection of freedom of the press did not eliminate it. Freedom of the press was held primarily to mean that there should be no censorship before publication, or "prior restraint." After publication, authors and printers could be held accountable for what was published. In the heightened tensions of the nation's first party system in the 1790's, the Federalists and Jeffersonian Republicans criticized each other in the press in terms that ranged from the vigorous to the scurrilous. Fearing that their opponents threatened the very stability of the government, the Federalists persuaded Congress to pass the Sedition Act of 1798. This act made it a crime to bring the president or Congress into disrepute. It also modified the law of seditious libel to allow truth as a defense and to permit juries to determine whether a publication was libelous. The act was employed in a very partisan manner: All those prosecuted under it were Republicans; all the judges were Federalists. Thomas Jefferson and his followers argued that the law was unconstitutional. The act expired in 1800, and after Jefferson's election to the presidency in 1800, Congress repaid the fines of those convicted under the act. The Sedition Act created a strongly negative reaction in public opinion. While the act never came before the Supreme Court and seditious libel was never formally repudiated, the increasingly democratic nature of American politics ensured that any government initiating a seditious libel prosecution would be subject to ridicule. For the next century little was heard of the crime.

*Associate Justice Brockholst Livingston, who joined the Supreme Court in 1807, had been a strong supporter of state prosecutions of seditious libel while he was on the New York Supreme Court.* (Collection of the Supreme Court of the United States)

**Later History of Seditious Libel.** Though the common-law crime of seditious libel was seldom used as the basis of prosecutions, the attitude that the federal government needed protection from the writings of subversives surfaced periodically in the twentieth century, particularly during times of crisis. During World War I, the Espionage Act of 1917 made a variety of forms of antigovernment expression illegal, particularly after it was amended by a new sedition act in 1918. During the Cold War, the Smith Act of 1940 was used to prosecute the leaders of the American Communist Party partly on the grounds that the party's publications had seditious purposes. As late as the 1960's, efforts were made by opponents of the Civil Rights movement to use the law of libel to silence their opponents in the press. The Supreme Court's decision in *New York Times Co. v. Sullivan* (1964), however, established the principal that political figures had to prove "actual malice" rather than mere inaccuracy to sustain a charge of libel.

Though seditious libel has never been declared a dead letter, the absence of its use and the relative rarity of other prosecutions utilizing the concept of sedition are a mirror of the extent to which American government has come to accept the view that vigorous public debate, including strong criticism of the government and its officials, is necessary to the existence of a free society.

*William C. Lowe*

# SELF-INCRIMINATION, IMMUNITY AGAINST

*Description:* One's right, before any compulsory forum, to resist testifying on any matter that might ensnare one in a criminal investigation or aid in one's own prosecution.

*Relevant amendment:* Fifth

*Significance:* Long regarded as the foundation of an accusatory system of justice, the immunity from self-incrimination imposes on the state the burden of presenting at trial proof of guilt without the participation of the accused. The Supreme Court's extension of this right into the pretrial stages of the criminal process has been controversial.

The right of the accused to refuse to testify against himself or herself gained acceptance in English common law after the seventeenth century, a period of strife that saw frequent reliance on the compulsory oath as an instrument of political and religious persecution. So venerated was this right in North America that it was included in the Fifth Amendment to the U.S. Constitution, which provided that "No person . . . shall be compelled in any criminal case to be a witness against himself." Because of its prominence in movies and television, it remains the defendants' right most identified in the popular mind.

Although the Constitution locates the right "in any criminal case," the Supreme Court extended it to any forum in which the individual might be compelled to testify, such as grand juries or legislative investigations. It is, however, limited to subjects on which the individual might be vulnerable to prosecution and therefore does not cover testimony that is merely humiliating or that exposes the witness to civil suit. Additionally, the right is limited to testimony and does not bar the compulsory production of nontestimonial evidence, such as fingerprints, photographs, blood samples, appearance in a lineup, or even providing voice exemplars. It is only the suspect's words that may not be used in evidence for his or her own undoing. The right can be asserted only on behalf of oneself and does not bar compulsory testimony against a relative or accomplice. Properly asserted, the right is absolute, but it can be circumvented by a grant of immunity from prosecution, on the theory that such immunity offers protection coextensive with the right. The right is frequently exercised when defendants decline to take the witness stand to avoid cross-examination. Understandably, this is a risky right to assert because juries might infer guilt from silence.

**Pretrial Confessions.** Assertion of immunity from self-incrimination at trial would be a hollow exercise if the suspect were compelled to confess to a criminal charge before trial and the confession later read into evidence by the prosecutor at trial. The National Commission on Law Observance and Enforcement, commonly known as the Wickersham Commission, in 1931 documented widespread use of physical brutality by police departments to extract such confessions, especially from members of groups outside the mainstream of society.

In *Brown v. Mississippi* (1936), the Supreme Court overturned the capital murder convictions of three African American defendants resting solely on confessions that had been extracted after brutal whippings at the hands of police. Aside from the inherent unreliability of such confessions, the Court sought to discourage such behavior on the part of the police. In *Chambers v. Florida* (1940), the Court formulated the voluntariness rule, requiring trial judges to assess the full circumstances surrounding pretrial confessions—not only allegations of physical brutality—to ensure that the suspects had voluntarily confessed to the charges against them. Such voluntariness was undermined by any circumstances tending to overbear on the suspect's free will, including various psychological "third degree" tactics. These cases rested on the due process clause of the Fourteenth Amendment but were subsumed under the right against self-incrimination in *Malloy v. Hogan* (1964).

The most notorious of this line of decisions was *Miranda v. Arizona* (1966). Experience with the voluntariness rule had revealed reluctance on the part of trial judges to bar confessions extracted by questionable techniques. Widespread complaints, especially by minorities, about police tactics in stationhouse backrooms and a growing egalitarian ethos on the Court led to replacement of the voluntariness rule. The Court ruled that prosecutors were barred from using any incriminating statements made by a suspect before trial unless procedures were already in place to ensure that confessions were based solely on the free will of the defendant. The Court did not specify what these procedures might be, but until the states developed effective alternatives, police would be required to read suspects the Miranda rights before any custodial interrogation. Failure to warn suspects of their right to remain silent and to inform them that statements they made might be used as evidence against them and that they had a right to counsel would result in the exclusion of any incriminating statements from trial. Although more than thirty years of empirical research has found *Miranda*'s impact on confessions to be negligible, the decision quickly became a lightning rod for attacks on the Court. Critics, such as presidential candidate Richard M. Nixon, accused the Court of favoring defendants at the expense of legitimate law enforcement techniques.

Since the 1970's the Court has tended to restrict the application of *Miranda*. In *Harris v. New York* (1971), the Court held that statements made in the absence of *Miranda* warnings, while barred from direct evidence, could be used for cross-examination if the accused took the witness stand. In *New York v. Quarles* (1984), the Court permitted the use of statements obtained by police if motivated by reasonable concerns for public safety. Other decisions have turned primarily on questions of when the suspect was under custody or what constituted an interrogation.

**Guilty Pleas.** In court, the immunity against self-incrimination is a "fighting right," meaning it does not become effective unless specifically asserted by the accused. It can be waived, however, and usually is. Over 90 percent of all felony convictions in the United States result from guilty pleas, usually pursuant to plea bargains. The effect of a guilty plea is the waiver of all trial and pretrial rights, including relief from self-incrimination. Trial judges are obliged to examine the guilty plea on record to verify that it is offered knowingly and intelligently, but this is pro forma. Usually, the guilty plea has been arranged by counsel. Nevertheless, the Court has come a long way from *Twining v. New Jersey* (1908), in which it held the right against self-incrimination not fundamental to a fair trial, as required by the Fourteenth Amendment, or *Palko v. Connecticut* (1937), in which the right against self-incrimination was pronounced not essential to justice. Whatever might be the practice of other nations, the immunity against self-incrimination is a fundamental component of U.S. law.

**Further Reading**

Berger, Mark. *Taking the Fifth.* Lexington, Mass.: D.C. Heath, 1980.
Bodenhamer, David J. *Fair Trial: Rights of the Accused in American History.* New York: Oxford University Press, 1992.
Helmholtz, R. H., Charles M. Gray, John H. Langbein, Eben Moglin, Hesury M. Smith, and Albert W. Altschuler. *The Privilege Against Self-Incrimination: Its Origin and Development.* Chicago: University of Chicago Press, 1997.
Levy, Leonard W. *Against the Law: The Nixon Court and Criminal Justice.* New York: Harper & Row, 1974.
\_\_\_\_\_. *Origins of the Fifth Amendment.* New York: Oxford University Press, 1968.

*John C. Hughes*

# SILVER PLATTER DOCTRINE

*Description:* The exception to the exclusionary rule that permitted federal prosecutors to introduce at trial evidence obtained illegally by state law enforcement agents.
*Relevant amendment:* Fourth

*Significance:* Until a 1960 Supreme Court ruling, federal prosecutors bypassed the requirements of the Fourth Amendment by using the silver platter doctrine to obtain admissible evidence against suspected criminals.

In *Weeks v. United States* (1914), the Supreme Court articulated what became known as the exclusionary rule : Evidence obtained in violation of the Fourth Amendment was inadmissible in federal court. This decision, however, did not apply to state courts. In fact, thirty-five years later, in *Wolf v. Colorado* (1949), the Court, while incorporating the Fourth Amendment into the Fourteenth Amendment, specifically rejected the notion that the exclusionary rule should be binding on the states. As a result, states were free to adopt or ignore the exclusionary rule.

This double standard gave rise to the silver platter doctrine. State law enforcement agents, often at the request of federal officers, conducted illegal seizures. The evidence obtained was then served up to federal authorities on a "silver platter" and was admissible in federal court because federal officers had not participated in its seizure. In *Elkins v. United States* (1960), the Court abandoned this exception, claiming that it undermined federalism. In *Mapp v. Ohio* (1961), the Court extended the exclusionary rule to state criminal prosecutions.

*Richard A. Glenn*

# SMITH ACT

*Description:* Officially known as the Alien Registration Act, the Smith Act in 1949 required aliens to register with the U.S. government and made it a crime to advocate overthrowing American governments by force
*Relevant amendment:* First
*Significance:* The Smith Act became the U.S. government's primary legal tool for attacking the American Communist Party during the early years of the Cold War

As World War II approached, fears of foreign-inspired subversive activity grew in the United States. Concerned especially that the buildup of American defenses might be threatened by sabotage, Congress reacted by passing the Alien Registration Act, which came to be more generally

known as the Smith Act for its major proponent, Congressman Howard
W. Smith of Virginia.

The Smith Act had two major thrusts. The first sought greater control
over aliens living in the United States. Under the act, aliens had to register with the government, be fingerprinted, carry identity cards, and report yearly. (The registration requirement was dropped in 1982.) Those
involved in what were regarded as subversive activities could be deported.
The other major provisions of the act were directed at disloyal activities.
These made it a crime for anyone to advocate the overthrow of the federal government or other American governments by force or violence, to
enter a conspiracy to advocate such a course of action, or to become a
knowing member of such a group. Penalties for those convicted under
the act included a ten-thousand-dollar fine, up to ten years in prison, or
both.

Though a wartime measure, the Smith Act was used relatively little during World War II. As postwar tension between the United States and the
Soviet Union developed into the Cold War, however, the act came to the
fore as concerns about the possibility of Communist subversion in the
United States rose. By the late 1940's, there were increasing concerns
about the activities of members of the American Communist Party and
sympathetic groups, and charges of communist penetration of the government were increasingly made. The administration of President Harry
S. Truman was charged with being slow to meet the communist challenge
at home. Partly in response, the Truman administration used the Smith
Act to attack the party's organization.

In 1948 Eugene Dennis and ten other communist leaders were arrested and charged under the act. They were convicted and sentenced to
prison. They appealed, arguing that the Smith Act was an unconstitutional violation of the First Amendment's protection of free expression.
Their appeal was denied by the Supreme Court in 1951.

Use of the Smith Act continued during the 1950's. Altogether, more
than 140 arrests were made under the act. Later Supreme Court decisions in *Yates v. United States* (1957) and *Brandenburg v. Ohio* (1969) broadened the extent of expression protected by the First Amendment, but the
Smith Act itself continued to be held as constitutional.

# SPEECH AND PRESS, FREEDOM OF

*Description:* Constitutional rights to speak freely and to publish one's views, free of government censorship.
*Relevant amendment:* First
*Significance:* Viewed by most scholars and citizens alike as the very foundation of all other constitutional rights, freedom of speech and freedom of the press are American ideals, indispensable to the democracy, and the subject of many Supreme Court cases.

When most Americans consider the U.S. Constitution, the Bill of Rights, or the Supreme Court, inevitably they think about freedom of speech and freedom of the press. These twin freedoms, expressly guaranteed in the First Amendment, represent the quintessential liberties on which the United States was founded. Asked to enumerate the rights protected by the Constitution, the vast majority of Americans would readily name free speech and free press. Asked to articulate what sets the United States apart from all other nations, most Americans would identify these same freedoms.

**The Struggle to Protect Freedom of Speech and Press.** Respect and pride for freedom of speech and freedom of the press are sincere and heartfelt—until tested in the harsh reality of the tumultuous and diverse culture, in which a wide array of political, religious, social, economic, ideological, racial, ethnic, and geographical constituencies are pitted against one another. In that crucible, pious fidelity to "free speech" and "free press" too often gives way to the inevitable qualification.

What inevitably follows is an ever-increasing list of exceptions to freedom of speech and freedom of the press, including not only the small group of exceptions recognized in the law, such as obscenity, libel, fighting words, false advertising, and criminal solicitation, but also newly proposed exceptions, such as hate speech, sexual harassment, offensive or sacrilegious art, and sexually explicit yet nonobscene photographs, magazines, videos, and Internet images.

When it comes to freedom of the press, the general public and the juries on which they serve sometimes ignore the First Amendment and hold books, films, and television shows financially liable for the acts of disturbed individuals and social miscreants who commit suicide, violent crimes, or general mayhem allegedly "inspired" by what they read or saw in a film or on television.

It is in this contentious atmosphere that the Supreme Court continues to serve its historic role in interpreting the meaning, scope, and limitations of freedom of speech and freedom of the press.

**The Meaning of Freedom of Speech and Press.** Generally speaking, "freedom of speech" refers to the right of individuals to freely express themselves, without fear of government restrictions. "Freedom of the press" refers more to the right of the publishers of newspapers, magazines, and books; the writers and producers of motion pictures and television productions; and the creators and distributors of CDs to sell and distribute these materials, free of government censorship. Beyond this general distinction, for constitutional purposes, scholarly analysis and Supreme Court decisions often merge the two concepts under the rubric "freedom of expression," frequently applying principles developed in one area to the other. In free press cases, civil libertarians and attorneys will readily cite precedents that advance constitutional protections in free speech cases, and vice versa.

Although the First Amendment speaks in absolute and unqualified terms ("Congress shall make no law abridging . . . freedom of speech or of the press"), the question has always been what is meant by "freedom of speech" or "freedom of the press." There is a school of thought, to which only two justices, Hugo L. Black and William O. Douglas, adhered, that holds that with respect to speech and the press, the First Amendment is absolute; it means what it says: "Congress shall make *no* law . . . "—not "some laws" or "almost no laws," but "no law." First Amendment absolutists simply cite the language of the First Amendment and accept no substitutes.

The other school of thought, to which all other justices have subscribed, believes that at the time the First Amendment was ratified, there were certain limited exceptions to freedom of speech and freedom of the press, which were already part of these concepts when they were included in the First Amendment. Thus, for example, in America in 1791, there were libel laws under which people could be punished for what they wrote or said about someone else if it was false and defamatory. Likewise, there were obscenity laws under which publishers could be fined or jailed for selling books or pictures deemed obscene under prevailing standards. Given the existence of these laws at the time the First Amendment was adopted and ratified, the majority view rejects the absolutist approach in favor of an interpretation that affords the broadest sweep of constitutional protection for all subject matter and forms of communications, subject only to limited exceptions.

Consequently, the Court has held that the First Amendment protects motion pictures, radio, television, cable, recordings and most recently the Internet, regardless of the fact that none of this technology existed when the First Amendment was written. No justice seriously argues that the First Amendment is frozen in the eighteenth century in terms of the forms of communications that existed at that time. Instead, the Court takes a functional view of freedom of speech and freedom of the press to encompass any form of communication that provides information much as books and newspapers did in 1791.

**Theories of Freedom of Expression.** A variety of theories have been offered for the protection of freedom of expression. One is that truth is best discovered by the free exchange of ideas. In his seminal 1644 work *Areopagitica,* John Milton confidently asked that if Truth and falsehood grappled, "Who ever knew Truth put to the worse, in a free and open encounter?" In 1919 Justice Oliver Wendell Holmes wrote that "the best test of truth is the power of the thought to get itself accepted in the competition of the market." No metaphor has proved more lasting in the defense of free expression than the "marketplace of ideas."

Another important rationale upholding freedom of expression is based on the principles of human dignity and autonomy. The opportunity to freely express oneself develops inner satisfaction and individual fulfillment. In this view, freedom of expression is worthy of constitutional protection as a step toward the realization of self-identity or what Justice Thurgood Marshall called "a spirit that demands self-expression." This rationale has nothing to do with the search for truth or the advancement of self-government. Instead, it justifies free expression based purely on its benefit to the individual.

At the other end of the spectrum is a rationale based on the common good rather than the good of the individual. Under this view, freedom of expression is indispensable to the progress of self-governance in a democratic society. For citizens to participate fully in their own government they need to exchange information and express their opinions on pending legislation, candidates, and public policy issues. Only open and unfettered communication, free of the distortions produced by government censorship, ensures the viability of democracy.

The final rationale supporting freedom of expression is closely related to the advancement of self-government but focuses on the value of dissent. Whereas the theory of self-governance looks at the role of free expression among those working *within* the system, the dissent rationale recognizes the value of those who work *outside* the system. Sometimes referred to as the "loyal opposition," dissident speech is protected because of the realization that by allowing opponents of the established order to peacefully and freely express themselves, the risk of violent opposition is reduced and hopefully eliminated. Tolerating, or even encouraging, dissent serves as a "safety value" preventing the political system from getting "overheated."

**Majority Rule and Minority Rights.** Disputes over freedom of expression generally pit the rule of the majority against the rights of the minority. The question is whether the expression of ideas deemed dangerous to the purpose of ensuring order, morality, loyalty, or some other important interest valued by society at large should be suppressed. Examples of these conflicts abound through the annals of the Supreme Court.

In the early 1970's, American Nazis announced their intent to conduct a march through Skokie, Illinois, a suburb of Chicago, inhabited by a large number of Jewish families, including survivors of the Holocaust. The march seemed purposely designed to deeply offend the Jewish community in Skokie. The city officials took various steps to block the march, but the Nazis, represented by the American Civil Liberties Union (ACLU), went to court, claiming they had a right to express their views, regardless of whether they gave offense. The ACLU was attacked for representing such despicable bigots and reportedly lost thirty thousand members. Nevertheless, the ACLU stood by the principle that regardless of whether it disagreed with the Nazis, it would defend their right to speak and march. Eventually, the federal courts agreed that the First Amendment protected the Nazis' freedom of expression. Ironically, having won the right to march, the Nazis chose not to hold the event.

Another issue is whether the government can deny funding to artists because of the controversial or offensive nature of their work. This issue was squarely presented in 1991 when Congress imposed content restrictions on the grants awarded by the National Endowment for the Arts (NEA), a federal agency established in 1965 to further the progress of the arts. Congressional leaders claimed that artists could create all the controversial art they wanted, they simply had no constitutional right to demand that the government pay for it. Civil libertarians countered that once the government decided to provide funds for artists through the NEA, it could not condition those funds on whether the government agreed or disagreed with the artistic, political, religious, social, or other messages communicated by the art. Eventually, the courts agreed with the artists and struck down the congressional restrictions. The Supreme Court held that the NEA could establish goals encouraging "decency" and respect for diverse American values but could not reject specific works of art based on their controversial content.

Every advance in technology has renewed the battle over freedom of expression. By the 1990's, the conflict was centering on the Internet and the revolutionary Worldwide Web. In 1996 Congress passed the Communications Decency Act (CDA) making it a crime to communicate "indecent" material to persons under eighteen years old. The ACLU promptly challenged the CDA, first before a federal three-judge panel and later before the Supreme Court.

The Court had never ruled on a case involving freedom of expression on the Internet. The CDA case squarely presented the question of whether the Internet would enjoy the same wide-open, robust constitutional protection accorded to books, newspapers, and magazines or the more restricted, narrow protection granted to television and radio. In other words, the Court had to decide whether the print model or the broadcast model would apply to the Internet. In 1998 the Supreme Court established the Internet model. The Court found that the Internet was a vast marketplace of ideas entitled to the widest possible constitutional protection. With respect to the CDA, the Court held that the adult population could not be reduced to what is acceptable for children. In the absence of effective age verification technology, the Court found that the responsibility for protecting children from indecent material on the Internet rested with their parents, not the government.

Even before the Internet, sexually explicit speech in books, art, films, and home videos has proven to be a perplexing subject for public debate and Court review. No other area of First Amendment litigation has prompted such heated and persistent controversy, pitting libertines against moralists. By 1968 the Court had adopted a three-part test for defining obscenity: sexually explicit material could not be banned unless it appealed to a prurient, or morbid, interest in sex; exceeded contemporary community standards; and was utterly without redeeming social value.

In 1973, in the case of *Miller v. California*, the Court recast the third prong (in an apparent effort to expand the scope of unprotected obscenity). Under *Miller*, material could be banned if it lacked "serious literary, artistic, political, or scientific value." Although one leading First Amendment scholar optimistically entitled his 1969 book *The End of Obscenity*, federal and state governments continue to prosecute material deemed obscene, while at the same time, the adult video business is thriving. Given the power and mystery of sex, on one hand, and the tendency of legislators to pass laws they believe are necessary to protect people from themselves on the other, the controversy over obscenity is unlikely to end in the near future.

The Court held that generally laws that punish defamation do not violate the First Amendment, except when it comes to public officials and public figures. Defamation, which encompasses libel (the written word, as well as radio and television), is defined as a false statement of fact that holds someone up to shame and humiliation. The defamation of a private person implicates little or no First Amendment concerns. However, allowing an individual or a publisher to be punished for attacking an elected official or a celebrity or famous person tends to suppress the sort of public criticism that is at the heart of the First Amendment.

In 1964 the Court faced a historic dispute that presented these important issues in the case of *New York Times Co. v. Sullivan*. At the height of the Civil Rights movement, a group called the Committee to Defend Martin Luther King took out an ad in *The New York Times* condemning racism and the actions of the officials in Montgomery, Alabama. One of the officials, L. B. Sullivan, sued for libel and won a $500,000 judgment against the *Times*. The Court overturned the verdict and established powerful protection for freedom of the press.

In a groundbreaking opinion by Justice William J. Brennan, Jr., the Court held that the freedom to criticize the government was so important, and the possibility that journalists might make innocent mistakes was so great, that defamation suits against public officials could not go forward unless the official proved that the defamatory statement was made with what the Court called "actual malice," that is, knowledge of falsity or reckless disregard for the truth. Nothing less, according to Justice Brennan's eloquent opinion, would serve the "profound national commitment to the principle that debate on public issues should be uninhibited, robust, and wide-open."

Freedom of speech encompasses not only what is spoken and written but also actions that are intended to communicate a message, such as burning a draft card to protest a war or burning a U.S. flag to express disagreement with government policy. Symbolic speech, as these expressive activities are called, is entitled to constitutional protection when it does not involve violence or destruction of private property, because it conveys, often in a most dramatic fashion, political, social, and other ideas.

In 1989, in *Texas v. Johnson*, Justice Brennan, speaking for the majority of the Court, characterized as "a bedrock principle underlying the First Amendment" that "the Government may not prohibit the expression of an idea simply because society finds the idea itself offensive or disagreeable." Justice Brennan suggested that there was "no more appropriate response to burning a flag than waving one's own."

One of the greatest threats to freedom of expression is prior restraint. This term refers to any effort by government to suppress speech even before it is published. The history of England is stained by examples of the Crown preventing books and newspapers from being printed. Indeed, the origin of modern copyright laws was a system of royal licensing with permission bestowed only on those publishers favored by the rulers. Many scholars argue that the essential purpose of the First Amendment was to prohibit prior restraint. If so, it has fulfilled that goal admirably because the Court has never upheld a prior restraint. In the landmark case involving the Pentagon Papers, a series of secret U.S. Defense Department studies on the Vietnam War, the Court rejected the request of the administration of Richard M. Nixon to enjoin *The New York Times* and *The Washington Post* from publishing the controversial reports. What the king of England could have done with a stroke of a pen, the First Amendment prohibited the U.S. government from doing.

**Speech Codes.** Although American campuses in the 1960's were a hotbed of freedom and openness, by the 1990's the antithesis emerged at many colleges and universities in the form of speech codes. These campus regulations prohibited, usually in broad and ambiguous terms, speech that was offensive to women and minorities. However, from the standpoint of freedom of expression, campus speech codes posed a serious threat. With little precedent and even less guidance, neither students nor faculty members could tell what sort of statements could get them in trouble.

Self-censorship out of fear of punishment is often referred to as the "chilling effect" caused by government regulation of speech. Because most people will steer clear of punishment, they will refrain from making statements or publishing material that is constitutionally protected for fear they may run afoul of the government. When this happens, freedom of expression suffers. This is one of the primary reasons that laws or regulations affecting speech must be written with great certainty and cannot be vague or ambiguous.

Campus speech codes were generally far from clear and certain. They usually spoke of speech that was "offensive," "degrading" or "hostile," terms that were highly subjective and lacked any objective definition. Consequently, the courts have consistently struck down campus speech codes when they were challenged on First Amendment grounds. Generally, the courts found that controversial ideas were at risk of being censored in the name of combating racism, sexism, and bigotry.

Justice Oliver Wendell Holmes wrote that the true purpose of the First Amendment was to protect the ideas Americans hate. Justice Louis D. Brandeis believed that the answer to offensive speech was *more* speech, not *less*. In other words, in a democratic society, committed to freedom of expression, the remedy to social evils is free and open debate.

**Further Reading**

Louis E. Ingelhart's *Press and Speech Freedoms in the World, from Antiquity Until 1998: A Chronology* (Westport, Conn.: Greenwood Press, 1998) takes an international approach, covering the concept of freedom of speech and press from ancient times until the modern period. Margaret A. Blanchard's *Revolutionary Sparks: Freedom of Expression in Modern America* (New York: Oxford University Press, 1992) also takes a historical approach, covering the concept from the beginning to the end of the twentieth century. *The First Freedom Today: Critical Issues Relating to Censorship and to Intellectual Freedom* (Chicago: American Library Association, 1984), edited by Robert B. Downs and Ralph E. McCoy, also covers the history of the concept but provides numerous essays examining the modern issues and controversies involving the First Amendment rights. Two books concentrating on the origin and meaning of the First Amendment are *The First Amendment: The Legacy of George Mason* (London: Associated University Presses, 1985), edited by T. Daniel Shumate, and George Anastaplo's *The Constitutionalist: Notes on the First Amendment* (Dallas: Southern Methodist University Press).

*Stephen F. Rohde*

# SPEEDY TRIAL

*Description:* Presentation of an accused person for trial within a reasonable amount of time to expedite justice and to prevent defendants from languishing in jail indefinitely.

*Relevant amendment:* Sixth

*Significance:* The Sixth Amendment to the U.S. Constitution ensures criminal defendants the right to a speedy trial but does not set a specific time limit between arrest and trial. The Supreme Court did not attempt to set specific guidelines for acceptable delays, preferring to examine the facts of each individual case.

The guarantee of a speedy trial for persons accused of criminal wrongdoing is a concept rooted in English common law. Although the Sixth Amendment to the U.S. Constitution guarantees the right to a speedy trial, it does not specify what length of time is appropriate. The Supreme Court has refrained from clearly separating permissible trial delays from unconstitutional delays, preferring instead to evaluate delays on a case-by-case basis according to a balancing approach. Under this approach, developed in *Barker v. Wingo* (1972), the Court considers the length and reason for the delay as well as whether the delay was to the defendant's advantage or disadvantage. The Court left the task of setting more definite time limits to state and federal legislatures. In 1974 Congress passed the Speedy Trial Act, which set a normal deadline of one hundred days between arrest and trial in federal courts; many states later passed similar laws.

Although the guarantee of speedy trial is derived from the Constitution, Court decisions interpreting the due process and equal protection clauses of the Fourteenth Amendment have provided for speedy trials in state criminal proceedings; for example, in *Klopfer v. North Carolina* (1967), the Court ruled unconstitutional a North Carolina law allowing the indefinite postponement of a trial. It also ruled in *Strunk v. United States* (1973) that dismissal of charges was the only acceptable remedy for violation of a defendant's right to speedy trial.

*Michael H. Burchett*

# STATES' RIGHTS

*Description:* Constitutional argument that state governments possess sovereignty, autonomous governing power that approximates the authority and status of the federal government.

*Relevant amendment:* Tenth

*Significance:* After the Articles of Confederation went into effect in 1781, the states began to assert a degree of independence from the federal government. The Supreme Court's interpretation of states' rights was not consistent, although policy making in the United States tended to be more local and diverse and less national and uniform.

The states' rights argument dates back to the founding of the United States and the first national constitution, the Articles of Confederation. The articles were drafted by delegates of the "states in Congress assembled" and explicitly provided for state sovereignty: "Each state retains its sovereignty, freedom, and independence." The U.S. Constitution of 1789, however, makes no mention of sovereignty, implies popular sovereignty in the Preamble's invocation of "We the people," and explicitly declares national supremacy in Article VI: "This Constitution, and the Laws of the United States which shall be made in Pursuance thereof . . . shall be the supreme Law of the Land . . . , any Thing in the Constitution or Laws of any State to the Contrary notwithstanding." The first Congress in 1789 proposed what came to be the Tenth Amendment in order to pacify the antifederalists, the states' rights advocates who opposed the Constitution of 1789. This amendment's language still serves as the principal constitutional grounds for states' rights arguments: "The powers not delegated to the United States by the Constitution, nor prohibited by it to the States, are reserved to the States respectively, or to the people."

**Determining States' Rights.** For two hundred years, constitutional questions have arisen when the national government's delegated powers and states' reserved powers have come into actual or potential conflict. Peaceful resolution of these disagreements required a legitimate and authoritative decision maker, and the candidates were the involved state or the national government (Congress or the Supreme Court). With few exceptions, the Court emerged as the final arbiter of states' rights in conflict with federal law. For example, in *McCulloch v. Maryland* (1819), the great nationalist, Chief Justice John Marshall, in the opinion for the Court, wrote that the supremacy clause of Article VI prevented Maryland from taxing the Second Bank of the United States. Two years later in *Cohens v. Virginia* (1821), the Court held that it and not the highest state court had final say on the meaning of the U.S. Constitution in a case involving a state conviction for selling federal lottery tickets.

Similarly in *Cooper v. Aaron* (1958), the Court said in a school desegregation case that it, not Arkansas officials, was "supreme in the exposition of the law of the Constitution." Some exceptions to the Court's primacy in determining the boundaries of states' rights and federal authority have been the Union's military dominance in the Civil War, Congress's authority to decide when general federal regulations apply to the states, and state supreme courts' decision-making power over matters of purely state law.

**Rejection of Radical States' Rights.** John C. Calhoun, an American statesman and author who died in 1850, provided the nation's most systematic and philosophical treatment of states' rights. His theory of the "concurrent majority" posited that no action of the national government would be legitimate unless each separate interest represented in Congress would forgo its inherent right of veto and assent to the policy. States' rights corollaries of this theory were that the states are sovereign, and as such, they adopted the Constitution and could repudiate the national compact whenever it would be in their interest.

This kind of states' rights argument was presented to the Court in *McCulloch* by Luther Martin, counsel for Maryland and an ardent states' rights advocate. According to Martin, Maryland could tax the Second Bank of the United States because the states are "truly sovereign" and "possess supreme dominion." The response of the Court, written by Chief Justice Marshall, was that the Constitution was the creation of the sovereign people, not of the states, and it was therefore superior to the states. In *Texas v. White* (1869), the Court again had occasion to rule on the theory that a state could renounce its membership in the Union. The Court rejected radical state sovereignty in ruling that the Constitution "looks to an indestructible Union." Therefore, Texas was not legally capable of secession.

**Era of Dual Federalism.** National supremacy rulings such as *McCulloch* and *Cohens* did not go uncontested. Strains of states' rights theory were present on the Court during the mid-nineteenth century chief justiceship

*A former Confederate officer, Associate Justice Horace Lurton supported a states' rights interpretation of the Tenth Amendment after he joined the Supreme Court in 1910.* (Collection of the Supreme Court of the United States)

of Roger Brooke Taney, but it was not until the early twentieth century that the Court gave support to a full-blown theory of states' rights known as "dual federalism."

Probably the high-water mark of this brand of states' rights was *Hammer v. Dagenhart* (1918). In this case, the Court found that an attempt by Congress to prohibit the labor of children in factories and mines violated the Tenth Amendment. The Court's rationale was that employment in these industries was a local matter reserved to state regulation by the Tenth Amendment.

Dual federalism was the term given to the Court's theory that the Constitution created a system of dual supremacy: The national government was supreme in the exercise of its delegated powers, but the states were equally supreme in their exercise of reserved powers over local matters. The Court's narrow interpretation of the reach of delegated powers, for example, the power to regulate interstate commerce, in effect defused the supremacy clause of Article VI. It was not until *United States v. Darby*

*Lumber Co.* (1941) that the Court overruled *Hammer* and said that the Tenth Amendment was not a check on the delegated powers of Congress. With the *Darby* decision, Marshall was in ascendancy and Calhoun in decline. The Court had entered a new jurisprudential period of economic nationalism in which federal regulatory power repeatedly displaced states' rights.

**Judicial New Federalism.** The administration of President Richard M. Nixon gave rise to the phrase "new federalism," the policy that the national executive and legislative branches should take steps to move power from the federal government back to the states. Subsequent presidential administrations continued to advocate new federalism policies.

The Court became part of this spirit when it initiated a period of "judicial new federalism" in *National League of Cities v. Usery* (1976). In this case, the Court declared that the Tenth Amendment prevented the federal Fair Labor Standards Act (1938), which contained minimum-wage and maximum-hour regulations, from being applied to state and local governments. Although the federal government could apply these general regulatory measures to businesses operating in interstate commerce, it could not apply such regulations to states acting in their governmental capacities. The heart of the Court's reasoning was that federal regulation of states struck at the states' integrity by impairing their ability to carry out their core governmental functions. The *Usery* rule was the Court's recognition once again of Tenth Amendment-based states' rights.

With judicial new federalism, the Court was saying something different from its "dual federalism" formulation of states' rights. With dual federalism, the Court said that the Tenth Amendment freed states to regulate local matters free from federal interference. With judicial new federalism, the Court said that the Tenth Amendment prevented application of a general federal regulatory measure to a state's "integral operations" which were the essence of "state sovereignty." After struggling for nine years to sort out what were and were not "attributes of state sovereignty" to determine what could be regulated by the federal government, the Court brought this era of states' rights to an end in *Garcia v. San Antonio Metropolitan Transit Authority* (1985). The Court overruled *Usery*, saying that its Tenth Amendment rationale had turned out to be "unworkable." Henceforth, the Court said, members of Congress and not the justices would decide when states' rights were a check on federal regulatory power.

**Era of Dual Sovereignty.** In his dissent in *Garcia*, Justice William H. Rehnquist said that the *Usery* rule of states' rights was "a principle that will, I am confident, in time again command the support of a majority of this Court." His prophecy essentially came true in *New York v. United States* (1992). In that case, the Court considered the application to the states of a congressional enactment, the Low-Level Radioactive Waste Policy Act of 1980. To encourage the states to provide disposal sites, Congress gave the states a choice between two mandates: accept the ownership and resulting liability for radioactive waste or regulate it according to federal guidelines. The Court ruled that both options violated the Tenth Amendment. Borrowing from *The Federalist* (1788), the *New York* majority said that the Constitution "leaves to the several States a residuary and inviolable sovereignty."

This core of state sovereignty, the Court said, is violated when Congress commands state legislatures to legislate. In *New York*, the Court did not overrule *Garcia*, distinguishing *Garcia*'s approval of a general federal law being applied to a state from *New York*'s condemnation of a direct federal mandate to a state legislature. Five years later, *Printz v. United States* (1997) extended the *New York* rule to a federal mandate to state administrative officials and gave this states' rights principle the name of "dual sovereignty." The issue in *Printz* was the constitutionality of the mandate of the federal Brady Handgun Violence Prevention Act (1993) that county and municipal chief law enforcement officers conduct a background check of would-be purchasers of handguns. To void the law, the majority used the Tenth Amendment principle of "dual sovereignty," which represented the Framers' intention to preserve "the States as independent and autonomous political entities." The *Printz* rule was categorical and absolute, thus "no case-by-case weighing of the burdens or benefits is necessary." The combined states' rights legacy of *New York* and *Printz* was that the "Federal Government may neither issue directives requiring the States to address particular problems, nor command the States' officers, or those of their political subdivisions, to administer or enforce a federal regulatory program." Apparently left undisturbed by *Printz*, however, was the holding of *South Dakota v. Dole* (1987) that the federal government could continue to use grants of money "with strings attached" to entice the states to do what the federal government could not directly mandate.

**Modern States' Rights Analysis.** In *New York*, Justice Sandra Day O'Connor wrote for the majority: "In the end, just as a cup may be half empty or half full, it makes no difference whether one views the question at issue in this case as one of ascertaining the limits of the power delegated to the Federal Government under the affirmative provisions of the Constitution or one of discerning the core of sovereignty retained by the States under the Tenth Amendment." Her point was that either analysis—the content of delegated powers or the content of reserved powers—could lead to the same end, enhanced states' rights. After *New York*, the Supreme Court used both approaches. In *Printz*, the majority stressed the Tenth Amendment in voiding the Brady Act. And in *United States v. Lopez* (1995), the Court focused on the limits of Congress's delegated powers in voiding the Gun-Free School Zones Act of 1990. In *Lopez*, the Court said that Congress's power to regulate interstate commerce extended only to "commercial" matters, which did not include guns at school.

**New State Constitutionalism.** A modern development in states' rights is a state supreme court using its state constitution to give greater protection to a fundamental right than that accorded the same right by the U.S. Supreme Court using the U.S. Constitution. The rationale for this practice is a long-standing principle of states' rights: the independent and adequate state grounds doctrine. In essence, this doctrine means that a state supreme court decision grounded solely in state law is final because the Supreme Court has no jurisdiction to review it. A corollary of the doctrine is that a state supreme court, compared with the U.S. Supreme Court, can be more protective, but never less protective, of an individual right.

Some applications of this states' rights doctrine have been state supreme courts acting opposite the U.S. Supreme Court to permit students to collect signatures on political petitions in shopping malls, to allow challenges to school funding schemes based on local property taxes, and to provide enhanced protection from police searches of automobiles.

**Further Reading**

The story of states' rights must begin with the theory's roots in the United States before 1787. For extended discussion of the antifederalists' arguments and the Founders' motives and compromises, see Alpheus T. Mason's *The States' Rights Debate: Antifederalism and the Constitution* (New York: Oxford University Press, 1972) and Raoul Berger's *Federalism: The Founders' Design* (Norman: University of Oklahoma Press, 1987). The standard original source for explaining the Framers' intent for state autonomy is *The Federalist* (1788) by Alexander Hamilton, James Madison, and John Jay. Readers should pay special attention to the tensions between Nos. 39, 27, and 44. A full appreciation of the states' rights doctrine must include some familiarity with its radical expression, which is detailed in John C. Calhoun's *A Disquisition on Government* (Indianapolis, Ind.: Bobbs-Merrill, 1953) and in *The Nullification Era* (New York: Harper & Row, 1967), edited by William W. Freehling. The eminent constitutional scholar Edward S. Corwin provides a clear exposition of the doctrinal evolution of national supremacy to dual federalism and back to national supremacy in *The Commerce Power Versus State Rights* (Princeton, N.J.: Princeton University Press, 1936). Sotirios Barber's *"National League of Cities v. Usery: New Meaning for the Tenth Amendment,"* in *The Supreme Court Review* (Chicago: University of Chicago Press, 1977), discusses the end of a modern dry period for states' rights. The demise of the *Usery* era and a justification for the new dual sovereignty era is found in Martin H. Redish's "Doing It with Mirrors: *New York v. United States* and Constitutional Limitations on Federal Power to Require State Legislation," *Hastings Constitutional Law Quarterly* (1993): 593. For the promise and results of the new state constitutionalism, see Justice William J. Brennan, Jr.'s "State Constitutions and the Protection of Individual Rights" in *Harvard Law Review* (1977): 489.

*James J. Lopach*

# STOP AND FRISK RULE

*Description:* The authority of the police, under certain circumstances, to approach and conduct an investigatory detention of a citizen and a limited search for weapons.
*Relevant amendment:* Fourth
*Significance:* In a 1968 case, the Supreme Court allowed police to use stop and frisk searches to investigate suspicious activity and to protect the safety of the public and themselves.

The Fourth Amendment prohibits unreasonable search and seizure by the police without a warrant. The Uniform Arrest Act of 1942 and some state statutes, including a New York law, allowed police officers to briefly detain a person for questioning if they suspected illegal activity and frisk them (run their hands over the outside of the suspect's clothing) in search of a weapon.

In *Terry v. Ohio* (1968), the Supreme Court held that police officers can stop a person briefly for the purpose of investigation if they have a reasonable, articulable suspicion that criminal activity is occurring. The Court did not define the term "reasonable suspicion" but placed it somewhere between a vague suspicion and probable cause. The duration of the stop and frisk is limited to the amount of time necessary to either confirm or eliminate the officer's suspicions about the suspect. The Court also stated that an officer may conduct a limited search or "pat down" of the suspect to ensure their safety and that of the public if they have reason to believe the suspect is armed and dangerous.

*Steven J. Dunker*

# SYMBOLIC SPEECH

**Description:** Communication by means other than oral speech or the printed word, usually through objects or actions that have some special significance, such as picketing, burning flags or draft cards, marching, and wearing protest armbands.

**Relevant amendment:** First

**Significance:** The Supreme Court held that nonverbal forms of expression are as fully protected as traditional means of expression when they are peaceful and pose no threat to public order; however, when they contain elements that might disrupt the peace or otherwise pose a threat to the community, they are subject to reasonable regulation.

The Supreme Court gradually developed a theory of how the First Amendment applies to so-called "symbolic speech." However, no doubt reflecting the complexity of the issue and the infinite forms that such expression may take, it did so on a case-by-case basis that left the exact boundaries concerning what forms of nonverbal communication are completely protected somewhat vaguely defined. Nonetheless, the Court has increasingly made clear that peaceful forms of nonverbal expression, just as with more traditional forms of expression, may not be forbidden on the basis of content, although reasonable regulations, if their intent is not to suppress, may be imposed on such communications.

**Flags.** The Court's first symbolic speech case was *Stromberg v. California* (1931), a conviction under a California law, passed during the Red Scare of 1919, that banned the display of red flags in an attempt to suppress procommunist organizations. The Court struck down the law on the grounds that to forbid the display of emblems used to foster even "peaceful and orderly opposition" to government was an unconstitutional violation of the First Amendment. This ruling clearly foretold the general direction of later Court decisions in the symbolic speech area, namely that nonverbal expression that was peaceful and served as a functional equivalent of ordinary speech or press was, from a constitutional standpoint, equivalent to them. It clearly established the general principle that symbols such as flags could legally be used to peacefully express political opposition. It also specifically contained the seeds of the Court's holdings in *Texas v. Johnson* (1989) and *United States v. Eichman* (1990) that peaceful flag burning and other forms of flag desecration for the purpose of expressing political protest were fully protected.

The Court's second important symbolic speech case also involved flags. In *West Virginia State Board of Education v. Barnette* (1943), the Court, citing *Stromberg* among other precedents, overruled its own decision in *Minersville School District v. Gobitis* (1940). It held that compulsory public school flag salutes and Pledge of Allegiance requirements were unconstitutional, on the grounds that a child required to attend public schools could not, without violating the First Amendment, be forced by public authorities to verbally or symbolically express sentiments "not in his mind." In rhetoric since cited by many scholars as among the most important and eloquent ever uttered by the Court, Justice Robert H. Jackson declared, "Compulsory unification of opinion achieves only the unanimity of the graveyard" and that it seemed "trite but necessary to say that the First Amendment to our Constitution was designed to avoid these ends by avoiding these beginnings." Jackson stated that the case was difficult not because of the principles involved but because the flag involved was that of the United States. He declared:

> Freedom to differ is not limited to things that do not matter much. That would be a mere shadow of freedom. The test of its substance is the right to differ as to things that touch the heart of the existing order. If there is any fixed star in our constitutional constellation, it is that no official, high or petty, can prescribe what shall be orthodox in politics, nationalism, religion, or other matters of opinion.

**Extensions of Protection.** In other rulings, the Court extended the mantle of First Amendment protection to many other forms of symbolic speech, including the right to peacefully picket in labor disputes in *Thornhill v. Alabama* (1940) and to peacefully march in support of civil rights in *Cox v. Louisiana* (1965). In a widely publicized 1969 case, *Tinker v. Des Moines Independent Community School District*, the Court upheld the right of schoolchildren to wear black armbands to express opposition to the Vietnam War, an activity that the Court termed "closely akin to 'pure speech'" and thus "entitled to comprehensive protection under the First Amendment" as long as it threatened no disruptions. The Court declared that "undifferentiated fear or apprehension of disturbance is not enough to overcome the right to freedom of expression" and that to justify suppression of expression, the government would have to show that its action was "caused by something more than a mere desire to avoid the discomfort and unpleasantness that always accompanies an unpopular viewpoint."

Court justices not only viewed such nonverbal expression as still essentially communicative in nature but also pointed out that symbolic speech might be the only way for the relatively powerless to gain public attention. In *Milkwagon Drivers Union v. Meadowmoor Dairies* (1941), the Court stated, "Peaceful picketing is the working man's means of communication." Justice William O. Douglas, dissenting in *Adderley v. Florida* (1966), noted, "Conventional means of petitioning may be, and often have been, shut off to large groups of our citizens [because] those who do not control television and radio, those who cannot afford to advertise in newspapers or circulate elaborate pamphlets may have only a more limited type of access to public officials."

Furthermore, the Court suggested that highly unorthodox and symbolic speech might especially deserve protection because it could communicate in an emotive way that ordinary speech and writing could not. Therefore, in *Cohen v. California* (1971), the Court overturned the conviction of a man who wore a jacket bearing the words "Fuck the Draft," declaring that words "are often chosen as much for their emotive as their cognitive force," and that "we cannot sanction the view that the Constitution, while solicitous of the cognitive content of individual speech, has little or no regard for that emotive function which, practically speaking, may often be the more important element of the overall message sought to be communicated."

The Court increasingly made clear that, just as ordinary written and oral political expression can virtually never be criminalized based on its content, neither can symbolic political speech be restricted on such grounds. In *Schacht v. United States* (1970), the Court struck down a law that forbade the unauthorized use of military uniforms in dramatic productions only when such use "tended to discredit" the military, and in *Boos v. Barry* (1988), it voided a law that banned picketing close to embassies only when the picket signs tended to bring the foreign government target into public "odium" or "disrepute."

**Unprotected Expressive Conduct.** However, in other symbolic speech cases, the Court declared that symbolically expressive conduct is not always as protected by the First Amendment as is pure speech. Therefore, in *Cox v. Louisiana*, the Court rejected the idea that the First Amendment and other constitutional provisions afforded "the same kind of freedom to those who would communicate ideas by conduct such as patrolling, marching and picketing on streets and highways" as was provided "to those who communicate ideas by pure speech."

In *United States v. O'Brien* (1968), the Court upheld a conviction under a 1965 law that outlawed draft card burning, noting, "We cannot accept the view that an apparently limitless variety of conduct can be labeled 'speech.'" Although the 1965 law was clearly intended to suppress dissent (failure to possess a draft card was already illegal and the congressional debate on the law was filled with references to draft card burners as filthy beatniks, communist stooges, and traitors), the Court upheld it on the strained grounds that it was designed not to hinder free expression but simply to foster the effective functioning of the draft (a purpose that required for its credibility the assumption that the draft administration retained no copies of the information contained on individuals' draft cards).

In *O'Brien*, the Court for the first time attempted to establish guidelines for determining when conduct could be constitutionally regulated if it was combined with an expressive element. In short, the Court held that restrictions on mixed conduct expression could be upheld if the regulation was within the government's constitutional power and furthered an important or substantial governmental interest that did not involve the suppression of free expression and "if the incidental restriction on alleged First Amendment freedoms is no greater than is essential to the furtherance of that interest." As applied twenty years later to flag desecration, one of the most contentious symbolic speech issues to ever arise, the *O'Brien* guidelines were held to require the protection of protest flag burning on the grounds that the reason behind attempts to outlaw such expression involved the suppression of free expression.

The Court's ruling in *Schenck v. Pro-Choice Network of Western New York* (1997) suggests that further symbolic speech cases will continue to be decided on a case-by-case basis and that the basis of the Court's ruling may continue to be difficult to determine. In *Schenck*, the Court upheld the constitutionality of a fifteen-foot fixed buffer zone banning antiabortion activists from protesting and distributing literature around the driveways and entrances to an abortion clinic but struck down a fifteen-foot "floating" buffer around clients and staff entering or leaving the clinic. It held that the first restriction was justified to ensure public safety and order and burdened speech no more than necessary to achieve that goal, but the second restriction burdened "more speech than is necessary to serve the relevant governmental interests."

**Further Reading**

Farish, Leah. *"Tinker v. Des Moines": Student Protest.* Springfield, N.J.: Enslow, 1997.

Goldstein, Robert Justin. *Saving "Old Glory": The History of the American Flag Desecration Controversy.* Boulder, Colo.: Westview Press, 1995.

Johnson, John. *The Struggle for Student Rights: "Tinker v. Des Moines" and the 1960's.* Lawrence: University Press of Kansas, 1967.

Tedford, Thomas. *Freedom of Speech in the United States.* State College, Pa.: Strata Publishing, 1997.

*Robert Justin Goldstein*

# TAKINGS CLAUSE

*Description:* Provision in the Fifth Amendment that prohibits the taking of private property for public use unless the owner is appropriately compensated.

*Relevant amendment:* Fifth

*Significance:* The takings clause is one of the most important and vigorously contested constitutional provisions, at the center of numerous cases before the Supreme Court. The clause pits fundamental capitalist principles of private ownership against the doctrines of state sovereignty and the public good.

The U.S. Constitution contains a number of provisions that seek to protect private ownership of property and property rights more generally. Chief among these is the takings clause of the Fifth Amendment. The clause provides that "private property [shall not] be taken for public use without just compensation." In including this provision, the Framers paid respect to a long-standing, basic individual right with roots in seventeenth century English legal tradition.

The takings clause seeks simultaneously to protect the property rights of individuals—crucial to the American capitalist economic system and its cultural value of individualism—and to ensure that the state is able to acquire private property when necessary in order to promote the public good. In other words, it is not a person's *property* that is inviolable; rather, a person is entitled to the *value* of that property in the event that the state has a compelling need to acquire ("take") it. Such state takings of property (usually land) follow the principle of eminent domain—essentially, that the government retains the ultimate right to secure private property for the good of the state because the existence of the state is a precondition of property itself. However, while the principles of eminent domain and just compensation work together neatly under the concept of the takings clause, the business of defining what specific instances warrant the exercise of eminent domain and what level of compensation is just, is fraught with controversy. The Supreme Court has issued a number of landmark decisions on these questions over the years.

**Condemnation.** Governments exercise eminent domain—that is, they take private property through a process of "condemnation"—in order to advance projects deemed to be in the interest of the public or the government. For example, state and local governments exercise eminent domain over private property that stands in the way of a planned road expansion, a proposed state building, a public works project such as a dam, or any of a number of other projects. Such condemnation of property typically is construed as a taking and thus requires payment of fair market value to the property owner. Eminent domain can be exercised by all levels of government, as well as some quasi-governmental entities such as public utilities.

Disputes may arise over what constitutes the fair market value for a property that is taken by the government through condemnation, but the principle of eminent domain is well established and seldom open to a constitutional challenge. As long as just compensation is provided, the threshold for a valid exercise of eminent domain is relatively low.

Sometimes a government may seize property without providing just compensation. For example, a number of laws at the state and federal level provide for the forfeiture of a person's assets under certain circumstances, including conviction for specified crimes. For example, federal laws permit the forfeiture of certain property, including boats and homes, that were purchased with illicit drug proceeds. Such laws have been challenged as unconstitutional, but generally it is the Eighth Amendment (which prohibits "excessive fines") that is invoked. Because seizures of this type are considered penalties, they do not require compensation.

There are several other circumstances under which the government can seize property without granting compensation. In certain cases, a government may destroy private property in order to preserve public health and safety. For example, the Court has long upheld the right of the state to demolish structures posing a fire hazard as in *Bowditch v. Boston* (1880), to destroy diseased trees that threaten the health of other trees as in *Miller v. Schoene* (1928), or otherwise to abate nuisances, all without compensation. In these cases, property is *not* seized for public use; rather, the state is performing a remediation action where a property owner has failed to meet requirements specified in laws and ordinances.

The takings issue becomes much more complicated when a government seeks not outright condemnation of property but rather to restrict its use. Regulating the use of property is a fundamental and indispensable facet of a government's police powers. Land use restrictions of various kinds have long been a recognized prerogative of government.

For example, federal, state, and local govern ments impose habitability standards for housing, hotels, mobile homes, and other structures. Local governments typically zone different sections of land under their jurisdiction for different uses, such as housing, retail businesses, or parks in order to impose order and promote compatible uses. Some such zoning ordinances restrict liquor stores or adult bookstores from areas near churches or schools. Zoning may also be used to restrict residential construction from floodplains and other hazardous areas. Local ordinances may limit noise from a factory or amphitheater in order to preserve quiet for nearby neighborhoods. Land developers may be required to provide open space for habitat conservation or public recreation. Easements may be required to facilitate public access to natural resources such as shorelines or parks. In these and myriad other ways, government exercises a long-accepted right to restrict the use of property.

**Regulatory Takings.** Governmentally imposed restrictions on the use of property, such as zoning restrictions, can be construed as "regulatory takings" when new restrictions are imposed on a piece of property after a person has purchased it. Presumably restrictions that exist on a property at the time of its purchase are reflected in the purchase price, and thus no governmental compensation is necessary.

The idea that regulatory (nonphysical) takings require compensation has evolved slowly and remains controversial. Until the early 1900's most courts rejected the argument, made by some property owners, that post-purchase regulatory takings warranted compensation under the Fifth Amendment. For example, in *Euclid v. Ambler Realty Co.* (1926), the Court rejected a property owner's argument that he deserved compensation for a local zoning ordinance that banned industrial development on his land. The Court held that the restriction was a valid exercise of police powers exercised by the government for legitimate reasons. *Euclid* thus upheld the constitutionality of zoning ordinances. At about this time, the Court began to recognize the possibility that zoning and other land use regulations, if restrictive enough, could indeed amount to takings deserving of just compensation. For example, in *Nectow v. City of Cambridge* (1928), the Court considered another ordinance prohibiting industrial development. In this case, the ordinance would permit only residential development on land under contract to be sold for industrial use. The Court found that the ordinance amounted to a taking because it allowed for "no practical use" of the particular parcel.

Many naturally sought guidance on identifying the point at which an otherwise legitimate government exercise of police powers becomes a taking under the Fifth Amendment. The issue was addressed, albeit incompletely, in the Court's opinion in *Pennsylvania Coal Co. v. Mahon* (1922). In that case, the first to address nonphysical takings, the Court found that "Government hardly could go on" if every governmental regulation that diminished the value of property had to be accompanied by compensation. Rather, "some values are enjoyed under an implied limitation and must yield to the police power." At the same time, however, "the implied limitation must have its limits or the contract and due process clauses are gone." In this case, the Court held that restrictions that prevented coal mining on a particular piece of property made that property virtually worthless, and therefore the owner deserved compensation. Justice Louis D. Brandeis issued a dissenting opinion, however, highlighting some difficult and controversial aspects to the Court's attempt at balancing public and private interests. Brandeis's dissent presaged many of the debates that would come into full bloom a half-century later.

For many decades after the 1920's the Court largely avoided takings cases, leaving them to be resolved by state and federal courts. Allowing for some variation among states and regions, legal development during much of the century generally took a fairly conservative approach to the takings clause, emphasizing the need for compelling, often extraordinary state interests in order to effect a taking without compensation. In the 1980's and 1990's, however, the Court heard and decided a number of landmark cases that generally had the effect of strengthening the government's ability to pursue regulatory takings, particularly with the goal of advancing environmental protection.

**Balancing.** In the 1980's the Court identified two major criteria for determining whether a taking had occurred. This approach, which the Court set forth in *Agins v. City of Tiburon* (1980), called for considering whether the restriction still permitted an economically viable use of the property and whether the regulation advanced a legitimate state interest. This approach is typically referred to as "balancing of public benefit against private loss." In the *Agins* decision, the Court determined that a local zoning ordinance that restricted but did not prohibit residential development did not constitute a taking.

It is important to note that denying a property owner the "highest and best" use of his or her property is not adequate grounds for a takings claim. Certainly a regulation eliminating all viable economic use would be considered a taking. This was illustrated in *Whitney Benefits v. United States* (1989), which held that federal legislation that deprived a mining company of all economic use of its property amounted to a taking without just compensation. Similarly, in *Lucas v. South Carolina Coastal Council* (1992), the Court found that the denial of a beachfront building permit effectively prohibited all economic use of the land and thus amounted to a taking deserving of compensation. (Lucas allowed an exception for nuisance abatement.) Aside from such extreme cases as *Whitney* and *Lucas*, however, it is somewhat difficult to establish whether a regulatory action or zoning ordinance permits "economically viable use." One case that did so is *Goldblatt v. Hempstead* (1962), wherein the Court found that an ordinance that effectively prohibited the operation of a gravel pit did nevertheless allow for other, economically viable uses for the property. A similar conclusion was arrived at in *Agins.*

In another landmark case from the 1980's, the Court ruled in *First English Evangelical Lutheran Church of Glendale v. County of Los Angeles* (1987) that even a temporary taking requires just compensation. In this case, a church sought to rebuild some structures on its property that were destroyed in a flood. The county, however, had adopted an interim ordinance preventing construction (including reconstruction) of buildings on the floodplain where the church's buildings had been located. The Court found that a taking, such as that created by the county ordinance, requires just compensation even when the taking is temporary. This decision closed a potential loophole of long-lived, though putatively temporary, land use restrictions.

**Open Space and Environment.** The increasing concern with environmental issues in the latter part of the twentieth century was accompanied by greater governmental regulation of private property to provide open space and public access to natural resources. Although the Court has generally supported such goals as legitimate public purposes, it has also had occasion to identify circumstances in which takings have resulted, thus requiring just compensation. For example, in *Kaiser Aetna v. United States* (1980), the Court held that requiring a landowner to provide public access to a private pond amounted to a taking deserving of just compensation. The Court pushed this decision further in *Nollan v. California Coastal Commission* (1987), holding that a state agency's demand for a coastal easement on private property amounted to a regulatory taking that required just compensation. In the case of *Nollan*, it was a public resource (the coastline of the Pacific Ocean), rather than a private pond, for which public access was required.

It would seem that the Court accepted a broad range of resource-related goals as legitimate grounds for the exercise of eminent domain. At the same time, the Court seemed to be viewing open space requirements and demands for easements as bona fide takings requiring just compensation. A distinction was generally drawn for open space requirements imposed on land developers whose proposed development would itself generate a need for such open space. For example, a housing development on agricultural land would increase the population of the area, thus arguably creating a need to preserve and create access to some open space, such as parks or greenbelts. Requirements for such environmental impact-mitigating measures might therefore not warrant compensation. However, in *Dolan v. City of Tigard* (1994), the Court struck down a city's requirement that a hardware store owner dedicate a portion of property for a trail in order to be permitted to expand the store. The Court held that the city had not satisfactorily established that the requirement was needed to offset any anticipated increase in traffic from the expansion. Dolan thus underscored the need to link mitigating measures to the actual impacts of a proposed project.

**Later Decisions.** In the late 1990's the Court seemed to continue its support for environmentally based regulatory takings, while maintaining or even expanding the requirement that such takings, when significant, require just compensation. The state has a right to insist on property restrictions that protect the environment, the Court seemed to say, but the state must be willing to pay when these restrictions significantly restrict use.

A major case from this period was *Suitum v. Tahoe Regional Planning Agency* (1997). In this case, a property owner sought to build a home on an undeveloped lot she had purchased fifteen years earlier. The lot, in Nevada near Lake Tahoe, fell under the jurisdiction of the Tahoe Regional Planning Agency (TRPA). The agency, charged with protecting environmental quality in the Lake Tahoe Basin, prohibited the development as likely to cause unacceptable environmental damage. TRPA essentially denied all economic use and offered as compensation "transferable development rights." Such rights could not be used to build on Suitum's lot but could be sold to a different landowner in the Tahoe basin where such development would not be prohibited. By purchasing those rights, the property owner could build a larger structure than otherwise allowed.

Suitum had been told by a lower court that her case was not "ripe"— that she had not accepted and tried to sell the transferrable development rights. However, the Supreme Court held that Suitum's case was indeed ripe and must be decided by the District Court of Nevada.

Transferable development rights are one of a number of the sometimes innovative, sometimes complicated, and frequently controversial approaches that were developed by various governmental bodies in order to regulate land use without running afoul of the Fifth Amendment. Other approaches involve development fees, open space dedications, habitat conservation plans, and statutory compensation programs.

**Further Reading**

One of the most focused recent works on the Supreme Court's treatment of takings is provided in George Skouras's *Takings Law and the Supreme*

*Court: Judicial Oversight of the Regulatory State's Acquisition, Use, and Control of Private Property* (New York: P. Lang, 1998). For a theoretical overview of the broader subject of property rights, see Tom Bethell's *The Noblest Triumph: Property and Prosperity Through the Ages* (New York: St. Martin's Press, 1998). Among general works on legal issues associated with property rights (including treatments of takings), see Jan Laitos's *Law of Property Rights Protection: Limitations on Governmental Powers* (Gaithersburg, Md.: Aspen Law and Business, 1998). On the subject of environmentally motivated takings, see Robert Meltz et al., *The Takings Issue: Constitutional Limits on Land Use Control and Environmental Regulation* (Washington, D.C.: Island Press, 1998), and Robert Innes et al., "Takings, Compensation, and Endangered Species Protection on Private Lands," *Journal of Economic Perspectives* (Summer, 1998): 35-52. A somewhat critical assessment of regulatory takings is provided by Gideon Kanner in "Just Compensation Is by No Means Always Just," *The National Law Journal* (March 24, 1997): A23. The Congressional Budget Office has put out a very understandable overview of regulatory takings, describing the current system for handling regulatory takings claims and evaluating various proposals for changing that system. See *Regulatory Takings and Proposals for Change* (Washington, D.C.: Congressional Budget Office, 1999).

*Steve D. Boilard*

# TIME, PLACE, AND MANNER REGULATIONS

*Description:* Permissible forms of prior restraint not based on content of expression that regulate when, where, and how expression may occur freely.

*Relevant amendment:* First

*Significance:* The Supreme Court usually considers the validity of time, place, and manner regulations in view of the forum in which the regulations are applied. Expressive activity occurring in a public, rather than private, forum receives the highest First Amendment protection.

In *Heffron v. International Society for Krishna Consciousness* (1981), Supreme Court Justice Byron R. White identified four characteristics of a valid time, place, and manner regulation: first, the restriction must be content neutral; second, the restriction must serve a significant governmental interest; third, the restriction must be no broader than would accomplish its purpose; and fourth, alternative means must exist to communicate the expression that is limited by the regulation. All four of the characteristics must be present for the regulation to be valid.

**Time, Place, and Manner.** The Court has allowed to stand ordinances that restrict loud noises at night when people are likely to be asleep and broadcast regulations that restrict indecent programming to safe harbor hours, between 10 P.M. and 6 A.M., when children are less likely to be in the audience.

The Court makes decisions regarding place according to the forum in which an activity occurs: a traditional public forum, a designated public forum, public property that is not a public forum, or private property. Traditional public forums are places that are accepted as sites where speeches may be made and people may assemble. Examples include public parks, street corners, and sidewalks. Speeches occurring in traditional public forums receive the highest First Amendment protection. In *Lovell v. City of Griffin* (1938), the Court made it clear that public streets are public forums. The city of Griffin, Georgia, had an ordinance requiring written permission from the city manager before distributing information in any form. The city argued that First Amendment protection applied to only the publication of information, not its distribution, but Chief Justice Charles Evans Hughes refuted that argument in the opinion he wrote for the Court.

Designated public forums are places specifically provided by the government for communication, assembly, and similar uses. These include government-owned auditoriums, meeting halls, fairgrounds, and student newspapers open to all students. Communication occurring in designated public forums receives First Amendment protection, but not as much as that occurring in traditional public forums; therefore, it is more subject to time, place, and manner regulations.

Some types of public property are not considered public forums and are closed to expressive activity on the part of the general public. Examples include airport concourses, prisons, and military bases. Private property is not a public forum; owners may decide who uses the property for expressive activity.

In *Grayned v. Rockford* (1972), the Court applied time, place, and manner regulations to demonstrations next to a school in session, saying the nature of the place, including the pattern of its typical activities, dictates the kinds of regulations of time, place, and manner that are reasonable. In its decision, the Court indicated that silent expression in a public library might be appropriate, although making a speech in the area where patrons are reading would not be. The manner of expression should be compatible with the normal activity of a particular place at a particular time.

**Problems in Application.** When time, place, and manner regulations were applied to commercial or religious speech (*Metromedia v. San Diego*, 1981) or obscene or indecent language, the Court generally found these restrictions invalid because they were content based. The same line of reasoning was used to invalidate the Communication Decency Act of 1996 (*Reno v. American Civil Liberties Union*, 1996). The Court generally frowns on ordinances that rely on the discretion of community officials to decide whether speech is allowed (*Schneider v. New Jersey*, 1939) because these deliberations often require officials to evaluate speech based on content.

In *Madsen v. Women's Health Center* (1994), the Court applied the third prong of the 1981 validity test in considering whether an injunction directed at protesters at an abortion clinic was narrowly tailored enough to accomplish its goals without restricting more expression than necessary. The Court decided that a 36-foot buffer zone around clinic entrances and a driveway was permissible and not over broad, but that a 300-foot buffer zone around the residences of clinic employees and a 300-foot no-approach zone around the clinic were over broad, and therefore impermissible.

**Further Reading**

Gillmor, Donald, Jerome Barron, and Todd Simon. *Mass Communication Law: Cases and Comment.* 6th ed. Belmont, Calif.: Wadsworth, 1998.

Pember, Don. *Mass Media Law.* Boston: McGraw-Hill, 1999.

Teeter, Dwight, Don Leduc, and Bill Loving. *Law of Mass Communications: Freedom and Control of Print and Broadcast Media.* 9th ed. New York: Foundation Press, 1998.

*Alisa White Coleman*

# UNPROTECTED SPEECH

*Description:* Speech that, if it falls into one or more of several categories, is treated by the Supreme Court as entitled to no (or lessened) constitutional protection because of the harm to society such utterances may cause.

*Relevant amendment:* First

*Significance:* The Court played a role in defining the categories of unprotected speech and in trying to achieve a balance between the interests of society and the liberty interests of the individual speaker.

In *Chaplinsky v. New Hampshire* (1942), the Supreme Court upheld the conviction of a Jehovah's Witness who called a city marshal a "racketeer and a Fascist." He was charged under a state law punishing offensive and derisive speech or name-calling in public. Writing for a unanimous Court, Justice Frank Murphy noted that there were limited classes of speech that could be prevented and punished without violating the Constitution. These classes included "the lewd and obscene, the profane, the libelous, and the insulting or 'fighting' words—those which by their very utterance inflict injury or tend to incite an immediate breach of the peace." He noted that these classes of speech were not necessary for the expression of ideas and were of such little social value that any benefit they imparted would be outweighed by society's interest in "order and morality."

*Justice Frank Murphy defined several classes of speech that are not protected by the Constitution.* (Library of Congress)

Justice Murphy's approach has been characterized as a two-tier theory of the First

Amendment. Socially valuable speech is protected, but certain categories are unworthy of constitutional protection. After *Chaplinsky*, as the Court became more sensitive to free speech issues, it emphasized narrowly and precisely defining these categories, as well as introducing into each of these categories (except obscenity) certain First Amendment exceptions.

**Obscenity.** In 1973 in *Miller v. California*, the Court announced its standard for obscenity. Writing for a five-justice majority, Chief Justice Warren E. Burger held that three requirements must be met to find material obscene. First, the average person, applying contemporary community standards, must find the material appealing to his or her prurient interest. Second, the material must depict sexual conduct in a patently offensive way. Third, material is obscene if, taken as a whole—not simply focusing on isolated passages or pictures in, for example, a book or magazine—it "lacks serious literary, artistic, political, or scientific value." In short, obscenity is "hard core" pornography.

Although the Court found no First Amendment value in obscenity, it consistently held that not all sexual depictions or utterances were the equivalent of obscenity. Thus, in *Sable Communications v. Federal Communications Commission* (1989), the Court stressed that the government's power to prohibit obscene speech does not extend to indecent speech. However, in other cases, the Court also recognized situations in which the government can ban profane or indecent language, including on television or radio broadcasts and at public elementary and secondary schools.

**Words Against Others.** Libel is any false and malicious statement made for the purpose of defaming (injuring the good name or reputation of) a living person. If the statement is spoken rather than written, the offense is called slander. Prior to 1964, such false statements were understood as totally unprotected by the First Amendment, but in that year, in *New York Times Co. v. Sullivan*, the Court began a process of applying First Amendment standards to certain types of libel actions. In essence, if a libel action is brought by a public official or a public figure (such as a well-known film star), that plaintiff must demonstrate that the false statement was made with actual malice, defined by the Court as knowledge of its falsity, or reckless disregard for truth or falsity.

Although *Chaplinsky* was not overruled, after that case, the Court never upheld a conviction solely for "fighting words" directed at public officials.

In *R.A.V. v. City of St. Paul* (1992), the Court held that bans on fighting words must be "content-neutral." That is, a city cannot ban only certain categories of hate speech, such as that which is race- or gender-based. The First Amendment requires an all-or-nothing approach.

**Incitement of Illegal Activity.** Although not mentioned in Justice Murphy's *Chaplinsky* listing, incitement to illegal activity was also traditionally considered unprotected speech. Much of modern First Amendment jurisprudence was developed in the context of speech advocating violent overthrow of the government, starting with Justice Oliver Wendell Holmes's famous clear and present danger test, enunciated in *Schenck v. United States* (1919). The challenge for the Court, from the Red Scare of the 1920's to the McCarthy era of the 1950's and the protests of the 1960's, has been to protect society's interests while also protecting political advocacy by unpopular dissidents.

In *Brandenburg v. Ohio* (1969), the Court put forward a standard that is highly protective of unpopular political speech and combines the best elements of the clear and present danger test with an approach—first enunciated in the World War I era by Judge Learned Hand—that focuses on the actual words of the speaker. According to the *per curiam* opinion in *Brandenburg*, the state may not "forbid or proscribe advocacy of the use of force or of law violation except where such advocacy is directed to inciting or producing imminent lawless actions and is likely to incite or produce such action." The Court reaffirmed its own earlier distinction between "mere abstract teaching" of the moral "propriety" or even "necessity" of resorting to force and violence, on one hand, and "preparing a group for violent action and steeling it to such action" on the other.

The Court also held that certain categories of speech, although not totally unprotected, may be entitled to lesser First Amendment protection. This group includes sexually explicit but nonobscene speech (in certain contexts), symbolic speech (communicative conduct such as marching, picketing, wearing arm bands, or burning a U.S. flag), and commercial speech (advertising and similar commercial expression).

### Further Reading

Abraham, Henry J., and Barbara A. Perry. *Freedom and the Court.* 7th ed. New York: Oxford University Press, 1998.

Greenwalt, Kent. *Fighting Words.* Princeton, N.J.: Princeton University Press, 1995.

Lewis, Anthony. *Make No Law: The Sullivan Case and the First Amendment.* New York: Random House, 1991.

*Philip A. Dynia*

# WITNESSES, CONFRONTATION OF

*Description:* The right of criminal defendants to have the witnesses against them testify in open court, face to face with them and the fact-finder, and to cross-examine those witnesses.

*Relevant amendment:* Sixth

*Significance:* As interpreted by the Supreme Court, the provision prohibits the prosecution from using evidence such as video testimony, written statements, affidavits, transcripts, and second-hand accounts. Banned also are unreasonable limits on defense questioning of prosecution witnesses.

The Sixth Amendment's confrontation clause fosters reliability and fairness in federal and state prosecutions. It allows criminal defendants to confront witnesses against them in open court, under oath or affirmation, face to face, and to cross-examine these witnesses. The scope of its protections, which benefit criminal defendants, has been defined by Supreme Court decisions citing history, reason, and practicality.

Normally, words may not be reported by others or in writing—that is, the witness must appear—and may be cross-examined under the full panoply of courtroom safeguards. However, the defendants' entitlements are qualified. For example, the separate, long-standing evidentiary rule against hearsay has numerous exceptions permitting second-hand or reported evidence, most of which, if they are deemed "firmly rooted" (rational and historically traditional), the Court has gradually been incorporating into the confrontation clause as in *White v. Illinois* (1992) and *Bourjaily v. United States* (1987). Thus, excited utterances, statements to physicians, coconspirator statements during and furthering the conspiracy, and the like can be reported, though the person who spoke them is not at trial to be confronted. These sorts of statements are presumed to be especially reliable and necessary. In *Idaho v. Wright* (1990), the Court ruled that some second-hand statements could be allowed if special facts demonstrated their reliability and necessity. In *Ohio v. Roberts* (1980), the

Court ruled that sometimes the litigators must demonstrate the unavailability of the witness for appearance at trial before second-hand statements could be admitted as evidence.

Once witnesses *are* produced at trial, defendants' opportunity to cross-examine them may similarly be confined within reasonable limits. In *Montana v. Egelhoff* (1996), the Court ruled that, for example, the judge may apply normal exclusionary evidence rules, recognize privileges, or prohibit unduly prejudicial, harassing, time-consuming, or misleading questioning. If a witness becomes ill or dies after giving testimony but before full cross-examination, the testimony might still be allowed to stand. In *Maryland v. Craig* (1990), the Court determined that if a specific child-witness will suffer trauma from confronting his or her accused molester, the child may testify on one-way closed-circuit television, despite some infringement of the face-to-face requirement, provided there is full opportunity to put questions to the witness and all can see the screen.

Thus, the rights conferred by the confrontation clause are not absolute but are qualified by countervailing concerns and may amount merely to a strong preference.

*Paul F. Rothstein*

# ZONING

*Description:* Premier land-use regulation method in the United States, which divides urban areas into different sectors or zones, with different uses and regulations and requirements.

*Relevant amendments:* First, Fifth

*Significance:* Most contested zoning legal issues were handled by one of the fifty state court systems and received final judgment in the state supreme courts; however, a few significant land-use cases found their way to the U.S. Supreme Court.

The police power, which is the right of government to regulate public health, safety, and welfare, gives zoning its legitimacy. State constitutions and statutes enable local governments to create their own zoning ordinances. Some states also created state zoning laws. The exact limits of the zoning power may seem fluid in time and place. Zoning power is ultimately what the courts determine. Conservative courts tend to limit the zoning power, and liberal courts tend to expand it.

*Euclid v. Ambler Realty Co.* (1926) was one of the most significant legal decisions by the Supreme Court in the history of zoning. Chief Justice George Sutherland concluded that each community had the right and responsibility to determine its own character. Zoning was a valid use of the police power as long as it did not disturb the orderly growth of the region or the nation. Justice Sutherland wrote, "But this village, though physically a suburb of Cleveland, is a separate municipality, with powers of its own and authority to govern itself . . . The will of its people determines, not that industrial development shall cease at its boundaries, but that such development shall proceed between fixed lines."

The Court made it clear that a municipality may determine the nature of development within its boundaries and plan and regulate the use of land as the people within the community may consider it to be in the public interest. Justice Sutherland introduced the concept that a community must also relate its plans to the area outside its own boundaries. Thus, the Court sustained a village zoning ordinance that prevented Ambler Realty from building a commercial structure in a residential zone. This case first established the constitutionality of all parts of comprehensive zoning.

The courts continued to support the rights of municipalities to zone, and conventional "Euclidean zoning" became almost universal in both urban and suburban areas. The power to zone as well as to use other, more flexible land-use controls, has an ideological dimension because it conflicts with the ability of property owners to use their property as they see fit. Typically, zones have been devoted to commercial, industrial, and residential uses, with different density requirements and other regulations.

**Relationship to Taking Cases.** In *First English Evangelical Lutheran Church of Glendale v. County of Los Angeles* (1987), the Court ruled that if landowners had been unduly burdened by land-use control regulations, they should be compensated by the government. Before this case, it was understood that a property owner might sue to have a regulation overturned. However, it was not required that compensation be paid for losses incurred while the regulation was actually in force. The Court's decision hinged on the last sentence of the Fifth Amendment, "nor shall private property be taken for public use, without just compensation." Undue restriction of use in the Court's view met the meaning of the word "taken" and therefore required compensation. Eventually when the case was sent back to a lower court, it was found that the taking had not oc-curred and that the church was not entitled to compensation. Despite the lower court's decision, the Court's ruling meant that a government might be forced to pay a large judgment if its actions were found to constitute a taking. Some feared the possibility that local governments might have to pay large judgments to litigants who could prove that zoning power had been overused.

Later, in *Lucas v. South Carolina Coastal Council* (1992) and *Dolan v. City of Tigard* (1994), the Court upheld the limiting of the government's au-thority to restrict the specific uses to which privately owned land could be devoted. For example, one opinion in the *Lucas* decision suggested that the one instance in which there might not need to be compensation (even though the property owner was deprived of all property use) was if that use might violate an established nuisance law. Some authorities spec-ulated that the legal basis of zoning might be trimmed back to being to-tally dependent on nuisance law. Land-use regulations in *Hadacheck v. Sebastian* (1915) had evolved from nuisance law but had been expanded well beyond these limited origins to a much more extensive notion of the public interest.

**Aesthetics and Exclusionary Zoning.** Many legal experts believe that zon-ing and other police power regulations may not be adopted when their sole basis lies in aesthetics. Proponents of this theory cite *Welch v. Swasey* (1909) and decisions rendered by most of the state supreme courts. How-ever, this view was challenged in *Berman v. Parker* (1954), in which Justice William O. Douglas, speaking for the unanimous Court opinion, stated, "If those who govern the District of Columbia decide that the Nation's Capital should be beautiful as well as sanitary, there is nothing in the Fifth Amendment that stands in the way." However, this case involved an effort to enjoin condemnation to preserve the natural beauty of urban renewal property. The Court was not confronted with a case in which police power was exercised in the form of a zoning ordinance and in which no compensation was paid. However, state courts have applied *Berman* in zoning cases. Douglas clearly affirmed that citizens need not tolerate an unsightly community and may take legal steps to change it.

Restrictive covenants, which discriminate against minority groups through race-based zoning ordinances, were declared unconstitutional by the Court in 1927 in *Buchanan v. Warley*. A Louisville, Kentucky, ordi-nance regulated the occupancy of city blocks; people of color could not reside in blocks where greater numbers of dwellings were occupied by whites and vice versa. This use of the police power was a violation of the Fourteenth Amendment because it prevented the use of property and deprived its owner of use without due process.

Years later the Court held in *Arlington Heights v. Metropolitan Housing Development Corp.* (1977) that a zoning ordinance does not necessarily violate the Constitution by restricting minority and low-income people; it must be shown that there was a deliberate exclusionary intention.

**Further Reading**

Babcock, Richard F. *The Zoning Game: Municipal Practices and Policies.* Madison: University of Wisconsin Press, 1966.

Crawford, Clan. *Strategy and Tactics in Municipal Zoning.* Englewood Cliffs, N.J.: Prentice Hall, 1979.

Kelly, Eric D. "Zoning." In *The Practice of Local Government Planning*, edited by Frank So. Washington D.C.: International City Management Association, 1988.

Mandelker, Daniel R. *Land Use Law.* 4th ed. Charlottesville, Va.: Michie, 1997.

Nelson, Robert H. *Zoning and Property Rights: An Analysis of the American System of Land-Use Regulation.* Cambridge, Mass.: MIT Press, 1980.

*G. Thomas Taylor*

# APPENDICES

# THE DECLARATION OF INDEPENDENCE

In Congress, July 4, 1776
The unanimous declaration of the thirteen United States of America

WHEN in the Course of human Events, it becomes necessary for one People to dissolve the Political Bands which have connected them with another, and to assume among the Powers of the Earth, the separate and equal Station to which the Laws of Nature and of Nature's God entitle them, a decent Respect to the Opinions of Mankind requires that they should declare the causes which impel them to the Separation.

We hold these Truths to be self-evident, that all Men are created equal, that they are endowed by their Creator with certain unalienable Rights, that among these are Life, Liberty, and the Pursuit of Happiness—That to secure these Rights, Governments are instituted among Men, deriving their just Powers from the Consent of the Governed, that whenever any Form of Government becomes destructive of these Ends, it is the Right of the People to alter or to abolish it, and to institute new Government, laying its Foundation on such Principles, and organizing its Powers in such Form, as to them shall seem most likely to effect their Safety and Happiness. Prudence, indeed, will dictate that Governments long established should not be changed for light and transient Causes; and accordingly all Experience hath shewn, that Mankind are more disposed to suffer, while Evils are sufferable, than to right themselves by abolishing the Forms to which they are accustomed. But when a long Train of Abuses and Usurpations, pursuing invariably the same Object, evinces a Design to reduce them under absolute Despotism, it is their Right, it is their Duty, to throw off such Government, and to provide new Guards for their future Security. Such has been the patient Sufferance of these Colonies; and such is now the Necessity which constrains them to alter their former Systems of Government. The History of the present King of Great Britain is a History of repeated Injuries and Usurpations, all having in direct Object the Establishment of an absolute Tyranny over these States. To prove this, let Facts be submitted to a candid World.

He has refused his Assent to Laws, the most wholesome and necessary for the public Good.

He has forbidden his Governors to pass Laws of immediate and pressing Importance, unless suspended in their Operation till his Assent should be obtained; and when so suspended, he has utterly neglected to attend to them.

He has refused to pass other Laws for the Accommodation of large Districts of People, unless those People would relinquish the Right of Representation in the Legislature, a Right inestimable to them, and formidable to Tyrants only.

He has called together Legislative Bodies at Places unusual, uncomfortable, and distant from the Depository of their public Records, for the sole Purpose of fatiguing them into Compliance with his Measures.

He has dissolved Representative Houses repeatedly, for opposing with manly Firmness his Invasions on the Rights of the People.

He has refused for a long Time, after such Dissolutions, to cause others to be elected; whereby the Legislative Powers, incapable of Annihilation, have returned to the People at large for their exercise; the State remaining in the meantime exposed to all the Dangers of Invasion from without, and Convulsions within.

He has endeavoured to prevent the Population of these States; for that Purpose obstructing the Laws for Naturalization of Foreigners; refusing to pass others to encourage their Migrations hither, and raising the Conditions of new Appropriations of Lands.

He has obstructed the Administration of Justice, by refusing his Assent to Laws for establishing Judiciary Powers.

He has made Judges dependent on his Will alone, for the Tenure of their Offices, and the Amount and Payment of their Salaries.

He has erected a Multitude of new Offices, and sent hither Swarms of Officers to harass our People, and eat out their Substance.

He has kept among us, in Times of Peace, Standing Armies, without the consent of our Legislatures.

He has affected to render the Military independent of and superior to the Civil Power.

He has combined with others to subject us to a Jurisdiction foreign to our Constitution, and unacknowledged by our Laws; giving his Assent to their Acts of pretended Legislation:

For quartering large Bodies of Armed Troops among us:

For protecting them, by a mock Trial, from Punishment for any Murders which they should commit on the Inhabitants of these States:

For cutting off our Trade with all Parts of the World:

For imposing Taxes on us without our Consent:

For depriving us, in many Cases, of the Benefits of Trial by Jury:

For transporting us beyond Seas to be tried for pretended Offences:

For abolishing the free System of English Laws in a neighbouring Province, establishing therein an arbitrary Government, and enlarging its Boundaries, so as to render it at once an Example and fit Instrument for introducing the same absolute Rule into these Colonies:

For taking away our Charters, abolishing our most valuable Laws, and altering fundamentally the Forms of our Governments:

For suspending our own Legislatures, and declaring themselves invested with Power to legislate for us in all Cases whatsoever.

He has abdicated Government here, by declaring us out of his Protection and waging War against us.

He has plundered our Seas, ravaged our Coasts, burnt our Towns, and destroyed the Lives of our People.

He is, at this Time, transporting large Armies of foreign Mercenaries to compleat the Works of Death, Desolation, and Tyranny, already begun with circumstances of Cruelty and Perfidy, scarcely paralleled in the most barbarous Ages, and totally unworthy the Head of a civilized Nation.

He has constrained our fellow Citizens taken Captive on the high Seas to bear Arms against their Country, to become the Executioners of their Friends and Brethren, or to fall themselves by their Hands.

He has excited domestic Insurrections amongst us, and has endeavoured to bring on the Inhabitants of our Frontiers, the merciless Indian Savages, whose known Rule of Warfare is an undistinguished Destruction, of all Ages, Sexes and Conditions.

In every stage of these Oppressions we have Petitioned for Redress in the most humble Terms: Our repeated Petitions have been answered only by repeated Injury. A Prince, whose Character is thus marked by every act which may define a Tyrant, is unfit to be the Ruler of a free People.

Nor have we been wanting in Attentions to our British Brethren. We have warned them from Time to Time of Attempts by their Legislature to extend an unwarrantable Jurisdiction over us. We have reminded them of the Circumstances of our Emigration and Settlement here. We have appealed to their native Justice and Magnanimity, and we have conjured them by the Ties of our common Kindred to disavow these Usurpations, which would inevitably interrupt our Connections and Correspondence. They too have been deaf to the Voice of Justice and of Consanguinity. We must, therefore, acquiesce in the Necessity, which denounces our Separation, and hold them, as we hold the rest of Mankind, Enemies in War, in Peace, Friends.

WE, THEREFORE, the Representatives of the UNITED STATES OF AMERICA, in General Congress, Assembled, appealing to the Supreme Judge of the World for the Rectitude of our Intentions, do, in the Name, and by Authority of the good People of these Colonies, solemnly Publish and Declare, That these United Colonies are, and of Right ought to be, FREE AND INDEPENDENT STATES; that they are absolved from all Allegiance to the British Crown, and that all political Connection between them and the State of Great Britain, is and ought to be totally dissolved; and that as Free and Independent States, they have full Power to levy War, conclude Peace, contract Alliances, establish Commerce, and to do all other Acts and Things which INDEPENDENT STATES may of right do. And for the support of this Declaration, with a firm Reliance on the Protection of divine Providence, we mutually pledge to each other our Lives, our Fortunes, and our sacred Honor.

# THE CONSTITUTION OF THE UNITED STATES OF AMERICA

We the People of the United States, in Order to form a more perfect Union, establish Justice, insure domestic Tranquility, provide for the common defence, promote the general Welfare, and secure the Blessings of Liberty to ourselves and our Posterity, do ordain and establish this Constitution for the United States of America.

### ARTICLE I.

SECTION 1. All legislative Powers herein granted shall be vested in a Congress of the United States, which shall consist of a Senate and House of Representatives.

SECTION 2. The House of Representatives shall be composed of Members chosen every second Year by the People of the several States, and the Electors in each State shall have the Qualifications requisite for Electors of the most numerous Branch of the State Legislature.

No Person shall be a Representative who shall not have attained to the Age of twenty five Years, and been seven Years a Citizen of the United States, and who shall not, when elected, be an Inhabitant of that State in which he shall be chosen.

Representatives and direct Taxes shall be apportioned among the several States which may be included within this Union, according to their respective Numbers, which shall be determined by adding to the whole Number of free Persons, including those bound to Service for a Term of Years, and excluding Indians not taxed, three fifths of all other Persons. The actual Enumeration shall be made within three Years after the first Meeting of the Congress of the United States, and within every subsequent Term of ten Years, insuch Manner as they shall by Law direct. The number of Representatives shall not exceed one for every thirty Thousand, but each State shall have at Least one Representative; and until such enumeration shall be made, the State of New Hampshire shall be entitled to chuse three, Massachusetts eight, Rhode Island and Providence Plantations one, Connecticut five, New York six, New Jersey four, Pennsylvania eight, Delaware one, Maryland six, Virginia ten, North Carolina five, South Carolina five, and Georgia three.

When vacancies happen in the Representation from any State, the Executive Authority thereof shall issue Writs of Election to fill such Vacancies.

The House of Representatives shall chuse their Speaker and other Officers; and shall have the sole Power of Impeachment.

SECTION 3. The Senate of the United States shall be composed of two Senators from each State, chosen by the Legislature thereof, for six Years; and each Senator shall have one Vote.

Immediately after they shall be assembled in Consequence of the first Election, they shall be divided as equally as may be into three Classes. The Seats of the Senators of the first Class shall be vacated at the Expiration of the second Year, of the second Class at the Expiration of the fourth Year, and of the third Class at the Expiration of the sixth Year, so that one third may be chosen every second Year; and if Vacancies happen by Resignation, or otherwise, during the Recess of the Legislature of any State, the Executive thereof may make temporary Appointments until the next Meeting of the Legislature, which shall then fill such Vacancies.

No Person shall be a Senator who shall not have attained to the Age of thirty Years, and been nine Years a Citizen of the United States, and who shall not, when elected, be an Inhabitant of that State for which he shall be chosen.

The Vice President of the United States shall be President of the Senate, but shall have no Vote, unless they be equally divided.

The Senate shall chuse their other Officers, and also a President pro tempore, in the Absence of the Vice President, or when he shall exercise the Office of President of the United States.

The Senate shall have the sole Power to try all Impeachments. When sitting for that Purpose, they shall be on Oath or Affirmation. When the President of the United States is tried, the Chief Justice shall preside: And no Person shall be convicted without the Concurrence of two thirds of the Members present.

Judgment in Cases of Impeachment shall not extend further than to removal from Office, and disqualification to hold and enjoy any Office of honor, Trust or Profit under the United States: but the Party convicted shall nevertheless be liable and subject to Indictment, Trial, Judgment and Punishment, according to Law.

SECTION 4. The Times, Places and Manner of holding Elections for Senators and Representatives, shall be prescribed in each State by the Legislature thereof; but the Congress may at any time by Law make or alter such Regulations, except as to the Places of chusing Senators.

The Congress shall assemble at least once in every Year, and such Meeting shall be on the first Monday in December, unless they shall by Law appoint a different Day.

SECTION 5. Each House shall be the Judge of the Elections, Returns and Qualifications of its own Members, and a Majority of each shall constitute a Quorum to do Business; but a smaller Number may adjourn from day to day, and may be authorized to compel the Attendance of absent Members, in such Manner, and under such Penalties as each House may provide.

Each House may determine the Rules of its Proceedings, punish its Members for disorderly Behaviour, and, with the Concurrence of two thirds, expel a Member.

Each House shall keep a Journal of its Proceedings, and from time to time publish the same, excepting such Parts as may in their Judgment require Secrecy; and the Yeas and Nays of the Members of either House on any question shall, at the Desire of one fifth of those Present, be entered on the Journal.

Neither House, during the Session of Congress, shall, without the Consent of the other, adjourn for more than three days, nor to any other Place than that in which the two Houses shall be sitting.

SECTION 6. The Senators and Representatives shall receive a Compensation for their Services, to be ascertained by Law, and paid out of the Treasury of the United States. They shall in all Cases, except Treason, Felony and Breach of the Peace, be privileged from Arrest during their Attendance at the Session of their respective Houses, and in going to and returning from the same; and for any Speech or Debate in either House, they shall not be questioned in any other Place.

No Senator or Representative shall, during the Time for which he was elected, be appointed to any civil Office under the Authority of the United States, which shall have been created, or the Emoluments whereof shall have been encreased during such time; and no Person holding any Office under the United States, shall be a Member of either House during his Continuance in Office.

SECTION 7. All Bills for raising Revenue shall originate in the House of Representatives; but the Senate may propose or concur with Amendments as on other Bills.

Every Bill which shall have passed the House of Representatives and the Senate, shall, before it becomes a Law, be presented to the President of the United States; If he approve he shall sign it, but if not he shall return it, with his Objections to that House in which it shall have originated, who shall enter the Objections at large on their Journal, and proceed to reconsider it. If after such Reconsideration two thirds of that House shall agree to pass the Bill, it shall be sent, together with the Objections, to the other House, by which it shall likewise be reconsidered, and if approved by two thirds of that House, it shall become a Law. But in all such Cases the Votes of both Houses shall be determined by yeas and Nays, and the Names of the Persons voting for and against the Bill shall be entered on the Journal of each House respectively. If any Bill shall not be returned by the President within ten Days (Sundays excepted) after it shall have been presented to him, the Same shall be a Law, in like Manner as if he had signed it, unless the Congress by their Adjournment prevent its Return, in which Case it shall not be a Law.

Every Order, Resolution, or Vote to which the Concurrence of the Senate and House of Representatives may be necessary (except on a question of Adjournment) shall be presented to the President of the United States; and before the Same shall take Effect, shall be approved by him, or being disapproved by him, shall be repassed by two thirds of the Senate and House of Representatives, according to the Rules and Limitations prescribed in the Case of a Bill.

SECTION 8. The Congress shall have Power To lay and collect Taxes, Duties, Imposts and Excises, to pay the Debts and provide for the common Defence and general Welfare of the United States; but all Duties, Imposts and Excises shall be uniform throughout the United States;

To borrow Money on the credit of the United States;

To regulate Commerce with foreign Nations, and among the several States, and with the Indian Tribes;

To establish an uniform Rule of Naturalization, and uniform Laws on the subject of Bankruptcies throughout the United States;

To coin Money, regulate the Value thereof, and of foreign Coin, and fix the Standard of Weights and Measures;

To provide for the Punishment of counterfeiting the Securities and current Coin of the United States;

To establish Post Offices and post Roads;

To promote the Progress of Science and useful Arts, by securing for limited Times to Authors and Inventors the exclusive Right to their respective Writings and Discoveries;

To constitute Tribunals inferior to the supreme Court;

To define and punish Piracies and Felonies committed on the high Seas, and Offenses against the Law of Nations;

To declare War, grant Letters of Marque and Reprisal, and make Rules concerning Captures on Land and Water;

To raise and support Armies, but no Appropriation of Money to that Use shall be for a longer Term than two Years;

To provide and maintain a Navy;

To make Rules for the Government and Regulation of the land and naval Forces;

To provide for calling forth the Militia to execute the Laws of the Union, suppress Insurrections and repel Invasions;

To provide for organizing, arming, and disciplining the Militia, and for governing such Part of them as may be employed in the Service of the United States, reserving to the States respectively, the Appointment of the Officers, and the Authority of training the Militia according to the discipline prescribed by Congress;

To exercise exclusive Legislation in all Cases whatsoever, over such District (not exceeding ten Miles square) as may, by Cession of particular States, and the Acceptance of Congress, become the Seat of the Government of the United States, and to exercise like Authority over all Places purchased by the Consent of the Legislature of the State in which the Same shall be, for the Erection of Forts, Magazines, Arsenals, dock-Yards and other needful Buildings;—And

To make all Laws which shall be necessary and proper for carrying into Execution the foregoing Powers, and all other Powers vested by this Constitution in the Government of the United States, or in any Department or Officer thereof.

SECTION 9. The Migration or Importation of such Persons as any of the States now existing shall think proper to admit, shall not be prohibited by the Congress prior to the Year one thousand eight hundred and eight, but a Tax or duty may be imposed on such Importation, not exceeding ten dollars for each Person.

The Privilege of the Writ of Habeas Corpus shall not be suspended, unless when in Cases of Rebellion or Invasion the public Safety may require it.

No Bill of Attainder or ex post facto Law shall be passed.

No Capitation, or other direct, Tax shall be laid, unless in Proportion to the Census or Enumeration herein before directed to be taken.

No Tax or Duty shall be laid on Articles exported from any State.

No Preference shall be given by any Regulation of Commerce or Revenue to the Ports of one State over those of another: nor shall Vessels bound to, or from, one State be obliged to enter, clear, or pay Duties in another.

No Money shall be drawn from the Treasury, but in Consequence of Appropriations made by Law; and a regular Statement and Account of the Receipts and Expenditures of all public Money shall be published from time to time.

No Title of Nobility shall be granted by the United States: And no Person holding any Office of Profit or Trust under them, shall, without the Consent of the Congress, accept of any present, Emolument, Office, or Title, of any kind whatever, from any King, Prince, or foreign State.

SECTION 10. No State shall enter into any Treaty, Alliance, or Confederation; grant Letters of Marque and Reprisal; coin Money; emit Bills of Credit; make any Thing but gold and silver Coin a Tender in Payment of Debts; pass any Bill of Attainder, ex post facto Law, or Law impairing the Obligation of Contracts, or grant any Title of Nobility.

No State shall, without the Consent of the Congress, lay any Imposts or Duties on Imports or Exports, except what may be absolutely necessary for executing its inspection Laws: and the net Produce of all Duties and Imposts, laid by any State on Imports or Exports, shall be for the Use of the Treasury of the United States; and all such Laws shall be subject to the Revision and Control of the Congress.

No State shall, without the Consent of Congress, lay any Duty of Tonnage, keep Troops, or Ships of War in time of Peace, enter into any Agreement or Compact with another State, or with a foreign Power, or engage in War, unless actually invaded, or in such imminent Danger as will not admit of delay.

**ARTICLE II.**

SECTION 1. The executive Power shall be vested in a President of the United States of America. He shall hold his Office during the Term of four Years, and, together with the Vice President, chosen for the same Term, be elected, as follows

Each State shall appoint, in such Manner as the Legislature thereof may direct, a Number of Electors, equal to the whole Number of Senators and Representatives to which the State may be entitled in the Congress: but no Senator or Representative, or Person holding an Office of Trust or Profit under the United States, shall be appointed an Elector.

The Electors shall meet in their respective States, and vote by Ballot for two Persons, of whom one at least shall not be an Inhabitant of the same State with themselves. And they shall make a List of all the Persons voted for, and of the Number of Votes for each; which List they shall sign and certify, and transmit sealed to the Seat of the Government of the United States, directed to the President of the Senate. The President of the Senate shall, in the Presence of the Senate and House of Representatives, open all the Certificates, and the Votes shall then be counted. The Person having the greatest Number of Votes shall be the President, if such Number be a Majority of the whole Number of Electors appointed; and if there be more than one who have such Majority, and have an equal Number of Votes, then the House of Representatives shall immediately chuse by Ballot one of them for President; and if no Person have a Majority, then from the five highest on the List the said House shall in like manner chuse the President. But in chusing the President, the Votes shall be taken by States, the Representation from each State having one Vote; A quorum for this Purpose shall consist of a Member or Members from two thirds of the States, and a Majority of all the States shall be necessary to a Choice. In every Case, after the Choice of the President, the Person having the greatest Number of Votes of the Electors shall be the Vice President. But if there should remain two or more who have equal Votes, the Senate shall chuse from them by Ballot the Vice President.

The Congress may determine the Time of chusing the Electors, and the Day on which they shall give their Votes; which Day shall be the same throughout the United States.

No Person except a natural born Citizen, or a Citizen of the United States, at the time of the Adoption of this Constitution, shall be eligible to the Office of the President; neither shall any person be eligible to that Office who shall not have attained to the Age of thirty five Years, and been fourteen Years a Resident within the United States.

In Case of the Removal of the President from Office, or of his Death, Resignation, or Inability to discharge the Powers and Duties of the said Office, the Same shall devolve on the Vice President, and the Congress may by Law provide for the Case of Removal, Death, Resignation or Inability, both of the President and Vice President, declaring what Officer shall then act as President, and such Officer shall act accordingly, until the Disability be removed, or a President shall be elected.

The President shall, at stated Times, receive for his Services, a Compensation, which shall neither be increased nor diminished during the Period for which he shall have been elected, and he shall not receive within that Period any other Emolument from the United States, or any of them.

Before he enter the Execution of his Office, he shall take the following Oath or Affirmation:—"I do solemnly swear (or affirm) that I will faithfully execute the Office of President of the United States, and will to the best of my Ability, preserve, protect and defend the Constitution of the United States."

SECTION 2. The President shall be Commander in Chief of the Army and Navy of the United States, and of the Militia of the several States, when called into the actual Service of the United States; he may require the Opinion, in writing, of the principal Officer in each of the executive Departments, upon any Subject relating to the Duties of their respective Offices, and he shall have Power to grant Reprieves and Pardons for Offenses against the United States, except in Cases of Impeachment.

He shall have Power, by and with the Advice and Consent of the Senate, to make Treaties, provided two thirds of the Senators present concur; and he shall nominate, and by and with the Advice and Consent of the Senate, shall appoint Ambassadors, other public Ministers and Consuls, Judges of the supreme Court, and all other Officers of the United States, whose Appointments are not herein otherwise provided for, and which shall be established by Law: but the Congress may by Law vest the Appointment of such inferior Officers, as they think proper, in the President alone, in the Courts of Law, or in the Heads of Departments.

The President shall have Power to fill up all Vacancies that may happen during the Recess of the Senate, by granting Commissions which shall expire at the End of their next Session.

SECTION 3. He shall from time to time give to the Congress Information of the State of the Union, and recommend to their Consideration such Measures as he shall judge necessary and expedient; he may, on extraordinary Occasions, convene both Houses, or either of them, and in Case of Disagreement between them, with Respect to the Time of Adjournment, he may adjourn them to such Time as he shall think proper; he shall receive Ambassadors and other public Ministers; he shall take Care that the Laws be faithfully executed, and shall Commission all the Officers of the United States.

SECTION 4. The President, Vice President and all civil Officers of the United States, shall be removed from Office on Impeachment for, and Conviction of, Treason, Bribery, or other high Crimes and Misdemeanors.

## ARTICLE III.

SECTION 1. The judicial Power of the United States, shall be vested in one supreme Court, and in such inferior Courts as the Congress may from time to time ordain and establish. The Judges, both of the supreme and inferior Courts, shall hold their Offices during good Behaviour, and shall, at stated Times, receive for their Services, a Compensation, which shall not be diminished during their Continuance in Office.

SECTION 2. The judicial Power shall extend to all Cases, in Law and Equity, arising under this Constitution, the Laws of the United States, and Treaties made, or which shall be made, under their Authority;—to all Cases affecting Ambassadors, other public Ministers and Consuls;—to all Cases of admiralty and maritime Jurisdiction;—to Controversies to which the United States shall be a Party;—to Controversies between two or more States; between a State and Citizens of another State; between Citizens of different States,—between Citizens of the same State claiming Lands under Grants of different States, and between a State, or the Citizens thereof, and foreign States, Citizens or Subjects.

In all Cases affecting Ambassadors, other public Ministers and Consuls, and those in which a State shall be Party, the supreme Court shall have original Jurisdiction. In all the other Cases before mentioned, the supreme Court shall have appellate Jurisdiction, both as to Law and Fact, with such Exceptions, and under such Regulations as the Congress shall make.

The Trial of all Crimes, except in Cases of Impeachment, shall be by Jury; and such Trial shall be held in the State where the said Crimes shall have been committed; but when not committed within any State, the Trial shall be at such Place or Places as the Congress may by Law have directed.

SECTION 3. Treason against the United States, shall consist only in levying War against them, or in adhering to their Enemies, giving them Aid and Comfort. No Person shall be convicted of Treason unless on the Testimony of two Witnesses to the same overt Act, or on Confession in open Court.

The Congress shall have Power to declare the Punishment of Treason, but no Attainder of Treason shall work Corruption of Blood, or Forfeiture except during the Life of the Person attainted.

## ARTICLE IV.

SECTION 1. Full Faith and Credit shall be given in each State to the public Acts, Records, and judicial Proceedings of every other State; And the Congress may by general Laws prescribe the Manner in which such Acts, Records and Proceedings shall be proved, and the Effect thereof.

SECTION 2. The Citizens of each State shall be entitled to all Privileges and Immunities of Citizens in the several States.

A Person charged in any State with Treason, Felony, or other Crime, who shall flee from Justice, and be found in another State, shall on Demand of the executive Authority of the State from which he fled, be delivered up, to be removed to the State having Jurisdiction of the Crime.

No person held to Service or Labour in one State, under the Laws thereof, escaping into another, shall, in Consequence of any Law or Regulation therein, be discharged from such Service or Labour, but shall be delivered up on Claim of the Party to whom such Service or Labour may be due.

SECTION 3. New States may be admitted by the Congress into this Union; but no new State shall be formed or erected within the Jurisdiction of any other State; nor any State be formed by the Junction of two or more States, or Parts of States, without the Consent of the Legislatures of the States concerned as well as of the Congress.

The Congress shall have Power to dispose of and make all needful Rules and Regulations respecting the Territory or other Property belonging to the United States; and nothing in this Constitution shall be so construed as to Prejudice any Claims of the United States, or of any particular State.

SECTION 4. The United States shall guarantee to every State in this Union a Republican Form of Government, and shall protect each of them against Invasion; and on Application of the Legislature, or of the Executive (when the Legislature cannot be convened) against domestic Violence.

### ARTICLE V.

The Congress, whenever two thirds of both Houses shall deem it necessary, shall propose Amendments to this Constitution, or, on the Application of the Legislatures of two thirds of the several States, shall call a Convention for proposing Amendments, which, in either Case, shall be valid to all Intents and Purposes, as Part of this Constitution, when ratified by the Legislatures of three fourths of the several States, or by Conventions in three fourths thereof, as the one or the other Mode of Ratification may be proposed by the Congress; Provided that no Amendment which may be made prior to the year one thousand eight hundred and eight shall in any Manner affect the first and fourth Clauses in the Ninth Section of the first Article; and that no State, without its Consent, shall be deprived of its equal Suffrage in the Senate.

### ARTICLE VI.

All Debts contracted and Engagements entered into, before the Adoption of this Constitution, shall be as valid against the United States under this Constitution, as under the Confederation.

This Constitution, and the Laws of the United States which shall be made in Pursuance thereof; and all Treaties made, or which shall be made, under the Authority of the United States, shall be the supreme Law of the Land; and the Judges in every State shall be bound thereby, any Thing in the Constitution or Laws of any State to the Contrary notwithstanding.

The Senators and Representatives before mentioned, and the Members of the several State Legislatures, and all executive and judicial Officers, both of the United States and of the several States, shall be bound by Oath or Affirmation, to support this Constitution; but no religious Test shall ever be required as a Qualification to any Office or public Trust under the United States.

## ARTICLE VII.

The Ratification of the Conventions of nine States, shall be sufficient for the Establishment of this Constitution between the States so ratifying the Same.

Done in Convention by the Unanimous Consent of the States present the Seventeenth Day of September in the Year of our Lord one thousand seven hundred and eighty seven and of the Independence of the United States of America the Twelfth. In Witness whereof We have hereunto subscribed our Names,

# AMENDMENTS TO THE U.S. CONSTITUTION

### AMENDMENT I.

Congress shall make no law respecting an establishment of religion, or prohibiting the free exercise thereof; or abridging the freedom of speech, or of the press, or the right of the people peaceably to assemble, and to petition the Government for a redress of grievances.

*[ratified December, 1791]*

### AMENDMENT II.

A well regulated Militia, being necessary to the security of a free State, the right of the people to keep and bear Arms, shall not be infringed.

*[ratified December, 1791]*

### AMENDMENT III.

No Soldier shall, in time of peace be quartered in any house, without the consent of the Owner, nor in time of war, but in a manner to be prescribed by law.

*[ratified December, 1791]*

### AMENDMENT IV.

The right of the people to be secure in their persons, houses, papers, and effects, against unreasonable searches and seizures, shall not be violated, and no Warrants shall issue, but upon probable cause, supported by Oath or affirmation, and particularly describing the place to be searched, and the persons or things to be seized.

*[ratified December, 1791]*

### AMENDMENT V.

No person shall be held to answer for a capital, or otherwise infamous crime, unless on a presentment or indictment of a Grand Jury, except in cases arising in the land or naval forces, or in the Militia, when in actual service in time of War or public danger; nor shall any person be subject for the same offence to be twice put in jeopardy of life or limb, nor shall be compelled in any criminal case to be a witness against himself, nor be deprived of life, liberty, or property, without due process of law;

nor shall private property be taken for public use without just compensation.

*[ratified December, 1791]*

## AMENDMENT VI.

In all criminal prosecutions, the accused shall enjoy the right to a speedy and public trial, by an impartial jury of the State and district wherein the crime shall have been committed; which district shall have been previously ascertained by law, and to be informed of the nature and cause of the accusation; to be confronted with the witnesses against him; to have compulsory process for obtaining witnesses in his favor, and to have the assistance of counsel for his defence.

*[ratified December, 1791]*

## AMENDMENT VII.

In Suits at common law, where the value in controversy shall exceed twenty dollars, the right of trial by jury shall be preserved, and no fact tried by a jury shall be otherwise re-examined in any Court of the United States, than according to the rules of the common law.

*[ratified December, 1791]*

## AMENDMENT VIII.

Excessive bail shall not be required, nor excessive fines imposed, nor cruel and unusual punishments inflicted.

*[ratified December, 1791]*

## AMENDMENT IX.

The enumeration in the Constitution, of certain rights, shall not be construed to deny or disparage others retained by the people.

*[ratified December, 1791]*

## AMENDMENT X.

The powers not delegated to the United States by the Constitution, nor prohibited by it to the States, are reserved to the States respectively, or to the people.

*[ratified December, 1791]*

## AMENDMENT XI.

The Judicial power of the United States shall not be construed to extend to any suit in law or equity, commenced or prosecuted against one of the United States by Citizens of another State, or by Citizens or Subjects of any Foreign State.

*[ratified February, 1795]*

## AMENDMENT XII.

The Electors shall meet in their respective states, and vote by ballot for President and Vice-President, one of whom, at least, shall not be an inhabitant of the same state with themselves; they shall name in their ballots the person voted for as President, and in distinct ballots the person voted for as Vice-President, and they shall make distinct lists of all persons voted for as President, and of all persons voted for as Vice-President, and of the number of votes for each, which lists they shall sign and certify, and transmit sealed to the seat of the government of the United States, directed to the President of the Senate;—The President of the Senate shall, in the presence of the Senate and House of Representatives, open all the certificates and the votes shall then be counted;—The person having the greatest number of votes for President, shall be the President, if such number be a majority of the whole number of Electors appointed; and if no person have such majority, then from the persons having the highest numbers not exceeding three on the list of those voted for as President, the House of Representatives shall choose immediately, by ballot, the President. But in choosing the President, the votes shall be taken by states, the representation from each state having one vote; a quorum for this purpose shall consist of a member or members from two-thirds of the states, and a majority of all the states shall be necessary to a choice. And if the House of Representatives shall not choose a President whenever the right of choice shall devolve upon them, before the fourth day of March next following, then the Vice-President shall act as President, as in the case of the death or other constitutional disability of the President.— The person having the greatest number of votes as Vice-President, shall be the Vice-President, if such number be a majority of the whole number of Electors appointed, and if no person have a majority, then from the two highest numbers on the list, the Senate shall choose the Vice-President; a quorum for the purpose shall consist of two-thirds of the whole number of Senators, and a majority of the whole number shall be necessary to a choice. But no person constitutionally ineligible to the office of President shall be eligible to that of Vice-President of the United States.

*[ratified June, 1804]*

## AMENDMENT XIII.

SECTION 1. Neither slavery nor involuntary servitude, except as a punishment for crime whereof the party shall have been duly convicted, shall exist within the United States, or any place subject to their jurisdiction.

SECTION 2. Congress shall have power to enforce this article by appropriate legislation.

*[ratified December, 1865]*

## AMENDMENT XIV.

SECTION 1. All persons born or naturalized in the United States and subject to the jurisdiction thereof, are citizens of the United States and of the State wherein they reside. No State shall make or enforce any law which shall abridge the privileges or immunities of citizens of the United States; nor shall any State deprive any person of life, liberty, or property, without due process of law; nor deny to any person within its jurisdiction the equal protection of the laws.

SECTION 2. Representatives shall be apportioned among the several States according to their respective numbers, counting the whole number of persons in each State, excluding Indians not taxed. But when the right to vote at any election for the choice of electors for President and Vice President of the United States, Representatives in Congress, the Executive and Judicial officers of a State, or the members of the Legislature thereof, is denied to any of the male inhabitants of such State, being twenty-one years of age, and citizens of the United States, or in any way abridged, except for participation in rebellion, or other crime, the basis of representation therein shall be reduced in the proportion which the number of such male citizens shall bear to the whole number of male citizens twenty-one years of age in such State.

SECTION 3. No person shall be a Senator or Representative in Congress, or elector of President and Vice President, or hold any office, civil or military, under the United States, or under any State, who, having previously taken an oath, as a member of Congress, or as an officer of the United

States, or as a member of any State legislature, or as an executive or judicial officer of any State, to support the Constitution of the United States,
shall have engaged in insurrection or rebellion against the same, or given
aid or comfort to the enemies thereof. But Congress may by a vote of two-
thirds of each House, remove such disability.

SECTION 4. The validity of the public debt of the United States, authorized by law, including debts incurred for payment of pensions and boun-
ties for services in suppressing insurrection or rebellion, shall not be
questioned. But neither the United States nor any State shall assume or
pay any debt or obligation incurred in aid of insurrection or rebellion
against the United States, or any claim for the loss or emancipation of any
slave; but all such debts, obligations and claims shall be held illegal and
void.

SECTION 5. The Congress shall have power to enforce, by appropriate legislation, the provisions of this article.

*[ratified July, 1868]*

## AMENDMENT XV.

SECTION 1. The right of citizens of the United States to vote shall not be
denied or abridged by the United States or by any State on account of
race, color, or previous condition of servitude.

SECTION 2. The Congress shall have power to enforce this article by appropriate legislation.

*[ratified February, 1870]*

## AMENDMENT XVI.

The Congress shall have power to lay and collect taxes on incomes, from
whatever source derived, without apportionment among the several
States, and without regard to any census or enumeration.

*[ratified February, 1913]*

## AMENDMENT XVII.

The Senate of the United States shall be composed of two Senators from
each State, elected by the people thereof, for six years; and each Senator
shall have one vote. The electors in each State shall have the qualifica-

tions requisite for electors of the most numerous branch of the State legislatures.

When vacancies happen in the representation of any State in the Senate, the executive authority of such State shall issue writs of election to fill such vacancies: *Provided,* That the legislature of any State may empower the executive thereof to make temporary appointments until the people fill the vacancies by election as the legislature may direct.

This amendment shall not be so construed as to affect the election or term of any Senator chosen before it becomes valid as part of the Constitution.

*[ratified April, 1913]*

### AMENDMENT XVIII.

SECTION 1. After one year from the ratification of this article the manufacture, sale, or transportation of intoxicating liquors within, the importation thereof into, or the exportation thereof from the United States and all territory subject to the jurisdiction thereof for beverage purposes is hereby prohibited.

SECTION 2. The Congress and the several States shall have concurrent power to enforce this article by appropriate legislation.

SECTION 3. This article shall be inoperative unless it shall have been ratified as an amendment to the Constitution by the legislatures of the several States, as provided in the Constitution, within seven years from the date of the submission hereof to the States by the Congress.

*[ratified January, 1919, repealed December, 1933]*

### AMENDMENT XIX.

The right of citizens of the United States to vote shall not be denied or abridged by the United States or by any State on account of sex.

Congress shall have power to enforce this article by appropriate legislation.

*[ratified August, 1920]*

### AMENDMENT XX.

SECTION 1. The terms of the President and Vice President shall end at noon on the 20th day of January, and the terms of Senators and Representatives at noon on the 3d day of January, of the years in which such terms would have ended if this article had not been ratified; and the terms of their successors shall then begin.

SECTION 2. The Congress shall assemble at least once in every year, and such meeting shall begin at noon on the 3d day of January, unless they shall by law appoint a different day.

SECTION 3. If, at the time fixed for the beginning of the term of the President, the President elect shall have died, the Vice President elect shall become President. If a President shall not have been chosen before the time fixed for the beginning of his term, or if the President elect shall have failed to qualify, then the Vice President elect shall act as President until a President shall have qualified; and the Congress may by law provide for the case wherein neither a President elect nor a Vice President elect shall have qualified, declaring who shall then act as President, or the manner in which one who is to act shall be selected, and such person shall act accordingly until a President or Vice President shall have qualified.

SECTION 4. The Congress may by law provide for the case of the death of any of the persons from whom the House of Representatives may choose a President whenever the right of choice shall have devolved upon them, and for the case of the death of any of the persons from whom the Senate may choose a Vice President whenever the right of choice shall have devolved upon them.

SECTION 5. Sections 1 and 2 shall take effect on the 15th day of October following the ratification of this article.

SECTION 6. This article shall be inoperative unless it shall have been ratified as an amendment to the Constitution by the legislatures of three-fourths of the several States within seven years from the date of its submission.

*[ratified January, 1933]*

## AMENDMENT XXI.

SECTION 1. The eighteenth article of amendment to the Constitution of the United States is hereby repealed.

SECTION 2. The transportation or importation into any State, Territory, or possession of the United States for delivery or use therein of intoxicating liquors, in violation of the laws thereof, is hereby prohibited.

SECTION 3. This article shall be inoperative unless it shall have been ratified as an amendment to the Constitution by conventions in the several States, as provided in the Constitution, within seven years from the date of the submission hereof to the States by the Congress.

*[ratified December, 1933]*

## AMENDMENT XXII.

SECTION 1. No person shall be elected to the office of the President more than twice, and no person who has held the office of President, or acted as President, for more than two years of a term to which some other person was elected President shall be elected to the office of the President more than once. But this Article shall not apply to any person holding the office of President when this Article was proposed by the Congress, and shall not prevent any person who may be holding the office of President, or acting as President, during the term within which this Article becomes operative from holding the office of President or acting as President during the remainder of such term.

SECTION 2. This article shall be inoperative unless it shall have been ratified as an amendment to the Constitution by the legislatures of three-fourths of the several States within seven years from the date of its submission to the States by the Congress.

*[ratified February, 1951]*

## AMENDMENT XXIII.

SECTION 1. The District constituting the seat of Government of the United States shall appoint in such manner as the Congress may direct:

A number of electors of President and Vice President equal to the whole number of Senators and Representatives in Congress to which the District would be entitled if it were a State, but in no event more than the least populous State; they shall be in addition to those appointed by the States, but they shall be considered, for the purposes of the election of President and Vice President, to be electors appointed by a State; and they shall meet in the District and perform such duties as provided by the twelfth article of amendment.

SECTION 2. The Congress shall have power to enforce this article by appropriate legislation.

*[ratified March, 1961]*

## AMENDMENT XXIV.

SECTION 1. The right of citizens of the United States to vote in any primary or other election for President or Vice President, for electors for President or Vice President, or for Senator or Representative in Congress, shall not be denied or abridged by the United States or any State by reason of failure to pay any poll tax or other tax.

SECTION 2. The Congress shall have power to enforce this article by appropriate legislation.

*[ratified January, 1964]*

## AMENDMENT XXV.

SECTION 1. In case of the removal of the President from office or of his death or resignation, the Vice President shall become President.

SECTION 2. Whenever there is a vacancy in the office of the Vice President, the President shall nominate a Vice President who shall take office upon confirmation by a majority vote of both Houses of Congress.

SECTION 3. Whenever the President transmits to the President pro tempore of the Senate and the Speaker of the House of Representatives his written declaration that he is unable to discharge the powers and duties of his office, and until he transmits to them a written declaration to the contrary, such powers and duties shall be discharged by the Vice President as Acting President.

SECTION 4. Whenever the Vice President and a majority of either the principal officers of the executive departments or of such other body as Congress may by law provide, transmit to the President pro tempore of the Senate and the Speaker of the House of Representatives their written declaration that the President is unable to discharge the powers and duties of his office, the Vice President shall immediately assume the powers and duties of the office as Acting President.

Thereafter, when the President transmits to the President pro tempore of the Senate and the Speaker of the House of Representatives his written declaration that no inability exists, he shall resume the powers and duties of his office unless the Vice President and a majority of either the principal officers of the executive department or of such other body as Congress may by law provide, transmit within four days to the President pro tempore of the Senate and the Speaker of the House of Representatives their written declaration that the President is unable to discharge the powers and duties of his office. Thereupon Congress shall decide the issue, assembling within forty-eight hours for that purpose if not in session. If the Congress, within twenty-one days after receipt of the latter written declaration, or, if Congress is not in session, within twenty-one days after Congress is required to assemble, determines by two-thirds vote of both Houses that the President is unable to discharge the powers and duties of his office, the Vice President shall continue to discharge the same as Acting President; otherwise, the President shall resume the powers and duties of his office.

*[ratified February, 1967]*

### AMENDMENT XXVI.

SECTION 1. The right of citizens of the United States, who are eighteen years of age or older, to vote shall not be denied or abridged by the United States or by any State on account of age.

SECTION 2. The Congress shall have power to enforce this article by appropriate legislation.

*[ratified July, 1971]*

### AMENDMENT XXVII.

No law, varying the compensation for the services of the Senators and Representatives, shall take effect, until an election of Representatives shall have intervened.

*[ratified May 7, 1992]*